Environmental Decision-Making

Volume Two

Edited by Yusuf J. Ahmad
Partha Dasgupta
Karl-Göran Mäler

Sponsored by the United Nations Environment Programme

HODDER AND STOUGHTON
LONDON SYDNEY AUCKLAND TORONTO

British Library Cataloguing in Publication Data

Environmental decision making.
Vol. 2
1. Environmental policy 2. Decision-making
I. Ahmad, Yusuf II. Dasgupta, Partha
III. Mäler, Karl-Göran IV. United Nations.
Environment Programme
333.7 HC79.E5

ISBN 0 340 34301 X

First published 1984

Represented in Nigeria and Cameroon by Nigeria Publishers Services Ltd, P. O. Box 62, Ibadan, Nigeria.

Printed in Great Britain for Hodder and Stoughton Educational, a division of Hodder and Stoughton Ltd, Mill Road, Dunton Green, Sevenoaks, Kent, by Biddles Ltd, Guildford, Surrey

Contents

Foreword vi

Chapter 1 Cost-Benefit Analysis: The Basic Facts
Karl-Göran Mäler 1

Chapter 2 Economic Valuation of Environmental Quality Aspects of Upland Agricultural Projects in Korea
Sung-Hoon Kim and John A. Dixon
Introduction 21
Case Study 22

Chapter 3 Blue Whales and Applied Control Theory
A. Michael Spence
Exploitation of the Lobster Fishery: Some Empirical Results
J. V. Henderson and M. Tugwell
Introduction 38
Case Study 1 43
Case Study 2 71

Chapter 4 The Trans-Alaska Pipeline: Environmental Consequences and Alternatives
John V. Krutilla and Anthony C. Fisher
Introduction 83
Case Study 84

Chapter 5 The Sixty-City Limit
Thomas D. Crocker, William Schulze, Shalul Ben-David and Allen V. Kneese
Introduction 114
Case Study 118

Chapter 6	Economic Growth and Climate: The Carbon Dioxide Problem William D. Nordhaus	
	Introduction	162
	Case Study	165
Chapter 7	A Socially Optimum Pricing Policy for a Public Water Agency Gardner Brown Jr. and C. B. McGuire	
	Introduction	176
	Case Study	179
Chapter 8	Atmospheric Corrosion of Materials V. Kucera, J. Ghullman and P. Swartlang	
	Introduction	198
	Case Study	200
Chapter 9	Regional Residuals Management Models	
	The Lower Delaware Valley Case Study Allen V. Kneese and Blair T. Bower	
	Introduction	222
	Case Study 1	229
	Case Study 2	257
Chapter 10	Option Value: Empirical Evidence from a Case Study of Recreation and Water Quality Douglas A. Greenley, Richard G. Walsh and Robert A. Young	
	Introduction	302
	Case Study	304
Chapter 11	Input-Output Analysis and Air Pollution Control Robert E. Kohn	
	Introduction	322
	Case Study	324

Acknowledgments

The editors and publisher are grateful to the following for giving permission to reproduce the case studies in this book:
'Economic Valuation of Environmental Quality Aspects of Upland Agricultural Projects in Korea' © John A. Dixon and Sung-Hoon Kim; 'Blue Whales and Applied Control Theory' by A. Michael Spence. First published in *Systems Approaches and Environmental Problems*, edited by Hans Werner Gottinger and published by Vandenhoeck and Ruprecht, Gottinger, Germany; 'Exploitation of the Lobster Fishery: Some Empirical Results' © J. Vernon Henderson. First published in 1979 by the *Journal of Environmental Economics and Management*, Academic Press Inc, New York, U.S.A.; 'The Trans-Alaska Pipeline: Environmental Consequences and Alternatives' by John V. Krutilla and Anthony C. Fisher. First published in *The Economics of Natural Environments* for the Resources for the Future by the Johns Hopkins University Press, Baltimore, U.S.A.; 'The Sixty-City Limit' by Thomas D. Crocker, William Schulze, Shalul Ben-David and Allen V. Kneese. First published in 1979 in *Methods Development for Assessing Air Pollution Control Benefit* by the United States Environmental Protection Agency, Washington D.C., U.S.A.; 'Economic Growth and Climate: The Carbon Dioxide Problem' by William D. Nordhaus. First published by American Economic Association in *American Economic Review* Vol. 67, No. 2, pp. 341–346 in February 1977; 'A Socially Optimum Pricing Policy for a Public Water Agency' © Gardner M. Brown Jr. and C. B. McGuire; 'Atmospheric Corrosion of Materials' by V. Kucera, J. Ghullman and P. Swartlang. First published in *The Costs and Benefits of Sulphur Oxide Control* by O.E.C.D., Paris, France in 1981; 'Regional Residuals Management Models' and 'The Lower Delaware Valley Case Study' by Allen V. Kneese and Blair T. Bower. First published in *Regional Scale Issues and Analyses* for Resources for the Future by the Johns Hopkins University Press, Baltimore, U.S.A.; 'Option Value: Empirical Evidence from a Case Study of Recreation and Water Quality' by Douglas A. Greenley, Richard G. Walsh and Robert A. Young. First published in *Quarterly Journal of Economics*, November 1981, Vol. 96, No. 4, pp. 657–673. Reprinted by permission of John Wiley and Sons, Inc, New York, U.S.A.; 'Input-Output Analysis and Air Pollution Control' by Robert E. Kohn. First published in *Economic Analysis of Environmental Problems*, edited by Edwin Mills, by National Bureau of Economic Research, Massachusetts, U.S.A. in 1975.

Foreword

The literature on social cost-benefit analysis of investment projects is large and growing. It may therefore be surprising that until recently only a few studies had addressed such issues in the context of projects in which environmental resources are a large component. No doubt this, in some measure, is due to the fact that any such investigation is best with analytical difficulties and estimation problems. But part of the reason must surely be that until recently environmental problems were not prominent on the agenda of public concern.

We take the view that environmental resources are not restricted to what are often called 'amenities', but that they encompass the class of all *regenerative natural resources*. This includes forests, fisheries, aquifers and soil, as well as of course clean air and drinking water. In this broader view, therefore, environmental problems are not restricted to an excessive discharge of pollutants. In this view a fishery requires public scrutiny not only when it is a deposit for industrial effluents; it demands scrutiny also if it is harvested at an excessive rate. Both situations present environmental problems. The merit in this broader view is conceptual unity. All problems concerning the control of natural regenerative resources display some strong similarities. It is good to exploit such similarities. Lesson learned from one may then be of use in the resolution of another. It helps to unify seemingly disparate problems concerning the control of resources.

However, having noted similarities, it is as well to recognise their differences. Different resource problems require different attention to detail, demand different emphases, and so on. The case studies gathered here, we believe, reflect well both the similarities and differences underlying resource management problems. The selection also reflects our broader view, and so a number of studies address problems in which there is no 'environmental pollution', as the term is usually understood.

The intention in collecting a set of such studies was to show how the methodology of social cost-benefit analysis can in practice be extended to environmental problems. We looked for case studies of regenerative natural resources and, for the most part, we wanted to include studies in which a menu of options is scrutinised. For this reason we have not included several outstanding case studies which evaluate a given project and do not consider project variants.

A short introduction is presented to each of the studies collected here.

To prepare the reader for the general approach to social cost-benefit analysis that is pursued in the studies a fairly long introduction has also been provided to each case study.

We are most grateful to Claes Thimren for fruitful discussion. The material prepared was typed with great speed and efficiency by Marion O'Brien of the London School of Economics and Margareta Blomberg and Marianne Widing, both of the Stockholm School of Economics. To them we are most grateful.

Yusuf J. Ahmad
Partha Dasgupta
Karl-Göran Mäler

1

Cost-Benefit Analysis: The Basic Facts

Karl-Göran Mäler

Introduction

Any project – whether it be an industrial investment, development of marketing activities, the building of a hydropower plant, establishing of a new educational programme or investments in pollution control – can in very broad terms be described in terms of its consequences. Building a hydropower plant, for example, can be described by specifying the quantities of the different inputs, cement, gravel, steel electrical machinery, manpower, electrical energy, wood, oil, etc., and the dates for the acquisition of these inputs, as well as the amounts of outputs over time, the site of the station and its interrelations with the environment. It is obvious that such a characterization of the hydropower plant will be quite complex and provide very little information to the ultimate decision-maker. Some aggregation of the consequences into more useful measures is therefore needed. For many of the variables describing the project, such an aggregation is carried out almost automatically, namely for those variables for which there exist reliable market prices. Instead of counting the number of tons of electrical wire or the number of nails of a certain size or the amount of cement needed, cost figures in monetary units are used. Likewise, on the output side, a revenue in monetary units is usually calculated whenever the produced goods are sold on a market. The reasons that market prices are accepted in most economies as tools for valuations are obvious. On a market one can voluntarily exchange one commodity for another, and the terms for that exchange, i.e. the prices, will represent the opportunity cost for the individual. By spending a certain amount on a particular commodity an individual is, in fact, abstaining from consuming those other goods that could have been bought at the ruling prices for the same amount. In this way market prices reflect the opportunity cost to the individuals and it is therefore natural to use them in evaluating cost and revenues from investments projects.

They are costs to society in the sense that their use in this particular project means that they will not be available in alternative uses which might enhance the welfare of society. They thus constitute opportunity costs. We include in this category not only the usual kinds of inputs like labour, raw materials, etc. but also negative effects on the environment or the possible reduction of supply of some amenity.

The benefits are those consequences that directly enhance the welfare of society – either through a higher output of a commodity or an improvement in environment quality or other increases in amenities.

The role of cost-benefit analysis

The theory of cost-benefit analysis provides a rigorous explanation for this use of market prices but also gives reasons for the failure of market prices to transmit correct information on the opportunity cost. Cost-benefit (C.B.) analysis theory also gives ways of mimicing market pricing where no markets exist so that non-priced goods (or bads) can be included in the analysis on the same footing as market goods. It is impossible to discuss these matters in any depth in this introductory chapter and we can only refer to specialised monographs.[1] We will, however, try to give a brief overview of the basic results from C.B. theory (sometimes leaving out lengthy motivations and arguments) and discuss some approaches to estimate environmental costs and benefits in view of this basic theory.

In order to simplify the exposition only one project will be considered, and the decision problem is whether this project should be undertaken or not. The comparison is thus to do nothing. In many (perhaps most) cases, the choice is not between to carry out a specific project or do nothing but between different projects. We will also comment upon this situation.

In order to structure our discussion let us consider a project which can be characterized in the following way. The time horizon is T, i.e. only effects appearing in time periods 1, 2, 3, . . . , T shall be taken into account. In general T depends on the nature of the project but we shall assume it is given. For each of the time periods there are consequences which we assumed can be measured. Thus, for each time period t there are two lists $x_{1t}, x_{2t}, \ldots, x_{nt}$ and $y_{1t}, y_{2t}, \ldots, y_{nt}$ of consequences measured in physical or other units. x_{1t} may be the amount of cement used, x_{2t} the amount of electricity consumed, x_{3t} the number of working hours hired. The list of x's is thus a list of inputs to the project. y_{1t} may be the amount of power produced in period t, etc. The list of y's is thus a list of outputs from the project. For each time period we thus have a list of consequences, or inputs and outputs, measured in some way. All these variables are of course not independent of each other. On the contrary, they are highly interdependent and their relationships are given by technical, geological, hydrological, biological and other constraints. We will not go deeper into the nature of these constraints being outside the domain of economists. In many of the case studies to be presented these constraints are in the focus of the analysis. Later, we will give a very brief discussion of some techniques for representing these constraints.

Given these lists of costs and benefits associated with a project, the aim of C.B. analysis is to aggregate these as far as possible in order to facilitate decision-making. Ideally we would like to aggregate all costs and all benefits to one single scalar measure so that when this measure is positive the project should be accepted and when it is negative it should be rejected. Very seldom, though, is it possible to carry out the evaluation that far, and in general it may be necessary to stop the aggregation before the dimensionality has been reduced to one. We will soon find good reasons underlying the difficulties that the analyst may encounter and that may prevent him from calculating one scalar measure.

In order to aggregate the different consequences a project gives rise to, we need a criterion on what constitutes an improvement in the welfare in society. The generally accepted starting point for such a criterion is the idea of consumer sovereignty. According to this idea no one else but the individual knows what is good and bad for him and he should be given complete freedom to make his own choices about his consumption pattern. There are of course many examples from everyday life where this idea is violated. Drug control is one example where consumer sovereignty is infringed upon. The limited rights of children in most societies is another case in point. Although many other examples may be given, the idea of consumer sovereignty is so pervasive in all societies when it comes to ordinary consumer goods, the design of investments etc. that it makes it a valid starting-point for C.B. analysis.

When applying C.B. analysis to project evaluation we are therefore interested in how each individual values the different consequences of the project, and it is those values that should be used in aggregating all the effects. More precisely we will define these individual values in terms of a numeraire, consumption in general or income. Thus the value to an individual of having more bread would be what he would like to give up in income to have more bread.

Our general definition is as follows: *The value to an individual of a consequence from a project is the amount he is willing to pay for having that consequence in case of a benefit or the amount he is willing to pay to avoid that consequence in case of a cost.*

This definition is from a purely theoretical point of view not satisfactory because it is asymmetric between costs and benefits. For our purpose the definition will suffice, however, because any problem due to this deficiency can be handled by *ad hoc* methods.

The example on the value of bread showed that the value to the consumer of one piece of bread is his willingness to pay for that bread. If the consumer cannot affect market prices, his willingness to pay for that piece will obviously be equal to the price of bread. Thus, we have reached the important conclusion that *whenever consequences from a project consist of goods and services bought and sold by consumers at certain prices, these prices represent the values that should be used in aggregating those consequences.*

However, this conclusion is based on the assumption that the individual can buy any quantity he demands. If he is rationed, either by disequilibrium in markets (unemployment, for example) or by government regulations (for instance, foreign exchange controls) the willingness to pay may not be equal to the current market price and *the market prices must be corrected for the disequilibrium.* In particular, the trade offs between different time periods may not be characterized by accurate market prices, i.e. interest rates. Therefore a special discussion of the choice of a discount rate is needed. Moreover, if the demand for certain goods for the project is so great that the prices are affected, other corrections may be needed.

One particular price is of utmost importance in any C.B. analysis, namely the interest rate. The interest rate (or rather the discount factor) tells us the value of one unit of consumption one year ahead in terms of present consumption. There are many reasons why not even a perfect capital market may yield an interest rate useful in C.B. analysis. Therefore a special discussion is warranted.

Moreover, in view of the pervasiveness of high inflation rates and high dependence on international financial markets in most developing countries, it seems advisable to include a discussion of some problems in making real profitability calculations of investment in contrast to nominal calculations.

One particular feature is uncertainty which creates certain problems in choosing a discount rate and a few comments and some references will be given on this particular issue.

The most important reason for cost-benefit analysis of environmental problems is the fact that most environmental consequences from a project are not valued at all on a market. Therefore special methods have to be developed in order to mimic the market when such consequences are to be measured, that is to estimate the willingness to pay for environmental improvements or for avoidance of environmental degradations.

Finally special considerations must be given to income distribution and employment inpacts and projects (see e.g. U.N.I.D.O. (1972)).

Technical constraints

If the project is described in terms of its consequences, as was discussed in the previous section, and if the problem is to reject or accept the project, then there is no need to discuss technical constraints. They are already incorporated in the description of the consequences. Even if there is more than one project and the problem is to decide which of the potential projects should be undertaken, there is no need to worry about technical constraints as long as the projects are described in terms of all their consequences.

However, when the number of alternatives is large it may not be possible to describe each of the alternatives in terms of their consequences in this way. In such cases it may be advantageous to represent the technological, biological and geological constraints in summary forms. The concept of a *production function* is particularly important. A production function describes the technical (or biological or geological) relations that must hold between inputs and outputs. In conventional economic analysis, a production function describes the relation between the quantity produced and the different quantities of factors of production which are utilized. We will assume that the reader is acquainted with this concept which is used in some of the case studies presented in this book. The concept of production function has, however, a more general interpretation. In some studies, the production function will take the form of a *growth function*. A growth function describes the growth of a renewable resource as a function of the size of the resource, the harvesting of the resource and other factors that may be relevant. Growth functions are used in the studies on fisheries and ground water presented in this volume. Moreover, similar functions are used to describe the relations between the discharge of various pollutants in a water course and the ensuing water quality. However, in relation to this larger application, the term *environmental model* is more used. The term environmental model also covers the diffusion models used by metereologists to predict the ambient concentrations in the atmosphere at various point in a region from known atmospheric emissions of different pollutants. Such environmental models are used in the Delaware case study, included in this volume. For a general discussion of production functions, and in particular growth functions, the reader is referred to Dasgupta, *The Control of Resources*.[2]

In some instances the conventional concept of a production function is not general enough. For example, whenever the interdependence between different economic sectors is judged important in connection with measures controlling environmental resources, *input-output techniques* may be useful. Input-output analysis is a technique which can be used to model the interactions between the different sectors in an economy. Basically it consists of the assumption that there are fixed proportions between the output in one sector and the various inputs (produced in other sectors) and the primary factors of production. The use of input-output analysis in environmental economics is illustrated in the case study by Kohn which is included in this collection and in which the interested reader can find further references.

A development of input-output analysis is *activity analysis*. This is an approach which is quite complex and we will not try to explain it here. However, it is based on a set of linearity assumptions and is also often called *linear programming*. In the above mentioned Delaware case study, an activity analysis approach was chosen combining engineering information with input-output data, and the production structure in the whole region around the Delaware estuary was described in terms of linear activities. Moreover, as the steady state diffusion model also turned out to be linear, just as the steady state solution to the environmental model of the estuary, the whole approach could be viewed as one big linear programme.

The use of market prices

One classical theorem in welfare economics says roughly the following: 'Assume we have an efficient allocation of resources in the economy. By efficient, we mean that it is impossible to reallocate the resources in such a way that no one is worse off and at least one individual is better off. If the preferences of the consumers are convex, if the production possibilities of producers are convex, and if all goods are sold and bought on markets at which no single individual can affect the prices, then the efficient allocation can be obtained as a market equilibrium by suitable redistributions of the initial wealth'. Conversely, 'any allocation that is the result of a competitive equilibrium is efficient given that all goods are sold and bought on a market'.

These two theorems give the basis for interpreting prices as measures of social opportunity costs. If the assumptions required in the theorems are satisfied, there would be no need for social cost-benefit analysis, because the prices would carry all relevant information on opportunity costs and consumers willingness to pay for goods.

The *raison d'être* for social cost-benefit analysis is, however, the fact that these assumptions are not realistic descriptions of existing economies. Most of our discussions in this introductory chapter will be concerned with situations where some of these assumptions are not accurate descriptions of reality. Such situations are denoted as *market failures*.

One of the assumptions necessary to make the fundamental theorem of welfare economics true is that *all markets equilibrate*. There are good reasons for some markets not to equilibrate, and this kind of market failure will be the focus of the discussion in this chapter. Whenever a market failure is observed, there is an à priori argument for replacing the existing market price with a *shadow price* or *accounting price* which better represents the social opportunity cost of the good.

There are several treatises on calculations of shadow prices or the valuation of goods and factors of production for which equilibrium markets are lacking. One basic reference is the previously mentioned *Guidelines for Project Evaluation*,[3] and we will follow the methodology exposed in that monograph. F. L. C. H. Helmers in *Project Planning and Income Distribution*[4] builds on the U.N.I.D.O. Guidelines and gives simple expositions of some of the more complicated developments.

The basic idea is very simple, however, and we will try to develop the analysis for a very simple case, namely the determination of the shadow price on foreign exchange. There are many reasons (most of which are not valid) for a government to control the price on foreign exchange. By doing that the possible equilibrium is the market for foreign exchange between different users is different from that under the price mechanism. The controlled exchange rate no longer indicates the true social value of a unit of foreign exchange and we therefore need a shadow price in order to handle transactions with foreign countries properly in a social cost-benefit analysis.

What is, then, the social value of a unit of foreign exchange? That depends in general for what purpose that unit is used. One more unit of foreign exchange could be used to increase imports marginally. The domestic value of the increase in imports made possible by an extra unit of foreign exchange is thus the social value of the shadow price on foreign exchange (assuming that the domestic value is calculated at 'proper' prices). On the other hand, one extra unit of foreign exchange could also be used for reducing exports and thereby increasing the domestic supply of goods. In this case the shadow price is equal to the domestic value of the increased domestic supply. If the extra unit of foreign supply is saved for future use, then the value would be the discounted future value calculated along the lines indicated above. In general, an extra unit of foreign exchange will be used both for increasing imports and for decreasing exports, and the shadow price will be a weighted average of export and import prices where the weights are based on information on how the extra unit is spent. For further details the reader is recommended to consult the above mentioned books.

Another important case is disequilibrium in the labour market. In general, the wage rate in the urban sector is higher than the subsistence level of income earned in agriculture in many developing countries. This creates an excess supply of labour which means that the ruling wage rate cannot convey proper information on the opportunity cost of labour. Instead a shadow wage has to be calculated. Such a shadow wage should represent both the sacrifices made in terms of production foregone and the compensation for harder work and a worse working environment (which may be negative if the project offers better environments and better working conditions than the alternatives). How this shadow wage is to be calculated is discussed in the specialized monographs mentioned above.

It should be noted, however, that the use of shadow wages (or any other shadow price) is really a second best solution to the allocation problem. If one uses a shadow wage which is lower than the prevailing market wage for the calculation of profitability for a particular project, one is not really comparing that project with all other projects but only with those that are using the same shadow wage. If all potential projects (including all private projects) were calculated with the same shadow wage quite a different ranking of the projects may result. It is therefore necessary to be quite careful in using shadow prices, trying to include as many as possible of the potential projects.

Large projects

So far, we have assumed that the project does not change any of the ruling prices. That meant that we could take the prices as given in evaluating the project. However, it is quite often the case that a project is so 'big' in some of its dimensions that prices are affected.

The classical example is the construction of a bridge. Before the bridge is built, the cost of crossing the river is very high (in some cases infinite because it is impossible to cross the river). After the bridge has been constructed, the cost of one more crossing of the river is very low and can approximately be assumed to be zero. Here the price of crossing the river has changed drastically due to the project. Similarly, a dam for irrigation may reduce the cost of water supply, or the opening up of a coal mine in an arid region, consuming huge quantities of water, may increase the cost of water supply.

The problem we have to solve is to determine which price to use in project evaluations when the price changes as a consequence of the project. Intuitively, one feels that some average of the pre-project price and the post-project price should be used. That this result is approximately true can be argued in the following way.

The demand curve for a good or service that is supplied by the project is shown in Figure 1.1.

Prior to the project nothing at all of the good is supplied, which can be represented by point A in the diagram. As a result of the project, price will go down to $\bar{p}$ and demand will increase from zero to $\bar{x}$. For the first unit of the good, consumers are willing to pay p_1. Thus the value of the first unit is p_1. They are only willing to pay p_2 for the second unit, and their

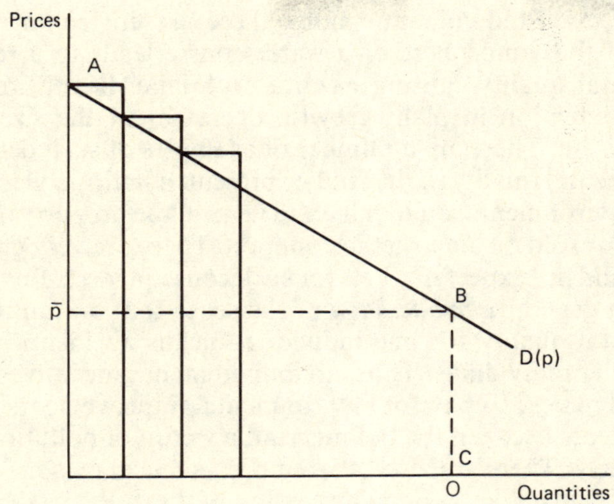

Figure 1.1

willingness to pay for two units is thus $p_1 + p_2$. Similarly, for three units they are willing to pay $p_1 + p_2 + p_3$.

Obviously, we can continue this line of thought until we have reached the quantity $\bar{x}$.But then the willingness to pay $p_1 + p_2 + \ldots$ can be approximated by the area under the demand curve, i.e. OABCO. This is the total willingness to pay for the quantity $\bar{x}$. If we assume that the demand curve is a straight line the area is equal to

$$\frac{(p_1 - \bar{p})\bar{x}}{2} + \bar{p}\bar{x} = \frac{p_1 + \bar{p}}{2}\bar{x},$$

i.e. the arithmetic average of p_1 and $\bar{p}$ times the quantity $\bar{x}$. This argument is not theoretically correct, because price changes induce changes in real income, which complicates the picture. However, Willig[5] has shown that often it is a reasonable approximation to neglect these complications.

We have carried out the discussion in terms of a price change on a good that is supplied by the project. We could also have looked at a price change for an input to the project and reached a similar conclusion.

Evaluating environmental consequences

In the previous section we discussed cases where market prices do exist but do not carry correct information on social opportunity costs. There are, however, many projects that carry important consequences that are not priced at all in any market. Such consequences are generally known as *external effects*. Predominant among these are environmental effects. Pollution of the atmosphere or a water course leads to a reduction of environmental quality causing hazards to human health, reduction of amenities, reduction in plant growth, decreases of the size of animal populations, etc. There are a number of examples of such deteriorations of environmental quality in the studies presented in this collection. These effects on environmental quality have in general the property that they are not bought or sold on a market in common. There are very good reasons why we should not expect markets for such consequences. Environmental quality is in general a *public good* in the sense that an improvement in environmental quality for one individual means an identical improvement for other individuals. Thus, no individual has incentives to reveal a positive willingness to pay for environmental improvements and voluntary agreements between the polluter and a victim of pollution would be highly unlikely. There are also other, more technical reasons for making such agreements unlikely. For a discussion of these, the reader is referred to Dasgupta and Heal[5], and Mäler[6].

But even if there are no market prices on most environmental consequences from a project, it is still possible to apply the same basic idea in order to evaluate environmental consequences as the one underlying the functioning of markets. The value of an environmental improvement is thus defined as the willingness to pay on the part of the individuals to obtain this improvement.

As discussed earlier, we are by this definition sidestepping some theoretical problems concerning the difference between the so-called compensating variation and the equivalent variation. By the compensating variation we mean the amount with which we have to compensate the individual for a change in the environment. For an environmental improvement, the compensating variation coincides with the willingness-to-pay concept, but for an environmental degradation the two concepts are different. The equivalent variation is the amount which is regarded equivalent to the environmental change by the individual. For an environmental degradation the willingness-to-pay concept coincides with the equivalent variation. Both these concepts are from a theoretical point of view correct measures of the individual's values. They are also in general not very different, but in some instances they may yield drastically different results.

Consider the case of an environmental degradation in the form of a dam construction which will flood a valley. One old man who has lived in the valley for all his life will be forced to move if the dam is constructed. His equivalent variation, or the amount one should reduce his income in order to expose him to an equivalent worsening of welfare, is bounded upwards by his income. On the other hand, his compensating variation is not bounded upwards and can be quite substantial. Although the two measures are radically different in this case, they both give valid measures of the welfare changes of the old man. The problem appears when we compare the welfare of this individual with the welfare of others, i.e. all those consumers of electricity who will gain by the construction of the dam. If we want to put special emphasis on the old man in the valley, we should choose to use the compensating variation, while if we want to treat him on an equal footing with the electricity consumer we should use the equivalent variation. For a detailed discussion on the concepts of equivalent and compensating variations, see Mäler, *Environmental Economics: A Theoretical Inquiry*, Johns Hopkins University Press, 1974. However, we will in the rest of this chapter ignore the difference between the two concepts and continue to use the willingness-to-pay concept.

As there are no markets for environmental quality, it is not possible to measure the value of environmental quality directly from market data. Instead, more roundabout methods have to be used. Roughly speaking, these methods can be classified into four classes:

1 Whenever the environmental quality change affects marketable outputs (or inputs) that part can be measured by using market prices.
2 Asking the individuals exposed to a change in the environment for their willingness to pay.
3 The change in environmental quality will induce shifts in individual behaviour. By measuring these shifts it may be possible to assess the willingness to pay.
4 Sometimes environmental quality changes will be capitalized in market prices such as property values and wages. By measuring these capitalization effects, the willingness to pay for an environmental improvement may be assessed.

These four groups are obviously not mutually independent but on the contrary to a large extent overlapping. For example, capitalization of environmental damage in land values obviously requires a change in individual behaviour, i.e. a desire to move from the degraded environment to a better one.

Before discussing these four groups of approaches, it is necessary to stress the importance of using a well defined concept of environmental change. These changes may be measured in several ways, depending on the specific problem at hand. Sometimes ambient concentrations of pollutants are used. Other times changes in biological populations or changes in landscape are appropriate variables. One should also not forget that sometimes an environmental quality change is best measured as a change in a probability distribution. For example, air pollution giving rise to health effects is best attacked from the point of view of a change in the probability distribution of morbidity and mortality. This is illustrated in the case on air pollution epidemiology.

Quite often, an environmental degradation or improvement leads to change in expenditures. For instance, increased particulate pollution may increase cleaning costs. Increased ambient concentrations of sulphur oxides may increase corrosion and thereby shorten the life of some materials. Increased acidification may result in reductions in the growth of biomass, both in agriculture and in forestry. All these examples are examples of *financial costs*, i.e. changes in expenditures that are associated with a change in environmental quality.

Generally, these financial costs are not difficult to estimate as long as we know the physical effects, i.e. the rate of corrosion, the reduction in biomass growth, etc. These are market prices that can be used to evaluate the cost of these effects.

However, in general there are other kinds of costs simultaneously with financial costs. To a certain degree it is possible to reduce the noise from a highway by retrofitting the windows, increasing the insulation, etc. The costs of these measures are easily calculated. However, this financial cost will not include the loss of amenity by not being able to open the windows, or by not being able to sit in the backyard enjoying a quiet evening. Thus, there is often a need to complement the financial cost estimates with estimates of amenity losses. Methods of doing that will be discussed next. Financial costs are treated in detail by Mäler and Wyzga[8] and Freeman.[9] One example included in the cases is the cost of corrosion due to sulphur dioxide emissions.

The most natural approach to find out the willingness to pay for an environmental improvement is of course to ask the concerned individuals directly. However, this approach has both theoretical and practical problems connected with it.

The classical problem is that there may be strong incentives for the individuals to distort their answers. Assume that the decision to improve the environment will be based on the responses from the individuals and that the individuals have to pay the amounts they have said were their willingness to pay for the improvement. It is then in the interest of the individual to give a low response, thus avoiding the possibility to pay his true willingness to pay and hoping that the responses from others would be sufficient to pay for the improvement. In this case, every individual has incentives to understate his willingness to pay for the improvement.

On the other hand, if the individual does not have to pay the amount he has responded with, but instead according to some tariff schedule independent of his response, he may have incentives to overstate his willingness to pay. In particular, if the questions are purely hypothetical, one should expect a bias upward of the stated willingness to pay. For a theoretical discussion of these incentives the reader is referred to Mäler, *Environmental Economics.*

More or less ingenious schemes have been invented to reduce the bias or completely eliminate it. So far those schemes are too complicated to be used (at the present, at least) in practice.

Only a few experiments on the quantitative importance of the possible bias have been carried out. The most interesting one was carried out by Peter Bohm.[10] His main result was that there seems to be very little bias, if there is any, in responses on willingness to pay for public goods.

From a practical point of view, there are important problems and in particular if the questions are purely hypothetical. Individuals are in these cases supposed to answer questions they have never been asked before and have had no reasons to make a real analysis of. In spite of these problems, some successful attempts have been made to estimate the willingness to pay by asking people through *bidding games*. These are special procedures which are used to reveal the willingness to pay for a particular amenity. The bidding game technique is presented in Schultz *et al.*,[11] and d'Arge *et al.*[12] It is also discussed in Freeman.[13]

Very often a change in the environment causes individuals to alter their behaviour. In fact, the financial cost estimates are quite often based on the fact that individuals do change their behaviour. The financial cost of particulate pollution is based on the assumption that the individuals increase their cleaning activities, i.e. change their behaviour. In a way, cleaning activities are substitutes to pollution reducton.

In general there may exist private marketable goods and services which are *substitutes* or *complements* or have other similar relations to environmental quality changes. By estimating the change in demand for these private goods, caused by a change in the environment, it is quite often possible to estimate the willingness to pay for environmental improvements. The discussion of this approach very easily becomes highly technical and the reader is referred to the books by Mäler and Wyzga[14], and Freeman.[15]

Sometimes environmental changes are capitalized in market prices. If, for example, air pollution gets worse in one district in a metropolitan area, one would expect land values in that district to fall in such a way that it corresponds to the willingness to pay for pollution abatement. If land values fall by less, people would move out of the district causing a further fall in land values. In equilibrium an individual would be indifferent between living in the different regions, requiring a complete capitalization of environmental quality changes. By measuring how land values depend on environmental quality variables, it would then be possible to assess the willingness to pay for pollution abatement.

The approach is, however, based on some quite restrictive assumptions. First, we have to assume perfect markets for land. Second, we have to assume either that all individuals are completely identical or that they live in completely segregated communities, so that all individuals in one community have the same preferences and the same income. Third, environmental changes must not be capitalized in any other prices. For a discussion of these assumption, see Mäler.[16] For a more positive attitude toward using land values, see Freeman.[17] Environmental differences may also be capitalized in wages. The case study on air pollution epidemiology uses an estimate of how risk of accidents affect wage rates to evaluate the health costs from air pollution.

Intertemporal trade-offs

By using the methods described in previous sections, it is possible to reduce the description of the project to a stream of net benefits:

$$B_0, B_1, \ldots, B_\tau, B_T$$

over the different time periods τ. Some of these may be negative. In fact we will assume that B_0 is negative, i.e. the society is experiencing a net cost in the first time period.

In order to make a judgement whether a project is worthwhile undertaking, it is necessary to weight the net benefits in the different time periods with each other. This is accomplished by computing the *present value* of the stream

$$PV = B_0 + \frac{B_1}{1+r_1} + \frac{B_2}{(1+r_1)(1+r_2)} + \ldots + \frac{B_T}{(1+r_1)(1+r_2)\ldots(1+r_T)}$$

If PV is positive, the project should be accepted; if negative it should be rejected. r_1, r_2, etc. are the interest rates by which future benefits are discounted to present values. r_1 is the interest rate in period 1, r_2 in period 2 and so on.

$1/1+r_1$ can be considered the amount we would be willing to *give up now* in order to have one unit of the numeraire (say \$) in period 1. In the same way $1/(1+r_1)(1+r_2)$ can be interpreted as the amount we are willing to give up now in order to get one dollar two periods ahead. The discount factors can thus be interpreted as prices on claims for one dollar due to be paid in future periods. The present value of a stream of net benefits can then be interpreted in the following simple way. B_τ is a claim on \$ B_τ to be paid in period τ. Multiplying B_τ with the price on a claim on \$1 in the same period gives the present value of B_τ.

It is a useful simplification to suppose that the interest rate will not change. We will therefore assume that

$$r_1 = r_2 = r_3 \ldots = r$$

and the formula for the present value simplifies to

$$PV = \sum_{\tau=0}^{T} \frac{B_\tau}{(1+r)^\tau} = B_0 + \frac{B_1}{1+r} + \ldots + \frac{B_T}{(1+r)^T}$$

The appropriate rate to be used in social cost-benefit analysis will be referred to as the *social rate of discount* or the *social interest rate.*

There are many controversies, both in the general discussion and among economists, about the choice of an interest rate. It has been argued that some consequences should be discounted at a certain rate while others should be discounted at a different rate. In particular, it has been argued that environmental consequences should be discounted at a zero rate while other consequences should be discounted at a positive rate. The argument being that the environment belongs to future generations as well as the present generation and discounting the environment may deprive our children of their heritage.

In view of our interpretation of the present value, this argument is not valid. The comparison between the environment and other consequences in each time period has already been made when the net benefit B_τ was computed. If the environment has a very great value fòr the generation living at time τ, that will be reflected in B_τ. The net benefit should correspond to the trade off between the environment and other goods that the generation living then is willing to make. This may be a very difficult thing to measure, but conceptually the net benefit should reflect the willingness to pay for the environment quality of the individuals living then. Obviously we do not know the preferences of future generations but that is a problem we have to live with, quite irrespective of the discounting procedures. We must, of course, use our best judgements about the willingness to pay for environmental improvements. But, and that is the important point, as soon as we have made an estimate of the value of the environment, all consequences of the project are directly comparable, and all constitute claims on resources which should be valued at the appropriate prices, i.e. they should be discounted.

The biggest controversy, however, is about the choice of an interest rate. The literature on this topic is huge and there is no good summary available. Ultimately, the choice of a discount rate is a political one. That does not mean that economic factors are irrelevant in determining the social discount rate. On the contrary, economic factors are important and often decisive inputs in determining a social rate of discount.

Before discussing those factors, it may be a good idea to briefly discuss some reasons for a positive interest rate. One such reason is myopia: people are nearsighted and may lack the necessary imagination to fully appreciate future consumption. In terms of marginal rates of substitution between consumption in different time periods, it means that when consumption is the same in two periods, the rate of substitution is greater than one. There is fairly good empirical evidence that people in general are myopic, but that does not necessarily mean that society as a whole should use a positive interest rate to discount future net benefits. In fact, quite a few distinguished economists have argued that society should free itself from nearsightedness and discard this reason for a positive interest rate. On the other hand, if society is the set of its citizens it should reflect the preferences of these citizens. If the citizens are myopic then so should the society be. Obviously, this is a political question and an important political element behind the choice of the social rate of discount.

Another reason for having a positive interest rate is the productivity of capital and the growth of the economy. If the economy is growing, those who benefit in the future from a project will be wealthier and consequently value one more unit of the numeraire less than it is valued at the present. But this amounts to the same thing as discounting future dollars at a positive interest rate. Finally, the fact that investment in other activities in general is profitable means that taking resources away for a particular project has an opportunity cost that must be taken into account.

How all these factors should be combined so as to produce a social rate of discount is a very difficult problem and the reader is referred to specialized literature on that topic. Here it suffices to stress the importance of the opportunity cost concept. If we could neglect all other aspects of the problem of choosing an interest rate, then the opportunity cost would be the decisive factor. With perfect capital markets and no taxes or other interventions, the ruling market rate would be the appropriate. However, with imperfect markets, corporate income taxes etc. the situation is not so simple. One has to try to find out which other activities are displaced by this particular project and estimate the opportunity cost for each of these displaced activities. If consumption is reduced, then the appropriate rate is the one consumers get on their savings. If private investments are displaced, then it is the total (i.e. corporate taxes included) returns that matter. If both private investments and private consumption are displaced, then one has to use some kind of weighted average of the two measures. The reader is referred to Robert Lind, *Discounting for Time and Risk in Energy Policy*, Johns Hopkins University Press (1982), for a more detailed discussion.

Before leaving intertemporal problems, there are three further remarks that must be made. First, all the discussions so far have been in *real terms.* In real life, inflation is a pervasive phenomenon, which must be taken into account. In particular the nominal interest rates are substantially higher than the real interest rates. Although it seems self-evident, too much bad reasoning in the past makes it necessary to stress that it is *the real rate of interest* that matters, not the nominal rate observed on credit markets.

Second, although the present value criterion is the basic investment criterion, it is possible to use derived criteria. One such criterion, which in most real applications is equivalent to the present value criterion, is *the internal rate of return* criterion. The internal rate of return is defined as the rate of discount that makes the present value equal to zero. It is thus defined as i in

$$0 = \sum_{\tau=0}^{T} \frac{B_\tau}{(1+i)^\tau}$$

If i is greater than the social rate of discount, r, the project is worth undertaking and if i is less than r the project should be rejected.

Third, very often a project is described by some average net benefit figure. To be more specific, assume that $B_0 = -K < 0$ and that $B_1 > 0$, $B_2 > 0, \ldots B_T > 0$. Then it is often the case that annual depreciations D of the original investment K is calculated and the annual benefits are calculated as

$$B_1 - D, B_2 - D, \ldots, B_T - D.$$

If these are positive, the project is accepted, and if negative rejected.

This procedure depends crucially on the way the depreciation charges are calculated. *This technique should not be used for project evaluation.* However, in some circumstances it may be useful to have an estimate of annual net benefits minus depreciation. In those calculations it is necessary to have a correct measure of depreciation. To be specific, assume that the project consists of investment K_0 in a certain structure with a certain lifetime T. Assume that the net benefits include the increased costs of maintenance and reduced production due to ageing of the structure. That enables us to look only at the physical lifetime of the structure.

The depreciation changes should be such that they reflect the fall in the value of the structure. If that is the case, $B_T - D$ will be the amount that can be spent on consumption without reducing the value of the total assets. In order to calculate the depreciation changes we thus have to calculate the value of the structure.

At the beginning of the time period t we have the choice of scrapping the structure and buying a new one (at the same cost K_0) or continue using the old structure. The value of the structure is obviously the difference between the cost of scrapping and buying a new one and keeping the old one. The cost C_s^t of scrapping the existing structure at period t is given by

$$C_s^t = K_0\left(1 + \frac{1}{(1+r)^T} + \frac{1}{(1+r)^{2T}} + \ldots\right) = K_0 \frac{(1+r)^T}{(1+r)^T - 1}$$

i.e. the investment cost at t plus the present value of making the same investment T years later, $2T$ years later, etc. The cost of keeping the structure, and replacing it at period T, and then a new structure at $2T - t$ etc. is given by

$$C_k^t = \frac{K_0}{(1+r)^{T-t}}\left(1 + \frac{1}{(1+r)^T} + \frac{1}{(1+r)^{2T}} + \ldots\right)$$

$$= \frac{K_0}{(1+r)^{T-t}} \frac{(1+r)^T}{(1+r)^T - 1} = K_0 \frac{(1+r)^t}{(1+r)^T - 1}$$

The value of the existing structure at period t is given by

$$K_t = C_s^t - C_k^t = K_0 \frac{(1+r)^T - (1+r)^t}{(1+r)^T - 1}$$

It follows that $K_T = 0$ and $K_0 = K_0$ as would be expected.

The depreciation changes D_t in period t are then given by

$$D_t = K_{t-1} - K_t = K_0 \frac{(1+r)^t - (1+r)^{t-1}}{(1+r)^T - 1} = K_0 (1+r)^t \frac{r}{(1+r)^T - 1}.$$

If depreciation changes are calculated according to this formula, $B_\tau - D_\tau$ will correspond to the consumption from the project in period τ that can be allowed without reducing the value of the capital asset.

Uncertainty

It is a truism that the future is concealed by uncertainty. The real problem is how to act in view of this uncertainty.

Let Y be the present value of the project. Y is not known now with certainty but is a stochastic variable with some probability distribution. It is thus possible that Y may be negative with a positive probability and positive also with a positive probability. Should the project be accepted? If we accept some very reasonable assumptions on rational decision-making,[18] it is possible to show that there exists a *utility function $U(Y)$ such that the correct criterion is to maximize the expected value of the utility function.* Unless we know the utility function (or at least some of its properties), this criterion is not very practicable.

However, in certain situations it is possible to conclude that the society should act as if it is *risk neutral.* By risk neutrality is meant that one is indifferent between a lottery ticket with a chance to win and a chance to lose and a certain outcome equal to the expected value of the lottery ticket. If society is risk neutral, the utility function is linear and we should try to maximize the expected value of Y. Situations in which this is true are when the present value Y is distributed among many individuals who share the benefits (if $Y > 0$) or the costs (if $Y < 0$) roughly equally.[19]

If environmental changes are an important aspect of the project this result is not valid because of the public good nature of the environment. It is not possible to divide the environment up among the citizens in a way that the result require.

Very often, uncertain projects are evaluated with uncertain variables replaced by their expected values, or *certainty equivalents*. This procedure, which is extremely simple, is based on some restrictive assumptions. One such assumption is that the technical constraints can be described by linear equations. However, it should be noted that if the project has irreversible impact on the environment, the use of certainty equivalents may lead the analyst astray. This is demonstrated in the last case study in this volume. In practical applications, the only way of including uncertainty may be to carry out sensitivity analysis in order to find out critical values for the project design parameters. Anyhow, it is better to be explicit about the uncertainty than to compute expected values with a very low information content.

Income distribution

The choice among projects have income distribution implications. Therefore these distribution implications are important in carrying out a social cost-benefit analysis. It is sometimes possible to include distributional values directly into the analyses by formulizing values on equity hold in the society. For a discussion of this approach the reader is referred to the book by Helmers.[20]

The most common way to handle the income distribution problem is, however, to compute the impact of the project on different income groups. Then it is up to the decision-maker to choose between the different alternatives, both with respect to their efficiency and equity.

Notes

1 *Guidelines for Project Evaluation* (1972), U.N.I.D.O., New York. Helmers, F.L.C.H., *Project Planning and Income Distribution*, Martinus Nijhoff Publishing, Boston, 1972.
Lesourne, J. (1975), *Cost Benefit Analysis and Economic Theory*, New York.
2 Dasgupta, P. (1983), *The Control of Resources*, Basil Blackwell Ltd., Oxford.
3 U.N.I.D.O., op. cit.
4 Helmers, op. cit.
5 Dasgupta, P. and Heal, G. (1979), *Economic Theory and Exhaustible Resources*, Cambridge.
6 Mäler, K.-G. (1974), *Environmental Economics – A Theoretical Inquiry*. Johns Hopkins University Press.

7 Willig, R. (1976), 'Consumer Surplus without Apology', *American Economic Review*, vol. 66, pp. 589–597.
8 *Economic Measurement of Environmental Damage*, O.E.C.D., 1976.
9 Freeman III, A. M., *The Benefits of Environmental Improvement*, Johns Hopkins University Press, 1979.
10 Bohm, P., 'An Approach to the Problem of Estimating Demand for Public Goods: An Experiment', *European Economic Review*, vol. 3, no. 2, 1972, pp. 111–130.
11 Brookshire, D., Ives, B. and Schultze, W., 'The Valuation of Aesthetic Preferences', *Journal of Environmental Economics and Management*, vol. 3, no. 4, pp. 325–346.
12 Schultze, W., d'Arge, R. and Brookshire, D., *Valuing Environmental Commodities: Some Recent Experiments*, University of Wyoming, unpublished, 1980.
13 Freeman, op. cit., p. 85.
14 Economic Measurement, op. cit., p. 82.
15 Freeman, op. cit., p. 62.
16 Mäler, K.-G., 'A Note on the Use of Property Values in Estimating Marginal Willingness to Pay for Environmental Quality', *Journal of Environmental Economics and Management*, vol. 4, 1977, pp. 355–369.
17 Freeman, op. cit., p. 108.
18 See, for example, Luce, R. D. and Raiffa, H., *Games and Decisions*, New York, 1977.
19 Arrow, K. and Lind, R., 'Uncertainty and the Evaluation of Public Investment Decisions', *American Economic Review*, 60, vol. 364–378.
20 Helmers, op. cit.

2

Economic Valuation of Environmental Quality Aspects of Upland Agricultural Projects in Korea

Dr Sung-Hoon Kim
Dr John A. Dixon

INTRODUCTION

The need to plan watershed developments in an *integrated* manner has long been recognized. The reasons are clear enough. While watersheds are fairly self-contained ecological systems, their components (e.g. uplands and downlands) are severely interlinked. The most critical sector of a watershed in the ecological sense is forest cover (the uplands). Such forests not only offer their direct yield to the rural population, they maintain ecological balance and water regime, prevent floods and droughts, wind and water erosion and sedimentation. Indeed, to take an analogy, an upland forest is related to the rest of the watershed in much the same way as *basic* industries are to the rest of an industrial economy.

Despite its importance, there have been very few attempts at conducting social cost-benefit analyses of integrated watershed development projects. This is easy to understand: the problems involved in carrying out such analyses are unusually difficult. (For a brief theoretical account of the issue involved, see Chapter 2, section 2.4 of Dasgupta (1982).)

The case-study by Kim and Dixon included here is *not* about an integrated watershed development project. Rather, it is aimed at locating the *least-cost* method of avoiding soil erosion and soil-nutrient losses in the hilly uplands in the districts of Icheon and Gochang, Korea. These losses are occurring because of the development of agricultural projects on, what were earlier, partially forested slopes. Kim and Dixon identify two broad categories of environmental losses due to this: first, the loss in productivity of the uplands, and second, the siltation of the paddy fields in the downlands.

In their study the authors in fact compare two methods (or projects) of avoiding soil erosion and nutrient losses. The first project consists simply of *replacing* the lost nutrients and soil in the uplands and clearing the silted paddy fields in the downlands. The total annual cost of this project is estimated to be won 268,963 (see page 31). Assuming a 15 year time horizon and a 10% discount rate the present value of the project's costs is therefore won 2,045,754 (see page 31). The alternative project the authors consider consists of the use of new management techniques; in particular that of straw mulching and vertical mulching combined with *some* soil and nutrient replacement. The present value of the costs associated with this project over the same time horizon and using the same discount rate is estimated to be won 1,074,249 (see page 33), or, slightly in excess of *half* the cost of the first project. The case study therefore makes a clear recommendation that the preventive medicine is better than the curative one.

This study, as the authors note, is not a complete cost-benefit analysis of environmental protection measures associated with conserving soil and its nutrients in these hilly slopes. The case-study does not estimate the *benefits* from preservation. It offers the prescription: if the soil in the uplands and its nutrients are to be preserved, then it is better to use new management techniques, in particular a combination of soil and nutrient replacement and straw and vertical mulching, than to rely exclusively on soil and nutrient replacement.[1] Therefore, the study implies that *if* the present value of social benefits from preservation exceeds the costs associated with the new management techniques, these techniques ought to be pursued.

Notes

1 The authors note (see page 33) that the new management techniques have the additional benefit of increasing the yield in the uplands by over won 580,000 per year.

CASE STUDY

Background information

Korea is a rapidly urbanizing country with a growing population and increasing needs for food. To meet its food needs Korea is putting more and more upland areas into agricultural production. As relatively flat farm land is lost to urban growth and industrial development, the development of hilly upland areas is seen as a major option for future expansion of agricultural production.

In this case study, 'uplands' refer to all cultivated uplands other than terraced rice paddy fields; most of these uplands are located on hillsides. Uncultivated uplands are classified as 'forest' lands (even though some of these lands are only marginally forested). About two-thirds of the total land area in Korea is classified as forest lands (see Table 2.1).

The total cultivated agricultural area is about 2.2 million hectares in Korea and the non-rice paddy field uplands account for about 40 per cent of this total. There are about 2.1 million farm families, and each farm is slightly larger than 1 hectare. Korea's population is over 38 million people and, since domestic production is insufficient to meet domestic demand, about 2 billion dollars worth of food is imported each year.

Table 2.1 *Land Use in Korea, 1978*

	Cultivated or Arable Land					
	Paddy-rice	*Upland*	*Total*	*Forest*	*Others*	*Total*
Area ('000 ha)	1,290	948	2,238	6,613	1,028	9,880
Percentage of Total Area (%)	13.1	9.6	22.7	66.9	10.4	100

– Arable land per capita—0.06 ha
– Forest land per capita—0.18 ha

Table 2.2 *Amount of Arable Land Converted to Non-Agricultural Uses, 1966–1981, Korea*

	1966–69	*1971–73*	*1976*	*1977*	*1978–81*
Converted Area (ha)	46,000	72,000	10,000	14,000	48,000*

* Estimate based on the 1976–1977 rate of decrease in arable land of 12,000 ha per year.

In the 1970–1978 period Korea's growth rate of population was 2 per cent per year, and real GNP per capita grew at 8.1 per cent per year. In order to meet the rapidly increasing demand for food and other agricultural products and to compensate for farmland lost to urban and industrial development (Table 2.2), the Government has embarked on an ambitious programme for upland development. The ultimate potential for further upland development of land with a slope of less than 30 per cent has been estimated by the Agriculture Development Corporation as 516 thousand hectares, divided among 2,400 parcels. Of this area less than 30 per cent has a slope of less than 15 per cent.

Environmental dimensions

In the past the performance of upland development areas has not been entirely satisfactory, mainly due to poor design and construction coupled with the inadequate soil management techniques used in cultivation. This resulted in heavy soil erosion and deterioration of the existing natural systems. Soil erosion and downstream deposition of silt have created serious damage to the environment as well as antagonism from paddy-growers. Some areas reclaimed by private initiative were abandoned as productivity fell due to the low level of fertility and moisture retaining capacity.

As a result, both policy-makers and farmers have had increasing doubts about the effects of upland development. Despite the need to expand the agricultural production base of Korea, the government seems ready to reduce its strong commitment to upland development.

In the past, little emphasis was given to environmental aspects in planning for and evaluating upland reclamation projects. Conventional cost-benefit analysis techniques were used, and only such positive products as increased production of food grains and fresh produce were included as benefits. Environmental factors such as soil erosion, water run-off, and siltation effects on downhill streams, rivers and paddy lands were ignored. Therefore, a comprehensive re-evaluation of upland agricultural projects is required to evaluate these environmental dimensions properly.

In this context, economic valuations of environmental effects of various soil management techniques are presented. These analyses are based on physical data obtained by the Office of Rural Development Soil Science Research Team in Icheon and Gochang where net areas of 272 and 325 hectares of hillside lands were initially developed in 1974 (Figure 2.1).

These areas are hilly uplands with an average slope of 15 per cent and red-yellow sandy loam soils. The fields were planted twice a year with one soybean and one barley crop. By using a Lysimeter, soil and nutrient loss rates were measured with the soybean barley cropping system under nine different types of soil treatments. The test plots were 10 metres long by 2 metres wide and had a 15 per cent slope.

Since the main environmental problems were rapid water run-off (causing soil erosion) and lack of deep percolation of rainwater into the fields, the soil management techniques were designed to slow run-off and increase water infiltration. The soil management techniques used included various forms of trenching, chiselling, mulching, and vertical mulching. The reduction in soil erosion between the control (check) plot and the other treatments is presented in Table 2.3. Annual soil losses were reduced by up to 90 per cent in some cases.

Table 2.3 *Soil Loss in Upland Areas – A Comparison of Existing Practices and New Management Techniques, 1976–1977* (in kg/0.1 ha)

			New Management Techniques							
Year	*Crop*	*Existing Practices (Control Plot)*	*Grass Band*	*Chiselling*	*Trenching*	*Vertical Mulching*	*Mulching*	*Mulch + Chisel*	*Mulch + Trench*	*Mulch + Vertical Mulch*
1976	Soybean	4,275	1,802	2,217	2,092	1,269	940	707	542	512
	Barley	432	52	188	212	100	70	70	58	52
	Annual Total	4,707	1,854	2,405	2,304	1,369	1,010	777	600	564
1977	Soybean	3,116	689	1,276	2,062	1,961	227	235	310	149
	Barley	246	20	184	211	221	3	3	0.3	1
	Annual Total	3,362	709	1,460	2,273	2,182	230	238	310.3	150
Annual	Average	4,035	1,282	1,933	2,289	1,776	621	508	455	357
	Index	100	31.8	47.9	56.7	44.0	15.4	12.6	11.3	8.9

Note: 1 *Are*(a) = 100 m^2; 1 hectare = 100 *Are*(a).

The different soil treatments used are defined in Table 2.4 and their annual costs are presented in Table 2.5.

The problem

In order to evaluate the trade-offs involved between the various improved agricultural practices, a *Replacement-Cost Approach* analysis will be used. This technique is briefly mentioned in Chapter 7 of the *Guide*.[1]

The replacement-cost approach is based on the premise that the costs of replacing productive assets that have been damaged because of pollution or improper on-site management can be measured. These costs are taken as a minimum estimate of the value of measures which will reduce pollution or improve on-site management practices.

In this case study the productive asset that has been damaged is the soil in the upland areas. Leaching of nutrients and soil erosion have both occurred and have decreased the value of the land by reducing its productivity. The cost of physically replacing lost soil and restoring lost nutrients is measured (the replacement cost); this cost is then used as the *minimum benefit* or *value* from steps taken to prevent these environmental problems. When the proposed preventive steps cost less than the replacement costs, the preventive measures are economically justified. The assumption is that these replacement costs are not greater than the value of the productive resources destroyed – that is, that the replacement is worth doing.

This approach is not the same as the Shadow Project Approach. If the services of an environmental resource (a field, a fishery) are lost because of a development project, one way to calculate the value of that resource is to estimate the cost of another project that would replace the lost resource. This 'shadow-project' is then used as a surrogate for the value of the threatened environmental service (a service that may be difficult to value). For example, if a lake shore land in a rural area is presently used for outdoor recreation but is required for an industrial development, a shadow-project evaluation would examine the cost of creating a similar lake and surroundings in another area. In the Korean example, a shadow project is not considered. Rather, detailed estimates of the costs of physically replacing productive assets (soil and nutrients) are made.

The data

In the case study two types of physical losses are considered – soil and nutrients. While these two losses frequently occurred simultaneously

Table 2.4 *Definitions of Soil Treatment Techniques*

1. Control plots of conventional soil management practice——Topsoil is ploughed to a depth of 20 centimetres for the first crop of the year; it is also limed and fused-phosphate is applied at a rate equivalent to 5 per cent phosphorous.

2. Gràss band——Weeping love grass is planted in bands 20 centimetres wide with 2 metres intervals.

3. Chiselling*——The soil surface is broken to a depth of 60 centimetres and a width of one metre by using tractor-attached bullet-headed driller. The bands are 2 metres apart.

4. Trenching*——A line of trenches is dug, 80 centimetres deep with a width of 20 centimetres, at 2 metres intervals. The trenches are filled in with loose soil.

5. Vertical mulching*——Trenches are dug as above but filled in part with rice-straw. The topsoil is treated as in the control plot.

6. Mulching——The surface is covered with rice-straws at a rate of 300 kg/10 *Are* after every seed-sowing.

Notes

* The so-called 'subsoiling technique' includes chiselling, trenching, and vertical mulching.

1 ha = 100 *Are*,

Table 2.5 *Costs of the Various Upland Soil Management Techniques (Won per hectare; US$1.00 = Won 690; and one man-day farm wage = Won 5,000)*

1. Control plot of conventional practices (incurred annually) (tiller ploughing + lime and phosphorous application)	W 35,000
2. Establishing grass bands (once every 3 years) (weeping love grass + 5 man-days labour)	W 125,000
3. Chiselling (once every 2 years) (tractor hire + 2 man-days labour)	W 110,000
4. Trenching (once every 2 years) (tractor hire + 4 man-days labour)	W 120,000
5. Vertical mulching (once every 4 years) (tractor hire + rice straw + 2 man-days labour + lime and phosphorous application)	W 185,000 (1st yr) W 85,000 (year 5, 9, 13 . . .)
6. Mulching (annual cost) (rice straw + 2 man-days labour)	W 90,000

(heavy rains leading to soil erosion and water run-off), in this analysis they are considered as separate elements.

Soil loss
The two sample survey areas (Icheon and Gochang) were measured for soil loss by the Research Bureau of the Office of Rural Development. They found average, annual soil losses of 40.35 tons per hectare, close to the theoretical loss of 39.9 tons per hectare estimated from the Universal Soil Loss Equation. The environmental effects of this erosion are considered later.

Nutrient loss
Average annual nutrient loss per hectare was calculated by use of a Lysimeter on trial plots. The losses were as follows:

Nutrient	*Rate of Loss (kg/ha)*
N	15.7
P	3.6
K	14.6
Ca	10.6
Mg	1.6
Organic Matter (O.M.)	75.4

Water run-off
During the two year observation period average annual run-off per hectare was 1,380 tons, or equivalent to roughly 1380 mm of rainfall. While average rainfall in Korea is about 1200 mm per year (see Table 2.11 and Figure 2.1), the sample areas had heavier rainfall than the average. A very high percentage of total rainfall was lost through run-off. The run-off caused the soil erosion and nutrient leaching.

The economic analysis

The analysis evaluates the environmental costs associated with present upland management practices and the benefits and costs of alternative soil management techniques. Soil erosion has resulted in the siltation of downstream paddy fields, especially in the first two years after establishing the upland area. To counteract this erosion, a number of treatments have been devised to stabilize the soil (Tables 2.4 and 2.5).

Table 2.3 shows the soil loss associated with soybean and barley production in upland areas under conventional and various proposed management practices. The type of crop grown, as well as rainfall quantity and timing, obviously affect the soil loss rates. With conventional practices, soil losses are high: over 40 tons per hectare. The use of new management techniques causes a dramatic drop in the erosion rates, especially when combined with the application of mulch.

Tables 2.6 and 2.7 show nutrient loss levels and water run-offs associated with the proposed new management practices.

Two concepts are considered in this case:

1 The cost of replacing the lost nutrients and soil in the upland areas and cleaning up the silted paddy fields downstream (the Replacement Cost).
2 The costs associated with the various new management practices. The use of these practices will reduce soil erosion and nutrient loss; the costs of implementing these practices and thereby reducing erosion need to be compared to the benefits of these actions, namely, the replacement costs foregone.

In this example only one new management technique is considered, that of combined straw mulching and vertical mulching. This combination gave the best results in physically controlling soil erosion (see Tables 2.3, 2.6 and 2.7).

In order to evaluate the two approaches, additional information is needed. The cost to recover and replace eroded soil in the upland fields is composed of truck rental and spreading costs. These charges are divisible and average won 2000 per ton of soil. The 1980 market values of nutrients (on an elemental basis) are given in Table 2.8. Labour costs for spreading nutrients and other materials average won 40 per kilogramme spread.

Soil and nutrient replacement are yearly phenomena. In addition, there are costs associated with implementing the new management technique as well as with the continued use of the conventional practice. The new technique, mulch plus vertical mulching, requires that appropriate measures be taken every 4 years. In the first year (year 1), the cost of vertical mulching is high: won 185,000 per hectare; in succeeding periods (years 5, 9, 13, etc.) the cost is reduced to won 85,000 per hectare since less labour and materials are required. In addition, there is a yearly expense for mulch of won 90,000 per hectare.

The conventional system only requires a recurring annual expenditure of won 35,000 for field maintenance and repair. However, the continuing erosion leads to down-stream siltation of paddy fields. This siltation creates damage and leads to decreased productivity; this loss is estimated at won 30,000 per year (60 litres of rice per hectare). A compensation payment is made from the upland to the lowland farmers to cover these losses.

A final cost under the conventional system is for supplemental irrigation. Assume that one-third of the annual run-off has to be replaced by commercial irrigation at an average cost of won 200 per ton of water. No irrigation is required under improved soil management practices.

Table 2.6 *Loss of Nutrient* (kg/0.1 ha/year)

		New Management Technique							
Components	*Existing Practice (Control Plot)*	*Grass Band*	*Chiselling*	*Trenching*	*Vertical Mulch*	*Mulching*	*Mulch + Chisel*	*Mulch + Trench*	*Mulch + Ver. Mulch*
Total N	1.572	0.643	1.132	1.141	0.869	0.634	0.485	0.404	0.494
P	0.358	0.041	0.187	0.121	0.080	0.033	0.014	0.010	0.013
K	1.459	0.700	1.120	1.193	0.922	0.689	0.544	0.454	0.556
Ca	1.061	0.296	0.670	0.587	0.432	0.283	0.201	0.165	0.203
Mg	0.162	0.039	0.105	0.096	0.072	0.049	0.036	0.029	0.036
Organic Matter	7.535	0.874	3.931	2.512	1.638	0.655	0.328	0.218	0.223

Table 2.7 *Amount of Run-off* (ton/0.1 ha/year)

		New Management Technique							
Year	*Existing Practice (Control Plot)*	*Grass Band*	*Chiselling*	*Trenching*	*Vertical Mulch*	*Mulching*	*Mulch + Chisel*	*Mulch + Trench*	*Mulch + Ver. Mulch*
1976	121.90	42.40	60.90	73.60	26.90	34.60	7.80	9.30	7.60
1977	153.92	67.76	87.78	102.31	66.22	26.31	28.92	19.22	19.91
Average	137.91	55.08	74.34	87.96	46.56	30.46	18.36	14.26	13.76
Index	100.	39.9	53.9	63.8	33.8	22.1	13.3	10.3	10.0

Table 2.8 *Market Values of Nutrients, 1980* (won/kg)

N	480
P	345
K	105
Ca	60
Mg	1,400
Organic matter	175

US$ = won 690.

Results

A Present Value of Net Benefits calculation was done comparing the two chosen alternatives: the present conventional practice and the new management technique of mulch plus vertical mulching. The analysis covered 15 years and used a 10 per cent discount rate (for sensitivity analysis purposes other discount rates, for example, 15 and 20 per cent, could also be used). Table 2.9 has details on crop yields for the different options and Table 2.10 lists 1980 prices for agricultural products in Korea. It is assumed that actual labour requirements for cultivation are the same under both options.

The present practices were evaluated first. This calculation gives the cost used in the Replacement Cost Approach, that is, how much it costs each year to replace lost soil and nutrients and maintain a given level of production. Based on the information given previously, these costs have 5 main components:

Field maintenance and repair	won	35,000
Compensation payments		30,000
Irrigation costs		92,000
Soil replacement		80,700
Nutrient replacement – materials		26,404
– labour		4,859
Total cost per hectare	won	268,963

This total cost, won 268,963, is an annual, recurring cost to maintain agricultural production and repair damages caused by soil erosion. The present value of these costs over 15 years at a 10 per cent discount rate is won 2,045,754.

The new management technique, vertical mulching plus mulching, has a different stream of costs associated with it. In a straight cost-comparison, the present value of these costs over 15 years will be

Table 2.9 *Crop Yields for Different Soil Management Techniques* (Non-irrigated uplands, kg per 0.1 ha)

Treatments	*Control Plot*	*Grass band*	*Chiselling*	*Trenching*	*Vertical Mulching*	*Mulching*	*Mulch + Chisel*	*Mulch + Trench*	*Mulch + Ver. Mulch*
Soybean	181	201	228	221	223	218	243	238	235
Barley	225	244	282	306	282	277	334	316	322

Table 2.10 *Agricultural Prices Received by Farmers, 1980*

Rice (won/100 l)	49,312
Barley (won/100 l)	23,224
Corn (won/100 l)	13,145
(Hulled) Peanut (won/100 l)	105,782
Soybean (won/100 l)	39,097
Sweet potato (won/3.75 kg)	491
Radish (won/3.75 kg)	269
Red pepper (won/0.6 kg)	2,730
Apple (won/18.75 kg)	5,043
Pear (won/18.75 kg)	5,039

Note: For rice, 100 l = 80 kg.
For all other crops, 100 l = 75 kg.

compared to those under the conventional practice. The fact that yields may even increase with the new technique (Table 2.9) is considered later.

The costs of the new technique are similar to those in the conventional approach for some items such as compensation, soil replacement and nutrient replacement. The amounts involved are much smaller, however, because of the very substantial decrease in soil erosion under the new management technique. There are no irrigation, field maintenance or repair costs but there are substantial land preparation and mulching costs:

Compensation payments	won	2,654
Soil replacement		7,140
Nutrient replacement – materials		4,016
– labour		610
Total recurring yearly costs	won	14,420
Land preparation – year 1	won	185,000
year 5, 9, 13		85,000
Mulch costs (annual)		90,000

The cost stream varies from year to year, with the largest cost occurring in year 1 and with periodic jumps in years 5, 9, and 13 when chiselling is redone. In other years the annual cost is only won 104,420. The present value of these costs over 15 years at a 10 per cent discount rate is won 1,074,249, or slightly more than half of the cost of the conventional technique. If the benefits from increased barley and soybean yields are added (see Tables 2.9 and 2.10) the attractiveness of the new approach increases. The value of increased yields is over won 580,000 per year.

This discussion will end here. It appears that the new soil management technique would be attractive even if yields were the same under both approaches (and even more attractive if the higher yield estimates are accurate). There may be some reasons why all farmers have not adopted the new technique. Possible reasons are listed here with indications of the types of data needed to answer the questions and suggestions for future research in this area:

1 Has the proper discount rate been used? Sensitivity analysis will illustrate how the results will change with higher and lower discount rates.
2 Are the costs charged to the conventional system actually cash costs that are paid by farmers? If compensation, soil replacement and irrigation are excluded, the yearly cost decreases over won 200,000 per hectare, which is a 75 per cent reduction. This change would make the conventional system less expensive than the new technique.
3 The new technique may require large cash expenditures for mulch plus vertical mulching. Is credit a constraint?
4 Will yields actually increase as indicated in Table 2.9? What can be realistically expected in farmers' fields?

Other questions can and should be asked to fully understand the implications and constraints of the proposed change. This example has shown how environmental aspects of an upland development programme have been incorporated in an economic analysis. The Replacement Cost Approach was used to determine the costs involved with an existing system and then compare these costs to those of a proposed alternative soil management technique. The fact that the new system appears economically very attractive from the social view may not assure its acceptance by farmers, however. The farmers must see it as attractive in terms of their own perceptions of costs. These costs include cash outlays, in kind contributions, and the timing of costs and benefits. If the social and private (farmer) perspectives vary, appropriate incentives may be required to secure adoption of the new system.

Universal soil loss equation

The Universal Soil Loss Equation (U.S.L.E.) relates a number of variables in predicting annual soil loss from any given piece of land.

The generalized form of the equation is:

$$A = R \cdot K \cdot LS \cdot C \cdot P$$

where: A = annual soil loss in tons per hectare
R = rainfall factor
K = soil erodibility factor

LS = length and slope factor
C = cropping factor
P = erosion control practice factor

In Icheon, one of the two sample areas, the variables had the following values:

R = 500
K = 0.25 for the sandy loam of Icheon
LS = 1.2 (average slope of 15°)
C = 0.35 for barley-soybean mix
P = 0.76 for contoured terraces

Therefore, $A = 500 \times 0.25 \times 1.2 \times 0.35 \times 0.76 = 39.9$ tons/ha/yr.

Standard reference works on soils explain how the U.S.L.E was developed and the ranges of values for the different parameters.

Table 2.11 *Rainfall Distribution by Region* (in m.m.)

Region	*January–May*	*June–August*	*September–December*	*Annual*
Seoul	248 (19.7%)	752 (59.7%)	260 (20.6%)	1,260 (100.0%)
Daejeon	257	669	238	1,164
Kwangju	309	593	321	1,223
Average	271 (22.3%)	671 (55.2%)	273 (22.5%)	1,215 (100.0%)

Table 2.12 *Soil Loss by Length and Slope*

Slope Angle	*Length of Slope* 10 m	20 m	30 m
10%	16.0	34.3	58.9
20	55.3	84.1	112.4
30	115.3	147.3	198.0

Table 2.13 *Soil Erodibility Factors (K) by Soil Type*

Soil	*Sand*	*Sand Loam*	*Loam*	*Clay Loam*	*Clay*
K Value	0.1	0.25	0.29	0.32	0.42

Table 2.14 *Crop Factors (C) by Cropping Pattern*

Cropping Pattern	*Naked Land*	*Corn*	*Soy-bean*	*Corn Soy-bean*	*Barley Soy-bean*	*Upland Paddy*	*Sweet Potato*	*Fodder Crops*
C Value	1.00	0.52	0.24	0.42	0.35	0.31	0.19	0.01

Table 2.15 *Erosion Control Practice Factors (P) by Management Technique*

Treatments	*Up and Down Cultivation*	*Contour Farming*	*Soil Profile Modification*	*Grass Band*	*Mulching*	*Mulching and Ver. Mulch*
P Value	1.00	0.76	0.45	0.16	0.05	0.04

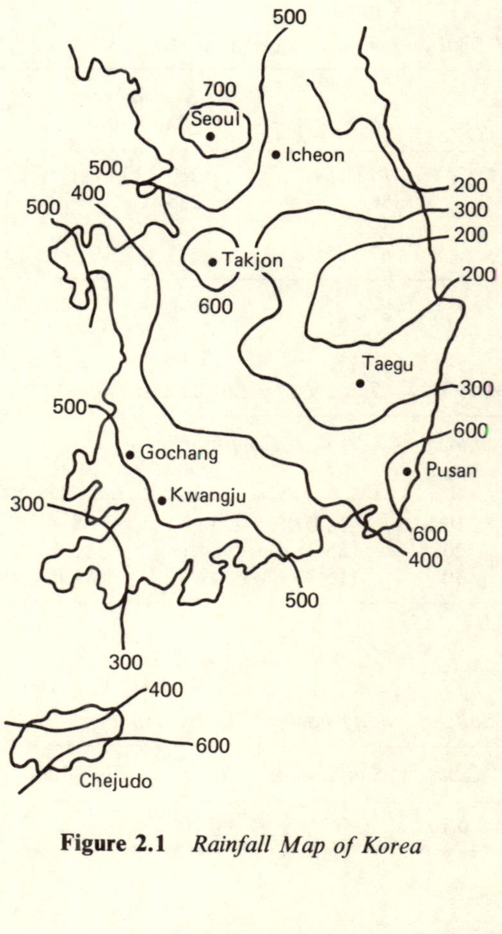

Figure 2.1 *Rainfall Map of Korea*

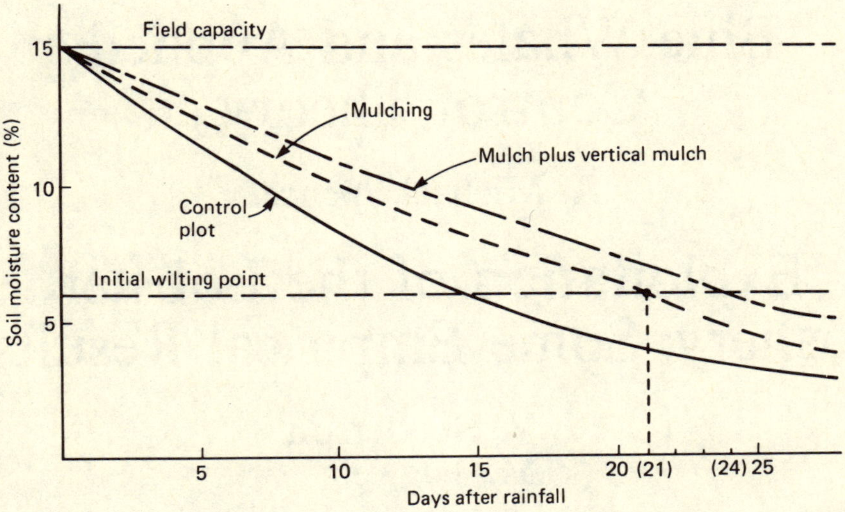

Figure 2.2 *Soil Moisture Changes as a Function of Time after Rainfall for Different Management Techniques*

Notes

1 *Environment, Natural Systems and Development: An Economic Valuation Guide* by M. M. Hupschmidt, D. E. James, A. D. Meister, B. T. Bower and J. A. Dixon. Published in June 1983 by Johns Hopkins University Press.

References

1 Kim, Sung-Hoon, *Economic Evaluation of Upland Reclamation Project*, Korean Rural Economic Research Institute, December 1977.
2 Choi, Jae-Sun, *Evaluation Study on Upland Reclamation Project under IBRD Loan*, Korean Rural Economic Research Institute, December 1978.
3 Kim, Don-Min, *Case Studies of Hillside Farms*, Korean Rural Economic Research Institute, September 1978.
4 The Agricultural Development Corporation, *Economic Analysis of Large-Scale Upland Reclamation Projects*, 1979 and 1980.
5 Im, J. N. *et al.*, *Studies on Soil Erosion Control in Newly Reclaimed Upland Soil*, a series of studies, Office of Rural Development, 1978–80.
6 Park, Johng-Moon, 'The Impact of the Reclamation and Utilization of Idle Hillside Lands on Future Food Production in Korea', *Journal of Korean Society of Soil Science and Fertilizer*, vol. II, no. 4, December 1978.
7 Um, Ki-Tae, 'Area of Potential Arable Land Distributed on Hillside', ibid.
8 Ahn, J. S. *et al.*, 'Engineering Aspect in Upland Reclamation', ibid.

3

Blue Whales and Applied Control Theory

A. Michael Spence

Exploitation of the Lobster Fishery: Some Empirical Results

J. V. Henderson
M. Tugwell

INTRODUCTION

The literature on fisheries is gigantic. Given the importance of the resource, this is not surprising. However, this in itself cannot explain why so much attention has been given to their *optimal* management. For this must presuppose that 'market' signals operate imperfectly in the case of fisheries, and therefore that some form of regulation is desired on their exploitation. The question then is: what form of regulation is desirable? To answer this one must model the unregulated industry in a fishery and then locate the optimal rate of exploitation. These two then enable one to find the regulation which, if imposed, will result in the optimal management by the industry in question.

The presumption that an unregulated industry is likely to harvest a fishery at an excessive rate was given a theoretical underpinning in a classic article by Gordon (1954). Gordon's basic argument has been refined by a number of authors, most notably by Smith (1968), in the process of providing an explicit intertemporal model of a fishery. Chapters 2 and 6 in Dasgupta (1982) provide a detailed account of these arguments. The essential idea in all this is simple. Fisheries are most often *common property* resources.

Since fisheries are in finite supply their social price is not nil. However, when they are common property firms are not obliged to pay a fee for harvesting them. In this case a resource with a positive social value is tapped as a free good. Even untrained intuition suggests that this will result in over-extraction. It also suggests that the social value (or the shadow price) ought to be imposed as a tax on fishermen. Alternatively, the intervention may be in the form of annual (or seasonal) quotas. Taxes and quotas have, not surprisingly, different distributional implications and they need to be borne in mind when judging the relative merits of these two polar forms of intervention (see Chapter 2, Dasgupta (1982)).

It is often suggested that a common property resource must necessarily be doomed in the long run (see Hardin 1968)). This is simply not so. Whether or not free-entry by firms results in the complete destruction of a common property resource depends, among other things, on the market price of the harvested resource relative to the cost of harvest. (See e.g. Smith (1968) or Dasgupta (1982), Chapter 6.) However, as we have noted above, what remains is that the rate of harvest from a common property is not optimal.

Each of the two case-studies presented below identifies the social benefit from harvests with the sum of consumers' and producers' surplus, which in turn are estimated on the basis of prevailing and projected market prices. It needs to be emphasized that this simplification does not make the studies any the less interesting. In many instances the cost-benefit analyst will wish to use accounting (or shadow) prices and also to appeal to distributional weights and/or employment premia in estimating social benefits. (See, for example, the interesting case study by Mishra and Beyer (1976) of the Ratnagiri Fisheries Project in India, which does precisely this.) He will finally wish to locate the best harvest policy by maximizing the present discounted value of net social benefits. Thus the *form* of the social benefit function will often be similar to the benefit functions used in the present case-studies. In fact it transpires that in a large class of cases the optimum policy consists of essentially two phases: first a transient phase, followed by second a stationary phase. By a stationary phase we mean a phase along which the harvest is constant and equals the rate of regeneration of the stock, so that along it the stock remains constant. In Dasgupta (1982), Chapter 6, the optimal stationary phase is described in some detail, and in Chapter 7 the transient phase is analysed for an important class of cases.

The case studies on fisheries included here are very interesting. A. Michael Spence, in his study, attempts both to develop principles of some generality regarding the optimal rate of exploitation of a renewable resource (Part II of Spence (1974), pp. 116–124; see also Dasgupta (1982) Chapter 7), and to determine the implications of these principles for *blue whales* (Part I of Spence (1974), pp. 97–115). Henderson and Tugwell (1979) in their article study the *lobster fishery* at two locations in Canada: Port Maitland and Miminegash. In addition to estimating the optimum rate of harvest at each of the two sites, Henderson and Tugwell compute the unregulated outcome under free-entry and show that the latter corresponds pretty closely to what was actually happening in the early 1960s in each of the two catchment areas. Henderson and Tugwell are therefore able to estimate the corrective taxes that need to be imposed on the fisheries.

In order to estimate shadow prices of renewable resources, such as a fishery, one requires, broadly speaking, four types of information: the natural growth function of the species in question; the technology of harvesting the resource (i.e. the cost function associated with harvesting the resource); the social objectives (which will have as an ingredient in many cases, the market price of the resource); and lastly initial conditions (i.e. stocks at the date the planning exercise is carried out). It is only over the past two decades or so that serious attempts have been made to estimate the first two for different fisheries.[1]

In order to estimate them one often has to rely on time series of harvest rates, efforts applied and prices. This is precisely what is done in the case studies presented here. The third type always contains a certain number of *ad hoc* elements such as the values chosen for the social rate of discount. But this should not be surprising. It is inherent in any planning problem, and the reasonable thing to do is to conduct *sensitivity analyses* of the results to alterations in the specifications of the parameters in the social benefit function. Information about the fourth type is difficult to obtain but theoretical considerations and empirical evidence can sometimes pin it down pretty well, as Henderson and Tugwell demonstrate.

In order to describe the central findings of these two studies we introduce some notation first. The subscript t denotes the date, S_t the stock, $H(S_t)$ the natural rate of 'increase' in the stock, X_t the harvest rate, E_t the total level of effort and $C(S_t, X_t)$ the total cost of harvesting at the rate X_t when S_t is the stock. If, as is assumed in the two case-studies, the marginal cost of effort is a constant, w, then $wE_t = C(S_t, X_t)$.

Let $B(X_t)$ be the flow of social benefits at t and r (> 0) the social rate of discount. Then it is possible to show that the socially optimal *stationary* catch policy must satisfy the following two conditions:

$$H(S) = X, \tag{1}$$

and

$$B_X(X) - C_X(S, X) = -C_S(S, X)/[r - H'(S)], \tag{2}$$

(where $B_X \equiv dB/dX$, $C_X = \partial C/\partial X$, $C_s = \partial C/\partial S$ and $H'(S) = dH/dS$.)

Equation (1) simply says that the annual rate of harvest must equal the net annual increment in the fish stock or, in other words, that the policy is a stationary one. Equation (2) is the social cost-benefit rule associated with the best stationary harvest policy. The left-hand side is the current net marginal benefit from harvest. The right hand side measures the social cost imposed by harvesting the last unit by way of increasing *future* harvesting costs because of the resulting reduced stock. (For a detailed discussion, see Dasgupta (1982), Chapter 6). In general one would wish to use accounting prices that differ from market prices in estimating the social benefit and cost functions $B(X)$ and $C(S, X)$. As mentioned above, the two case studies presented below rely exclusively on market prices. But the *qualitative* properties of their findings are of general interest – as is indeed the methodology that is pursued in estimating the growth function $H(S)$ and the cost function $C(S, X)$ from time series.

We now proceed to discuss the findings in some detail.

Spence (1974)

Spence works in discrete time. Thus he expresses his 'growth' equation as:

$$S_{t+1} = H(S_t) - X_t, \quad \text{with } X_t \leqslant H(S_t), \tag{3}$$

and assumes that the 'production function' (i.e. the cost function) is of the form

$$X_t = H(S_t)[1 - e^{-\lambda E_t}]; \quad \lambda > 0, \tag{4}$$

and that the natural growth function of whales is of the form

$$H(S_t) = AS_t^a; \quad A, a > 0. \tag{5}$$

(Actually, as he says on page 49, form (5) gave the best fit out of several functional forms for $H(S)$ that he used on the data.)

The estimated values of the constants in (4) and (5) are: $\lambda = 0.0019$, $a = 0.8204$ and $A = 2.213$ (see Spence (1974), p. 5). With these values it is readily checked that *maximum sustainable yield* (MSY) is 9890 whales per year and the stock sustaining it is 45,177 whales (p. 52). Table 3.3 on page 56 presents a sensitivity analysis of the optimum stationary phase to variations in the cost of effort relative to the market price of whales. Using a 5% discount rate, Spence shows that it is only if this relative price is about 18 that MSY is approximately optimal in the long run. However this is not otherwise the case. There are two reasons why MSY is not a desirable policy, even in the long run, and they pull in opposite directions. The first is that a positive social rate of discount favours early extraction over a delay. This pulls in the direction of a long run stock falling short of that which sustains MSY. The second is that harvest costs are less when the stock is larger and thus there are cost advantages in letting the stock grow beyond the MSY level. In Table 3.3 Spence brings these considerations out rather beautifully. q/p is the ratio of the rental on a vessel (the marginal cost of effort) and the market price of a blue whale. For $q/p < 18$ the optimum stationary stock is less than 45,000; for $q/p > 18$ it is more.

A main purpose of Spence's paper is to prove that when current stocks are low, the optimum transient policy is to *cease* harvesting until the stock reaches the optimal stationary level. In Table 3.4 (p. 59) Spence assumes that current population is 1639 blue whales, and considering a set of values of the relevant parameters computes that the optimum number of years of moratorium range from 5 to 17 years.

Henderson and Tugwell

This analysis assumes that the lobster fisheries' regeneration rate is given by a quadratic function (or the logistic function). Thus

$$H(S) = \alpha S - \beta S^2, \quad \alpha, \beta > 0. \tag{6}$$

Furthermore, Henderson and Tugwell assume a Cobb-Douglas catch function:

$$X = AS^{\mu}E^{\nu}, \quad A, \mu, \nu > 0. \tag{7}$$

and so from (7)

$$E = A^{-1/\nu}X^{1/\nu}S^{-\mu/\nu}, \tag{8}$$

(the cost function).

We summarize the findings for the Port Maitland fishery only. The growth function (6) is estimated to have $\alpha = 1.80167$ and $\beta = 0.00051$, (p. 75). The parameters of the catch function (8) are: $A = 2.26$, $\mu = 0.44$ and $\nu = 0.48$ (p. 77). In addition, it is assumed that lobster price is $485 per thousand lbs., the marginal cost of effort is $1,421 per hundred traps (Table 3.5, p. 79), and that $r = 0.06$ per year.

We now refer to equations (1) and (2) above. Using these figures in the two equations, it is simple to compute, as Henderson and Tugwell do in Table 3.5, that the optimum stationary stock is 3.05 million lbs. and that optimum stationary catch is 0.745 million lbs. Compare this with the stock sustaining MSY, which is 1.766 million lbs. (p. 76). The point is, as the authors fully recognize, the values of 0.44 and 0.48 for the Cobb-Douglas coefficients in the catch function (5) means that there are severely diminishing returns to both stock and effort. Aiming at a large stock saves on harvest costs.

The free-entry common property solution is taken by the authors to be the point at which the price of lobsters equals the *average* cost of harvest. ($C(S, X)/X$). In Table 3.5 (p. 79) they note that the free entry stationary lobster stock is 2.49 million lbs. and they compare this with the figure of 2.47 million lbs. estimated to have been the average lobster stock during 1959–1963. This demonstration is striking.

The optimum tax on lobster catch is estimated to be about $270 per thousand lbs. of catch. This is about 56% of the revenue of $485 per thousand lbs., implying thereby that the distortion at the free-entry common property solution is significant.[2]

Notes

1 For example, in their well-known study, Mishra and Beyer (1976) concentrate on the second and third types only and merely compute the present social value of a *given* harvesting policy. They do not *compare* alternatives.

2 Readers may wish to ignore the mathematical part of this paper (pp. 73–4). The optimum tax formula which Henderson and Tugwell use is discussed in Dasgupta (1982), Chapter 6, section 6.6 (equation 6.19).

CASE STUDY 1

Abstract

The paper has two parts. The first deals with the optimal use of the blue whale population, an example of a self-renewing natural resource. It applies the control theory developed in the second part. The control theory section investigates the class of problems for which the solution is to move as rapidly as possible to a stationary optimal value of the state variable and stay there. My aim has been to carry out an applied control problem in the environmental area from formulation of objects through the specification of a model, estimation and finding the optimal strategy. I also wanted to show that at least some control problems have reasonably simple solutions that have some chance of being implemented.

Introduction

This paper is really two complementary pieces of analysis. The first deals with the blue whale, one of the many animals on our lengthening list of endangered species.[1] It stems from a long standing interest in the appropriate uses of economically valuable, self-renewing natural resources, of which the blue whale will serve as an example. It is a common belief that the environmentalist interested in the preservation of a species, and those interested in extracting the most from that species that is economically valuable to man, are in fundamental conflict. This at best is a half truth. The optimal use of many self-renewing natural resources from a purely economic point of view is to maintain the level of the resource at a level that is far away from the point at which we would be in danger of running out of it. In the case of the blue whale, this means that the best use of the resource, even if one is only interested in the products it generates, is to maintain the whale population at levels which make extinction virtually impossible.

The second part deals with control theory. It attempts to characterize classes of control problems that have solutions of the following type. First, one identifies a stationary optimal level for the state variable (in the whale problem it is the population). Then, no matter where one is now, one proceeds as rapidly as possible to the stationary optimum value of the state variable, and stays there forever. Apart from any inherent interest such problems may have, solutions of this type are of interest because they are simple, and therefore possibly easier to explain and to implement than are problems in which the optimal strategy is to move in the direction of the ideal state much less precipitously. There are two reasons for combining these two parts into one. The first is that I need the control theory results in order to justify the strategic proposals in the whale problem. There is no need to be mysterious about these. The argument based on the control theory is simply that since the current population of blue whales is disasterously low, the optimal strategy is to cease whaling for this species altogether for whatever period of time is required to allow the population to rise to an identifiable ideal level, and then maintain it at that level by arranging to catch only the surplus that results in each year from natural population growth. The second reason for putting the papers together lies in a desire to carry out a piece of applied control theory which is nevertheless reasonably rigorous.

If the case is convincing that the best use of the whale population on purely economic grounds is to let it grow for several years as fast as possible, the environmentalist should be happy since that is presumably what he would regard as optimal with only the safety of the species in mind.

Each part of the paper can be read in isolation. The first part uses historical data on boats and catches to estimate both a growth equation and a production function for blue whales. It then argues that in the case of whales, the appropriate measure of the value of the resource to man in purely economic terms is the present value of the differences between the market value of the products of the blue whales caught, and the costs of catching them. And finally it appeals to part II to find the best intertemporal patterns for catches, and the economic value of the resource when the optimal strategies are adopted. Very roughly, the best strategy is to forbid blue whaling for a period ranging from seven to twenty-one years depending upon some cost data which I was unable to locate at the time of writing.

Part II attempts to identify the classes of control theory problems, both continuous and discrete, that have solutions consisting of going to a stationary optimal value of the state variable as fast as possible and staying there. Paths which have this last property I call *most rapid approach paths*. With that definition, the question addressed in part II can be stated quite precisely: 'For what classes of control theory problems are most rapid approach paths optimal?'

International whaling

Brief history

The blue whale is the world's largest creature. A fully grown adult can weigh as much as 26 elephants or 350,000 pounds. Because they occupy this unique position among the world's living things, it is especially important that extinction of the species be prevented. Blue whales are not the only threatened whale species, but they are at present among those in the greatest danger. In 1964 they were dangerously close to extinction. Since then, international regulation and a unilateral ban by the United States on both capturing the animal and selling the products has probably helped.

The golden age of blue whaling was the decade 1928–1938, when catches went as high as 26,000 whales in a single year. The war saw little whaling and the post war period saw a more or less steady decline in the size of catches. In the early 1960s, catches were becoming insignificant by comparison with their previous levels.

Two economic factors have complicated the problem of protecting the species. One is that there are several whaling nations, conspicuously Japan, Norway, the U.S.S.R. and until recently, the U.S.A. One can imagine that it is in their collective interest to allow the blue whale population to grow so that the resources required to capture each whale are reduced. But implementation of the collective interest requires effective international regulation. The latter appears to have been difficult to achieve in the past. In its absence, the economic incentive for the individual whaling nation to restrict its catch is weak, because the benefits are diffused among all the whaling nations. The whale population, like clean air or water, is a public good. It tends to be undersupplied by the people who value it, acting as individuals.[2]

The second factor concerns the profitability of the industry. One might have guessed that, as the population fell, a point would be reached where the catch per boat was low enough to render the cost of the boat (fully manned) higher than the value of the catch. Unfortunately, whale boats do not specialize by species and as the blue whale population falls, efforts are transferred more or less continuously to the capture of other species. Only the last in the string of species is likely to be protected by profitability considerations.

The blue whale produces oil, blubber, meat and a variety of other products including an ingredient in perfume.

Policy criteria and decisions

The fundamental decision concerns the intertemporal pattern of catches of the blue whale. The decision should be made with at least two criteria in mind. One is the value of having the species around, that is to say, not having it become extinct. The second is the value of the products of the whales caught, not of the costs of capturing them. The two criteria are environmental and economic respectively.

The environmental problem is solved by maintaining the whale population at a sufficiently high level that extinction becomes a remote possibility. I shall argue that in the course of optimally utilizing the resources on purely economic grounds, the population will be increased in precisely the manner required to solve the extinction problem. For analytical purposes therefore, one can concentrate on the economic problem.

In principal, it is quite easy to measure the cost of catching the whales. In a similarly straight forward manner, one can find the value of the products generated by the catch in any given year. The difference between the value of the products and the costs are the profits of the industry.

Whale products are typically close substitutes for other products. The essence for certain perfumes is something of an exception. Because of this close substitutability, the demand curve is very elastic. In economists' terms, the consumer surplus is negligible or at least small. Hence, unlike other markets where demand is less elastic, profits in the whale industry are a reasonable, rough measure of the economic value of the industry. Of course they may not be called profits. In the Soviet Union, they are government revenues. In any case, the amount by which the value of the products at market prices exceed the cost of catching and processing the whales is a measure of the economic value of the industry. Producer surplus, rather than the small consumer surplus, constitutes the economic value of the industry.

Let Π_t be industry profits in year t and let r be the discount rate. The previous argument leads to the conclusion that the appropriate economic objective is to maximize the present value of the stream of industry profits.

$$\overline{\prod} = \sum_{t=0}^{\infty} = \frac{\Pi_t}{(1+r)^t} \tag{1}$$

A model

In order to proceed with the analysis, we require a descriptive model of the industry. Such a model includes at least two elements. One is the production function. The inputs are the whale population (analogous to capital) and boats. The output is the catch. The following notation is defined:

x_t = the whale population in year t,
m_t = the number of fully equipped boats in year t, and
c_t = the number of whales caught in year t.

For the moment, the production function can be written

$$c_t = P(x_t, m_t). \tag{2}$$

The second crucial relationship is the growth equation for the whale population. For this study I shall ignore the age distribution of the population and simply keep track of the population's size. The available data really do not permit a more sophisticated treatment (see below). The growth equation can be written

$$x_{t+1} = G(x_t, c_t), \tag{3}$$

the population in year $t+1$ depends on the population in year t and the size of the catch.

We now have to pick functional forms for G and P which have acceptable properties. It seems reasonable to assume that in the absence of whaling, the population would grow according to an equation like the following

$$x_{t+1} = H(x_t), \tag{4}$$

The catch can be thought of as a deduction from the population of the next year:

$$x_{t+1} = H(x_t) - c_t. \tag{5}$$

For the moment H is left unspecified. However we might expect it to have the properties of the curve in Figure 3.1. At A there is an unstable equilibrium. Below A, the whales have difficulty finding mates and the population declines to zero. Above A, and in the absence of whaling the population rises to B, a stable equilibrium and an upper limit to the number of whales. At that point they, in some sense, exhaust the environment.

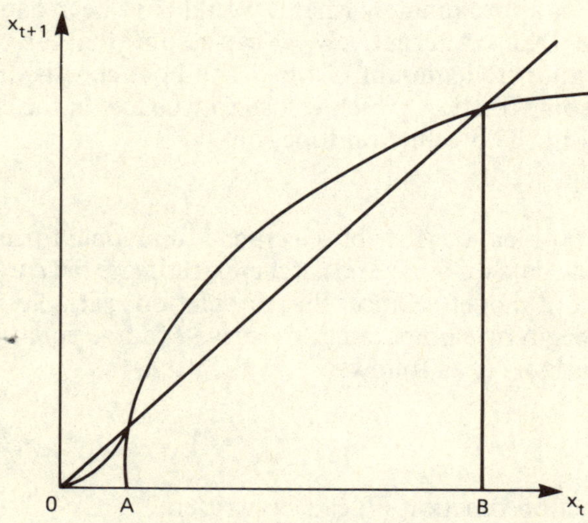

Figure 3.1 *Growth Function*

Turn now to the production function. It is tempting to give it a simple Cobb-Douglas form[3]

$$c_t = Ax_t^{\alpha} m_t^{\beta}. \tag{6}$$

This however is a serious mistake. Among other things it implies that c_t can be made arbitrarily large by raising m_t. But that is nonsense, for c_t cannot be larger than $H(x_t)$. The discrete representation is an approximation to a continuous model. Hence, within a period, there are substantial diminishing returns to boats, which prevent c_t from being larger than $H(x_t)$. In light of this fact, it seems reasonable to specify the production function in the following way

$$c_t = H(x_t)[1 - e^{-\lambda m_t}]. \tag{7}$$

Notice that when $m_t = 0$, $c_t = 0$, and as $m_t \to \infty$, $c_t \to H(x_t) \to x_{t+1}$. In no case is $c_t > x_{t+1}$.

The data

In order to estimate the production function and the growth equation, it would be nice to have time series data on boats, catches and the size of the population. The data on boats and catches are shown in Table 3.1. Data on population size are unavailable for obvious reasons.

A word about boats is in order. As noted earlier, whale boats do not specialize in particular species. This suggests that the equivalent number of boats devoting full time to catching blue whales would be less than the numbers shown. To some extent this is true. However, the blue whale, because of its size, is particularly valuable. Hence, when a blue whale is sighted, it is not passed up. Therefore, my working hypothesis is that the blue whale catch is approximately what it would have been had the boats caught only blue whales. Alternatively, we can assume that the presence of other species reduces the amount of time each boat spends on catching blue whales by some fraction, which will simply be lost in the estimate of the parameter λ in the production function.

Estimation

The estimation problem consists of selecting a functional form for $H(x)$, and then using the data on boats and catches to estimate the parameters of the two equation models. Since the population variable x_t is not observable, we begin by eliminating it to arrive at a one equation model. First define a variable z_t as follows:

$$z_t = \frac{c_t}{1 - e^{-\lambda m_t}}. \tag{8}$$

Then the production function (7) can be written

$$z_t = H(x_t). \tag{9}$$

Table 3.1 *Data on Boats and Catches, 1909–1960*

Year	*Number of Boats*	*Size of Catch*	*Year*	*Number of Boats*	*Size of Catch*
1909	149	316	1931	100	6 705
1910	178	704	1932	186	19 067
			1933	199	17 486
1911	251	1 739	1934	242	16 834
1912	246	2 417	1935	312	18 108
1913	254	2 968	1936	254	14 636
1914	182	4 527	1937	357	15 035
1915	151	5 302	1938	362	14 152
1916	94	4 351			
1917	130	2 502	1945	158	3 675
1918	141	1 993	1946	246	9 302
1919	154	2 274	1947	307	7 157
1920	112	2 987	1948	348	7 781
			1949	382	6 313
1921	142	5 275	1950	468	7 278
1922	174	6 869	1951	430	5 436
1923	194	4 845	1952	379	4 218
1924	234	7 548	1953	368	3 009
1925	235	7 229	1954	386	2 495
1926	233	8 722	1955	419	1 987
1927	222	9 676	1956	395	1 775
1928	242	13 792	1957	417	1 995
1929	337	18 755	1958	420	1 442
1930	280	26 649	1959	399	1 465
			1960	418	1 987

Source: *International Whaling Statistics*, published in Oslo, Norway, by the Committee for Whaling Statistics.

Then, substituting for x_t and x_{t+1} in the growth equation, we have

$$z_{t+1} = H(z_t e^{-\lambda m_t}). \tag{10}$$

The next step was to experiment statistically with different functional forms for $H(x)$. Among the ones I tried were Ax^a, $ax+bx^2$ and $A+B(\log x)$. The form

$$H(x) = Ax^a. \tag{11}$$

produced a substantially better fit than any of the others. With the form above, the one equation summary of the model (10), can be written

$$z_{t+1} = Az_t^a e^{-\lambda a m_t}. \tag{12}$$

For estimating purposes, it is convenient to write it in logarithmic form:

$$\log(z_{t+1}) = \log A + a(\log z_t) - \lambda a m_t. \tag{13}$$

This would be a straight forward linear estimation problem were it not for the fact that the parameter λ appears in the definition of the variable z_t. I handled this problem in the following way. I picked a λ and generated the corresponding time series z_t. I then estimated log A, a and (λa) using least squares and equation (13). This of course, generated an estimate of λ which differed from the one I started with. The process was repeated with different starting λ's until the value was found that made the starting λ equal to the estimated one from the regression. That value was

$$\lambda = .0019 \tag{14}$$

The results of the regression are shown in Table 3.2.

Table 3.2 *Summary of Statistical Results*[4]

$$\lambda = .0019$$

Equation estimated

$$z_{t+1} = A + a(\log(z_t)) - (\lambda a)m_t,$$

where

$$z_t = \frac{c_t}{1 - e^{-\lambda m_t}}$$

Parameter	*Estimated Value*	*Standard Deviation*	*t-Value*
A	2.213		
a	.8204	.059	13.9
λa	.00156	.0055	2.839

$R^2 = .85618$

Variance-Covariance Matrix of a and λa

	a	λa
a	.00348	$-.93(10)^{-5}$
λa	$-.93(10)^{-5}$	$.302(10)^{-6}$

Durbin Watson Statistic = 2.092

The estimated equations are:

1 Production function

$$c_t = 8.356x_t^{.8204}(1 - e^{.0019m_t}). \tag{15}$$

2 Growth equation

$$x_{t+1} = 8.356x_t^{.8204} - c_t. \tag{16}$$

I would have preferred a form for $H(x)$ which reflected the hypothesized existence of the extinction level discussed earlier (the current form does not have this property – it is concave everywhere). On the other hand, only very recent and limited data apply to this part of the curve, so that even if correctly specified, the lower end could not be accurately estimated. The form Ax^a fits well and has the limited virtue of a small number of parameters.

Figure 3.2 depicts the estimated growth function $H(x)$. With no whaling, the population would rise to 136,000 and stay there.

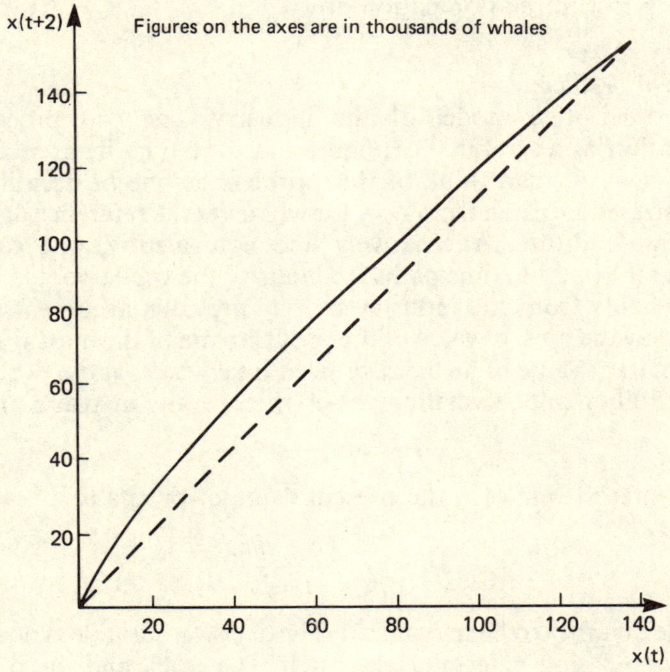

Figure 3.2 *Growth Equation*

The maximum sustainable catch and the historical record

With the estimated equations, it is possible to compute the largest catch that could possibly be sustained indefinitely without running the population down. This quantity is of interest as a check on our estimator. For if the historical record fails to show periods in which the catch exceeded the estimated maximum sustainable one, we have a problem. Such a failure would suggest the population as not depleted, when in fact we know it has been run down to very low levels.

A catch is sustainable if it leaves the population size unaltered. Let x^* be the stable population level and c^* be the sustainable catch. From the growth equation, with $x_t = x_{t+1} = x^*$, we have

$$c^* = 8.356(x^*)^{.8204} - x^*. \tag{17}$$

The x^* that maximizes the sustainable catch is 45,177, and the maximum sustainable catch is 9890.

A series of catches larger than c* would inevitably run the population down. It was the period 1930 to 1939 when the catches exceeded c^* by as much as 10,000 (in 1932). In that period the population must have been falling. There was probably some recovery during the Second World War, but not enough to permit the smaller catches in the post war period from continuing to run the population down.

The control problem

With a descriptive model of the industry, one can proceed to a consideration of its optimal configuration over time from an economic point of view. We can think of this problem as one of deciding on the optimal size of the catch from now (or whatever the reference date is) into the indefinite future. Alternatively and equivalently, one can try to determine the optimal time paths for boats or the whale population itself.

The benefits from the industry by our previous argument are to be measured by the present value of the profit stream of the industry. If we let p = the market value of an average sized blue whale, and q = the annual cost of a fully-manned whaling vessel, then profits in year t are

$$\Pi_t = pc_t - qm_t. \tag{18}$$

With an interest rate of r, the present value of profits is

$$\overline{\Pi} = \sum_{t=0}^{\infty} \frac{pc_t - qm_t}{(1+r)^t}. \tag{19}$$

This is the quantity to be maximized. The decision variable is boats. Boats and the population determine the catch. The catch and the population determine the new population.

Therefore, in formal terms, the problem is to

$$\underset{\langle m_t \rangle_{t=0}^{\infty}}{\text{maximize}} \sum_{t=0}^{\infty} \frac{(pc_t - qm_t)}{(1+\gamma)^t}$$

subject to

$$\begin{aligned} &(1)\ c_t = 8.356 x_t^{.8204}(1 - e^{-.0019 m_t}) \\ &(2)\ x_{t+1} = 8.356 x_t^{.8204} - c_t \\ &(3)\ m_t \geqslant 0 \text{ for all } t \\ &(4)\ x_0 = 1639 \end{aligned} \tag{20}$$

Because of the kinds of data that were easily available, I have taken 1960 as the starting date. In that year, the catch was 1987 whales and the number of boats was 418. Hence the model indicates that the population in 1960 was 1639 whales. Thus, one of the constraints in our problem indicates that the starting population is 1639. That is the implication of the fourth constraint.

Several remarks need to be made at this stage. I have had some difficulty in acquiring the requisite information on the values of p and q. As a result, the analysis that follows is carried through for unspecified p and q, and optimal configurations are given for a range of reasonable values. One estimate of the market value of a blue whale was six thousands dollars, but I am not confident of this figure. My uncertainty is even greater with respect to the annual cost of a whaling vessel.

A second remark concerns the starting population, and the accuracy of the model in the low ranges of the population. I have already suggested that the model is misspecified in the bottom ranges of the population. Hence, the predicted time paths for the population should be viewed with a certain amount of scepticism. I shall, however, defer dealing with this problem until the basic outline of the solution is presented.

The third remark concerns the pricing of whale boats. As noted earlier, whaling vessels do not completely specialize by type of whale. Hence, one could plausibly argue that the full cost of a boat should not attributed to the blue whale industry alone. The point is correct. Therefore, the decision variable in the problem above, is to be taken as the number of full-time boats that would be optimal. If boats do not specialize, then actual numbers will exceed the computed optimal numbers by a fraction which is the inverse of the percentage of a full-time boat's total catch that is in fact taken by a whaling boat. One can easily see that from the point of view of optimally controlling the size of the whale population, the crucial magnitude is the size of the catch. We are only interested in boats in so far as they constitute the principal cost in the industry. Thus, to summarize, we are charging to the blue whale industry, the cost of the fleet of boats specialized in blue whaling that would be required to generate the desired catch.

With those remarks, the control problem is well-posed, and based on a model of the technology and biology of the industry. The latter in turn is based upon the available data, and some hypotheses about functional forms in equations that describe production and biology. One could, of course, carry out a descriptive analysis of the industry, showing how the whale population is a public good that is run down because of the competitive structure of the industry and the absence of effective regulation. Limitations of space prevent such an investigation here. The solution to the problem posed above should provide appropriate guides for future regulation.

Characterizing solutions to the problem

The problem is a control theory problem. It is the analogue of capital theory problems in economics. Some kinds of pollution problems have similar structural features. The common feature of all these problems is the presence of a stock that is being built up or run down over time according to the decisions that are made. The stock in the whale problem is the whale population itself. Our problem is to determine how the population should be built up or run down over time.

Rather than digress at length on the mathematics of solving this problem let me simply try to characterize the features of the solution, leaving the formal argument to the second part of the paper. Even without a great deal of formal argument, one can guess that there is an optimal level for the population, that is to say, a level which we would choose if we could snap our fingers and make it come true. I shall refer to the best population size as the *stationary optimum.* A reasonable guess would be that it is the level of the population at which the annual natural increase in the size of the population before the catch is taken, is largest (the population corresponding to the maximum sustainable catch). This is not quite right, for reasons associated with discounting and the interest rate, and with the costs of boats, but it conveys the idea of a stationary optimum.[5]

Now suppose we can identify a stationary optimum. It is almost certain to be larger than the 1960 population which was disasterously low on both economic and ecological grounds. Having identified a stationary optimum one might then guess that the best policy is to stop catching blue whales altogether and to let the population rise to stationary optimum. At that point it is desirable to take a catch which just creams off the natural population increase, leaving the population the same in the next year. In terms of the whale population, what has just been described is a most rapid approach path. It is the strategy which takes one from the current population level to a stationary optimum as fast as possible. One can do no better than reducing the catch to zero, if one's aim is to achieve the stationary optimum in the shortest possible time.

Not only is the most rapid approach path about the simplest one can think of, it also turns out to be the optimal strategy in our problem. This assertion requires some non-trivial argument, and that is what is undertaken in part II. If the reader will take that argument on faith, then we now known what we are looking for. It is simply necessary to compute two things. The first is the stationary optimum. The second is the number of years of zero catches required to move the population up to that optimal level. Of course, one will also want to compute the size of the catch required to sustain the stationary optimum, and the associated number of boats. These last two figures fall naturally out of the growth equation and the production function respectively.

Those unfamiliar with control theory will undoubtedly find the strategy just described at least reasonable. But those familiar with control problems are used to solutions in which the approach to the stationary optimal level of the stock is considerably less precipitous than the most rapid approach path. In general, control theory problems do not have most rapid approach path solutions. Part II is an attempt to characterize the class of control problems that do have solutions exhibiting this kind of maximum haste in getting to stationary optima.

Stationary optima

Henceforth, the stationary optimal level of the population is denoted by $\bar{x}$. In addition, for illustrative purposes and concreteness, the discount rate r is taken to be 0.05.

How does one find the stationary optimum? My aim here is simply to give an intuitive explanation of the calculations, and to show that while the stationary optimum does depend upon the discount rate, it does not have anything to do with the starting level of the population. Suppose that we start with a population x^*. Depending upon how we select the number of boats in the current year, we will increase or decrease the population for next year. Let the population for next year be $\bar{x}$. And suppose that once that population is achieved, it is maintained forever. Profits in the current year will depend upon x^* and $\bar{x}$, denoted by $\Pi^0(x^*, \bar{x})$. Future profits depend upon $\bar{x}$, and are the same from next year on. Denote them by $\Pi(\bar{x})$. As we raise $\bar{x}$ we raise future profits, and lower those in the current year, because raising $\bar{x}$ means restricting the catch in the current year.

Now the present value of profits is simply

$$\Pi^0(x^*, \bar{x}) + \frac{1}{r}\Pi(\bar{x}). \tag{21}$$

The second term is the present value of profits from next year on. Given x^*, one can maximize with respect to $\bar{x}$, by setting

$$\Pi_2^0(\mathrm{x}^*, \bar{\mathrm{x}}) + \frac{1}{r}\Pi'(\bar{x}) = 0. \tag{22}$$

If it turned out that $\bar{x} - x^*$, then one would not wish to change the level of the population at all. The $\bar{x}$ that satisfies the equation

$$\Pi_2^0(\bar{x}, \bar{x}) + \frac{1}{\mathrm{r}}\Pi(\bar{x}) = 0, \tag{23}$$

is the stationary optimum. It is simply the level of the population such that increasing it in the next period takes out more in current profits than it generates in future profits, and decreasing it yields less in current profits than it removes in future profits. That is really all there is to it. What remains is the computation.

With an interest rate of five per cent, the stationary optima in our

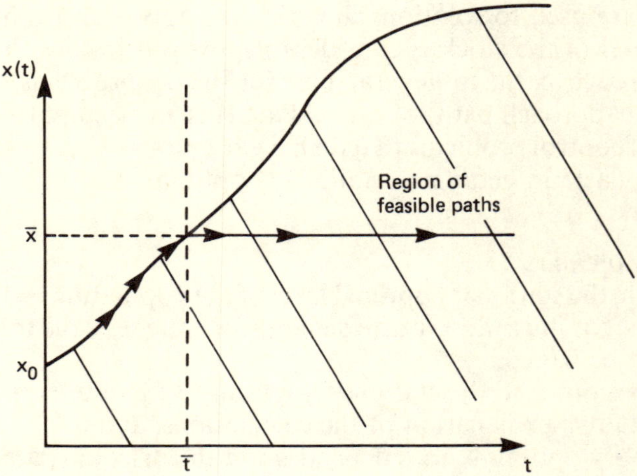

Figure 3.3 *A Most Rapid Approach Path*

problem depends upon p and q according to the formula, whose derivation is given in part II:

$$(.00869)\bar{x} - (.05675)\bar{x}^{.8204} = \frac{q}{p} \tag{24}$$

The stationary optimum depends upon r and the ratio q/p. The solutions to (24) for various values of q/p along with the stationary values of c and m (denoted by $\bar{c}$ and $\bar{m}$) are shown in Table 3.3. The values of $\bar{c}$ and $\bar{m}$ are

Table 3.3 *Stationary Optima in Relation to q/p for r = .05*

q/p	*Population*	*Boats*	*Catch*	*Catch per Boat*	*Profits per Year per Dollar of Operating Cost*
0	34,421	129	9,635	74.6	–
9	40,000	115	9,834	85.5	8.34
18	45,000	104	9,890	95.1	4.21
28	50,000	95	9,845	104	2.7
49	60,000	77	9,501	122	1.47
73	70,000	63	8,870	141	.94
98	80,000	50	8,002	159	.63
124	90,000	39	6,930	177	.43
151	100,000	29	5,681	195	.29
180	110,000	20	4,276	213	.19
209	120,000	12	2,732	227	.09
240	130,000	4.3	1,062	246	0.25
250	136,000	0	0	–	–

computed from constraints (1) and (2) once x is found, simply by substituting $x_{t+1} = x_t = \overline{x}$, in those constraints. Graphs of $\overline{x}$, $\overline{c}$ and $\overline{m}$ as a function of q/p are shown in Figures 3.4, 3.5 and 3.6.

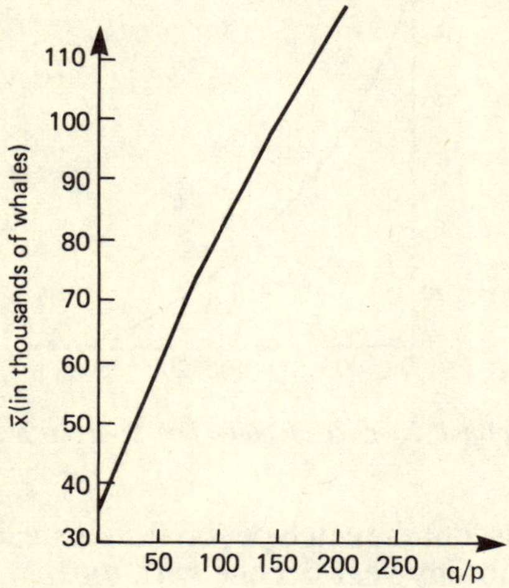

Figure 3.4 *Stationary Optima as a Function of q/p*

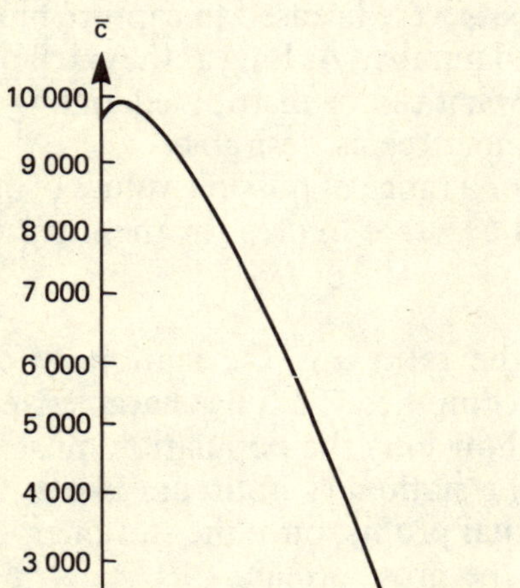

Figure 3.5 *Optimal Size of Catch as a Function of q/p*

Several points are worthy of note. The optimal value of $\overline{x}$ rises with q/p. As the cost of boats rises relative to the value of the whale, the optimal stationary level of the population rises, thereby making it easier to catch whales. The optimal number of boats declines with q/p. The catch rises for

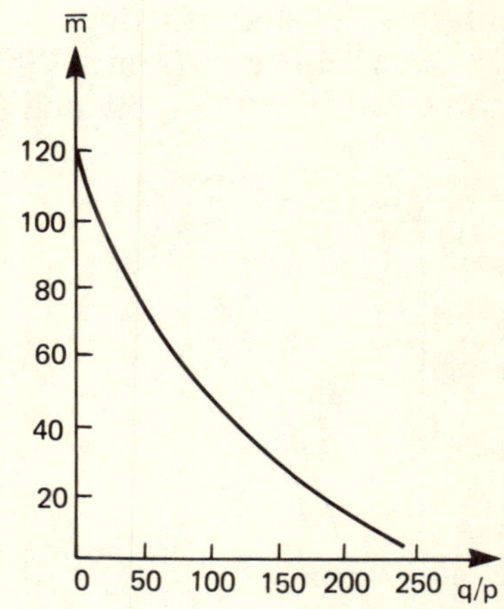

Figure 3.6 *Optimal Number of Full-Time Boats as a Function of q/p*

a while and then falls, but the catch per boat rises steadily with q/p. Profits per dollar of costs in any year decline with q/p.

The figure for boats is not meant to suggest that the whaling industry should only send out that many boats per year, but rather that if only a certain number of boats were licensed to capture blue whales full-time, it should be the specified number. As long as the catch per year is maintained at the appropriate level, it can be distributed among boats in the whaling fleet in whatever manner seems desirable.

Figures are given for a range of possible values of q/p because I have not yet been able to find accurate figures for these prices.

Optimal strategies

For each value of the ratio q/p, the stationary optimal level of the population has been computed. To fully characterize an optimal strategy, one must determine how long the population must be left to grow at its natural rate before the stationary optimum is reached. In addition, one can compute the annual profits, once the stationary level is reached, and the present value of the profit stream.

Table 3.4 gives the results of some calculations on the assumption that a blue whale is worth 6000 dollars. Thus in addition, if $q/p = 28$, then $\bar{x} = 50$, $\bar{c} = 9845$, and profits per year at the stationary optimum are 57.4 million. Starting from a population of 1639, one must wait seven years before catching anything. The present value of the profits of the industry are 806 million dollars.

Figure 3.7 shows the estimated time path of the population beginning at $x_0 = 1639$. It is the natural growth path of the population, the one that is achieved when catches are zero. From it, one can read for each stationary

Table 3.4 *Sample Calculation for the Optimal Path $r = .05$; $x_0 = 1639$; $p = 6000$*

q/p	x *Thousands*	*Catch*	*Boats*	*Profit/Yr. at x (millions)*	*Number of yrs. with No Catch*	*Present Value Profits (millions)*
0	344	9,635	129	57.8	5	906
28	50	9,845	95	57.4	7	806.5
124	90	6,930	39	41.5	12	462.7
209	120	2,732	12	16.4	17	343.9

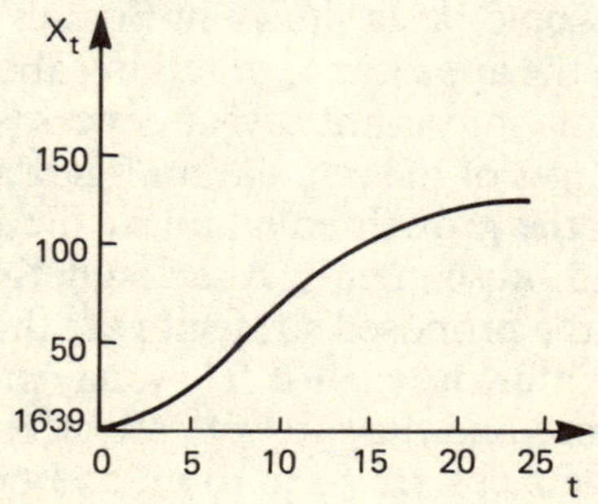

Figure 3.7 *Time Path of Whale Population with No Catch ($x_o = 1639$)*

optimum level of the population, the number of years of zero catches required to reach that level. In conjunction with earlier graphs, it completely characterizes the optimal strategies.

A reasonable guess is that the annual cost of a boat is about four hundred thousand dollars. With a blue whale price or market value of six thousand dollars, the ratio q/p would be 66. Thus the stationary optimum from Figure 3.4 would be about 67,000, the catch 9,000, the number of fulltime boats about 63, and the required waiting time is nine years.

Concluding remarks

The analysis carried out here is intended as a guide to further work and to the design of regulatory measures. It is incomplete in several respects. The precise technology relating to boats needs further work. More importantly, since the equations in the model are merely estimates, they can be modified and improved over time as additional data are obtained. As they are modified, one's perception of the location of the stationary optimum will change, and plans will be adjusted accordingly.

I have conducted the analysis by referring explicitly to the whale population throughout. This seemed the most intuitive way to discuss the problem. But it is hazardous at best. Biologists may be able to show through census taking that the population differs from the figures cited here. One can, in fact, drop the population out of the analysis altogether. It was, after all, introduced primarily to specify the estimating equations of the descriptive model. Once these have been selected, all that matters is the relationship between catches and boats in successive years. In short, we could have maximized the present value of industry profits, subject to the one dynamic constraint

$$\frac{c_{t+1}}{1-e^{-\lambda m_{t+1}}} = A\left[\frac{c_t e^{-\lambda m_t}}{1-e^{-\lambda m_t}}\right]^a. \tag{25}$$

The solutions would be exactly the same. The optimal stationary values for catches and boats would be as shown in Figures 3.5 and 3.6. But one would not have to give the appearance of talking about something that is not observable. The most important caveat concerns the accuracy of the model for the lower ranges of the population. The data did not permit us to accurately estimate the growth equation at the low levels that were approached in 1960 and subsequently. As a result, the figures that inspire the least confidence in the proposed strategies are those for waiting times until the stationary optimum is reached. They may in fact, be much longer than those estimated here, and they are very sensitive to the starting value for the population. Two steps are open to us, and both should be taken. The first is to make use of the considerable expertise of the biologists who have studied whale populations and advised the International Whaling Commission. The second is to avoid deciding in advance how long to wait, but rather to send out or licence one or two boats per year to catch blue whales (once the danger of extinction has passed). By observing the catch per boat, one can determine whether the stationary optimum has been reached. Small samples of this type, taken in each year, will not significantly delay the reaching of the stationary optimum.

Finally, let me return to the extinction problem. We began by ignoring the extinction problem in the determining the best use of the population. It turns out, that the best use on economic grounds that can be made of the blue whale population is to stop catching altogether until the population has risen to levels at which the danger of extinction is presumably removed. Had we ignored the economic value of the resource and simply minimized the probability of extinction, we would have prescribed the same strategy. Thus there is no conflict. The pursuit of economic or environmental ends leads to similar conclusions.

Part II
Most rapid approach paths in control theory

The continuous case

Suppose that we have a problem in one state variable x, and one control variable m, of the following form:

$$\text{maximize} \int_0^\infty u(x, m)e^{-rt}\, dt$$

subject to

$$\begin{aligned} &\text{(i)}\ \dot{x} = F(x, m) \\ &\text{(ii)}\ 0 \leqslant m \leqslant m^* \\ &\text{(iii)}\ x(0) = x_0. \end{aligned} \tag{26}$$

It is assumed throughout that $F_x > 0$, $F_m > 0$, that $F(x, 0) \geqslant 0$ and equals zero only if $x = 0$, that $F(x, m^*) \leqslant 0$ and equals zero only if $x = 0$.

Definition: A path $x(t)$ is called admissible if it satisfies the three constraints in the problem, that is to say, if there is an $m(t)$ such that $x(t)$ and $m(t)$ together satisfy the three constraints.

To properly introduce the subject matter of this section, it is necessary to define a most rapid approach path.

Definition: A path $z(t)$ is called a most rapid approach path with respect to x_0 and x^* if $z(0) = x_0$ and it satisfies the appropriate one of the following conditions:

for $x_0 < x^*$: $\dot{z} = F(z, 0)$ when $z < x^*$
$\quad = 0$ otherwise
for $x_0 > x^*$: $\dot{z} = F(z, m^*)$ for $z > x^*$
$\quad = 0$ otherwise
for $x_0 = x^*$: $\dot{z} = 0$.

The quantity x_0 is the starting point and x^* is where one ends up. If x_0 is below x^*, you get up to x^* as fast as possible by setting $m = 0$. Once there, you stay there. And conversely for $x_0 > x^*$.

This section develops conditions on u and F which yield most rapid approach paths solutions to the problem stated above. It is perhaps advisable to state the conclusions in advance. A problem of the type described above has a most rapid approach path solution if the objective function is implicitly a function of x alone. This will happen if either $u_m = 0$, or if u is implicitly linear in $\dot{x}$. And finally u is implicitly linear in x if $u = a(x)F(x, m) + b(x)$ for some functions a and b. The necessary and sufficient marginal condition for this to be true is

$$\frac{u_{mm}}{u_m} = \frac{F_{mm}}{F_m}. \tag{27}$$

In short, for continuous control problems, the solution is a most rapid approach path if either $u_m = 0$ or the above condition holds. Similar results hold for discrete models, and they will be dealt with after the continuous results are established.

Let me deal first with the case $u_m = 0$, and then show that the other case can be reduced to this one. Our assumption is that $u(x, m) = v(x)$ for some function v. It is assumed that

$$v'(x) = 0 \tag{28}$$

has a solution, $\bar{x}$. This will be the stationary optimum. It is further assumed that $v''(x) < 0$. Under these assumptions, the most rapid approach path with respect to x_0 and $\bar{x}$ is the optimal path. It is clear that the most rapid approach path is admissible. Let the most rapid approach path be $z(t)$, let $y(t)$ be any other admissible path, let s be a scalar between zero and one, and let $w(t) = sz(t) + (1-s)y(t)$, a simple linear combination of z and y. Now consider

$$I(s) = \int_0^\infty v(w)e^{-rt}\,dt. \tag{29}$$

By differentiating with respect to s, we find that

$$I'(s) = \int_0^\infty v'(w)[z-y]e^{-rt}\,dt. \tag{30}$$

I will now establish that I' is positive. The argument is carried out for the case $x_0 < \bar{x}$. The other cases follow by almost identical arguments. If $x_0 < \bar{x}$, then $z(t) < \bar{x}$ for $t < \bar{t}$ and then $z(t) = \bar{x}$. Moreover, for $t < \bar{t}$, $y(t) < w(t) < z(t) < \bar{x}$. Thus in the interval $(0, t)$, $[z-y] > 0$, and $v'(w) > 0$, because of the concavity of v. For $t \geqslant \bar{t}$ either

$$\begin{aligned} z-y > 0 &\text{ and } v'(w) > 0, \text{ or} \\ z-y < 0 &\text{ and } v'(w) < 0. \end{aligned} \tag{31}$$

Therefore, the integrand is non-negative everywhere, and is zero only on intervals where $z \equiv y$. Thus, unless $z \equiv y$ for all t, the integral is positive. Therefore $I'(s) > 0$. This means that $I(1) > I(0)$, or simply that z is preferred to y.

But since y was selected arbitrarily among the class of admissible paths, z is the optimal path. The arguments for the cases in which x_0 equals or exceeds $\bar{x}$ are the same and need not be repeated here.

It is perhaps worth noting that the intermediate paths w in the argument above need not be admissible paths, but the argument does not depend on assuming that they are admissible; they merely serve as stepping stones in showing that z is preferred to any other admissible path y.

The argument above shows that if u does not depend upon m, then the optimal path is a most rapid approach path. A concavity condition is required. Convexity would make the most rapid approach path a minimum. We turn now to a less restrictive case.

The first constraint in the initial problems, $\dot{x} = F(x, m)$, can be thought of as defining m as a function of x and $\dot{x}$. Thus, we can think of the function u as being implicitly a function of x and $\dot{x}$. Now, simply for the sake of argument, let us suppose that u is linear in $\dot{x}$, so that

$$u = a(x)\dot{x} + b(x) \tag{32}$$

We shall consider when this will happen below. Under these conditions, the objective function in the problem can be written

$$\int_0^\infty [a(x)\dot{x} + b(x)]e^{-rt}\,dt. \tag{33}$$

Now, define the function $c(x)$ as follows

$$c(x) = \int_0^\infty a(s)\,ds. \tag{34}$$

It is fairly clear that $dc(x)/dt = a(x)\dot{x}$. Hence the objective function can be written

$$\int_0^\infty \left[\frac{dc(x)}{dt}\right]e^{-rt}\,dt + \int_0^\infty b(x)e^{-rt}\,dt. \tag{35}$$

Now if one integrates the first term by parts, the result is a revised version of the objective function

$$c(x_0) + \int_0^\infty [rc(x) + b(x)]e^{-rt}\,dt. \tag{36}$$

The first term is just a constant. The second term is an integral, but the $\dot{x}$ is missing. In fact, if we let $v(x) = rc(x) + b(x)$, we have the case we previously dealt with. The integrand in the objective function, ignoring the discounting term, depends only upon x.

It follows that the proposition just proved, that the optimal path is a most rapid approach path, applies here. More precisely, if $rc' + b' = 0$ has a solution $\bar{x}$, and if $rc + b$ is concave, then the solution to the problem is the most rapid approach path with respect to x_0 and $\bar{x}$. Note that $c'(x) = a(x)$, so that the equation defining the stationary optimum $\bar{x}$ can be written $ra(\bar{x}) + b'(\bar{x}) = 0$.

To summarize briefly, if u does not depend upon m, or if u is implicitly linear in $\dot{x}$ (the latter case really includes the former), then the solution to the control problem has the most rapid approach property.

The next step is to determine when u is implicitly linear in x. Actually, it is a relatively straight forward matter to verify that the derivative condition

$$\frac{u_{mm}}{u_m} = \frac{F_{mm}}{F_m} \tag{37}$$

is necessary and sufficient for the linearity condition. For, if this is integrated twice with respect to m, one finds that

$$u = a(x)F + b(x) \tag{38}$$

for arbitrary a and b. But since $\dot{x} = F(x, m)$, u is linear in $\dot{x}$.

The converse argument is simpler still. With m implicitly a function of x and $\dot{x}$,

$$\frac{\partial^2 u}{\partial \dot{x}^2} = \frac{u_{mm}}{F_m^2} - u_m \frac{F_{mm}}{F_m^3} \tag{39}$$

This equals zero if $u_{mm} \equiv 0$ or the stated derivative condition (37) holds.

Depending upon the problem, one would check the derivative condition (37) or visually inspect to see if u can be expressed in the form $a(x)F(x, m) + b(x)$. The problem is simplest when $u_m = 0$. In any case, if either condition is verified, the a and b such that $u = aF + b$ can be found. Then the stationary optimum is computed by finding the $\bar{x}$ that satisfies $ra(\bar{x}) + b'(\bar{x}) = 0$. Finally, the differential equation is used to compute the length of time required for the state variable to reach the stationary optimum.

It should be emphasized that these are sufficient conditions. They are not necessary conditions. Even when the conditions above are not met, the constraints on m may be sufficiently stringent to cause one to be on the boundary all the time, in approaching the stationary optimum. But what distinguishes this class of problems, and in this they are unique, is that the most rapid approach property of the solution holds regardless of the stringency or lack of it in the boundary constraints on the control variables.

Put another way, it is the class of concave problems for which it is known that the solution approaches the stationary optimum as fast as possible, independent of the precise upper and lower bounds on the control variable.

Discrete case

Though similar to the continuous case, the discrete case does not follow automatically by the most obvious analogy, from the continuous case. Hence it is developed fully here. The type of problem of interest can be written

$$\text{maximize} \sum_{t=0}^{\infty} \frac{u(x_t, m_t)}{(1+r)^t}.$$

subject to

$$\begin{aligned} x_{t+1} &= F(x_t, m_t) \\ 0 &\leqslant m_t \leqslant m^* \\ x_0 &\text{ is fixed.} \end{aligned} \tag{40}$$

As before, x is the state variable and m the control variable. The assumptions are that $F_x > 0, F_m < 0$, that $F(x, 0) \geqslant x$ and equals x only if x is zero, and that $F(x, m^*) < x$, and equals x only when x is zero. Admissible paths are those which satisfy the constraints.

Definition: A path z_t is called a most rapid approach path with respect to x_0 and $\bar{x}$, if $z_0 = x_0$, and the appropriate condition below is satisfied:

$$\begin{aligned} \text{for } x_0 < \bar{x}\text{: } z_{t+1} &= F(z_t, 0) \text{ if } z_{t+1} < \bar{x} \\ &= \bar{x} \text{ otherwise} \\ \text{for } x_0 > \bar{x}\text{: } z_{t+1} &= F(z_t, m^*) \text{ for } z_{t+1} > \bar{x} \\ &= \bar{x} \text{ otherwise} \\ \text{for } x_0 = \bar{x}\text{: } z_t &= \bar{x}. \end{aligned}$$

In the discrete case, there may be an intermediate period in which the control variable equals neither of its extremes nor the level which will sustain the state variable at $\bar{x}$. It is the period in which the transition from rapid ascent or descent is made to the stationary level.

We begin by establishing that if $u_m = 0$, so that $u = v(x)$ for some function v, then the optimal path is a most rapid approach path. The argument is similar to that given for the continuous case. Assume that $v(x) = 0$ has a solution $\bar{x}$ and that v is concave. Then the most rapid approach path with respect to x_0 and x is optimal.

Let z_t be the most rapid approach path, let y_t be any other admissible path and let $w_t = sz_t + (1-s)y_t$, where $0 \leqslant s \leqslant 1$. Let

$$I(s) = \sum_{t=0}^{\infty} \frac{v(w_t)}{(1+r)^t}. \tag{41}$$

Note that $I(0)$ is the value of the objective function for the path y_t, and $I(1)$ is the value on the path z_t. The derivative of $I(s)$ with respect to s is simply

$$I(s) = \sum_{t=0}^{\infty} \frac{v(w_t)[z_t - y_t]}{(1+r)^t} \tag{42}$$

The argument is completed for the case $x_0 < \bar{x}$. Because z_t is the most rapid approach path, one of the following sets of inequalities holds for every t:

$$\begin{aligned} y_t \leqslant w_t \leqslant z_t \leqslant \bar{x} &\text{ and } v'(w_t) \geqslant 0 \\ y_t \geqslant w_t \geqslant z_t = \bar{x} &\text{ and } v'(w_t) \leqslant 0. \end{aligned} \tag{43}$$

Hence the terms in the summation defining $I'(s)$ are all non-negative, and at least one is positive unless $y_t = z_t$ for all t. Therefore $I(1) > I0)$, and z_t is preferred to y_t. Since y_t was an arbitrarily selected admissible path, we have shown that the most rapid approach path is optimal.

To summarize, if $u_m = 0$, then the solution to the discrete problem is a most rapid approach path. Now the question arises, as it did in the continuous case, is to more general circumstances or conditions on u and F, that still guarantee that the rapid approach property holds. The first constraint permits us to regard m_t implicitly as a function of x_t and x_{t+1}. Hence u is implicitly a function of x_t and x_{t+1} as well. Now the most direct analogy with the continuous case might suggest that the rapid approach property holds if

$$u = a(x_t)[x_{t+1} - x_t] + b(x_t). \tag{44}$$

Unfortunately, this is incorrect. With u, as given above, the rapid approach property will hold only if $a'(x) = 0$. The reason for this will become apparent below.

The analogue in the discrete case of the condition that u be linear in $\dot{x}$ in the continuous case, is the following condition:

$$u = a(x_t) + b(x_{t+1}). \tag{45}$$

The reason is not hard to find. For if u is implicitly additively separable in x_t and x_{t+1} as shown above, then the objective function can be written

$$a(x_0) + \sum_{t=0}^{\infty} \frac{a(x_t) + (1+r)b(x_t)}{(1+r)^t}. \tag{46}$$

Now let $v(x) = a(x) + (1+r)v(x)$. Then the objective function can be written

$$a(x_0) + \sum_{t=0}^{\infty} \frac{v(x_t)}{(1+r)^t}. \tag{47}$$

Formally the problem is now as if $u_m = 0$. But we have just shown that in this case, the optimal path is a most rapid approach path. Hence when u is implicitly additively separable in x_t and x_{t+1}, the optimal path has the same property. Moreover, the stationary optimum satisfies $v(x) = a'(x) + (1+r)b'(x) = 0$. The required second order condition is that $a'' + (1+r)b'' < 0$. One can now see why if u can be expressed as in (45), then the rapid approach property holds if $a' = 0$. For if $a' = 0$, the additive separability property holds.

We turn now to conditions that ensure that u is implicitly additively separable in x_t and x_{t+1}. It is clear that if u can be written in the form

$$u(x, m) = a(x) + b(F(x, m)), \tag{48}$$

for some functions a and b, then the property will hold, for $F(x_t, m_t)$ just equals x_{t+1}. On occasion, this condition may be verified by inspection. However, it is convenient to have a necessary and sufficient marginal condition that can be checked mechanically. The condition is both different and somewhat more complicated than in the continuous case. If

u is implicitly additively separable in x_t and x_{t+1}, then its cross-partials with respect to these two variables must be zero. It is easily verified that

$$\frac{\partial u}{\partial x_t} = u_x - u_m \frac{F_x}{F_m}. \tag{49}$$

Hence

$$\frac{\partial^2 u}{\partial x_t \, \partial x_{t+1}} = \frac{\partial}{\partial m}\left(u_x - u_m \frac{F_x}{F_m}\right)\frac{\partial m}{\partial x_{t+1}}. \tag{50}$$

The cross partial will be zero if $(u_x - u_m F_x/F_m)$ does not depend upon m. That is perhaps the easiest way to state the condition. The argument can be reversed. If $u_x - u_m F_x/F_m$ does not depend upon m, then for some $n(x)$,

$$\frac{u_x - n(x)}{u_m} = \frac{F_x}{F_m}. \tag{51}$$

If we let $s(x, m) = u(x, m) - \int_0^x n(s)ds$, then the above equation implies that

$$\frac{w_x}{w_m} = \frac{F_x}{F_m}.$$

Therefore w and F have the same isoquants (to use an economist's term), and as a result

$$w = b(F), \tag{52}$$

for some monotonic function b. But then with $a(x) = \int_0^x n(s)\, ds$, $w = u - a$, or simply

$$u = a(x) + b(F(x, m)). \tag{53}$$

To summarize, the condition that $(u_x - u_m F_x/F_m)$ not depend upon m is both necessary and sufficient for u to be additively separable in x_t and x_{t+1}. Therefore, all problems for which the condition holds have optimal solutions that are most rapid approach paths.

What the discrete and continuous problems have in common is the fact that the most rapid approach property applies to the solution to the control problem if the objective function can be written in such a way that it only depends upon the state variable. They differ in the conditions which make that objective function implicitly a function of the state variable alone. In the continuous case, we require that

$$u = a(x)F(x, m) + b(x), \tag{54}$$

or equivalently, that

$$\frac{u_{mm}}{u_m} = \frac{F_{mm}}{F_m}. \tag{55}$$

Either condition makes the u linear in x which in turn enables us to write the objective function depending only on x. In the discrete case, it is necessary that u be additively separable in x_t and x_{t+1}. This is ensured if

$$u = a(x) + b(F(x, m)) \tag{56}$$

or equivalently, if

$$\frac{\partial}{\partial m}\left[u_x - u_m \frac{F_x}{F_m}\right] = 0. \tag{57}$$

I should like to conclude by demonstrating that the control problem associated with the whale problem of part I has the most rapid approach property. In that problem, $u = pc_t - qm_t$, $x_{t+1} = H(x_t) - c_t$, and $c_t = H(x_t)[1 - e^{-\lambda m_t}]$. By eliminating c_t and m_t, we find that

$$u = \left[pH(x_t) - \left(\frac{q}{\lambda}\right)\log(H(x_t))\right] + \left[\left(\frac{q}{\lambda}\right)\log(x_{t+1}) - px_{t+1}\right]. \tag{58}$$

By inspection, u is additively separable in x_t and x_{t+1}. Therefore, the control problem is likely to have a most rapid approach path optimum. There remains a second order condition and the computation of the stationary optimum. Let

$$a(x) = pH(x) - \left(\frac{q}{\lambda}\right)\log(H(x)), \tag{59}$$

and

$$b(x) = \left(\frac{q}{\lambda}\right)\log(x) - px.$$

With these definitions,

$$u = a(x_t) + b(x_{t+1}). \tag{60}$$

Therefore, from the previous results, the stationary optimum is the solution to the equation

$$a'(x) + (1 + r)H(x) = 0. \tag{61}$$

Finally, the second order condition must be checked. For this purpose, we insert the functional form for $H(x)$. It was $H(x) = Ax^a$. With that specification

$$a(x) + (1 + r)b(x) = px^a - p(1 + r)x + (1 + r - a)\left(\frac{q}{\lambda}\right)\log(x) - \left(\frac{q}{\lambda}\right)\log(A). \tag{62}$$

Since $(1 + r - a) > 0$, every term is either concave in x, linear in x, or a constant. Hence the function is concave and the second order condition is satisfied. This completes the argument that the whale problem has a most rapid approach path solution, a fact that was asserted and used in the analysis of part I.

Discussion

U. Olin

I would like to comment on Professor Bruckmann's observation concerning incorrect discounting of future gains and losses as a reason for excessive exploitation of self-renewable resources. In the meantime Dr. Bossel has brought up the same problem but some elaboration may still be in order.

What constitutes the correct discounting of the future is often a very difficult question to answer. To begin with, we have to consider whose future we are talking about. What is economical from the macroeconomic point of view may spell disaster for the individuals or groups most directly involved. Additionally, competition is a continual process. If you do not maintain or advance your position at all times, you may fall behind and this will easily cause irreparable damage to your career or to the organization involved, as the case may be. This problem is of course particularly accute for politicians, who play a crucial role in the handling of most important economic problems. The conclusion is that the usefulness of economic models depends entirely on the extent to which theory can be incorporated into the institutional process, on which their implementation hinges.

M. Lipsicas

You are dealing with a *practical* environmental problem which necessarily involves value judgments. One could (and I am not advocating this approach!) consider the blue whale as a 'factory' converting plankton to whale products. In this sense the whale is a totally different resource to an exhaustible resource such as oil, or even to a trout (as introduced by Professor Bruckmann). One could nowadays, technologically, replace this economic function of the whale completely by setting up a factory to process plankton chemically and, in fact, the end product may be of more economic value than whale products. This approach might even, as a side product, save all whales from extinction!

F. Hanssmann

1 How general is the result of 'no conflict between extinction and economic objectives'? Does this not depend on rates of regeneration as well as investment opportunities *outside* the whaling industry?
2 Would not dynamic programming be sufficient to solve the control problem?

G. Bruckmann

I should like to make two comments.

1 You are certainly right that *mathematically* the optimal solution of the profit problem also takes care of the extinction problem, i.e. that it suffices to show that if profits, *in the long run*, are maximized if one

stops whaling until the population has reached 70,000 there exists no extinction problem any more.

In practice, however, there are (at least) two obstacles. One is expressed by the well known 'prisoner's dilemma' according to which each whaling nation 'optimizes' its profits by *not* obeying any international agreement. The other obstacle lies in the fact that man tends to assess incorrectly the expectation of future losses or profits; the expectation of whaling in 1985 from 70,000 whales weighs less than the expectation of whaling from 2,000 whales in 1973.

2 It may well be that the optimum solution *both* for the profit and for the extinction problem lies outside the system, e.g. by shifting in the whaling industry from hunting to farming. From that point of view, it might be preferable to devote brains, efforts and resources not to talking the whaling industry into not hunting the blue whale for 10 years, but to develop the technology to farm the blue whale instead. Of course, this might give rise to new problems, e.g. that a farmed population is ecologically less stable than a hunted population in some ecological equilibrium.

E. Zahn

Using only economic criteria may not lead to a desirable solution of the whole problem. The reason is the trade-off between short-term and long-term perspectives.

The whole industry, like any other industry, tends to follow a strategy of short-term profit maximization. As more whales are caught the population decreases which tends to reduce the profit margin. The industry will counteract by trying to reduce the costs of control by using more efficient equipment. Thus a certain profit margin can be kept which in effect will result in a lower optimal whole population x.

This strategy of counteracting which – of course – can only be followed up to a certain point, makes it easy to always forget the long-term implications. In the long-run such behaviour tends to lead to a crisis, as many examples in reality show.

P. Leyhausen

It is quite true that in the way described you may avoid extinction while at the same time attaining your economic objective. However, the method has two considerable side effects: first it interferes with both the natural age group composition of the population the long term consequences of which cannot nearly be forecast; second it introduces biased selection pressures, e.g. if only animals of a certain size are taken, this automatically puts a selective premium on slow growth, as growing slowly obviously will be of survival value. This will also, to a degree, defeat the economic objective in the long run.

Notes

1 Public interest was drawn to endangered whale species by McVay in 1966. Since then there has been a spate of articles and newspaper reports on the progress in international regulation. In 1971 Small wrote a book on the blue whale and the industry.

2 Space limitations have prevented the inclusion of a descriptive analysis of the historical performance of the industry. But very roughly, its competitive structure was the cause of the depletion of the resource. Monopolistic control of the industry by some firm or country would have been preferable on efficiency grounds. It is interesting to note that other natural resources in the ocean are being depleted for a similar reason – the lack of well-defined ownership of the resource. Of particular interest are the so-called 'cod wars' where the struggle is precisely over the property right (see Jensen (1973) and Shapley (1972)).

3 This was done in an earlier study by the author.

4 The equation was estimated leaving out 1939–45 for which period accurate data is not available.

5 Authorities in Peru estimated the maximum sustainable catch of anchovies and regulated the industry to achieve this catch and level of the population (see Idyll (1973)).

References

The Committee for Whaling Statistics (ed.) (1930–73), *International Whaling Statistics*, Oslo, Norway.

Idyll, C. P. (1973), 'Anchovy Crisis', *Scientific American*, June.

Jensen, A. C. (1973), 'Cod: A Case of Supervised Neglect', *Natural History*, January.

McVay, Scott (1966), 'The Last of the Great Whales', *Scientific American*, August.

Shapley, D. (1972), 'Icelandic Fishing: Science Awash in the Great Codfish War', *Science*, December.

Small, G. L. (1971), *The Blue Whale*, Columbia University Press, New York.

CASE STUDY 2[1]

In this paper biomass equations and a production function for two lobster areas in Canada are estimated. The equations are used to calculate fishing solutions when the fishery is optimally exploited and when utilization of the fishery is unregulated. The solutions are compared and social welfare losses are examined.[2]

When utilization is unregulated, solutions are nonoptimal for two reasons. First, fishermen do not properly account for the effect of their fishing on future stocks of fish and thus they tend to nonoptimally deplete the stock of fish. Second, when effort is applied to the fishery, fishermen receive not just the marginal product of their effort but they also appropriate the rents accruing to the resource. This extra return on effort in any time period tends to lead fishermen to enter the industry until the rents are dissipated and effort is paid the value of its average rather than marginal product. This type of over-utilization of the fishery results in a social wastage of effort in any period.

This paper represents the only paper we know of in which the biomass equation and production function are separately estimated and combined to find equilibrium and optimal solutions. Thus while the model is very simplistic the results are most suggestive and demonstrate the numerical magnitudes involved in fishing solutions and the way for further empirical work.

The model

The biomass equation

The growth and number of lobsters in an area is dependent on their environment: temperature, food sources, and predators. A maximum naturally sustainable population exists determined by food availability and crowding which affects reproduction, cannibalism, and growth. Up to the maximum population level, population growth will occur at various rates. Taking an aggregative approach to this relationship which ignores the details of death, reproduction, and age structure, we postulate a local quadratic relationship between population and population growth measured in pounds of fish.[3]

$$dX/dt \equiv \dot{X} = aX - bX^2 \qquad (1)$$

where X is population in time t and $\dot{X}$ is the gross change in area population. Maximum population is a/b. Maximum growth is $a/2b$.

If there is fishing, catch in time t, Q, reduces the population so that net growth is $\dot{X} - Q$. In a stationary fishing solution $\dot{X} = Q$, or catch exactly matches the gross growth in lobster stock in each period. A biomass equation is illustrated in Figure 3.8, plotting growth in the stock against the stock.

The production function

Lobster catch in an area is a function of the stock of lobsters and fishing effort as measured by the number of traps or man days. A variety of other factors such as water temperature and season length which are represented in this theoretical section by a parameter A affect catch. These effects are analyzed in the empirical sections below. The production function is

$$Q = AX^{\alpha}E^{\beta}, \qquad (2)$$

where E is effort and A is a shift factor.

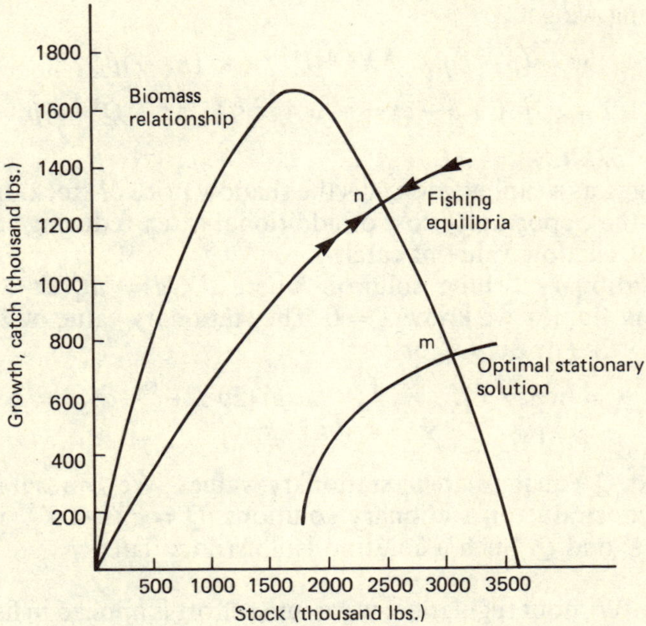

Figure 3.8 *The Bioeconomic Relationships*

Theoretical solutions

The optimal solution The optimal solution for a fishing area is that which maximizes the present value of profits. Such a solution could be reached by assigning ownership of the fishery to one private entity or through government regulation. The present value of profits is

$$\int_0^\infty e^{-\delta t}(pQ - wE)\,dt, \tag{3}$$

where p is the price of catch, w the price of effort, and δ the discount rate. Maximization is constrained by the equation of motion for the system where net additions to the stock of fish are $\dot{X} - Q$, or $aX - bX^2 - Q$, and by the production relationship which we rewrite as $E = A^{-1/\beta}X^{-\alpha/\beta}Q^{1/\beta}$.

Thus the current value Hamiltonian for the maximization problem is

$$H = e^{-\delta t}[(pQ - wA^{-1/\beta}X^{-\alpha/\beta}Q^{1/\beta}) + \lambda(aX - bX^2 - Q)],$$

where λ is the costate variable. Necessary conditions for an optimum are that at any point in time

$$\frac{\partial H}{\partial Q} = (p - w\beta^{-1}A^{-1/\beta}X^{-\alpha/\beta}Q^{1/\beta-1}) - \lambda = 0,$$

$$\partial(e^{-\delta t}\lambda)/\partial t = -\partial \dot{H}/\partial X = -e^{-\delta t}[-wA^{-1/\beta}X^{-\alpha/\beta-1}Q^{1/\beta}\alpha/\beta + \lambda(a - 2bX)].$$

Rearranging we get

$$w = (p-\lambda)\beta A^{1/\beta} X^{\alpha/\beta} Q^{1-\alpha/\beta} \equiv (p-\lambda)\beta Q/E, \tag{5}$$

$$\dot{\lambda} - \lambda(2bX + \delta - a) = -wA^{-1/\beta} X^{-\alpha/\beta-1} Q^{1/\beta}\alpha/\beta, \tag{6}$$

where $\dot{\lambda} = \partial\lambda/\partial t$.

Viewing X as a capital good, λ is the shadow price of stock. In Eq. (5), λ relates to the opportunity cost of additional catch reducing stock. Thus $p-\lambda$ is the shadow value of catch.

In a stationary fishing solution where $dX/dt = dQ/dt = 0$ by differentiating Eq. (5), we know $\lambda = 0$. The stationary value of λ in Eq. (6) equals its value in Eq. (5), or

$$\lambda = (wA^{-1/\beta} X^{-\alpha/\beta-1} Q^{1/\beta}\alpha/\beta)(2bX + \delta - \alpha)^{-1} = p - (wA^{-1/\beta} X^{-\alpha/\beta} Q^{\alpha/\beta-1}\beta^{-1}) \tag{7}$$

for X and Q equal to their stationary values. We can substitute the biomass constraint on stationary solutions, $Q = aX - bX^2$, into (7) to solve for X and Q. Such a solution is illustrated later.

Free entry Without regulation, we assume effort is applied in fishing until the rent to the fishery is dissipated, or effort receives its average product. Then

$$w = pQ/E \equiv pA^{1/\beta} X^{\alpha/\beta} Q^{1-1/\beta}. \tag{8}$$

Rearranging, for any X, Q is given by

$$Q = (wp^{-1} A^{-1/\beta} X^{-\alpha/\beta})^{\beta/\beta-1} \tag{9}$$

Equation (9) is illustrated of the graph of Q_{equil} in Figure 3.8. The curve represents the equilibrium Q for any X. Thus a stationary equilibrium occurs at n where $Q = \dot{X}$. To the left of $n\dot{X} > Q$, so that X is increasing and we are always moving toward n. To the right of $n\dot{X} > Q$, so that X is decreasing and we are always moving toward n. Thus in a market situation, equilibrium stock and catch move monotonically toward their values at n.

Empirical estimates

The biomass equation

We estimate the biomass Eq. (1) by ordinary least squares for two lobster areas in the Maritimes accounting for 5–6% of Canada's total catch. Clearly the two areas must be treated separately since the environments in terms of area size, food availability, temperature, etc., will be different. To find values for stock, a certain number of lobsters in both areas were tagged each year before the fishing season and stock is estimated from the percentage of tagged lobsters in the catch. (Stock at the beginning of the lobster season is defined to be that year's catch in pounds multiplied by the ratio of total tagged lobsters to tagged lobsters caught.) For this to be a reasonable estimate of the stock we must assume that tagged and untagged lobsters are cought at the same rate.[4] The gross change in stock in a year is the catch plus the net change in stock (the estimated change in stock between two seasons calculated from taggings).

The data on stock and catch is only for lobsters larger than the minimum legal catch size (carapace length of $2\frac{1}{2}''$ for Miminegash and $3\ 3/16''$ for Port Maitland). Thus, by estimating the biomass equation with our data, we are estimating the growth function for the existing stock of harvestable fish, assuming that current catches do not influence the number of recruits in the future. Apparently for certain species such as lobster, this is not an unreasonable assumption as long as annual catches do not fluctuate too much. This would suggest that the annual growth of stock is a constant (the influx of recruits) plus a growth function for the existing greater-than-legal-size stock. Our estimates of various forms of such a function were unsuccessful. Thus the simple quadratic function presented below with a constant term of zero should be viewed as the function that provides the best local fit of our data and that best describes the growth of the existing stock of harvestable fish within the ranges observed. These problems clearly limit the interpretation of optimal solutions presented later, as will be discussed.

The biomass equations are estimated to be:

Port Maitland (1954–1969)

$$\dot{X} = \underset{(6.30)}{1.80167\,X} - \underset{(4.70)}{0.00051\,X^2} \qquad R^2 = 0.42 \qquad DW = 1.72$$

Miminegash (1957–1971)

$$\dot{X} = \underset{(4.40)}{1.27024\,X} - \underset{(1.69)}{0.00039\,X^2} \qquad R^2 = 0.08 \qquad DW = 1.97$$

The t statistics are in parentheses, although due to measurement errors in X they may not be especially meaningful. The Port Maitland equation is graphed in Figure 3.8. By our locally fit equation, maximum growth is 1766 thousand lb and the natural equilibrium stock is 3532 thousand lb. For Port Maitland, while the sample points are quite variable, they are all to the right of the maximum growth point, which makes our locally fit function more palatable for application in this region.

The production function

The production function is taken from Tugwell's extensive investigation of the production function. The function was estimated from 22 observations from various fishing areas in Nova Scotia, covering the years 1953 to 1960. When estimates of stock are available, the only measure of effort is simply the number of traps fished. We have no information on men, boats, and equipment but must implicitly assume some fixed relationships between these and traps – i.e. a fixed rate of fishing of traps. In Tugwell's work when there is information on both traps and numbers of fishermen, the latter variable is almost always insignificant whereas traps are almost always significant. Thus our assumption may not be too restrictive. We include season length in our equation, because it varies considerably over the 22 observations. We include average bottom temperatures and temperatures lagged which also vary considerably over the 22 observations.[5] This is an important variable since lobsters move around much more, covering more territory, as temperature rises. The production function in estimated form is

$$\ln Q = -1.57 + \underset{(4.23)}{0.48 \ln E} + \underset{(4.56)}{0.44 \ln X} + \underset{(1.32)}{0.16 \ln D} + \underset{(2.81)}{0.45 \ln T_t} + \underset{(2.81)}{0.30 \ln T_{t-1}} \qquad R^2 = 0.94$$

where Q is lobster landings in thousands of pounds, E is fishing effort in hundreds of traps, X is lobster stock in thousands of pounds, D is season length in days, and T_t, T_{t-1} are average seasonal bottom temperature in degrees Centigrade. The t statistics are in parentheses. Note there are strong diminishing returns to both labour and the biomass. The small effect of changing season length holding traps fished and stock fixed is due to two facts. Longer seasons are associated with the winter months when the level of daily activity is quite low. Second in most situations even with short seasons, fishermen do not fully utilize the full season. They harvest most of the lobster crop in much less time than the maximum allowed.

There are several possible sources of statistical bias in this production function. The best known problem is that effort is chosen according to the productivity rule in Eq. (8), and, therefore, in the production function, the error term and the independent variable $E(t)$ are correlated. It can also be argued that since our stock data are estimated from catch the error term and $X(t)$ are correlated. However, this seems unlikely since stock is estimated from the *ratio* of tagged catch to total catch (see above) and hence does not depend on the absolute level of catch or variations in catch due to factors in the error term. Note that it is not possible to properly simultaneously estimate the biomass equations and production function since there is almost no overlap in observations.

In using the production function in our calculation below we insert the season length and average seasonal temperature for the two areas we are examining. The season lengths for Port Maitland and Miminegash are, respectively, 185 and 61 days and the average seasonal temperatures are, respectively, 6.34 and 8.87°C. Inserting these values in the production function we get a measure of the normal shift factor A in Eq. (2) for one two areas.[6] The production functions for the two areas become.

Port Maitland

$$Q = 2.26\, E^{0.48}\, X^{0.44}$$

Miminegash

$$Q = 2.51\, E^{0.48}\, X^{0.44}.$$

Prices

To solve the model presented in Section 1, we need information on prices. We have excellent month-by-month data on the landed price of lobsters. In the results presented below the difference between the Port Maitland and Miminegash average price occurs because the Port Maitland season is in the winter and spring when prices are high and the Miminegash season is in the summer and early fall when prices are low.[7]

Our problem is finding values for w, the opportunity cost of effort. One way to calculate the opportunity cost of effort is to assume the prevailing fishing situation is one of complete rent dissipation. Then effort is paid its average product and this equals opportunity cost. Therefore, the opportunity cost of effort is simply total revenue divided by the number of traps. We follow this simplistic procedure. However, survey data from 1961 in Rutherford *et al.* allow us to check the empirical validity of this assumption.

In Rutherford *et al.*, for our lobster areas, expenses per fishing enterprise are recorded. First, we evaluate capital and equipment costs in annual, or rental terms. Capital stock valued at current prices per enterprise for lobster plus other fishing activities is given. We calculate an annual implicit rental for all activities on boats and shore equipment, based on interest payments at 6% and depreciation at 17.5% for boats and engines and 7.5% for shore equipment (rates suggested in Rutherford *et al.*). Part of this annual rental is charged to lobstering according to the fraction of time items used in lobstering as opposed to other activities. Then an annual rental on gear used solely for lobstering is calculated given a depreciation rate of 15%.

We subtract these calculated capital rentals to be charged to lobster fishing from total revenue. The residual is the return to the operators or fishermen. If this residual equals the opportunity wage of fishermen in other activities, our assumption of complete rent dissipation where opportunity cost equals average product is justified. For Port Maitland this is certainly the case.

The residual return to lobster operators in Port Maitland was

$35.32/week in 1961. Operators spent 35% of their annual time lobstering, 21% in other fishing, 19% in other employment, and 25% unemployed. The weekly return to lobstering was $35.32, to all fishing was $47.00, to other employment was $42.00, and to all annual activities was $38.55. Therefore, an opportunity cost of time of $35.32 seems reasonable. For Miminegash where 27% of one's time was spent lobstering and 45% was spent unemployed in 1961, the return to lobstering per week was $60.54 versus an annual average weekly income of $42.98. Our opportunity cost of effort, set at the average product of effort in lobstering, may be too high for Miminegash.

In the solutions below, the discount rate used is 0.06 because that is the figure used in calculating the opportunity cost of effort.

Solutions to the models

Given our estimates of the biomass equations and production functions, we calculate stationary solutions for optimal and equilibrium solutions, based on prices prevailing in 1961. Although our solutions are for stationary situations, we believe the equilibrium solutions are comparable with the actual situations prevailing in the lobster areas in 1961. First, the assertion of rent dissipation as discussed in the above paragraphs seems reasonable. Second, given discussions with local officials of the Department of Fisheries in Canada, it appears that p/w was constant for the last part of the 1950s and for the first half decade of the 1960s. That is, given a fixed price ratio we should have been approaching a stationary equilibrium with free entry. Free entry solutions are obtained by solving Eqs. (1), (2), and (9) for Q, E, and X. As stated above, for Port Maitland, the equilibrium solution is at n in Figure 3.8. Optimal stationary solutions for Q, X, and E are obtained by solving Eqs. (1), (2), and (7). A curve of optimal stationary X, Q combinations for Port Maitland is represented in Figure 3.8. Given the biomass, the actual solution on the curve is at m. (Note that unlike the free entry solution, this curve is, of course, not an approach path since it assumes $\lambda = 0$.)

Our numerical solutions for 1961 are presented in Table 3.5. There are two main features. First, the free entry solutions for both catches and stocks and the actual situations in the areas are similar, differing at the most by 12% and as little as 1%. Despite the inadequacy of the biomass equation in terms of low explained variance, errors in measurement, and being defined for greater than legal size lobsters and the bias inherent in estimating the production function, our model predicts very well.

The second feature is the extent to which the optimal solution dominates the free entry solution. Comparing the two stationary equilibria, although the free entry solution has higher catches (179 and 117% of

Table 3.5 *Results*

	Port Maitland			*Miminegash*		
Biomass equation	$dX/dt + Q = 1.80167\,X - 0.00051\,X^2$			$dX/dt + Q = 1.27024\,X - 0.00039\,X^2$		
Production function	$Q(t) = 2.26\,E^{0.48}\,X^{0.44}$			$Q(t) = 2.51\,E^{0.48}\,X^{0.44}$		
Lobster price/thousand lb	\$485			\$370		
Opportunity cost/hundred traps	\$1,421			\$950		
	Optimal Solution	*Free Entry*	*Actual Average 1959–1963*	*Optimal Solution*	*Free Entry*	*Actual Average 1959–1963*
Lobster stock (thousand lb)	3,050	2,490	2,467	2,450	1,125	1,273
Lobster catch (thousand lb)	745	1,330	1,183	801	936	1,094
Effort (100s traps)	112	454		122	365	
Ratio: catch/stock	0.25	0.53	0.48	0.33	0.83	0.86
Shadow price of future stock (λ)	36	n.a.	n.a.	68	n.a.	n.a.
Optimal tax/thousand lb catch	270	n.a.	n.a.	225	n.a.	n.a.
(Annual resource savings: value of trap savings less value of reduced catch	\$202,173	n.a.	n.a.	\$180,470	n.a.	n.a.

the optimal solutions for Port Maitland and Miminegash, respectively), the associated effort is much greater (405 and 300% of the optimal solutions, respectively) because the equilibrium stocks are smaller. The resource savings from being at the optimal solution – the savings in traps less the value of the reduced catch – are very large. For Port Maitland it is $202,173 per year. These savings are 62% of the total value of the optimal catch.

To sustain the optimal solution through government regulation, catch could be taxed. With free entry and no regulation, effort is employed so that $w = pQ/E$. We want effort employed so that in Eq. (5) $w = (p-\lambda)\beta Q/E$. Thus we want to redefine p through taxation so that $p-t = (p-\lambda)\beta$ where t is a unit tax price. Thus the stationary $t = p - \beta(p-\lambda)$, where the stationary value of λ is defined in Eq. (7). From Table 3.5, for Port Maitland λ = $36/thousand lb and the unit tax is $270/thousand lb. This is 56% of revenue.

If the biomass effects and the dynamics of the problem are ignored, it is interesting to note that in our situation the results are minimally affected. We set $\lambda = 0$ in the stationary solution and examine only the problem of applying effort to an unpriced resource in any period. Setting the unit tax equal to $t = p(1-\beta)$, we move to a solution for Port Maitland where $X = 3015$ thousand lb, $Q = 796$ thousand lb, and $E = 13{,}100$ traps: Profits in this situation are $199,908, representing a loss of only 1% relative to the optimal solution where $\lambda > 0$.

Our final comment concerns the adjustment process. Our equations satisfy the assumptions in Brown. Thus in moving from the free market to optimal solution, starting at the initial X, λ should decline continuously and X increase continuously to their stationary values. This would imply a declining schedule of unit taxes to the stationary tax. In applying Eqs. (1), (2), (5), and (6) to our empirical results to solve for the optimal approach path, unfortunately the assumption of continuous time and adjustment does not hold up because the changes in Q, X, and E from period to period are noninfinitesimal. (This also presents a problem in the production function because X varies over the fishing season given the pattern of X and Q over the season. Given X and Q are large, our specification of costs and production is not very sophisticated.) If we formulate a discrete adjustment process in our nonlinear model (where $\dot{\lambda}_t \approx \lambda_t - \lambda_{t-1}$ and $\dot{X}_t \approx X_{t+1} - X_t$), we do converge to the stationary solution (but a cyclical adjustment path can be involved). As a practical matter and ignoring distributive considerations, given the limitations of our specification and estimation, for Port Maitland, for example, we would suggest an immediate move to the stationary solution at m. This would involve, for $X_0 = 2490$ thousand lb, setting t_0 such that Q_0 was reduced from the free market 1330 to 770 thousand lb, yielding an X of 560 thousand lb so that $X_1 = X_{\text{opt}} = 3050$ thousand lb. This would require an initial tax of

t_0 = \$217/thousand lb, followed by a tax in all succeding periods of \$270/thousand lb.

The suggestion that a regulator should move the fishing solutions to their optimal levels as quickly as possible is based upon the assumption that current resources in fishing can be immediately shifted to other uses (equipment sold off at prevailing prices and fisherman reemployed at the same compensation). This assumption may not be met and a more sophisticated economic and political approach might suggest a more graduated phasing out of the excess resources committed to fishing.

Conclusions

Our calculations indicate that the welfare losses from nonregulation of the lobster fishery are about 20 and 30% of the value of the current or free market catch in the areas we studied. The calculation of optimal solutions based upon the fitted biomass equations concerns reductions in the rate of harvest of stocks of greater than legal size lobsters, assuming that the annual influx of recruits is unaffected by catch. More sophisticated data could indicate that a reduction in the rate of harvest would stimulate recruits and bring even greater benefits from regulation.

Notes

1 This article was first produced as Working Party No. 78–80, Brown University.

2 We are indebted to Gordon Douglas for his help in estimating the biomass equation and compiling references. We are also indebted to Herbert Mohring, Anthony Scott, and two anonymous referees for their helpful comments on earlier versions of this paper.

3 See Lotka and Beverton and Holt on this formulation. It would be desirable to incorporate water temperature into the analysis. Lobsters grow and mature much more quickly in warmer water. It takes about 80 molta (shell changes) for a lobster to reach sexual maturity at a weight of about 1 lb and a carapace length (body length excluding tail and claws) of around 3 inches. This molting to maturity takes 8 years in Nova Scotia, 5 to 6 years in Massachusetts, and 2 years in controlled high-temperature laboratory conditions. To incorporate temperature would require specifying some of the lag structure to account for the effect of previous bottom temperatures on current population growth.

4 See Paloheimo on using tagged lobsters to estimate stock.

5 The inclusion of T_{t-1} is difficult to defend. However it is the specification of the production function with the other variables present that is available. For any area T_{t-1} and T_1 should be highly correlated.

6 To avoid introducing uncertainty into the production process, we assume that *within* an area there is negligible variation in average seasonal *bottom* temperature. This assumption appears to be reasonable.

7 Our figures were obtained from Rutherford *et al.* and D.B.S. Canada, *Monthly Review of Canadian Fisheries Statistics*, Queen's Printer.

8 Note that stationary catch follows to zero as stationary X falls below 1750 thousand lb. Below 1750, profits are negative. This means that if the biomass equation shifted leftward such that X (where $X = 0$) fell below 1750, this fishing area would not be profitable to fish.

References

Bell, F. W. (1972), 'Technological Externalities and Common Property Resources', *Journal of Political Economics.*

Beverton, R. J. H. and Holt, S. V. (1957), 'On the Dynamics of Exploited Fish Populations', *Fisheries Investigations*, vol. 29, Ser. 2, Ministry of Agriculture, Fisheries and Food, London.

Brown, G. (1974), 'An Optimal Program for Managing Common Property Resources', *Journalof Political Economics*, vol. 82, pp. 163–74.

Cheung, S. (1970), 'The Structure of a Contract and the Theory of a Non-Exclusive Resource', *Journal of Law and Economics.*

Clark, C. W. (1976), *Mathematical Bioeconomics*, John Wiley & Son Ltd, New York.

Gordon, H. S. (1954), 'The Economic Theory of a Common Property Resource: The Fishery', *Journal of Political Economics*, vol. 62, pp. 124–42.

Hughes, J. T., Sullivan, J. J. and Shleser, R. (1972), 'Enhancement of Lobster Growth', *Science*, vol. 177.

Lotka, A. J. (1956), *Elements of Mathematical Biology*, New York.

Rutherford, J., Wilder, D. and Frick, H. (1967), *An Economic Appraisal of the Canadian Lobster Fishery*, Fisheries Research Board of Canada, Ottawa.

Scott, A. (1956), 'The Fishery: The Objectives of Sole Ownership', *Journal of Political Economics*, vol. 63, pp. 116–24.

Spence, M. (1973), *Blue Whales and Applied Control Theory*, Technical Report No. 8, Stanford University.

Tugwell, M. (1974), *Common Property Resource Management: The Maritime Lobster Fishery*, unpublished Ph.D. thesis, Queen's University, Canada.

4

The Trans-Alaska Pipeline: Environmental Consequences and Alternatives

John V. Krutilla
Anthony C. Fisher

INTRODUCTION

We have so far only studied cases which have aimed at quantifying costs and benefits in monetary terms and by doing that evaluate the desirability of a certain project or programme. However, it will very often be the case that it is impossible to quantify all the relevant aspects in one single measure. This may be because we simply lack methods of estimating environmental damage. It may also be the case when we believe that present markets (and in particular markets for future claims) are functioning so badly that any reliance on market prices is very doubtful. We also know that irreversible environmental changes create problems of their own which may make a complete cost-benefit analysis very difficult. Thus it is easy to imagine situations where it is not feasible to carry out a complete analysis of all costs and benefits. But as the included case study demonstrates, the machinery developed for cost-benefit analysis may still be very valuable in organizing the information available in a way that facilitates good decisions.

One way cost-benefit analysis may be valuable is that it may provide the decision-maker with a minimum or maximum shadow price on environmental resources. Assume we are studying a project with an environmental damage which we, however, cannot quantify. Assume also that the quantified effects from the project give a surplus. This surplus can then be interpreted as the maximum value of the environmental damage which would permit the project. The question the decision-maker has to answer is then whether the actual value of the damage is greater or smaller than this value. The problem has then been reduced to a binary choice which is in general simpler to handle than the original problem.

Another way cost-benefit analysis may facilitate a decision is by organizing the alternatives in such a way that the environmental consequences are the same for alternatives in the same group. It would then be possible to find a ranking of some of the alternatives. In extreme cases we may end up with a ranking of all but one alternative, i.e. the alternative of doing nothing. This is the approach taken in the Charles Cicchetti study of the Trans-Alaska Pipeline (Charles Cicchetti, *Alaskan Oil: Alternative Routes and Markets*/Baltimore 1972). This study was summarized in Chapter 9 in John Krutilla's and Anthony Fisher's book *The Economics of Natural Environments* (Baltimore 1975).

CASE STUDY

Introduction

In November of 1973 Congress amended the Mineral Leasing Act of 1920 and provided authorization for the Trans-Alaska pipeline (T.A.P.) to short circuit some difficult legal issues pending before the courts. This marked the end of a long period of deferred action due to the controversy over the environmental impact from exploiting and transporting oil that had been discovered on the North Slope of Alaska's Brooks Range.

The planned transport facility, a hot oil pipeline destined to cross arctic tundra and some very active seismic zones in its near-800 mile length, has many and varied environmental hazards that are discussed in section 2. In the light of these problems, environment and conservation-conscious citizen groups had intervened to ensure that an adequate environmental evaluation be undertaken before a permit was issued for rights of access across federal lands. The process of undertaking the necessary studies and sorting out the legal tangles that ensued took nearly $3\frac{1}{2}$ years. One of the important studies that played a significant role in identifying and evaluating the alternatives, and in illuminating related public policy issues, was Charles Cicchetti's *Alaskan Oil: Alternative Routes and Markets*, from which the materials and analyses of this chapter are largely drawn.

Since completion of Cicchetti's study early in 1972, when the decision on the pipeline was still pending, several important developments have occurred. The decision for which the Cicchetti analysis was relevant[1] has since been made in favour of the Trans-Alaskan route. The price of imported crude – an element in the analysis – has roughly quadrupled in the wake of the Arab oil embargo and the O.P.E.C. pricing policy. Nevertheless, to the extent that the inflation in construction costs has not offset the rise in imported crude prices, the change in the price structure between the time of analysis and the present reinforces Cicchetti's conclusions. And despite the fact that the decision to proceed with T.A.P.

has been made, the analysis as an illustrative case is both valid and valuable. Accordingly, while most of the issues to which this chapter is addressed are now moot from the decision standpoint, the study is presented as part of a series of cases illustrating the kind of analyses that can and should be undertaken in environmentally relevant areas that involve public decisions.

In the case studies in chapters 5 to 9 of *Economics of Natural Environments* by Krutilla and Fisher, problems in which it was possible to develop meaningful estimates of the costs of environmental modification or estimates of at least significant portions of the benefits that attach to retaining a natural environment in an undisturbed state were addressed. It was discovered that in many instances it is possible to counsel in favour of preserving an environment even in the absence of all the information that would be potentially relevant in very close decisions. In some cases studied, the non-environmental costs alone were sufficient to justify rejection of an extractive or developmental project. In other cases, while non-environmental opportunity costs alone were not sufficient to reject a developmental project, estimates of readily evaluated opportunity returns from environmental amenities precluded by development were sufficient to tip the balance without an exhaustive analysis of all environmental costs.

In this chapter, the problem addressed was basically of a different order of evaluative difficulty. Quantitative evaluation of environmental impact, or the probability of environmental damage from the pipeline expressed in monetary terms, defined the analyst's best efforts. The problem of deciding whether the undertaking was warranted in the face of environmental hazards ultimately was an ethical and political one. In this instance the analyst found it difficult to argue on the basis of the objective scientific evidence that the costs of this resource extractive activity, including the expected costs of the environmental damage, outweighed the economic benefits. But in any event, there remained the question of the relative economic and environmental costs of alternative routes and markets. The study of the Trans-Alaska pipeline, then, was an exercise in carrying out the requirements of the National Environmental Policy Act [sections 102 (c) and (d)] to evaluate the alternative transportation possibilities in the face of the need to raise and bring to market the North Slope oil. Because of our utter inability to assess environmental costs of the pipeline in monetary terms, as well as prospective changes in the value of North Slope oil over time, no attempt was made to fit the Cicchetti analysis into a formal dynamic framework. Instead, we mainly reports the results of analysis carried out independently, with some simplifying assumptions.

North Slope oil discovery and environmental implications

Between 1968 and 1970, exploration for petroleum on the North Slope of the Brooks Range in Alaska led to the discovery of a major oil field. Proven reserves of the Prudhoe Bay field approximate 10 billion barrels as estimated by the American Petroleum Institute. Because the field is on the arctic side of Alaska, the problem of bringing oil from Prudhoe Bay to market is a serious one. Several transportation routes and modes, such as an all-water route involving ice-breaking tankers, an overland oil pipeline crossing Canada in large part, and a combination overland route across Alaska, completed by tanker transshipment from the south of Alaska to West Coast ports in the United States, were considered. Ultimately, the oil companies involved, operating through the Alyeska Pipeline Service Company, favoured transportation by a pipeline from Prudhoe Bay across Alaska to the southern port city of Valdez for transport to the 'lower 48'. The planned Trans-Alaska pipeline will be 789 miles in length and will require 373 miles of new service road along the portion between the north bank of the Yukon River and Prudhoe Bay.

While a great deal of the general region south of the Yukon River is essentially undeveloped, the presence of the highway between Valdez and the proposed Yukon crossing reflects some strip development of the area through which the pipeline will pass. The region to the north of the Yukon River, however, is completely roadless. Here is to be found the largest expanse of authentic wilderness remaining within the continental United States. It is over this region that the large (quarter of a million head) arctic caribou herd migrates and where we find the large (9 million acre) Arctic National Wildlife Range.

The objection of environmentalists to the intrusion of additional development and extractive activities into the last really vast, authentic, wilderness remaining in the United States can be readily understood. In addition to the disruption of an area that has escaped, to date, evidence of the activity of a highly industrial society, the nature of the potential disturbances occasioned by the pipeline and its construction is of some significance. The pipeline will pass through something like 750 miles of territory characterized by permafrost. Permafrost is a condition in which the soil and related materials at or near the surface of the ground remain permanently at or below the freezing temperature of water. In an undisturbed state, permafrost protected by tundra vegetation will remain in a relatively stable condition. Modification of the environment by construction activities disturbing the tundra, however, can cause thawing of the permafrost by changing the thermal balance at the surface. This can be caused by gravel pads, damage to the organic surface layer, or disturbed surface drainage. Another hazard to the stability of the permafrost will come from burying the hot oil pipeline itself. Such instability in the soils and related materials could cause pipeline displacement, resulting in serious damage to it (U.S. Dept. of Interior, 1972, vol. 2, pp. 7–10, 97), although those who favour the construction of a hot pipeline argue that design specifications could be stipulated to withstand the stresses that are likely to be imposed.

The difficulty, of course, is that design and construction costs mount disproportionately as the safety factor is increased. Doubtless the pipeline will be built with specifications short of those that will guarantee a zero probability of pipeline damage and oil spill in the arctic tundra. It is worth noting that each mile of pipeline is reported to contain double the amount of oil involved in the Santa Barbara spill of 1969 (Aspin, 1971). Moreover, the pipeline will cross several major navigable rivers and as many as 350 additional smaller streams. Potential problems with spring ice breakup and ice jams raise difficult questions which may never be answered adequately for the assured protection of the arctic environment.

While minimum-risk construction of the pipeline facility across permafrost may be the most challenging engineering problem, the hazard of earthquake damage is another serious problem. Approximately 70 per cent of the southern portion of the route lies within 25 miles of a recorded epicenter (Lewis, 1971). There have been 23 large earthquakes with Richter ratings of 6 or higher during the past 70 years in the vicinity of the T.A.P. route. Moreover, the most frequently mentioned tanker route from Valdez to the U.S. West Coast will pass through areas with a notable concentration of previously recorded epicenters (Cicchetti, 1972, p. 39). To sum up, the Department of the Interior's findings on exhaustive investigation were as follows:

> Seismic shaking or surface faulting accompanying a large shock could rupture the pipeline directly or cause failure in the foundation material that could lead to rupture. Furthermore, large earthquakes could trigger landslides and sea waves that could jeopardize the integrity of the pipeline. (U.S. Dept. of Interior, 1972, vol. 2, p. 11)

Accordingly, the problem appears to be, quoting Cicchetti (1972):

> The as-yet unresolved controversy is whether it is possible to construct a pipeline that can withstand major earthquakes in this range along the proposed route and – short of such an accomplishment – whether a system of shutoff valves, retaining dikes, or walls can be constructed to contain or minimize the damage to the wilderness and the many streams and rivers the proposed pipeline will cross. (pp. 39–40)

The hazards to the environment of transporting North Slope oil through the Trans-Alaska pipeline are not confined to the area along the pipeline route. Upon delivery at Valdez, the oil will be transferred to ocean-going oil tankers for delivery to West Coast ports. Roughly two million barrels of oil per day will be moved across Prince William Sound, with about half that amount moving through Puget Sound. The Department of the Interior's assessment of the treacherous weather and navigation conditions attending this tanker route is sobering. A translation of the hazardous conditions into annual equivalent spills suggests an amount of up to 140,000 barrels per year (U.S. Dept. of Interior, 1972, vol. 4, p. 474).

Quite aside from oil spills that occur as a result of tankers running aground or colliding, and similar large-scale adverse events, there will be a continuous low-level contamination of the terminal port waters. There are two sources of this low-level contamination. First normal spillage associated with loading and unloading operations involving the prospective 2 million barrels a day, and second the discharging of ballast water from tankers on return to Prince William Sound. There is great variation in the estimates of the likely amount and effect of this contamination, but the higher range estimates provide grounds for grave concern about the Prince William Sound fisheries among a group of Cordova fishermen economically dependent on them. The concern is of sufficient gravity to have resulted in a legal action seeking to prevent the use of Prince William Sound for these operations.

To sum up, it is doubtless true that the problem of transporting oil from Prudhoe Bay across Alaska and thence from the port of Valdez on Prince William Sound to the Puget Sound and California ports is attended by enormous risks of environmental damage. There is no question that the risks can be reduced by increasing expenditures for engineering design and construction features directed toward fail-safe characteristics in the transport system. It must be acknowledged, however, that engineering and construction costs become prohibitive in any economic sense before fail-safe features are incorporated which would guarantee that there was no possibility of breaching the integrity of the pipeline under the difficult permafrost and seismic conditions, or that there was a zero probability of offshore marine mishaps, given the treacherous weather and navigation conditions. What this suggests is that it is certain that there will be somewhere, sometime during the period of oil exploitation from the Prudhoe Bay field, an accidental spill of some kind involving the transport system. But, of course, the severity of the environmental impact could not really be assessed with sufficient precision, given information on engineering and construction safety stipulations existing at the time the analysis was undertaken. It has not been meaningful to attempt any serious quantitative (monetary) estimates of the environmental impact from accidental breaches of the transport system's physical integrity.

Aside from the environmental impacts from breaks in the pipeline or offshore oil spills, of course, there are other environmental impacts such as the unevaluated effects on the caribou herds, the low-level contamination of offshore waters from normal operations, and the like. Even here

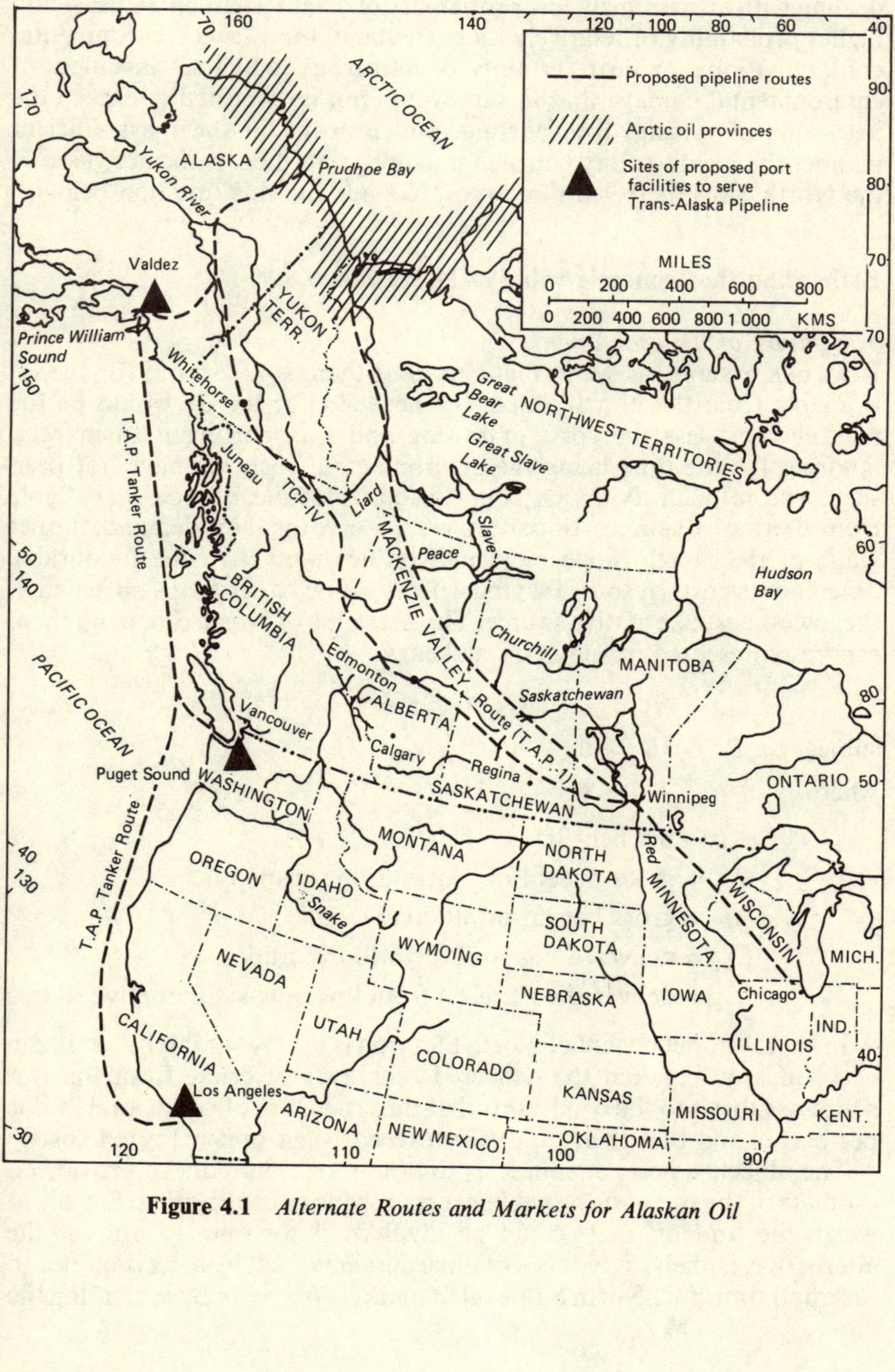

Figure 4.1 *Alternate Routes and Markets for Alaskan Oil*

we are dealing with risks and probabilities rather than certainty as to the impact on the environment. There is no general consensus whether we are dealing with an extremely low probability of an environmental disaster; a higher probability of relatively more frequent lower level environmental contaminations; or near certainty of numerous individual instances of environmental damage that in sum would not be expected to exceed the net value of raising, transporting, and utilizing in the most efficient manner the Prudhoe Bay petroleum. How great, then, is the net value of the North Slope petroleum reserves? We address this question below.

Estimating the economic value of North Slope oil[2]

The nature of the evaluation

If we can assume, as we in fact can, that there is a demand for the oil available from the North Slope, the net value of the oil would be the market value less the costs of raising and transporting it to market, ignoring for the time being the environmental costs we have not been successful in quantifying. Of course if oil of identical grade is available from alternative sources, since both would serve the same demand, the net value of the North Slope oil would be no more than the favourable difference in costs (resource savings) if any, using North Slope oil in lieu of the lowest cost alternative source. The net value of North Slope oil, then, can be represented in summary as below:

$$b = C_A - C_{NS} \qquad (1)$$

subject to: $B_{NS} = B_A \geqslant C_{NS}$

where

b = net benefits
B_{NS} = gross benefit of North Slope crude oil
B_A = gross benefit of alternative oil
C_{NS} = delivered cost of North Slope crude
C_A = delivered cost of oil from lowest cost alternative source

In short, the net benefit of North Slope oil is the favourable difference in cost[3] (if any) between the delivered real costs of crude from the two sources, subject to the conditions that the crudes are of comparable value per barrel, and that their unit value exceeds their unit delivered costs.

The objective here, of course, is to obtain relevant data to provide an estimate of the size of b, the net benefits or value of the Prudhoe Bay oil, to weigh the tradeoff that would be involved if we were to opt for the alternative, namely, avoidance of environmental risk by a decision not to raise and transport North Slope oil to market. We begin by estimating the delivered cost of oil from an alternative source to the market (West Coast) identified by the T.A.P. promoters. Secondly we consider the delivered cost of North Slope crude to the market and obtain the difference which provides our estimate of the net value of the oil as transported by T.A.P. and tanker to West Coast markets.

Delivered cost of crude from alternative sources

The most likely alternative source of low-cost crudes to serve the intended Alaskan Oil–T.A.P. market at the time of analysis was the Persian Gulf petroleum fields. To calculate the delivered cost of the most economic foreign alternative to Alaskan oil via T.A.P. and tanker to the West Coast, Iranian Light 34° A.P.I. (1.4 per cent sulphur) was selected as the specific reference crude. Table 4.1 is a summary of values prepared in connection

Table 4.1 *Average Costs for Persian Gulf Oil Delivered to U.S. Coastal Ports (dollars per barrel)*

	Iranian Light 34° A.P.I. (1.4% sulphur)	
	1971	*1975*
Production[a]	0.10	0.11
Payments to foreign governments[b]	1.11	1.27
Other costs[c]	0.30	0.30
FOB price at destination	$1.51	$1.68
Transportation costs[d]	0.74	0.45
Total cost to U.S. (delivered)	$2.25	$2.13
U.S. tariff	0.105	0.105
Delivered price	$2.36	$2.24
Average	$2.30	

Notes

[a] See M. A. Adelman, *The World Petroleum Market* (Johns Hopkins Press, 1972). Adelman's calculation is best viewed as an overall average for the Persian Gulf and not necessarily for the Iranian Light 34° A.P.I. that is used in this analysis.

[b] See *Platt's Oligram Price Service*, August 25, 1971; and *Oil and Gas Journal*, June 21, 1971, for crude price postings in 1971 and 1975. Payments to foreign governments are based on a calculation of 49 per cent of the posted price that has been approximately determined by Mikesell for Iran. See Raymond F. Mikesell, *Foreign Investment in the Petroleum and Mineral Industries: Case Studies of Investor – Host Country Relations* (Johns Hopkins Press, 1971), especially p. 247.

[c] These costs include all other transportation and gathering costs and payments made to determine the F.O.B. price at point of destination. This F.O.B. price was estimated to be $1.30 in New England Council and others, 'Rebuttal Statement of the New England Parties on Oil Import Controls to the Cabinet Task Force on Oil Import Control', submitted to the Cabinet Task Force, August 15, 1969. At the old posting of $1.80 and Adelman's production costs of 10¢, this would mean a difference of 30¢, which is denoted as 'other costs.'

[d] A high and low cost for transportation are shown to be consistent with the Cabinet Task Force calculations.

with Cicchetti's analysis of delivered costs of imported crudes.[4]

Although the 1971 estimated delivered price, as indicated in the table, was \$2.36 per barrel, the U.S. tariff of 10.5 cents per barrel is an internal (U.S.) monetary transfer and hence should not be included in the real cost of imported oil delivered to U.S. coastal ports. An additional adjustment of 12 cents per barrel was based on the 8° A.P.I. difference in specific gravity (at 1.5 cents/1° A.P.I.), thus leaving an adjusted delivered real cost of crude comparable to the North Slope crude of \$2.13 per barrel (Cicchetti, 1972, p. 21, and footnotes 18 and 19).

Transportation cost of Alaskan oil moved via T.A.P. and tanker

Since all of T.A.P. capacity must be built in advance of any movement of petroleum from Prudhoe Bay to Valdez, it represents a fixed capital outlay irrespective of the level of throughput or rate of utilization. The original Alyeska throughput schedule assumed a 5-year buildup beginning with a 350,000 barrel per day throughput in the first year, ultimately reaching capacity throughput (2 million barrels per day) in the fifth year. Alternatively, an accelerated throughput, assuming capacity operation beginning in the first year, represented a utilization rate that would effect a per-unit transport cost reduction because the fixed costs could be allocated at capacity utilization rates from the outset. A second consideration in estimating the transport cost per barrel was the difference in the time distribution of capital outlays, and oil deliveries. To deal with the latter problem, Cicchetti reduced both the costs and the barrels of oil delivered to time-equivalent, or present-value, terms. Below are given both the present-value computation model for obtaining the present equivalent of oil throughput and the results of the computations.

$$PV_{1971} = \sum_{t=1}^{T} DTP_t(365)(1+i)^{-t} \tag{2}$$

where

PV_{1971} = the present equivalent of the throughput

DTP_t = the average daily throughput in year t

i = the rate of discount

T = the shorter of either the useful life of the transportation system or the expected production period

Table 4.2 presents the results of the computations employing this present equivalent conversion model. It gives the relevant equivalent throughput estimates for the two alternative schedules at each of three discount rates; 10 per cent is used as the rate for the basic computations, with alternatively 8 and 12 per cent used for testing the sensitivity of the conclusions to the estimates of appropriate discount rate.

To obtain the estimated capital cost per barrel, the data displayed in

Table 4.2 must be divided into the estimates of capital outlays for T.A.P. The latter range from \$1.75 billion to \$2.5 billion and are displayed in the upper portion of Table 4.3.[5] In the lower portion of the table are displayed the results of the division, giving the capital costs in cents per barrel.

In addition to the per barrel fixed capital charges, there is an estimated operating cost of about 13 cents that must be added to the figures given in Table 4.3 (Cicchetti, 1972, pp. 11–12). Finally, while these costs cover delivery of the oil from Prudhoe Bay to Valdez, there is an additional charge required to cover the tanker leg of the trip from Valdez to the ports in the 'lower 48'. Transported in U.S. bottoms, as required by the Jones Act, an estimated 35 cents per barrel appeared appropriate for this leg of the trip (see Cicchetti, Table 7). The sum of these costs, representing the total real transport cost of North Slope oil to a West Coast port, is shown in Table 4.4.

Table 4.2 *Present Equivalent Barrels of Oil Throughput* (billions of barrels)

Total Undiscounted Throughput	*Alyeska Throughput*	*Accelerated Throughput*
	16.74	18.25
1971 equivalent at 8%	5.16	6.19
1971 equivalent at 10%	4.04	4.98
1971 equivalent at 12%	3.22	4.08

Source: Cicchetti (1972), p. 11.

Table 4.3 *Capital Costs per Barrel for T.A.P. and Terminal Facility*

	Investment (\$ billion, 1971)			
Discount Rate	*1.75*	*2.00*	*2.25*	*2.50*
	Alyeska throughput schedule (cents per barrel)			
8%	33.9	38.8	43.6	48.5
10%	43.3	49.4	55.7	61.9
12%	54.4	62.2	69.9	77.7
	Accelerated throughput schedule (cents per barrel)			
8%	28.3	32.3	36.4	40.4
10%	35.2	40.2	45.2	50.2
12%	42.9	49.1	55.2	61.3

Source: Cicchetti (1972), p. 13.

Table 4.4 *Transport Cost of North Slope Oil to Los Angeles via Trans-Alaska Pipeline and Tanker of U.S. Registry*

	Investment ($ billion, 1971)			
Discount Rate	*1.75*	*2.00*	*2.25*	*2.50*
	Alyeska throughput schedule (dollars per barrel)			
8%	0.82	0.87	0.92	0.97
10%	0.91	0.98	1.04	1.10
12%	1.02	1.10	1.18	1.26
	Accelerated throughput schedule (dollars per barrel)			
8%	0.76	0.80	0.84	0.88
10%	0.83	0.88	0.93	0.98
12%	0.91	0.97	1.03	1.09

Note: The estimates in this table are based on tanker costs of 35 cents per barrel and terminal operating cost of 13 cents per barrel.

A final cost element was necessary in order to determine the net savings in the delivered cost of crude from the North Slope compared with the most economical alternative (Persian Gulf) source. This related to the cost of raising and collecting the oil in the field in preparation for transporting is to tidewater at Valdez. Various estimates were presented within a reasonable range and we shall employ the average, 24.5 cents, as used by Cicchetti (p. 22). Table 4.5 displays the total real cost of raising, collecting, and transporting North Slope crude to the Los Angeles market.

Estimated net 1971 *value of North Slope oil*

If we substitute in equation (1) \$2.13 as the cost (C_A) of equivalent grade Persian Gulf crude delivered to Los Angeles, using selected values from Table 4.5 as the values of C_{NS}, we can obtain the per barrel savings in costs of North Slope oil over equivalent grade crude from the most economical alternative source.[6] Next, if we wish to get an aggregate net 1971 value of North Slope oil, we can multiply this difference per barrel by the corresponding 1971 equivalent barrels of oil obtained by equation (2), displayed in Table 4.2. These computations are performed and the results shown in Table 4.6. Of course, all of the computations assume that the measure of value per barrel, the price differential, remains the same over the life of the project. Admittedly this was a strong assumption, but as we noted earlier, the myriad uncertainties surrounding the future course of delivered oil prices, especially from the Middle East, did not permit the substitution of an alternative trend with any degree of confidence. Accordingly, the assumption of a steady flow of benefits was made in the interest of simplicity, and for lack of more defensible assumptions.

Table 4.5 *Total Real Cost of Delivering North Slope Oil to Los Angeles via Trans-Alaska Pipeline and Tanker of U.S. Registry*

	Investment ($ billion, 1971)			
Discount Rate	*1.75*	*2.00*	*2.25*	*2.50*
	Alyeska throughput schedule (dollars per barrel)			
8%	1.06	1.11	1.16	1.21
10%	1.16	1.22	1.28	1.34
12%	1.27	1.35	1.42	1.50
	Accelerated throughput schedule (dollars per barrel)			
8%	1.01	1.05	1.09	1.13
10%	1.08	1.13	1.18	1.23
12%	1.15	1.22	1.28	1.34

If we take the discount rate of 10 per cent for our comparative estimates, we see that the savings in costs using North Slope oil will range from a low of around $3.19 billion as a 1971 worth (capital cost of $2.5 billion and Alyeska throughput schedule) to a high of around $5.2 billion (capital costs of $1.75 billion and accelerated throughput schedule). Corresponding variations for discount rate changes between 8 and 12 per cent are presented for inspection. The values given in Table 4.6 will vary from $3.2 billion to $6.9 billion, depending on assumed investment in the pipeline, rate of discount, and throughput schedule. Observing the case of variation in all variables except for the discount rate held at 10 per cent will

Table 4.6 *Aggregate Net Present (1971) Value of Savings in Costs, North Slope Oil Compared with Lowest Cost Alternative*

	Pipeline investment ($ billion, 1971)			
Discount Rate	*1.75*	*2.00*	*2.25*	*2.50*
	Alyeska throughput schedule ($ billion, 1971)			
8%	5.52	5.26	5.01	4.75
10%	3.92	3.68	3.43	3.19
12%	2.77	2.51	2.29	2.03
	Accelerated throughput schedule ($ billion, 1971)			
8%	6.93	6.69	6.44	6.19
10%	5.23	4.98	4.73	4.48
12%	4.00	3.71	3.47	3.22

give the $3 billion to $5 billion range noted above. This represents a net resource cost savings apart from other potential desirable characteristics (national security advantage?). It was this magnitude of net present value that would have been foregone if a decision had been made to forego exploitation of North Slope oil in the interest of environmental protection.

The question turns essentially on whether the public interest in avoiding the expected deleterious effects of T.A.P. and tanker transport – which involves both an assault upon the northern Alaskan wilderness as well as other environmental insults associated with oil spills – was sufficinet to trade off $3 billion to $5 billion of benefits through resorting to other, higher cost sources of petroleum. There are doubtless some persons who would have unhesitatingly subscribed to the belief that it was. There are others who thought otherwise, noting additional considerations such as national security achieved from reduced reliance on imported foreign sources and the associated adverse environmental impacts from expected oil spills associated with transportation of Persian Gulf oil to the United States. The merits of one position over the other cannot be effectively demonstrated, of course, since they depend as much on values and ethical predispositions as on the objective probabilities attaching to the risks involved.

In the absence of scientific and related objective information that would yield more demonstrable conclusions, there was a need for a consensus to be reached by public debate, which in fact was conducted through various media. In this debate, at least two potentially important issues, among others, were sorted out. One was the question of whether the Prudhoe Bay oil field should be exploited or not. The second was, assuming that a decision was to be made to do so, whether the choice of transport mode and market was appropriate. It was on the assumption that the first issue would be resolved in the affirmative that the second question was addressed. The analysis that resulted is presented in the next section.

Evaluating alternative routes and markets

The nature of the evaluation

The previous section discussed the economic advantage of raising and transporting oil from the North Slope to the West Coast market by means of T.A.P. and tanker, as proposed by the promoters of T.A.P. We looked to the most economical alternative source, the Persian Gulf petroleum fields, to determine whether or not the market could be supplied as economically without disturbing the arctic environment. Since both sources would serve the same market, the price of the Iranian reference crude could be adjusted for comparability with North Slope oil to represent benefits which were then equivalent per barrel of crude. To determine the relative economics of the two as sources of oil for the Los Angeles market, we needed only to compare the costs. Since there was a savings in cost favouring the North Slope source, we were able to develop estimates of the net value of the North Slope oil to compare with the anticipated environmental impact. In this case the expected environmental damages would need to be on the order of \$3 billion to \$5 billion before the damages could be considered in excess of benefits.

Such an analysis is useful for comparing the expected benefits of a given proposal with its expected costs. But it is not inconceivable than an equal, or even greater, benefit might be achieved at a lesser economic and environmental cost by considering an alternative route and market. This issue will be addressed below, but first it is important to consider the difference in the nature of the evaluation when the same source of oil is destined to supply, alternatively, different markets by different transport routes and modes, in contrast with the case in which different sources of oil and transport modes are used to provide oil for the same market. In the previous case the gross benefits at market were the same for both sources of oil; production and transport costs differed. In the case we consider below, production costs are going to be the same for oil destined or different markets, but the market value of the petroleum per barrel may differ, apart from the difference induced by transportation cost differentials. Understanding why the clearing prices in different markets might differ by an amount that is more or less than the transportation cost differentials requires some background on the institutional features of the domestic petroleum industry, along with other related factors. First, however, we shall indicate how the rationale for the analysis will differ in this case from the evaluation in the previous section. Here we shall seek, not an estimate of the net value of the North Slope oil field, but rather an evaluation of the relative economics of alternative routes and markets. That is, for the net benefit of T.A.P. to be positive,

$$(B^i_{NS} - C^i_{NS}) > (B^j_{NS} - C^j_{NS}) \quad (3)$$

where

B^i = the gross value or benefit of a barrel of oil at market i served by T.A.P. and tanker

C^i = the total cost of a barrel of North Slope oil delivered at market i

B^j = the gross value or benefit of a barrel of oil at the alternative market, j, served by the alternative transport mode and route

C^j = the total cost of a barrel of North Slope oil delivered at market j.

In short, if T.A.P. is to emerge as the most economical route and transport mode serving the most economical market, the net benefits of T.A.P., the left-hand expression, must be greater than the net benefit of the alternative route, mode and market, or the value of the expression to the right of the inequality.

Gross benefits or market value of oil in alternative markets

To understand why the gross benefit of a barrel of oil might differ in different markets, one must understand the administered nature of the price structure in the domestic petroleum products market. The United States has not been self-sufficient in oil for some time, relying in part on imported Canadian, Indonesian, Persian Gulf, and Venezuelan oil.[7] However, on the presumption that more intensive exploration for oil would occur if the domestic producers would have greater profit incentives, the institution of the oil import quota was adopted to artificially restrict the amount of imported oil and thus provide for a generally higher level of prices for petroleum products in the United States. A feature of the Mandatory Oil Import Quota Program is the division of the United States into five Petroleum Administration for Defense (P.A.D.) Districts. P.A.D. District I and especially P.A.D. Districts II and V are the most relevant for our purpose. Included in P.A.D. District V are Alaska, Hawaii, and the Pacific coastal states, along with Arizona and Nevada. All of the Midwestern states east of the Rockies and west of the Appalachians (excluding, of course, the Gulf Coast states) are included in P.A.D. District II. We shall refer to District II as the Chicago market. In District I are all of the Atlantic coastal states; we shall use New York as the reference market. The policies adopted with respect to the amount of petroleum to be imported under the quota programme in the different districts gave rise to price differentials, in addition to the differences in prices attributed to transportation cost differentials among different markets.

In P.A.D. District V, domestic production was completely protected against foreign competition at a predetermined historical price ($3.17 per barrel of 26°–26.9° A.P.I. crude for reference purposes). If the quantity of oil demanded at that price exceeded the amount supplied from domestic sources and Canada (the latter of which is limited by the throughput capacity of the Trans-Mountain pipeline from the Alberta fields to the Puget Sound), the difference was permitted to be supplied from foreign imports. Given the domestic production in District V and the capacity limitation on Canadian petroleum entering District V, the foreign imports have been representing about 12.2 per cent of the total up to at least mid-1973, at which time the restrictions on imports were relaxed in light of the 'energy crisis'.

Administration of the import quotas in the districts east of the Rocky

Mountains was quite different and resulted in a different clearing price in eastern markets. Petroleum products (excluding residual fuel oil) permitted under the import were set at 12.2 per cent of domestic production, a percentage that happens to be quite coincidentally equal to that in Distict V. Canadian crude oil in this case, however, is figured as part of the foreign imports governed by the quota. Finally, the domestic production was influenced by state demand prorationing restrictions. Prorationing results in higher cost domestic production than otherwise possible for any given quantity supplied. Producers with both high and low marginal costs, within limits, were assigned a given allowable monthly production level. This resulted in a higher rate of output from high-cost wells than would have been required if there were no output restrictions on low-cost wells. Accordingly, petroleum supplied from domestic sources east of the Rockies was marketed generally at a higher price than if it had been market determined in the absence of prorationing restrictions.

The result of the prorationing and the effects of the operation of the Mandatory Oil Import Quota Program, produced a substantial price differential between the Pacific Coast District V ($3.17/barrel) and the Districts (I and II) east of the Rockies ($3.81 and $4.06) respectively.[8] The significance of these price differentials is that the value of the North Slope oil is not independent of the market in which it is sold. An examination of transportation costs to different markets must be undertaken for comparison of cost differentials with corresponding price differentials before a judgment can be made regarding the economics of alternative routes and markets. But, first there was need for some adjustments to the reference price due to the different values placed on crude oil of the same specified gravity and sulphur content, other things being equal, in different markets.

Consumers value products made from crude oil differently in different markets. Petrol bulks dominate in the product mix of refineries on the West Coast. Because it represents a product from the lighter end, the lighter the crude oil used, the more economical is the production of gasoline from it. A higher proportion of fuel oil for home heating is demanded in the Midwest and as this represents a refinery product toward the heavier end, the heavier North Slope crudes are relatively more valued by midwest refineries and consumers than is true on the West Coast. A rough indication of this is the difference in penalty per degree A.P.I. specific gravity on the West Coast (6–7 cents) compared with the Midwest (2 cents). On the other hand, the North Slope crude may be lighter than the 26.9° A.P.I. used for reference purposes, and thus, for example, the Alyeska Service Company suggested a 5 to 10 cent per barrel downward adjustment for Alaskan oil in Midwest markets (Cicchetti, 1972, pp. 78–79).

Another matter of potential significance was that domestic crudes supplying the Midwest market are typically of lower sulphur content than anticipated for North Slope crudes. A difference of 11 cents per barrel existed between a barrel of West Texas Sour and West Texas Intermediate Sweet, other things remaining equal. Accordingly, there could be a total downward adjustment of up to 18 cents per barrel from the reference price for North Slope oil in the Midwest market, as suggested by Alyeska representatives. This would have reduced the reference price to $3.63. On the other hand, early analysis of North Slope crude indicated that it scored particularly high with hydrocracking refining techniques then being introduced in the Midwest and thus the adjustment for the sulphur difference could be in the opposite direction. Taking into account factors that were not considered by Alyeska, the upper bound reference price as estimated by Cicchetti was placed at $3.93 per barrel.

Delivered cost of crude to alternative markets

Having bracketed a range for the market value, or gross benefit, of North Slope oil in the Pacific Coast and Midwest markets, it remained to determine whether the difference in transport costs from the North Slope to Chicago was greater than the difference in the value of petroleum in the two markets.[9] The estimated cost of delivering North Slope crude to Los Angeles market was presented earlier, and is used below in our comparison of cost and value differentials. But first estimates of costs involved in delivering North Slope crude oil to Midwest markets are required.

Obtaining a valid estimate of the construction and operating costs of a Trans-Canadian pipeline (T.C.P.) was difficult and perhaps unduly complicated. The reason is that the estimates which were available in published sources vary a great deal because vastly different assumptions were made in what were regarded as preliminary estimates. Some involved assumptions that both gas and oil pipelines would be built, with costs of such facilities giving estimates highest in the range. Others were prepared with an eye to combining current facilities, i.e. looping existing pipelines, using rights-of-way supporting existing facilities, or combining gas and oil transport facilities with joint costs allocated in some reasonable proportions. The Cicchetti estimates were developed with an eye to maintaining comparability in assumptions with T.A.P., and thus the same investment per mile (excluding port transhipment facilities) was used as in the estimates developed for T.A.P. (1972, table 14, p. 62). Investment costs in the Prudhoe Bay to Edmonton leg of the route run from $2 billion to $2.75 billion and are displayed in Table 4.7.

Investment in transport facilities for the Edmonton to Chicago leg of the route also varied widely, depending on the nature of the assumptions with respect to possibly looping or using existing facilities or excess capacity on the Interprovincial pipeline. An investment of only $0.1

Table 4.7 *Capital Costs for Trans-Canada Pipeline from North Slope to Edmonton*

	Investment ($ billion, 1971)			
Discount Rate	*2.00*	*2.25*	*2.50*	*2.75*
	Alyeska throughput schedule (dollars/barrel)			
8%	0.39	0.44	0.49	0.53
10%	0.50	0.56	0.62	0.68
12%	0.62	0.70	0.78	0.86
	Accelerated throughput schedule (dollars/barrel)			
8%	0.32	0.36	0.40	0.45
10%	0.40	0.45	0.50	0.55
12%	0.49	0.55	0.61	0.68
	Accelerated throughput schedule following 2-year delay (dollars/barrel)			
8%	0.38	0.42	0.47	0.52
10%	0.49	0.55	0.61	0.67
12%	0.62	0.69	0.77	0.85

Source: Cicchetti (1972), p. 63.

billion represented the lower end of the range while an estimated $3.5 billion represented the highest estimate. The estimates used here, following Cicchetti, are the ones that were advanced in various early oil company reports (Atlantic-Richfield, 1971) adjusted to 1971 price levels, with a spread ranging from $1.0 billion. Capital costs per barrel based on this range of estimated investment outlays are displayed in Table 4.8.

With capital charges for the two legs of the North Slope to Chicago T.C.P. as given above, operating costs need to be included for total transportation costs per barrel. The three major oil companies involved in North Slope oil exploitation estimated operating costs for the North Slope–Edmonton–Chicago line, operating at full capacity, or 2 million barrels per day, to be approximately $0.30 per barrel. Components of their cost estimation are displayed in Table 4.9.

Given the two sets of capital outlays – one of four estimates for the North Slope to Edmonton leg of the Trans-Canada pipeline, and one of three estimates for the Edmonton to Chicago leg, we have a combination of twelve estimates of capital costs per barrel which, combined with the 30-cent estimated operating costs per barrel gives a set of estimates of total transportation costs from the North Slope to Chicago by the Trans-Canada pipeline as displayed in Table 4.10. These costs now can be compared with the estimated costs transporting North Slope crude from

Table 4.8 *Capital Costs for Trans-Canada Pipeline when Full Throughput is Sent from Edmonton to Chicago*

	Investment ($ billion, 1971)		
Discount Rate	*0.60*	*0.80*	*1.00*
	Alyeska throughput schedule (dollars/barrel)		
8%	0.12	0.16	0.19
10%	0.15	0.20	0.25
12%	0.19	0.25	0.31
	Accelerated throughput schedule (dollars/barrel)		
8%	0.10	0.13	0.16
10%	0.12	0.16	0.20
12%	0.15	0.20	0.25
	Accelerated throughput schedule following 2-year delay (dollars/barrel)		
8%	0.11	0.15	0.19
10%	0.15	0.19	0.24
12%	0.19	0.25	0.31

Source: Cicchetti (1972), p. 66.

Prudhoe Bay through Valdez to Los Angeles by means of the Trans-Alaska pipeline and tanker combination. The latter estimates are given in Table 4.4.

With the transport cost estimates provided, along with the estimated range of values for the North Slope crude in each of the two markets, we can carry out the evaluation implicit in equation (3). This can be performed for any of the twelve combinations of investment costs; however, in the interest of minimizing detail, the display is reduced to a comparison of only four estimates for each of the markets – for any given discount rate. This is done by selecting the middle estimate of investment outlays ($0.8 billion) for Edmonton to Chicago leg to combine with each of the four investment outlay estimates of the North Slope to Edmonton leg for the Trans-Canada pipeline, as the difference per barrel among transport costs estimates for the Edmonton–Chicago leg is quite small and thus permits the reduction of detail with minimum reduction of information (see Table 4.8). In Table 4.11 are shown the differences between the value per barrel of North Slope oil in each market and the corresponding transportation cost.[10]

If it is understood that the difference in value per barrel of North Slope oil between the West Coast ($3.17) and the minimum estimated value for

Table 4.9 *Operating Costs per Barrrel for Full Capacity Throughputs*

	North Slope to Edmonton		*Edmonton to Chicago*
Expenses for personnel, materials, maintenance, service, administration, oil measurement losses, and fuel (Can. $)	35,300		41,220
Depreciation (Can. $)	42,400		14,830
Total annual operating costs (Can. $)	77,700		56,050
Maximum annual throughput (mil. bbl.)	547.5		547.5
Operating costs/bbl. at maximum throughput (Can. ¢)	14.2		10.2
Linear increase in costs/bbl. to a throughput level of 2MMb./day (Can. ¢)[a]	18.9		13.6
		32.5	
Conversion to U.S. dollars, Can. $1 = U.S. 1971 $0.93 (U.S. ¢)	17.4		12.6
		30	

Source: Canadian Bechtel, Ltd., *Mackenzie Valley Pipeline Research Limited, Preliminary Report* (June 1970).

Note: n.a. = not applicable. Monetary costs of property taxes and interest have not been included above.

a If costs are expected to increase linearly when throughput is increased from 1.5 MMb./day, the assumption is that savings fromeconomies of scale are offset by additional pumping costs. This assumption has been utilized generally in the estimates found in the various Arctic pipeline costs reports prepared for or by the oil industry.

the Midwest ($3.63) was $0.46, it is clear that the difference in the transport costs per barrel to the two markets was substantially less. When both differences are taken into account, it is seen that the net difference favoured the Trans-Canadian pipeline route and the Midwest market by a large margin. Indeed, were we to compare the differences between the market value on the Pacific Coast, and the lowest estimated transport cost to that market, with the highest estimated transport cots associated with the Trans-Canada pipeline and the lowest estimated market value in the Midwest (for comparable discount rates), we would see that there still remained a substantial margin of advantage in the selection of the Midwest market and the Trans-Canada pipeline route, factors other than those considered in the analysis remaining equal.

One of the factors not considered in the analysis to this point, however, does not remain equal. This factor concerns the differential environmental impact of the alternative routes to the different markets. To quote the U.S. Department of Interior (1972) environmental impact study:

> One factor involved in viewing potential Trans-Alaska-Canada Alternative routes from an environmental impact standpoint is the potential oil and gas resource situation of the entire Arctic and prospective future pipeline

Table 4.10 *Transport Cost for Trans-Canada Pipeline from North Slope to Chicago via Edmonton*

Discount Rate	*Investment ($ billion, 1971)*											
	2.6	*2.8*	*3.0*	*2.85*	*3.05*	*3.25*	*3.10*	*3.30*	*3.50*	*3.35*	*3.55*	*3.75*
	Alyeska throughput schedule (dollars/barrel)											
8%	0.81	0.85	0.88	0.86	0.90	0.93	0.91	0.95	0.98	0.95	0.99	1.02
10%	0.95	1.00	1.05	1.01	1.06	1.11	1.07	1.12	1.17	1.13	1.18	1.23
12%	1.11	1.17	1.23	1.19	1.25	1.31	1.27	1.33	1.39	1.35	1.41	1.47
	Accelerated throughput schedule (dollars/barrel)											
8%	0.72	0.75	0.78	0.76	0.79	0.82	0.80	0.83	0.86	0.85	0.88	0.91
10%	0.82	0.86	0.90	0.87	0.91	0.95	0.92	0.96	1.00	0.97	1.01	1.05
12%	0.94	0.99	1.04	1.00	1.05	1.10	1.06	1.11	1.16	1.13	1.18	1.23
	Alyeska throughput schedule following 2-year delay (dollars/barrel)											
8%	0.79	0.83	0.87	0.83	0.87	0.91	0.88	0.92	0.96	0.93	0.97	1.01
10%	0.94	0.98	1.03	1.00	1.04	1.09	1.06	1.10	1.15	1.12	1.16	1.21
12%	1.11	1.17	1.23	1.18	1.24	1.30	1.26	1.32	1.38	1.34	1.40	1.46

Table 4.11 *Estimated Difference Between Market Value and Transport Cost per Barrel of North Slope Oil for Pacific Coast Compared with Midwest Markets*

	Investment ($ billion, 1971)							
Discount Rate	*1.75*	*2.00*	*2.25*	*2.50*	*2.08*	*3.05*	*3.30*	*3.55*
	Alyeska throughput schedule (dollars/barrel)							
	Pacific Coast market $(B^i_{NS}-C^i_{NS})$				Midwest market $(B^j_{NS}-C^j_{NS})$ [a]			
8%	2.35	2.30	2.25	2.20	2.78	2.73	2.68	2.56
10%	2.26	2.19	2.13	2.07	2.63	2.57	2.51	2.45
12%	2.15	2.07	1.99	1.91	2.46	2.38	2.30	2.22
	Accelerated throughput schedule (dollars/barrel)							
8%	2.41	2.37	2.33	2.29	2.88	2.84	2.80	2.75
10%	2.34	2.29	2.24	2.19	2.77	2.72	2.67	2.62
12%	2.26	2.20	2.14	2.08	2.64	2.58	2.52	2.45

[a] B^i_{NS} or the benefit of North Slope oil in the Midwest market, was taken to be the minimum ($3.63) estimate in the range for these calculations.

> development. This is important because the fewer the corridors, pipelines, or other transport systems which might ultimately be used, the lesser would be the injury to nature.

and, again:

> The mountain chains are major obstacles to movement and construction. Less severe, but nevertheless important are the topographic hindrances imposed by the intervening hills. plateaus and uplands. If only topography were considered, the most favourable corridor from Prudhoe Bay to Edmonton would follow the coastal plain lowlands and interior plains around the outer margins of the mountains. . . .
>
> On the basis of recorded earthquakes . . . it appears that each of the (T.C.P.) corridors traverses areas of much lower seismic activity and risk than the proposed Trans-Alaska pipeline. In particular, all the new corridors avoid the very high seismic zone in the Prince William Sound area. . . . (vol. 2, p. 115ff.)

One of the two possible Trans-Canada routes would move across the mountains to the Fairbanks area and then follows the right-of-way of the Alcan highway, thus making use of an already disturbed area. Offsetting considerations here are that the route would traverse some of the active seismic zones in the Fairbanks area, and would not exploit the possibility of consolidating both Prudhoe Bay oil and gas transport systems and corridors with those most likely to be introduced by the discovery and exploitation of Canadian arctic petroleum resources. A disadvantage of the consolidation of the Alaskan and Canadian transport facilities through Northern Canada is the hazard that one variant poses to the 9-million-acre Arctic National Wildlife Range, which borders Canada and adjoins the Beaufort Sea. On balance, however, it was the conclusion of the Department of Interior study that the routes through Northern Canada would be superior to the Trans-Alaska pipeline on environmental grounds (U.S. Dept. of Interior, 1972, vol. 2, p. 320ff.).

To summarize then, it appeared that given the decision to exploit the Alaskan oil, the use of the Trans-Alaska pipeline for transporting it to market was the least desirable method on two counts. First, it was not economic compared with alternative transport routes and markets, and second, it was inferior on environmental grounds as well.

This conclusion has implications for the net value of the Alaskan oil. That is, if the Trans-Canada pipeline and the Midwest market provide for a net gain in their favour, the additional net benefits per barrel of oil will be reflected in a larger net value of the Prudhoe Bay field than initially estimated ($3 billion to $5 billion) in section 3. There are some qualifications in reaching this judgment, however, to which we give attention in the next section.

Consideration of some factors not remaining equal

Given the indicated advantages of the Trans-Canada pipeline, other factors remaining equal, the question can be advanced as to why these advantages could not have been perceived as readily by the Alyeska Service Company as by an economic analyst.

Assuming the analysis itself is correct, there may be many reasons for a divergence between private and social benefits and costs or between pecuniary and real benefits and costs that could lead private parties to opt for actions quite advantageous to themselves that would be less than socially optimal. There are in this instance a whole set of institutional restrictions on free market operation that leave numerous opportunities for private parties, working within the policies and laws affecting their activities, to take advantage of actions that would not be feasible within an unconstrained socally optimal course of action. As an example, it is known that members of the Alyeska Service Company were alert to the possibility of diverting some (or all) of Alaskan oil to Japanese markets rather than to the West Coast under an import-for-export plan. That is, the Alaskan oil sent to Japan was expected to be marketed at roughly the world price of $2 per barrel, thus reducing the oil companies' per barrel tax liability on North Slope oil to the state of Alaska. Compensating for the lower price of oil sold in Japan was the higher price of oil sold in New York ($4.06 per barrel), imported from Venezuelan fields under the import-for-export arrangement, and the opportunity of avoiding provisions of the Jones Act requiring shipment in higher cost U.S. bottoms. There is no need to detail the numerous possibilities under which the returns to the Alyeska Pipeline Service Company, given existing laws, policies, and institutional arrangements, would exceed returns from pursuing the alternative environmentally (and economically) most desirable course of action. These have been examined in rich detail in Cicchetti's study;[11] thus we note them only in passing. There was one factor, however, relating to another real element in the problem, which does not fit neatly into the distinction between private and social nonconformities in objectives.

One implicit assumption, or factor taken to be remaining equal, in our evaluation of the alternative transport modes and markets, was that access to a Canadian right-of-way would not be delayed compared with the time that would be required for a similar right-of-way across lands in Alaska. Given the fact that access across public lands was required in Alaska, and that this required compliance with the National Environmental Policy Act and a provision on rights-of-way of the Mineral Leasing Act of 1920,[12] it was not clear that seeking a permit through Canada would necessarily involve a longer period of negotiation and preparation than the attempt to obtain a permit from the Department of the Interior for a right-of-way to build a service road and line across public lands in Alaska.[13] Assuming, however, that the problem of obtaining access across lands in Canada, involving as it does a foreign power, would incur additional delays, the economics of the alternative routes and markets would be changed, and with sufficient delay in the Canadian over the Alaskan route, actually reversed.

Simply in order to gain perspective on this problem, let us assume that the time required to obtain access rights-of-way, build, and put into operation a transport facility across Canada would involve 2 years in excess of the time the T.A.P. facility could otherwise be put into operation. We can observe the effects of this in Table 4.12 which is drawn from the appropriate section of Table 4.10.

At first sight, the change in the difference between market value and transport cost, assuming an accelerated throughput schedule but with a 2-year delay for the Trans-Canada pipeline, appears to have an effect that only approximates the difference between the Alyeska throughput and the accelerated throughput schedules examined before. Comparing the differences, we see that even at the lowest estimated market value in the Midwest, i.e. $3.63, the accelerated schedule with a 2-year delay in operation of the Canadian facility still has a large favourable net advantage over T.A.P. with the assumed accelerated throughput schedule when viewed in the net difference per barrel perspective. However, a 2-year delay implies that the benefits will not be received as soon, and this will have an effect equivalent to a reduction in number of 1971 barrels for

Table 4.12 *Estimated Difference Between Market Value and Transport Cost per Barrel of North Slope Oil for Trans-Alaska Pipeline and Trans-Canada Pipeline with 2-Year Delay*

Discount Rate	*Investment ($ billion, 1971)*							
	1.75	*2.00*	*2.25*	*2.50*	*2.08*	*3.05*	*3.30*	*3.55*
	Accelerated throughput schedule Pacific Coast market (dollars/barrel) $(B^i_{NS} - C^i_{NS})$				Accelerated schedule with 2-year delay Midwest market (dolars/barrel) $(B^i_{NS} - C^i_{NS})$; $B^i_{NS} = \$3.63$			
8%	2.41	2.37	2.33	2.29	2.80	2.76	2.71	2.66
10%	2.34	2.29	2.24	2.19	2.65	2.59	2.53	2.47
12%	2.26	2.20	2.14	2.08	2.46	2.39	2.31	2.23
					$(B^i_{NS} - C^i_{NS})$; $B^i_{NS} = \$3.93$			
8%					3.10	3.06	3.01	2.96
10%					2.95	2.89	2.83	2.77
12%					2.76	2.69	2.61	2.53

the delayed throughput.[14] To give an indication of the magnitude of the effect, we compare the two in Table 4.13.

The effect of a 2-year delay at discount rates in the range of 8 to 12 per cent can be seen to be rather substantial. If the favourable difference in the per barrel net benefit for the Trans-Canada pipeline and Midwest market is weighted by the unfavourable difference in the time equivalent barrels that a two-year delay would occasion, the comparison of the Trans-Alaska and Trans-Canada pipelines becomes much more difficult. The combined effects of the difference in time-equivalent barrels and the net benefits per barrel for the two alternative routes and markets are illustrated in Table 4.14. Here it is readily seen that at a discount rate of 10 per cent, there is no unambiguous way in which to distinguish the economic superiority of one over the other, when the Trans-Canada pipeline is assumed to be delayed 2 years longer that T.A.P. At the lowest

Table 4.13 *Time-Equivalent Barrels of Oil Throughput*

	Accelerated Throughput	*Accelerated Throughput with 2-year Delay*
	(billions of barrels)	
Total Undiscounted Throughput	*18.25*	*18.25*
1971 Equivalent at 8% discount	6.19	5.31
1971 Equivalent at 10% discount	4.98	4.12
1971 Equivalent at 12% discount	4.08	3.25

Table 4.14 *Comparative 1971 Equivalent Values of Trans-Alaska Pipeline and Trans-Canada Pipeline Delayed a Differential 2-Year Period*

Discount Rate	*Investment ($ billion, 1971)* 1.75	2.00	2.25	2.50	2.08	3.05	3.30	3.55
	Acelerated throughput schedule Trans-Alaska pipeline and tanker ($ billion, 1971)				Accelerated schedule with 2-year delay Trans-Canada pipeline; Midwest market ($ billion, 1971) $B^i_{NS} = \$3.63$			
8%	14.92	14.67	14.42	14.18	14.87	14.66	14.39	14.12
10%	11.65	11.40	11.16	10.91	10.92	10.67	10.42	10.18
12%	9.22	8.98	8.79	8.49	8.00	7.77	7.51	7.25
					$B^i_{NS} = \$3.93$			
8%					16.46	16.25	15.98	15.72
10%					12.15	11.91	11.66	11.41
12%					8.97	8.74	8.48	8.22

estimated market value of North Slope oil in the Midwest market ($3.63), the 1971 net value of T.A.P. and tanker in the Los Angeles market exceeds the Canadian alternative route and Midwest market by approximately three-quarters of a billion dollars. Alternatively, at the higher estimated market value of North Slope oil in the Midwest market ($3.93), the 1971 net value of T.C.P.-transported North Slope crude in the Chicago market exceeds the Trans-Alaskan alternative route and Los Angeles market by approximately half a billion dollars. At lower discount rates, the Trans-Canada alternative will naturally appear to improve slightly, whereas at higher discount rates the nondelayed alternative will benefit differentially.

Accordingly, it is conceivable that expectation of a differential delay, along with the need to consider compensation to Canada for rights-of-way may have figured significantly, along with other incentives to consider a non-Canadian route and West Coast markets.[15] It may well have seemed reasonable at the time of the proposed Trans-Alaska pipeline that a longer time would be required for the Canadian than for the Alaskan route, and that would have made a significant difference in the relative economics. Whether the same rationale will hold in retrospect is uncertain, but even if as little as a 2-year delay were anticipated, assuming accelerated throughput schedules for the two routes, the relative economics would leave little to choose between them. Even so, the lesser environmental impact of the Trans-Canadian pipeline would remain at issue, and here we would encounter the inconsistency between private and public objectives and values.

Conclusions

The decision to raise and transport North Slope oil across arctic tundra and seismically active zones represented an option having environmental impact of such potentially large magnitude that it may appear questionable whether conventional economic analysis can be applied without severe qualifications. The smaller scale the decision, the more applicable is cost-benefit analysis. On the one hand, from the standpoint of the total energy supply situation, perhaps, North Slope oil might be considered a relatively modest increment to total petroleum resources. On the other hand, from the standpoint of new investment in energy supplies, or of environmental impact, we cannot be too comfortable relying ultimately on techniques of marginal or incremental analysis.

In addition to the limitations of the analysis for the reasons cited above, we are dealing with a problem having monumental imponderables. These appear not only with respect to the more conventional variables in benefit-cost analysis, e.g., the trend in future relative price of imported foreign crudes, hence the relative benefits of North Slope oil (for simplicity assumed to remain constant in the analysis) but also in connection with the uncertainty attending potentially massive damage in a particularly fragile environment. These considerations counsel viewing the economic analysis with perhaps greater circumspection than in the more typical problems represented by the previous cases analyzed.

Since it is ultimately not clear whether we are talking about a fairly high probability of numerous relatively low-level contaminations on the one hand, or a low probability of an ecological catastrophe, it may be that neither expected values of benefits and costs nor the present-value criterion are as defensible, as welfare-analytic concepts, as they were in the more customary problems we have addressed. A very low probability of an ecological catastrophe can be expected to yield a relatively modest 'expected value' in terms of environmental costs; yet should it occur, and the effects continue in perpetuity, the costs to future generations may well be so extreme that we would elect to reject economic comparisons based on expected present values. The deficiencies of the present-value criterion involving intergenerational resource allocations were discussed in section 2 of Chapter 4 of *The Economics of Natural Environments* by Krutilla and Fisher. It was there illustrated that changes in the vantage point from which present values are to be calculated, i.e., from one generation to the next, make the present-value criterion a possibly ambiguous policy guide. This may not be all that serious in cases where the variance about the expected values is not great and the magnitude of the decision impacts is also relatively modest. But these conditions are not so likely to obtain in the case of raising and transporting North Slope oil to markets. For this reason the economic analysis of the costs and gains, under the severe qualifications cited above, must be considered as only a part of the input in reaching a public decision in this case in particular. The outcome of the political process, if resulting from free and open public debate of the issues, with the economic considerations entering as part of the relevant information for public choice, is doubtless a more reliable guide to decision in this matter than exclusive reliance on economic information on relative costs and gains, when undertaken under the rather severe conditions of this case.

Yet while the issue whether to raise and transport North Slope oil may be debatable, once given the decision, the selection of market and route seems clearly to favour the Trans-Canadian alternative. Here the T.C.P. alternative dominates T.A.P.; i.e., it appears to have been preferable not only environmentally but economically as well. Accordingly, while economic analysis may not be definitive on the first issue, it does provide useful evidence on the second.

Notes

1 The Cicchetti proposed alternative, a Trans-Canada pipeline, was reflected in the Bayh-Mondale amendment which failed passage in the Senate by a tie-breaking vote cast by then Vice-President Spiro Agnew.

2 This section is based entirely on the analysis presented in Chapter 1 of Cicchetti's study, *Alaskan Oil*.

3 The term *real*, associated with the delivered costs, is used to distinguish between real costs of production and transportation, and 'pecuniary' costs associated with taxes and similar transfer of funds among individuals, rather than net resource costs to society. In the case of North Slope oil, severance and other taxes would be excluded from the *real* delivered costs. Since severance taxes or royalties paid foreign governments on imported crudes represent deferred claims against resources within the U.S. economy, such taxes would represent real costs in the delivered price of foreign, or imported, crudes.

4 These data appear as Table 9, page 20 of Cicchetti (1972).

5 These data are, of course, much out of date, owing both to the delays encountered before final clearance to begin construction, the required improvements stipulated for safety reasons in the design of the system, and, of course, the course of inflation in construction (and other) costs. These costs have been more than matched by the price behaviour of foreign oil following the Arab-Israeli conflict of October 1973, the Arab oil embargo and the O.P.E.C. pricing policy adopted in the wake of the embargo. The analysis is presented using the original data since the changes in costs and prices tend to reinforce rather than reverse the results of Cicchetti's analysis.

6 Although the real resource costs of raising and transporting Persian Gulf oil to U.S. markets were not affected by the October war, the price to importers and hence real costs to them was increased. What the ultimate long-run cost

to importing countries may turn out to be if O.P.E.C. cartel agreements do not hold fast is not predictable. The price, however, is not likely to result in a delivered cost of less than $2.13; hence this figure represents a lower bound estimate. Any departures in the upward direction not offset by equivalent increases in costs simply reinforce the conclusions of Cicchetti's analysis.

7 Oil imports were about 30 per cent of domestic production in 1970.

8 See Cicchetti (1972), Appendix A, Table A-5, page 131.

9 Since the difference in market price (25 cents per barrel) between Chicago and New York is equivalent to the difference in transport costs per barrel from Chicago to New York, the two will cancel out, and it is necessary to compare only one of the districts, i.e. The Midwest, with the Pacific Coasts in evaluating alternative routes and markets.

10 The estimated production cost was not included in the data shown in these tables because this would be equal for each market, since it depends on the same source of petroleum. Accordingly, the *differences* between corresponding estimates in the two sets presented in Tables 4.11 and 4.12 are not affected.

11 See Cicchetti (1972), especially Chapters 4 and 5.

12 Provisions of the Mineral Leasing Act restricted the width of rights-of-way to 24 feet, a limitation that was inconsistent with the proposed methods of construction contemplated for T.A.P. until the action taken by Congress on 16 November 1973, amending the original provisions of the Act.

13 In 1970 the Environmental Defense Fund, the Friends of the Earth and the Wilderness Society joined in a legal action seeking an injunction against the issuance of a permit pending the filing of an environmental impact statement under provisions of PL 91–190, 91st Congress. Following the filing of a final environmental impact statement, the courts, without ruling on the environmental issue, ruled on the inconsistency of the plans involving a right-of-way exceeding limits imposed by the Mineral Leasing Act of 1920. Subsequently Congress liberalized the provisions for width of rights-of-way across public lands to enable the project to meet rights-of-way provisions, following which all formal opposition to the T.A.P. ceased.

14 Compare equation 2 and Table 4.2.

15 Cicchetti does not emphasize this point by virtue of his conclusions derived from analysis of the relative size of the Pacific Coast and the Midwest and East Coast Markets. A two million barrel per day throughput would approximately double the supply of crude oil on the West Coat, but would increase the supply east of the Rockies by only approximately 17 per cent. Accordingly, he assumes the Alyeska throughput schedule for delivery of crude from Prudhoe Bay to be applicable to the Pacific Coast market, and recognizes on the other hand that the total supply of Alaskan oil could be readily absorbed in the Midwest and Eastern markets with an accelerated throughput schedule following a 2-year delay. Cicchetti concludes that the payments to Canada could increase costs by as much as 20 per cent and the delay compared with the Trans-Alaskan pipeline could go up to 3 years without tipping the balance away from the Trans-Canada pipeline and Midwest and Eastern markets (Cicchetti, 1972, page 121).

References

Adelman, M. A. (1972), *The World Petroleum Market*, Johns Hopkins University Press, Baltimore,

Aspin, L. (1971), 'It's Not Too Late to Stop the Alaska Pipeline – Maybe', *Not Man Apart*, vol. 1, no. 8.

Atlantic-Richfield Co. (1971), *The Trans-Canadian Alternative Route*, memorandum submitted to the Department of the Interior, 10 September 1971.

Canadian Bechtel Ltd. (1971), *Mackenzie Valley Pipeline Research Limited Preliminary Report*.

Cicchetti, C. J. (1972), *Alaskan Oil: Alternative Routes and Markets*, Johns Hopkins University Press, Baltimore.

Lewis, C. R. (1971), *Comments on the Draft Environmental Impact Statement for the Trans-Alaska Pipeline*, submitted to the Department of the Interior.

Mikesell, R. F. (1971), *Foreign Investment in the Petroleum and Mineral Industries: Case Studies of Investor-Host Country Relations*, Johns Hopkins University Press, Baltimore.

U.S. Department of the Interior (1972), *Final Impact Statement Proposed Trans-Alaska Pipeline*, vols. 2 and 4.

5

The Sixty-City Limit

Thomas D. Crocker, William Schulze, Shalul Ben-David, Allen V. Kneese

INTRODUCTION

One of the major damages from pollution stems from the effects of human health. In an O.E.C.D. study on sulphur dioxide emissions, the benefits from controlling sulphur emissions were totally dominated by health effects (the study probably underestimated these effects). On the other hand measuring effects on human health in monetary units has created quite a lot of discussion and not few misunderstandings.

Traditionally, estimation of health benefits from pollution control has proceeded in three stages. In a first stage the effects on ambient environmental quality from pollution control programmes have been quantified. This has mainly involved atmospheric dispersion models but also general ecological models. In a second step a dose-response relation has been estimated describing the causal effects on mortality and morbidity from different exposures to pollutants. The third step has involved assessing a monetary value to the predicted reductions in mortality and morbidity. This has most often meant that the analysis has computed the reduction in the cost of medical care and the increase in production made possible by the pollution control programme.

We will not consider the first step in this introduction, although the construction and use of environmental models may be the most important input in cost-benefit analysis. Such model constructions belong, however, to meteorology and ecology rather than economics.

Estimation of dose response relations has been pioneered by economists, and the information available at present stems mainly from the work of economists and we will give a very brief survey of that work together with some critical comments.

The assessment of a monetary value as suggested above has been very much criticized and most economists would now agree that the basic philosophy behind putting a price tag on health effects should not be the calculation of medical care costs or the value of production foregone but the willingness in order to pay to reduce the risk of having pollution induced health effects.[1] We will elaborate on this in some detail because it gives the rational of including health effects in cost-benefit studies.

The study we have chosen to include, is an edited version of chapter IV in E.P.A., *Methods Development for Assessing Air Pollution Control Benefits*, Volume 1, 'Experiments in the Economics of Air Pollution Epidemiology', by Thomas D. Crocker, William Schulze. Shalul Ben-David and Allen V. Kneese. The study contains a detailed discussion of the problems connected with specification and simultaneity that arise when dose response relations are estimated. It then continues by assessing a monetary value on health effects by using estimated willingness to pay for increases in safety. The study is based on the estimates of safety values obtained by Shervin Rosen and Richard Thaler ('The Value of Saving a Life: Evidence from the Labor Market', in N.E, Terleckyj, ed. *Household Production and Consumption*, New York 1975). In order to make the included case study self contained, we will briefly survey the article by Rosen and Thaler.

The pioneering studies in the field of pollution epidemiology were carried out by Lester Lave and Eugene Seskin. In a series of papers, starting 1970, they have tried to estimate dose response relations by using econometric techniques.[2]

Usually cross section data over different regions or cities are used. Assume that it has been possible to measure mortality and morbidity rates in these different regions and that it also has been possible to measure exposure to pollutants. It is then possible to estimate by different regression techniques the relation between mortality and morbidity rates and the exposure to pollutants. However, it is by no means obvious how exposure to pollutants should be measured – would it be daily average concentrations, or hourly averages? Which pollutants should be included? Moreover, not only exposure to pollution but other variables that vary over the regions may affect the mortality and morbidity rates. For example, it is widely recognized that smoking habits differ between urban and non-urban regions and, as smoking is of importance for health, it is one variable that should be included in the regression.

The study we have chosen also includes dietary variables. Kerry Smith has shown that the specification of the relation to be estimated is very important for the final analysis of dose-response relationships. The study therefore tries more explanatory variables such as dietary variables.

Another feature of the selected case study is that for the first time simultaneity problems of estimating dose-response relations are recognized. Such problems may arise because people may move from one region to another because of different exposures to pollution. In order to handle this situation a fully interdependent model is needed.

Needless to say the estimated relations are very uncertain but using the information they contain is by far much better than to neglect the connection between pollution and health.

The modern approach to assess the monetary value of health effects is to ask how much people are willing to pay to reduce the probability of getting a pollution induced desease. Health effects do not differ in this respect from any other pollution effects. The value or the benefits of a pollution control programme is by definition the amount the exposed people are willing to pay to have these positive health effects. This approach has been put against the traditional one where the reduction in financial costs due to health effects has been used to assess the value of positive health effects.

The two approaches may, however, not be incompatible with each other. Consider an individual who at the present has a small probability p of getting a pollution induced desease. An air pollution control programme would reduce that probability to $p' < p$. How much would the individual be willing to pay for that reduction? Assume that the medical cost to the individual if he catches the desease is A and that his loss of income is B. If the control programme is realized his expected medical costs will fall with $(p-p')A$ and his expected income will increase with $(p-p')B$. If the individual is risk neutral he would be willing to pay at least $(p-p')A+(p-p')B$ for having the control programme. He may very well be willing to pay more, but we have at least a lower boundary for the benefits from the air pollution control programme which may be sufficient for making the decision on realizing the programme or not.[3]

However, it may be that this lower boundary is very low compared with the actual benefits. Schultze and Gerking[4] write 'For similar safety programmes estimates based upon willingness to pay measures are about ten times higher than those based upon productivity changes'. If this is a general phenomenon it is obviously necessary to use the willingness to pay approach directly instead of estimating a lower boundary by looking at financial costs only.

There are in principle two ways of estimating the willingness to pay for improved safety. One way would be to ask people directly about their willingness to pay. This approach is connected with quite a lot of problems. It has been included as a separate case study on option values (which deals with water quality planning and not health effects, though the approach is the same). The other way is to estimate the value of improved safety from observing people's behaviour. If a person is fully informed about the relevant probability distributions one would expect that his behaviour would be influenced by this information. If it is more risky to live in one region than in another, one would expect individuals to move from the first region to the second. With perfect markets this change in the demand for real estates will then be capitalized in changes in property values. By studying property values and estimate how they are related to pollution levels it would then be possible to estimate the willingness to pay to reduce pollution. This approach has been used very frequently[5] but it has also been criticized very much.[6]

The same line of thought can also be applied to the choice between jobs with different risks. With completely homogeneous workers who are fully informed and with a perfect labour market the wages in equilibrium adjust so that wage differentials exactly compensate the workers for differences in risk. By estimating the influence of risk on wages in different professions it would then be possible to find the willingness to pay to reduce the risk.

This is the approach taken by Rosen and Thaler (op. cit.). Of course, it is not possible to maintain the hypothesis that the workers constitute a homogeneous population and that wage differentials can be completely explained by differences in risk. Therefore they include variables for job characteristics and worker characteristics. Their basic data contained in a 1967 study of the extra risks associated with some very hazardous occupances was based on insurance records and earnings data. The interested reader is referred to their original article. Suffice it to say that in the end they found that jobs with extra risks of .001 pay $ 3.52 per week more than jobs with no risks.

One can now assume that this figure is characteristic for all individuals and all kind of risks. Thaler and Rosen themselves use the figure to calculate the willingness to pay for safety belts in the U.S. The case study on epidemiology we have included has used the same estimate to calculate the willingness to pay for reduced health damage from air pollution exposure.

Is it possible to use the estimates reported in the case study outside the United States? It is obvious that any estimate of the willingness to pay in the U.S.A. is relevant only for that country and it should not be possible to use that estimate in other parts of the world. The estimated dose-response relations can, however, be used elsewhere if care is taken in onterpreting the results and if differences between U.S.A. and the region under study that may affect health are carefully made explicit. The use in one country of dose-response relations which were estimated for another country has occurred. In an O.E.C.D. study on sulphur emissions, the health benefits from pollution control in Western Europe have been estimated using American dose-response relations.

Notes

1 This was first discussed by E. J. Mishan in 'Evaluation of Life Limb: A Theoretical Approach', *Journal of Political Economy*, December 1971. See also K.-G. Mäler and R. Wyzga, *Economic Measurement of Environmental Damage*, O.E.C.D., Paris, 1976.

2 See K. V. Smith, 'Mortality – Air Pollution Relationships: A Comment', *Journal of American Statistic Association*, vol. 70, pp. 341–43, June 1975.

3 For a more detailed discussions see Mäler-Wyzga, op. cit.
4 See W. Schultz and S. Gerking, 'What Do We Know about Benefits of Reduced Mortality from Air Pollution Control?', *American Economic Review*, May 1981.
5 For a survey and discussion, see Freeman, *The Benefits of Environmental Improvement*, Johns Hopkins University Press, 1979.
6 See K.-G. Mäler, *A Note on the Use of Property Values in Estimating Marginal Willingness to Pay for Environmental Quality*.

CASE STUDY

Objectives of the experiment

The identification of substances in the environment which affect human health, and accurate quantifications of their effects, is extremely difficult. Often there are multiple substances involved, there may be long latency periods before effects are seen, and the amount and time of exposure is often unknown. There are three general approaches to identifying such substances and quantifying their impact – all more-or-less imperfect. In the first, laboratory animals are exposed to large doses of the suspect substance and, if effects appear, an effort is made to extrapolate them to the human population. The correct manner in which to execute the second step is not well established. The second approach is to develop aggregate cross-sectional data, usually for cities or standard metropolitan areas, on a number of variables which might be associated with mortality rates or illness rates and then to use regression analysis in order to discover statistically significant associations. A third approach is to gather very detailed data on individuals and again to use statistical analysis to determine the effect of various factors including environmental exposures on individualized measures of health status.

The purpose of the research reported in this chapter is to explore both the possibilities and limitations of the second approach mentioned above – aggregate epidemiology – in the estimation of human dose-response functions which include exposure to air pollution. The principal advantage of the use of aggregated data on cities or metropolitan areas is quite simply the widespread availability and low cost of such data as opposed to data generated from animal experiments or collected on individual human beings through specialized surveys. However, the use of aggregated data creates a number of special problems.

First, one ideally wishes to estimate a dose-response relationship or function as shown in Figure 5.1. Based on *a priori* considerations one would suppose that for human populations, risk of death for an individual would be a function of medical care, age of the individual, the genetic endowment of the individual, the behaviour of the individual – does he or

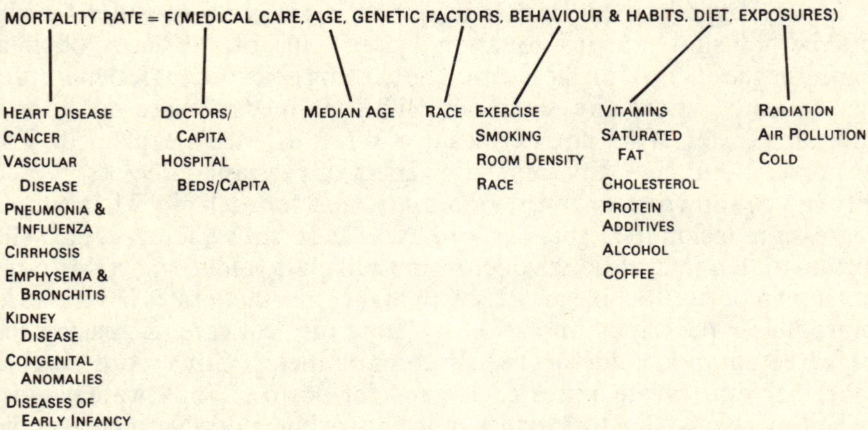

Figure 5.1 *Hypothetical Human Dose-Response Function*

she exercise, smoke, etc. – the diet of the individual, and exposures to possibly harmful substances or circumstances. However, aggregate epidemiology provides no data on individual risks or characteristics but only data for population characteristics as a whole. Thus, aggregate mortality rates in, for example a city are used as a proxy for risk of death in the estimation of an individual dose-response function where it is implicitly assumed that individuals can be represented by the *average* individual in each city. Thus, in using the data set developed below for sixty U.S. cities to estimate a dose-response function of the form shown in Figure 5.1, it is implicitly assumed that each city represents one average individual. However, the list of assumptions required to allow such aggregation (all relationships must be perfectly linear, etc.) are not likely to be met in practice. Thus, one must recognize that estimated results are biased to an unknown extent by the very use of aggregated data.

A second problem arises from the fact that aggregate epidemiology must rely on secondary data. Since the investigator must depend on data already collected, he cannot add a question to a survey nor can he vary the design of an animal experiment to test the importance of a new variable. In the past this problem has led to the exclusion of data on important variables such as smoking, diet and exercise from aggregate epidemiological studies (see, for example, Lave and Seskin (1977) and Schwing *et al.*, (1974)). We have been able to gather some data – not necessarily good data – on both smoking and diet and, as we show below, these are important omissions from previous studies. The current study still excludes any measure of exercise.

Finally, aggregate epidemiological studies are likely to suffer from a number of simultaneous equation biases. One of the most obvious concerns the effect of medical care. The existing epidemiological literature has failed to show any significant effect of medical care on human mortality rates. This counterintuitive result is easily explained. For example, in our sixty city sample, no effect of per capita doctors in each city can be shown on aggregate mortality rates for each city when simple regression techniques such as ordinary least squares are used. The explanation is that, although doctors most likely do reduce mortality rates (as shown below), people in cities with higher mortality rates have in turn more illness per capita and seek out more medical care, increasing the observed number of doctors in such communities. In other words, higher mortality rates create a greater demand for doctors. Thus, we have two offsetting effects – doctors reduce mortality, while mortality increases the demand for doctors – and simple regression analyses cannot untangle them. Several statistical techniques are available for coping with simultaneous equation problems. We use a very simple approach, two-stage least squares, a technique described in a little detail below.

A second simultaneous equation problem may arise because of multiple causes of death. Cities with high coronary death rates may likely have lower cancer death rates because people die of heart attacks before they have a chance to die of cancer. In this situation, factors which, for example, show up positively correlated with coronary disease may show up with a spurious negative correlation with cancer rates. This simultaneous equation problem is likely to work 'through' the age variable in that median age is determined in part by mortality rates of individual diseases, while, in turn, age is used to explain mortality rates. We therefore have also employed two-stage least squares on the age variable, but with no impact on the estimated equations so these results are not reported here. An alternative approach to the problem, which we do not employ, is the use of age-specific mortality rates.

A third possible source of simultaneous equation bias occurs because people make voluntary choices over location. Migration in and out of our sixty city sample is effectively disregarded. People may, for example, contract an air pollution related disease and, on a physician's advice, move from a highly polluted area to an unpolluted area, only then to die. A false negative association between air pollution and pollution-related mortality might then be shown. Although in the past we have included a net migration variable (see Kneese and Schulze (1977)) which was statistically significant, we have excluded such a variable in this analysis because it defies interpretation in a dose-response function context.

We now turn to development of methodology for estimating the value of reducing health risks and for the effect of medical care on human health. This latter section focuses on the role of economics in aggregate epidemiology.

Value of life versus value of safety

The direct costing approach employed by economists for evaluating the mortality costs of diseases which result from environmental exposures is straightforward but difficult to quantify fully (see, for example, Kneese and Schulze (1977)). First, the population at risk must be known. Second, the increased risk of mortality ssociated with environmental exposures must be quantified either through epidemiology or through extrapolation from animal experiments. Third, the amount of money or the value that individuals place on safety (avoiding risk of death) must be known. Multiplying these three values together then gives an approximation of the incremental benefits of reducing such exposures. This cost or benefit is not in any way related to a 'value of life' which is most likely unmeasurable, but rather focuses on a concept of the value of safety (alternatively 'cost of risk') to individuals where risks are statistically small.

Economists in the past have attempted to value human life as the sum of present value of the future earnings over an individual's lifetime (see Lave and Seskin (1970 and 1977)). This approach, however, is no longer viewed as acceptable. In the first place, it assumes that the value of life can, in fact, be measured – a point certainly open to debate. Second, it implies that the lives of children, housewives, retired and other unemployed individuals are worth less than the lives and employed heads of households.

Two measures can be used to value safety or risk to life which are based on the economic concepts of equivalent variation (E.V.) and compensating variation (C.V.). An E.V. measure of the value of life is the amount of money an individual would require to escape from or prevent certain death; in theory, a rational individual would part with all his available wealth to save his life. C.V., in contrast, measures the compensation required to induce an individual to accept voluntarily a situation where the probability of death is increased. As the probability of death approaches unity, the C.V. measure can be taken as an estimate of the value the individual places on his life. Logically, though, the value of life measured this way must be infinite, because as the probability of death approaches certainty, the probability of enjoying any compensation offered (and thus the value of the compensation) approaches zero. Thus, neither E.V. (which requires coercion) nor C.V. (which makes the value of life immeasurable) provides a wholly satisfactory way of estimating the dollar costs of mortality in real world situations that involve risk. An elaboration of the C.V. concept, however, can provide a useful measure of the compensation necessary to induce an individual to accept a *slight* increase in the probability of death.

Mishan (1971) was the first to distinguish between the concept of cost of risk, which is ethically appealing, and earlier efforts to value human life based on lost earnings, which, as a methodology, has strange and intuitively objectionable features. The latter measure of the 'value' of human life has now been rejected by economists both on theoretical and, to some extent, on ethical grounds. Thaler and Rosen (1975), using wage differentials between jobs varying in the level of job-associated risk of death, were the first to estimate explicitly the value of safety. In other words, workers in high risk jobs receive higher wages, and a value of safety can be imputed by examining risk-related wage differentials. Unfortunately, however, their study dealt with a high risk class of individuals. The Thaler and Rosen (1975) estimate suggests that in current dollars a small reduction in risk over a large number of individuals which saves one life is worth about $340,000. Another study (Blumquist (1977)), which examines seat belt use, suggests that the figure might be $260,000. This study first estimates how people value their own time and then imputes a value of safety from the amount of time a sample of individuals spent in buckling up seat belts. These results may be biased downward because individuals seem to perceive risks differently when an element of personal control, such as driving an automobile, is involved. Finally, Smith (1975) in a study similar to the one by Thaler and Rosen (1975) has suggested that, for a more typical population and for job-related risks, the figure may exceed $1,000,000. Clearly, the cost of risk is not precisely known, and perhaps will never be, since attitudes – risk preferences – presumably can change over time, between groups, and can even vary in diffrent situations But, we at least have a range of values with which to make order-of magnitude estimates of the costs of environmental risks. This range of values does not, however, overlap the value-of-life estimates based on lost earnings. For example, Lave and Seskin (1977) use a value in the thirty to forty thousand dollar range for a life lost. The Thaler and Rosen (1977) value of safety is, for example, about an order of magnitude larger than the Lave and Seskin (1977) lost earnings number.

The theoretical basis of a value of safety or cost of risk concept can be shown briefly as follows: Assume that an individual has utility function, $U(W)$, where utility is an increasing function of wealth, W. If risk or death is Π, expected utility is $(1-\Pi)U(W)$. If we hold expected utility constant, we have $(1-\Pi)U(W) = \text{constant}$, and the total differential of this equation is:

$$-U(W)d\Pi + (1-\Pi)U'(W)dW = 0 \tag{1}$$

where the prime denotes differentiation. Holding utility constant then implies that the increase in wealth (or income or necessary to offset an increase in risks:

$$dW/d\Pi = U/[U'(1-\Pi)]. \tag{2}$$

This is the compensating variation measure of the cost to an individual attributable to an increased risk of death. Analysis of the last expression can be simplified we assume a constant elasticity of utility with respect to wealth, η, such that $U(W) = \eta$ and consequently $\eta = (dU/dW)\,(W/U)$. Then (2) can be written as:

$$dW/d\Pi = W/[\eta(1-\Pi)]. \qquad (3)$$

The right-hand side of (3) suggests several interesting points about the value of safety or cost or risk. First, if we assume that the elasticity of utility is less than one, people are risk averse. This in turn implies that since the risk of death is positive ($\Pi > 0$) that $(dW/d\Pi) > W$. In other words, if an individual is risk averse, his life, in terms of the risk premium necessary to get him to accept risk, is worth more to him than his wealth. Second, from (3) as wealth increases, the risk premium required to accept an increase in risk voluntarily, $dW/d\Pi$ must increases with age, *ceteris paribus*. Thus, one would expect older people to act in a more risk averse manner than younger individuals (require greater compensation to voluntarily take a risky action), both because of increased income and because of increased initial age-related risk of death.

This model contrasts for a number of reasons with the value of lost earnings approach previously used in economic analysis. First, if lost income itself is the measure, the 'value of life' measured through lost earnings obviously cannot exceed wealth (see Conley (1977)). Second, increased wealth will increase the lost earnings measure as well as the cost of risk measure. However, the cost of risk measure may not increase proportionately if a different utility function is used. Third, the lost earnings measure must *decrease* with age at some point as individuals get older because the expected remaining earnings must decrease, while the cost of risk, as we argued above, will likely increase. Finally, it is clear from (3) that as Π approaches unity, $dW/d\Pi$ approaches infinity. In other words, the compensation required to induce an individual to accept a certainty of death voluntarily is infinite. The lost income measure has no similar property. Nevertheless, the implication is that *small* increases in risk may be valued in terms of comprensation required to induce individuals to accept such risks voluntarily. Individuals, of course, rationally accept small risks on a daily basis, presumably on the basis of some monetary or psychic return.

Given the analysis above, the current methodology of multiplying value of safety numbers times experimentally or epidemiologically determined environmental risks can then be justified as follows: assuming a utility function $U(W)$ where W is wealth, if risk of death is Π, the marginal cost of risk, as derived earlier, is $(dW/d\Pi)\overline{U} = U/U'(1-\Pi)$, where $\overline{U}$ is a constant utility level. If risk, Π, is a function of pollution, X, where utility functions are identical for N individuals, one would wish to maximize expected utility,

$$N[1-\Pi(X)]U(W), \tag{4}$$

subject to a constraint on total wealth, $\overline{W}$, or income of society

$$\overline{W}-NW-C(X^0-X)=0 \tag{5}$$

which is allocated to individual wealth, assumed identical for purposes of exposition, (NW), and costs of controlling environmental pollution from the initial level X^0, $[C(X^0-X)]$. Noting that $\Pi_X > 0$, and $C' > 0$, the first order conditions are (where λ is the multiplier on (5) and L denotes the Lagrangian):

$$\partial L/\partial W = N(1-\Pi)U' - N\lambda = 0$$

$$\partial L/\partial X = -N\Pi_X U - \lambda C' = 0$$

These imply:

$$N\,[U/U'(1-\Pi)]\Pi_X = C' \tag{6}$$

or that the number of individuals, N, times the marginal cost of risks, $[U/U'(1-\Pi)]$, times the marginal effect of pollution on risk, Π_X, equals the marginal cost of control, C'. Clearly, this model abstracts from many welfare theoretic problems but it does imply that estimation of the left-hand side of (6) as suggested at the beginning of this section is a legitimate approximation of the incremental benefits of environmental control.

In summary, the direct costing of mortality has the advantage of focusing attention on one positive output of environmental agencies which has clear economic value – safety. It is important, however, to distinguish between the value of safety to consumers which does have measurable economic value – environmental agencies may be viewed as selling safety to the public – as opposed to techniques which claim to measure the value of human life. Cost-benefit arguments for environmental programmes should and can rest on demonstrable increases in public safety delivered at costs comparable to what the public is willing to pay for safety, not on claims as to the value of human life. However, the assessment of the risk of mortality associated with environmental exposures such as air pollution – whether based on animal experiments or epidemiological studies – remains difficult and uncertain and is central to the direct costing methodology. Surprisingly, perhaps, the authors feel there is likely to be less professional debate as to the economic measure of the dollar value of safety than as to the quantification of environmental health effects. We now turn to the possible role of economic analysis in the epidemiology of air pollution.

A methodological basis: does economics matter?

The question posed above could be rephased 'does rational human behaviour matter in the estimation of dose-response functions?'

Economists would certainly answer in the affirmative; individuals are likely to respond to illness with numerous ameliorative measures. Clearly, such measures must be accounted of a properly specified dose-response function is to be estimated. What follows is a simplified economic model of human behaviour in response to health risks which in turn allows specification of appropriate statistical techniques for estimating a human dose-response relationship.

Let Π denote risk of death for an individual where that risk can be reduced by medical care which we denote D, synonymous with our empirical measure, doctors per capita. Thus, risk can be written as a function, $\Pi(0)$, where $d\Pi/dD = \Pi' < 0$. If the price of medical care is p and income is denoted Y, then utility, U, can be written $U(Y-pD)$, a function of income net of expenditures on medical care, pD. In an uncertain world, economic analysis assumes that an individual will choose to maximize expected utility – the odds of remaining alive $(1-\Pi)$ times the utility level U – or

$$[1-\Pi(D)]\,U(Y-pD), \tag{7}$$

so the first order condition for the quantity of medical care chosen when rearranged is:

$$\frac{U}{(1-\Pi)U'} = \frac{p}{-\Pi'} \tag{8}$$

The term on the left-hand side of (8) is easily recognizable from the previous section as the marginal value of safety (or compensation required to voluntarily accept a small increase in risk), while the term on the right is the marginal cost of increased safety through medical care. Thus, this model of human behaviour implies that an individual will choose a level of medical care which equates his or her marginal value of safety to the marginal cost of reducing risk through medical care. Of course, an individual's perception of risk and of the ability of medical care to reduce risk of death may be imperfect. However, from (8) it is easy to show that individuals who are more risk averse, i.e. those with a large marginal value of safety, will seek more medical care than those who are less risk averse.

An explicit set of functional forms will simplify interpretation. Let us again (as in Section 4.2) assume a constant elasticity of utility with respect to income, η, so $U-(Y-pD)^{\eta}$. Also assume a linear (approximate) dose-response relationship, $\Pi = \Pi_0 + \Pi' D$, where $\Pi' < 0$ is now a fixed coefficient and Π_0 is a positive constant. Equation (8) can then be written as:

$$D = \left(\frac{\eta}{\Pi'}\right) - \left(\frac{1}{\Pi'}\right)\Pi + \left(\frac{1}{P}\right)Y \tag{9}$$

which is a demand equation for medical care. If we take the supply price of medical care to be fixed $P = P^*$ (infinitely elastic supply of medical care), the individual demand for medical care, doctors per capita for example, is then a linear increasing function of total risk Π, since $(-1/\Pi') > 0$, and of income Y, since $1/P^* > 0$. Of course, we wish, as our principal objective for policy purposes, to estimate the dose-response function:

$$\Pi = \Pi_0 + \Pi' D; \tag{10}$$

in particular, we wish to obtain an unbiased estimate of Π', the effect of medical care on mortality and of the effect of other variables such as air pollution. However, any attempt to directly estimate (10) is doomed to failure. This occurs because the equation specified for statistical estimation (equivalent to 10 where α_0 amd α_1 are parameters for estimation)

$$\Pi = \alpha_0 + \alpha_1 D + \mu_\Pi \tag{11}$$

has a disturbance term μ_Π which is not independent of D. In other words, μ_Π is correlated with D. This is easy to show if we specify the demand equation for doctors (equivalent to 4.9 above with parameters β_0, β_1 and β_2) as stochastic:

$$D = \beta_0 + \beta_1 \Pi + \beta_2 Y + \mu_D \tag{12}$$

as well, with a disturbance term μ_D. Now suppose some factor (random) embodied in μ_Π causes Π to rise in (11). But if Π rises, by (12), D must increase since, from (9), $\beta_1 > 0$ and D, through P_1, depends on Π. Thus, D depends on μ_Π through (12) and D and v_Π are correlated. Now, if in estimating (11) this correlation is not accounted for, not only will estimates of α_1 and α_0 be biased, but if we had included other factors which affect morality such as diet or pollution in (11), coefficients on these variables would be biased as well. It is also true that if simultaneous equation biased is present and not accounted for, it becomes possible that the estimated effect of medical care, α_1, will appear not significantly different from zero or even of the wrong sign (note we assume that $\alpha_1 < 0$; that doctors reduce mortality).

We can break the dependence of D on μ_Π by first substituting (10) into (9), or (11) into (12), to obtain a reduced form equation for medical care,

$$D + \frac{\eta}{2\Pi'} - \frac{\Pi^0}{2\Pi'} + \frac{1}{2P^*} Y \text{ or } D = \gamma_0 + \gamma_1 Y + \mu_r \tag{13}$$

where μ_r is the disturbance term in the reduced form. This equation can be legitimately estimated since the income variable is exogenous, determined outside the relevant system of equations, and the endogenous variables D and Π, those determined within the system, do not appear on the right-hand side of (13). Now, if we estimate (13) and obtain unbiased estimates of the two coefficients $\gamma_0 = (\eta/2\Pi')/(\Pi/2\Pi')$ and $\gamma_1 = (1/2P^*)$ we can use these along with data on income, Y, to generate a new variable, estimated medical care, D, where

$$D = \gamma_0 + \gamma_1 Y. \tag{14}$$

Note that this new variable, D, generated from data on Y does not depend on μ_Π and can be used instead of actual data on D to estimate a dose-response function:

$$\Pi = \alpha_0 + \alpha_1 D + \mu_\Pi \tag{15}$$

This estimated equation gives a consistent estimate of α_1 or Π'. In fact, if the hypothesis that doctors are both important and effective in reducing mortality rates is correct, α_1 should show up negative and significantly different from zero as estimated in (15). Note, however, that if individuals perceive that doctors are effective, they will have a strong incentive to seek medical help when ill, thus making a direct least squares estimate of the effect of medical care as specified in (11) impossible.

The procedure we have outlined above, two-stage least squares, has been used successfully in many instances to resolve simultaneous equation problems and has the advantage of requiring minimal additional data. In general, if an unbiased estimate of a structural equation (one equation is a simultaneous system) is desired, one need only use ordinary least squares to estimate each of the endogenous variables as a function of all of the exogenous variables in the model (estimate a set of reduced form equations). Then, using the data on the exogenous variables, an estimated data set for each of the endogenous variables is created. Consistent structural equations can then be obtained by replacing each endogenous variable on the right hand side of a structural equation by its estimated equivalent using ordinary least squares.

The sixty-city data set: selection of variables

In this section, we describe the data set itself and also examine some properties of the data with special emphasis on collinearity and consequent implications on the variety and kinds of hypotheses which can be appropriately tested.

Tables 5.1–5.4 present a listing of the variables available for analysis along with the year of the variable, units, mean, standard deviation (S.D.), and sources for the data by number, where the number refers to the listing of sources at the end of the chapter. Table 5.1 includes total mortality rate calculated from 1970 data on mortality by city divided by the 1970 census population. Disaggregated mortality data by disease category – heart, vascular, pneumonia and influenza, emphysema and bronchitus, cirrhosis, nephritis and nephosis, congential anomalies, early infant diseases, and cancer – were also collected for 1970, and divided by 1970 census population to develop mortality rates; exceptions are the congential

Table 5.1 *Mortality Variables*

	Variable	*Year*	*Units*	*Mean*	*S.D.*	*Sources*
Mortality Variables						
MO70	Total Mortality	1970	deaths/1000 pop.	11.283	2.161	(18)(6)
HA70	Heart Disease	1970	,,	4.126	1,078	(18)(6)
VA70	Vascular Disease	1970	,,	1.566	0.395	(18)(6)
PN70	Pneumonia & Influenza	1970	,,	0.375	0.114	(18)(6)
EM70	Emphysema & Bronchitis	1970	,,	0.178	0.059	(18)(6)
CI70	Cirrhosis	1970	,,	0.238	0.106	(18)(6)
NE70	Nephritis & Nephrosis	1970	,,	0.058	0.027	(18)(6)
C/B%	Congenital Anom/Births	1970	%	0.473	0.105	(18)(6)
I/B%	Early Infancy/Births	1970	%	1.294	0.333	(18)(6)
CA70	Cancer Mortality	1970	deaths/1000 pop.	1.958	0.402	(18)(6)

Table 5.2 *Dietary Variables*

	Variable	*Year*	*Units*	*Mean*	*S.D.*	*Sources*
Dietary Variables						
NTRI	Nitrites in Food	1955	g/yr/cap	1.27	0.14	(2)(4)(27)
NTRA	Nitrates in Food	1955	g/yr/cap	69.86	9.05	(2)(4)(27)
SFAT	Saturated Fatty Acids[a]	1955	g/yr/cap	16220.00	874.65	(2)(3)(4)
PROT	Protein[a]	1955	g/yr/cap	26557.00	1314.00	(2)(3)(4)
CHOL	Cholesterol[a]	1955	g/yr/cap	234.81	6.98	(2)(3)(4)
CVIT	Vitamin C[b]	1955	g/yr/cap	16.96	1.46	(2)(3)(4)
CALO	Calories	1955	keal/yr/cap	1149.7	56.27	(2)(3)(4)
COFF	Coffee	1955	kg/yr/cap	5.83	0.70	(2)(3)(4)
ALCO	Alcohol ($ value)	1955	$/yr/cap	17.30	6.06	(2)(3)(4)
XFRO	Total Protein	1965	g/yr/cap	39845.	706.46	(28)
XFAT	Total Fats	1965	g/yr/cap	57512.	1795.7	(28)
XCAR	Carbohydrates	1965	g/yr/cap	123490.	3623.0	(28)
XASA	Ascorbic Acid	1965	mg/yr/cap	42281.	2364.2	(28)
6NTI	Nitrites in Food	1965	g/yr/cap	1.14	.16	(4)(28)(27)
6NTA	Nitrates in Food	1965	g/yr/cap	52.67	2.47	(4)(28)(27)
6SFT	Saturated Fatty Acids[a]	1965	g/yr/cap	16315.	976.3	(3)(4)(25)
6PRO	Protein[a]	1965	g/yr/cap	28128.	1603.4	(3)(4)(28)
6CHL	Cholesterol[a]	1965	g/yr/cap	219.9	5.80	(3)(4)(28)
6CAL	Calories	1965	kal/yr/cap	1171.1	27.63	(3)(4)(28)
6CVT	Vitamin C[b]	1965	g/yr/cap	18.65	1.3	(3)(4)(28)
6COF	Coffee	1965	kg/yr/cap	5.40	.18	(3)(4)(28)
6ALC	Alcohol ($ value)	1965	$/yr/cap	25.97	6.45	

[a] Includes only animal products.
[b] Includes only vitamin C content for fruits and vegetables eaten fresh.

Table 5.3 *Social, Economic, Geographic, and Smoking Variables*

	Variables	*Year*	*Units*	*Mean*	*S.D.*	*Sources*
Social, Economic, Geographic						
MDOC	Medical Doctors	1970	M.D.'s/100,000	162.8	54.2	(19)
IN69	Median Income	1969	\$/yr/Household	10763.	1060.	(6)
EDUC	Education	1969	% > 25 yrs w/H.S. diploma	55.3	7.4	(6)
DENS	Crowding in Homes	1969	% > 1.5 persons/room	0.022	0.013	(8)
COLD	Cold Temperatures	1972	days temp < 0 0°C.	86.9	47.7	(9)
NONW	Nonwhite Population	1969	Fraction	0.226	0.154	(6)
MAGE	Median Age of Population	1969	Years	28.82	2.74	(6)
Smoking Variables						
C156	Cigarettes	1956	packs/yr/cap[a]	183.52	26.66	(22)(4)
CI68	Cigarettes	1968	packs/yr/cap[b]	165.80	23.25	(7)(1)

[a] Data for states, 1960 census population used.
[b] Data for states, 1970 census population used.

Table 5.4 *Air Pollution Variables*

	Variable	*Year*	*Units*	*Mean*	*S.D.*	*Sources*
Air Pollution						
SU66	Sulphate	1966	$\mu g/m^3$	10.67	5.44	(20)
AM66	Ammonium	1966	$\mu g/m^3$	1.15	1.42	(20)
NI66	Nitrates	1966	$\mu g/m^3$	1.96	0.68	(20)
PA66	Suspended Particulates	1966	$\mu g/m^3$	114.83	33.97	(20)
NO69	Nitrogen Dioxide	1969	ppm	0.076	0.034	(11)
PA70	Suspended Particulates	1970	$\mu g/m^3$	102.30	30.11	(13)
SO70	Sulphur Dioxide	1970	$\mu g/m^3$	26.92	22.20	(13)
NI70	Nitrate, annual mean	1971–73	$\mu g/m^3$	3.13	0.92	(14)
NI90	Nitrate, 90th %-tile con.	1971–73	$\mu g/m^3$	5.21	1.80	(14)
SU70	Sulphate, annual mean	1971–73	$\mu g/m^3$	10.65	4.01	(14)
SU90	Sulphate, 90th %-tile con.	1971–73	$\mu g/m^3$	17.69	7.62	(14)
LEAD	Lead	1970	$\mu g/m^3$	1.33	0.54	(16)
CO74	Carbon Monoxide	1974	mg/m^3	11.86	3.50	(15)
BETA	Beta Radioactivity	1966	PC_1/m^3	0.261	0.091	(20)

anomalies and early infant disease categories which were divided by the number of births in each city for 1970 in order to define an appropriate mortality rate. Mortality data for 1970 were chosen because reliable city population estimates are available for that year as opposed to more recent data requiring use of non-census year city population estimates in place of actual data. The disaggregation of total mortality by disease may not be appropriate. However, only data on city mortality was available, as indicated in Table 5.1.

Table 5.2 describes per capita dietary data by city for the years 1955 and 1965. The procedure used to construct the dietary data sets was somewhat involved. Food consumption estimates were first constructed for each of the 60 cities, using data on a sample of about 3,000 urban households, distributed among eight income brackets, for four regions of the United States, collected by the Department of Agriculture for 1955 and 1965. The results are regionally-specific weighted averages of consumption of various foods by families in each income bracket, multiplied by the fraction of each city's population in each income bracket. Data for specific dietary factors were then generated by multiplying the consumption rate of 49 foods by their respective concentrations of a given substance. A number of additional variables are available from the Department of Agriculture for 1965 as opposed to 1955. These include total protein, total fats, and total carbohydrates. As such, these variables provide a better indication of broad dietary patterns as opposed to the 1955 data set.

Table 5.3 describes our data on socioeconomic, geographic, and smoking variables. The socioeconomic and geographic variables were chosen for their consistency for estimating the aggregate dose-response function hypothesized in previous sections. Both the income and education variables are hypothesized to enter the demand equation for medical care, *not* the dose-response function. We must therefore employ the two-stage least squares estimation technique outlined above. Doctors per capita was chosen as the best available indication of available medical care, both in terms of preventative and ameliorative care. Alternative variables such as hospital beds per capita were judged inferior, in that underutilization of hospital facilities is a common problem and adjustments for utilization factors would prove troublesome. Also, if one assumes a less than perfectly elastic supply of medical care, the doctors per capita variable is an appropriate supply side variable in that it reflects patient loads for doctors in a particular city. The possible importance of age and cold temperatures in a dose-response relationship are clear. However, the nonwhite and crowding variables may be more difficult to interpret. The nonwhite variable would ideally control to some extent for genetic variations in the population. Obviously, however, this variable may well proxy for education, poverty, habits, etc. Similarly, crowding would ideally be an indication of possible contagion but may really proxy for poverty, old age, or even race. Thus, the role of these variables should be interpreted with great care.

Cigarette consumption was estimated from cigarette tax revenues for each state in which a sample city was located; the result is thus a statewide average that includes rural populations. Per capita cigarette consumption was estimated using the total state population over 16 years of age both for 1956 and 1968. It should be noted that both our dietary and our smoking variables are quite crude, reflecting problems in utilizing secondary data. However, the possible importance of their effects on human health may justify use of even these measures. We also attempted to develop a measure of total exposure to radiation, collecting data on beta radioactivity in air, terrestrial gamma radiation, and cosmic ray exposures, but have to this point been able to account for only about half of the average individual annual dose associated with medical exposures. As a result, no suitable total exposure variable is available at this time.

Table 5.4 presents the air pollution variables available for testing. All data are annual geometric means for each city unless otherwise specified. Unfortunately, hydrocarbon data was only available for about ten of our sample cities and are excluded for this reason. Finally, as noted above, Table 5.5 presents our data sources.

In summary, data available for testing include: first 1970 mortality rates for total mortality and for major disease categories; second data on dietary patterns for 1955 and 1965; third data on medical doctors and socioeconomic factors for 1970 or a nearby year; fourth data on smoking patterns for 1956 and 1968; and fifth data on air quality for each city for 1970 or a nearby year.

Since only 60 observations are available, we must obviously select a subsample of the available explanatory variables for hypothesis testing. To allow straightforward statistical tests of the significance of estimated coefficients, it is necessary to make the selecion of included variables *a priori* rather than testing each of the variables in various combinations for significance and excluding some on the basis of relative significances. Techniques do exist for testing significance where pre-testing has been employed but the standard *t*-statistic is no longer applicable.

The first problem in specifying the final data set is a decision on including lagged variables. Given a highly mobile U.S. population, the question becomes 'do people now living in a city represent the same sample as individuals who lived in cities 14–15 years before (the lags on smoking and diet, respectively)?' If the answer is no, and if people carry their dietary and smoking characteristics with them as they move, the most recent available data is likely to better represent long-term dietary and smoking patterns of individuals in a particular city. For these reasons, in this study, we use the available data closest to 1970 throughout. However, it may well be, for diseases with long lags such as cancer, that lagged variables are superior in any case. The real answer is, of course, to account properly for mobility – a near impossibility when using aggregate data.

The second consideration in specifying variables for inclusion is multicollinearity. Typical, multicollinearity problems can be avoided if the simple correlations between explanatory variables are less than 0.4 to 0.6. Tables 5.5 and 5.6 present simple correlation matrices for 1965 diet and air quality variables, respectively.

Table 5.5 *Simple Correlation Matrix for 1965 Diet Variables*

	XPRO	XFAT	XCAR	XASA	6NTI	6NTA	6SFT	6PRO	6CHL	6CVT	6COF	6ALC
XPRO	1.00	0.46	−0.01	0.53	−0.64	0.43	0.16	0.29	0.67	0.88	−0.14	0.70
XFAT	0.46	1.00	0.85	−0.17	0.34	0.74	−0.62	−0.41	0.50	0.12	−0.09	−0.28
XCAR	−0.01	0.85	1.00	−0.33	0.66	0.58	−0.66	−0.46	0.33	−0.33	−0.22	−0.71
XASA	0.53	−0.17	−0.33	1.00	−0.69	−0.16	0.86	0.93	0.58	0.79	−0.59	0.58
6NTI	−0.64	0.34	0.66	−0.69	1.00	0.20	−0.66	−0.67	−0.36	−0.77	0.25	−0.93
6NTA	0.43	0.74	0.58	−0.16	0.20	1.00	−0.47	−0.31	0.46	0.20	0.16	−0.13
6SFT	0.16	−0.62	−0.66	0.86	−0.66	−0.47	1.00	0.96	0.26	0.55	−0.39	0.54
6FRO	0.29	−0.41	−0.46	0.93	−0.67	−0.31	0.96	1.00	0.51	0.63	−0.53	0.50
6CHL	0.67	0.50	0.33	0.58	−0.36	0.46	0.26	0.51	1.00	0.64	−0.48	0.21
6CVT	0.88	0.12	−0.31	0.79	−0.77	0.20	0.55	0.63	0.64	1.00	−0.16	0.81
6COF	−0.14	−0.09	−0.22	−0.59	0.25	0.16	−0.39	−0.53	−0.48	−0.16	1.00	0.03
6ALC	0.70	−0.28	−0.71	0.58	−0.93	−0.13	0.54	0.50	0.21	0.81	0.03	1.00

Table 5.6 *Simple Correlation Matrix for Air Quality Variables*

	AM66	NI66	SU66	NO69	PA66	PA70	SO70	NI70	NI70	LEAD	CO74	SU70	SU90
AM66	1.00	−0.16	0.78	0.28	0.51	0.32	0.52	−0.15	−0.08	0.04	0.14	0.66	0.64
NI66	−0.16	1.00	0.07	0.36	0.24	0.08	0.04	0.48	0.44	0.51	0.19	0.07	−0.01
SU66	0.78	0.07	1.00	0.34	0.68	0.43	0.72	0.08	0.11	0.07	0.28	0.86	0.73
NO69	0.28	0.36	0.34	1.00	0.30	0.09	0.35	0.31	0.33	0.40	0.21	0.37	0.21
PA66	0.51	0.24	0.68	0.30	1.00	0.69	0.50	0.11	0.12	0.19	0.36	0.53	0.53
PA70	0.32	0.08	0.43	0.09	0.69	1.00	0.25	0.17	0.11	−0.00	0.36	0.37	0.31
SO70	0.52	0.04	0.72	0.35	0.50	0.25	1.00	0.20	0.28	0.10	0.50	0.74	0.56
NI70	−0.15	0.48	0.08	0.31	0.11	0.17	0.20	1.00	0.92	0.18	0.24	0.19	0.04
NI90	−0.08	0.44	0.11	0.33	0.12	0.11	0.28	0.92	1.00	0.20	0.24	0.22	0.14
LEAD	0.04	0.51	0.07	0.40	0.19	−0.00	0.10	0.18	0.20	1.00	0.20	0.00	−0.08
CO74	0.14	0.19	0.28	0.21	0.36	0.36	0.50	0.24	0.24	0.20	1.00	0.34	0.25
SU70	0.66	0.07	0.86	0.37	0.53	0.37	0.74	0.19	0.22	0.00	0.34	1.00	0.85
SU90	0.64	−0.01	0.73	0.21	0.53	0.31	0.56	0.04	0.14	−0.08	0.25	0.85	1.00

Table 5.6 shows that a very high level of collinearity is probably present among dietary variables. It appears so high, in fact, that the problem becomes one of finding a set of dietary variables which is sufficiently non-collinear to allow reasonable estimation of individual coefficients. Perhaps the broadest indicators of dietary patterns are the total protein (XPRO), total fat (XFAT) and total carboydrate (XCAR) variables. Protein and fat will tend to indicate high consumption of meat and nuts, while high carbohydrate consumption will indicate consumption of grains, fruits, vegetables, and refined sugars. However, total carbohydrate and total fat have a correlation coefficient of 0.85, too high to allow inclusion of both variables in an estimated equation. However, if we replace total fats (XFAT) with animal fat (6SFT), a good proxy for consumption of saturated fats, the correlation between fat (now animal fat) and carbohydrates drops to 0.66, which although still high, will likely cause less difficulty. Thus, we include these three diet variables as broad indicators of dietary patterns where, however, it must be clearly recognized that the estimated coefficients on these variables may well include the effect partially or totally of a number of other highly collinear dietary variables. For example, total protein (XPRO) has a correlation with cirrhosis, one might justifiably doubt that a causal relationship exists between protein and cirrhosis as opposed to one between alcohol and cirrhosis.

Table 5.6 suggests that multicollinearity may well be a problem within the air quality data set as well. Given previous research (see, for example, Lave and Seskin, 1977), the air quality measures of most concern are those for NO_2, SO_2, sulphate, and particulates, so we focus on these variables here. However, our measures of SO_2 and sulphate for 1970, the year of the mortality data, are highly collinear – SO70 and SU70 have a simple correlation of 0.74 – so any separation of their relative importance is likely impossible. As a result, we use SO_2 (SO70) as a proxy variable for both pollutants. Note also that among the included air pollution variables, NO_2 (NO60), particulates (PA70), and SO_2 (SO70), collinearity problems may exist with respect to ammonium, carbon monoxide and lead (some correlations greater than or equal to 0.4). Since we exclude these variables here (as have most previous investigators) some unknown contribution from these pollutants may be included in estimated coefficients on NO_2, SO_2, and particulates.

A complete correlation matrix for our choice of included variables is presented in Table 5.8 with the exception of the doctors per capita variable for which we use two-stage least squares. Several interesting collinearity issues are apparent here as well, not necessarily as a multicollinearity problem since the highest simple correlation is 0.66 within the data set, but rather as an indication of problems of exclusion of variables in previous studies. For example, SO_2 (SO70) shows a correlation of 0.59 with animal

Table 5.7 *Simple Correlation Matrix for Included Variables*

	NONW	MAGE	IN69	EDUC	DENS	COLD	C168	XPRO	XCAR	6SFT	NO69	SO70	FA80
NONW	1.00	0.02	−0.26	−0.22	0.40	−0.04	0.02	0.02	0.23	0.02	0.22	0.29	0.30
MAGE	0.02	1.00	0.08	−0.14	−0.30	0.01	−0.05	0.22	−0.24	0.32	0.21	0.25	0.13
IN69	−0.26	0.08	1.00	0.49	−0.32	0.02	0.05	0.20	−0.23	−0.05	0.12	−0.12	−0.25
EDUC	−0.22	−0.14	0.49	1.00	−0.22	0.04	−0.28	0.26	−0.35	−0.13	−0.16	−0.34	−0.24
DENS	0.40	−0.30	−0.32	−0.22	1.00	−0.38	−0.08	0.03	0.39	−0.26	0.08	−0.03	−0.07
COLD	−0.04	0.01	0.02	0.04	−0.38	1.00	0.03	−0.60	−0.38	0.34	−0.03	0.35	0.34
CI60	0.02	−0.05	0.05	−0.28	−0.08	0.33	1.00	−0.24	−0.01	0.09	0.17	0.23	−0.08
XPRO	0.02	0.22	0.20	0.26	0.03	−0.60	−0.24	1.00	−0.01	0.16	0.11	−0.08	−0.31
XCAR	0.23	−0.24	−0.23	−0.35	0.39	−0.38	−0.01	−0.01	1.00	−0.66	−0.18	−0.33	−0.03
6SFT	0.02	0.32	−0.05	−0.13	−0.26	0.34	0.09	0.16	−0.66	1.00	0.16	0.59	0.12
NO69	0.22	0.21	0.12	−0.16	0.08	−0.03	0.17	0.11	−0.18	0.16	1.00	0.35	0.09
SO70	0.29	0.25	−0.12	−0.34	−0.03	0.35	0.23	−0.08	−0.33	0.59	0.35	1.00	0.25
PA70	0.03	0.13	−0.25	−0.24	−0.07	0.34	−0.08	−0.31	−0.03	0.12	0.09	0.25	1.00

Table 5.8 *Complete Listing of Data Used*

	MO70	VA70	HA70	PN70	EM70
	11.283	1.566	4.216	0.375	0.178
	2.161	0.395	1.078	0.114	0.059
1 BIRMG AL	14.008	2.758	3.925	0.349	0.216
2 MONTG AL	10.136	1.619	2.954	0.195	0.127
3 PHOEN AZ	8.598	1.040	2.884	0.359	0.279
4 TUCSN AZ	10.151	1.327	3.347	0.373	0.422
5 LROCK AK	11.480	1.927	4.155	0.271	0.098
6 LONGB CA	12.074	1.782	5.106	0.332	0.212
7 OAKLD CA	11.792	1.628	4.500	0.281	0.195
8 SANDI CA	7.658	1.214	2.728	0.165	0.148
9 SFRAN CA	13.112	1.808	4.618	0.440	0.187
10 HARTF CF	11.246	1.329	4.025	0.405	0.171
11 NEWHA CT	11.111	1.314	4.597	0.392	0.116
12 WATER CT	11.219	1.814	4.897	0.324	0.176
13 WASHG DC	11.700	1.249	3.845	0.590	0.132
14 ATLAN GA	11.809	1.636	3.596	0.515	0.157
15 CHICA IL	12.317	1.363	5.555	0.413	0.117
16 ECHIG IN	12.239	1.894	4.300	0.447	0.128
17 INDIA IN	8.171	1.280	2.889	0.247	0.117
18 SBEND IN	10.814	1.847	3.735	0.334	0.127
19 DESHO IO	11.117	1.685	4.517	0.314	0.239
20 DUBUQ IO	10.945	1.685	4.718	0.858	0.128
21 TOPEK KA	9.247	1.528	3.720	0.264	0.168
22 WICHI KA	8.393	1.276	3.052	0.253	0.199
23 LEXNG KY	9.377	1.443	3.588	0.342	0.065
24 LOUIS KY	13.539	2.150	5.057	0.387	0.293
25 NEWOR LA	12.408	1.523	4.829	0.361	0.158
26 BALTI MD	12.614	1.242	4.921	0.350	0.152
27 DETRO MI	12.184	1.375	4.615	0.436	0.197
28 GDRAP MI	11.986	1.771	4.604	0.385	0.182
29 MINNE MN	12.661	2.125	4.784	0.414	0.193
30 KCITY MO	11.513	1.668	3.431	0.333	0.199
31 STLOU MO	15.602	2.134	6.130	0.546	0.222
32 OMAHA NB	9.153	1.417	3.501	0.328	0.204
33 CAMDN NJ	12.696	1.307	5.383	0.439	0.224
34 JCITY NJ	12.946	1.305	5.703	0.526	0.196
35 NEWRK NJ	11.616	1.043	4.712	0.382	0.133
36 ALBUQ NM	8.230	0.993	2.162	0.308	0.205
37 NYORK NY	11.526	1.148	4.710	0.514	0.119
38 AKRON OH	10.609	1.503	3.805	0.240	0.200
39 CINNC OH	13.385	1.686	5.299	0.522	0.214
40 COLUM OH	9.489	1.416	3.378	0.302	0.187
41 DAYTN OH	11.925	1.646	4.425	0.427	0.250
42 TOLED OH	11.141	1.701	4.343	0.380	0.221
43 YTOWN OH	13.063	1.953	4.929	0.486	0.196
44 TULSA OK	8.561	1.345	2.943	0.244	0.148
45 PLAND OR	13.517	2.287	4.843	0.384	0.243
46 PHILA PN	12.553	1.376	4.486	0.405	0.148
47 PITTS PN	14.062	1.873	6.127	0.498	0.115

Table 5.8 (*Contd.*)

	MO70	VA70	HA70	PN70	EM70
48 REDDG PN	15.198	2.407	6.412	0.297	0.160
49 PROVI RI	13.727	1.663	5.731	0.379	0.156
50 CHATI TN	15.141	2.242	5.895	0.554	0.202
51 MEMPH TN	9.358	1.536	3.222	0.269	0.159
52 DALLS TX	8.423	1.108	2.834	0.261	0.159
53 HOUST TX	7.803	1.001	2.614	0.266	0.119
54 PASSA TX	5.018	0.526	1.613	0.202	0.112
55 SANAN TX	8.131	1.217	2.606	0.266	0.125
56 SALTC UT	11.246	1.478	3.684	0.273	0.262
57 NFOLK VA	8.008	1.085	2.939	0.260	0.094
58 RICHM VA	12.503	1.899	4.627	0.501	0.140
59 SEATT WA	12.047	1.850	4.372	0.377	0.213
60 CHARL WV	14.321	1.510	6.028	0.727	0.280
	CI70	**NE70**	**CNB%**	**INB%**	**CA70**
	0.238	0.058	0.473	1.294	1.958
	0.106	0.027	0.105	0.333	0.402
1 BIRMG AL	0.116	0.116	0.465	1.327	2.343
2 MONTG AL	0.112	0.112	0.243	1.335	1.732
3 PHOEN AZ	0.205	0.029	0.246	0.975	1.499
4 TUCSN AZ	0.198	0.027	0.688	0.995	1.719
5 LROCK AK	0.188	0.045	0.478	1.299	1.942
6 LONGB CA	0.290	0.028	0.482	1.045	2.049
7 OAKLD CA	0.358	0.047	0.401	1.250	2.090
8 SANDI CA	0.191	0.030	0.467	1.058	1.316
9 SFRAN CA	0.646	0.049	0.368	0.934	2.493
10 HARTF CT	0.329	0.032	0.506	1.519	1.987
11 NEWHA CT	0.211	0.022	0.513	1.758	2.004
12 WATER CT	0.333	0.037	0.396	1.189	1.999
13 WASHG DC	0.489	0.081	0.401	1.937	2.000
14 ATLAN GA	0.213	0.131	0.355	1.539	1.789
15 CHICA IL	0.289	0.062	0.430	1.612	2.038
16 ECHIG IN	0.298	0.106	0.561	1.794	2.022
17 INDIA IN	0.140	0.058	0.441	1.254	1.573
18 SBEND IN	0.159	0.080	0.549	1.450	2.142
19 DESMO IO	0.130	0.020	0.619	1.381	1.919
20 DUBUQ IO	0.096	0.064	0.413	1.570	1.894
21 TOPEK KA	0.104	0.024	0.392	0.940	1.568
22 WICHI KA	0.116	0.036	0.506	1.465	1.454
23 LEXNG KY	0.176	0.037	0.359	0.934	1.517
24 LOUIS KY	0.288	0.055	0.436	1.237	2.304
25 NEWOR LA	0.189	0.091	0.609	1.497	2.158
26 BALTI MD	0.394	0.063	0.456	1.417	2.228
27 DETRO MI	0.413	0.067	0.470	1.320	2.126
28 GDRAP MI	0.187	0.035	0.579	1.183	2.155
29 MINNE MN	0.214	0.028	0.544	1.258	2.281
30 KCITY MO	0.187	0.049	0.384	1.318	1.871
31 STLOU MO	0.268	0.090	0.475	1.449	2.562
32 OMAHA NB	0.184	0.043	0.486	1.362	1.776

Table 5.8 (*Contd.*)

	CI70	NE70	CNB%	INB%	CA70
33 CAMDN NJ	0.419	0.068	0.319	1.716	2.048
34 JCITY NJ	0.426	0.111	0.412	1.687	2.241
35 NEWRK NJ	0.290	0.092	0.489	1.997	1.663
36 ALBUQ NM	0.254	0.025	0.518	1.132	1.276
37 NYORK NY	0.352	0.055	0.424	1.245	2.151
38 AKRON OH	0.160	0.051	0.430	1.291	1.968
39 CINNC OH	0.190	0.053	0.474	1.040	2.510
40 COLUM OH	0.143	0.041	0.456	0.946	1.740
41 DAYTN OH	0.177	0.078	0.506	1.224	2.048
42 TOLED OH	0.190	0.044	0.506	0.127	1.964
43 YTOWN OH	0.243	0.086	0.865	1.259	2.389
44 TULSA OK	0.130	0.036	0.491	1.188	1.586
45 PLAND OR	0.314	0.044	0.588	0.874	2.425
46 PHILA PN	0.219	0.066	0.535	1.713	2.170
47 PITTS PN	0.277	0.071	0.490	1.510	2.426
48 REDDG PN	0.251	0.023	0.676	1.149	2.818
49 PROVI RI	0.262	0.084	0.600	1.327	2.690
50 CHATT TN	0.218	0.076	0.556	2.105	2.469
51 MEMPH TN	0.154	0.056	0.572	1.143	1.644
52 DALLS TX	0.165	0.034	0.512	1.297	1.397
53 HOUST TX	0.166	0.039	0.436	1.264	1.311
54 PASSA TX	0.101	0.011	0.526	0.789	0.941
55 SANAN TX	0.194	0.064	0.377	1.182	1.373
56 SALTC UT	0.222	0.080	0.296	0.765	1.558
57 NFOLK VA	0.146	0.052	0.411	1.447	1.322
58 RICHM VA	0.248	0.072	0.377	1.684	1.959
59 SEAIT WA	0.266	0.053	0.416	1.075	2.174
60 CHARL WV	0.392	0.098	0.421	0.843	2.671

	MAGE	CI68	MDUC
	28.820	165.798	162.807
	2.737	23.247	54.226
1 BIRMG AL	29.700	136.604	142.00
2 MONTG AL	27.700	136.604	80.400
3 PHOEN AZ	27.500	128.693	148.500
4 TUCSN AZ	26.800	128.693	166.600
5 LROCK AK	29.600	150.591	229.800
6 LONGB CA	32.700	157.477	186.800
7 OAKLD CA	31.400	157.477	239.600
8 SANDI CA	25.800	157.477	149.400
9 SFRAN CA	34.20	157.477	239.600
10 HARTF CT	27.800	201.869	195.100
11 NEWHA CT	27.800	201.869	327.300
12 WATER CT	31.300	201.869	377.300
13 WASHG DG	28.400	137.765	302.400
14 ATLAN GA	27.200	159.601	159.500
15 CHICA IL	29.600	189.522	161.400
16 ECHIG IN	27.700	191.140	68.700

Table 5.8 (*Contd.*)

	MAGE	CI68	MDUC
17 INDIA IN	27.100	191.140	141.400
18 SBEND IN	29.600	191.140	120.300
19 DESMO IO	28.600	158.907	175.500
20 DUBUQ IO	25.000	158.97	105.300
21 TOPEK KA	28.000	146.046	127.500
22 WICHI KA	27.000	146.046	111.500
23 LEXNG KY	24.600	203.395	98.900
24 LOUIS KY	30.100	203.395	159.500
25 NEWOR LA	27.900	182.361	209.100
26 BALTI MD	28.700	166.384	200.400
27 DETRO MI	29.300	202.620	152.700
28 GDRAP MI	27.100	202.620	125.900
29 MINNE MN	29.100	166.797	156.800
30 KCITY MO	29.500	166.797	156.600
31 STLOU MO	31.400	164.695	144.800
32 OMAHA NB	26.700	152.560	160.100
33 CAMDN NJ	27.500	148.636	158.200
34 JCITY NJ	30.700	148.636	101.900
35 NEWRK NJ	25.900	148.636	195.400
36 ALBUQ NM	25.100	157.395	188.100
37 NYORK NY	32.400	152.273	250.200
38 AKRON OH	28.500	183.177	143.400
39 CINNC OH	28.800	183.177	157.000
40 COLUMN OH	25.400	183.177	186.300
41 DAYTN OH	27.800	183.177	113.500
42 TOLED OH	28.700	183.177	128.600
43 YTOWN OH	31.600	183.177	128.600
44 TULSA OK	28.700	111.392	143.400
45 PLAND OR	32.600	170.820	186.200
46 PHILA PN	30.900	147.692	207.000
47 PITTS PN	33.400	147.692	144.300
48 REDDG PN	36.900	147.692	112.400
49 PROVI RI	32.100	191.745	157.000
50 CHATT TH	31.100	160.097	120.700
51 MEMPH TN	26.100	160.097	167.900
52 DALLS TX	27.200	171.593	154.800
53 HOUST TX	26.000	171.593	144.500
54 PASSA TX	24.400	171.593	144.500
55 SANAN TX	24.800	171.593	119.600
56 SALTC UT	27.700	100.734	193.600
57 NFOLK VA	24.000	172.618	93.600
58 RICHM VA	29.500	172.618	231.100
59 SHATI WA	31.900	143.939	185.300
60 CHARL WV	34.600	181.301	89.700

	DENS	NONW	IN69	EDUC	COLD
	0.022	0.226	10762.895	55.298	86.900
	0.013	0.154	1059.562	7.439	47.654
1 BIRMG AL	0.037	0.422	8692.000	45.400	48.000

Table 5.8 (*Contd.*)

	DENS	NONW	IN69	EDUC	COLD
2 MONTG AL	0.037	0.336	9933.000	51.600	29.000
3 PHOEN AZ	0.027	0.067	11329.000	60.100	13.000
4 TUCSN AZ	0.032	0.052	9922.000	63.100	22.000
5 LROCK AK	0.017	0.251	10438.000	56.500	51.000
6 LONGB CA	0.013	0.082	11804.000	62.000	1.000
7 OAKLD CA	0.023	0.407	11279.000	66.100	7.000
8 SANDI CA	0.019	0.111	11664.000	65.300	0.0
9 SFRAN CA	0.027	0.286	12507.000	66.100	11.000
10 HARTF CT	0.029	0.292	10011.000	59.100	147.00
11 NEWHA CT	0.015	0.274	10444.000	56.800	102.000
12 WATER CT	0.015	0.105	11500.000	49.900	102.000
13 WASHG DC	0.048	0.723	12189.000	68.500	114.000
14 ATLAN GA	0.034	0.516	10656.000	53.400	45.000
15 CHICA IL	0.026	0.344	13527.000	53.900	132.000
16 ECHIG IN	0.047	0.284	10068.000	53.600	132.000
17 INDIA IN	0.017	0.184	12260.000	56.000	122.000
18 SBEND IN	0.010	0.147	11431.000	54.200	131.000
19 DESMO IO	0.010	0.062	11350.000	68.000	151.000
20 DUBUQ IO	0.018	0.003	11274.000	54.600	152.000
21 TOPEK KA	0.011	0.096	10830.000	64.800	122.000
22 WICHI KA	0.013	0.107	10940.000	63.200	122.000
23 LEXNG KY	0.026	0.174	10033.000	60.100	94.000
24 LOUIS KY	0.019	0.241	9980.000	46.900	91.000
25 NEWOR LA	0.055	0.045	10246.000	45.800	13.000
26 BALTI MD	0.017	0.470	10035.000	44.600	90.000
27 DETRO MI	0.016	0.445	11015.000	52.100	126.000
28 GDRAP MI	0.007	0.120	11242.000	54.000	157.000
29 MINNE MN	0.010	0.064	11127.000	66.100	167.000
30 KCITY MO	0.017	0.228	11306.000	60.100	106.000
31 STLOU MO	0.044	0.413	9268.000	48.000	118.000
32 OMAHA NB	0.013	0.106	11605.000	62.700	144.000
33 CAMDN NJ	0.018	0.402	8627.000	50.600	89.000
34 JCITY NJ	0.026	0.222	10285.000	36.300	79.000
35 NEWRK NJ	0.040	0.560	8637.000	55.100	84.000
36 ALBUQ NM	0.022	0.043	10926.000	66.200	122.000
37 NYORK NY	0.029	0.234	11632.898	51.800	79.000
38 AKRON OH	0.007	0.178	11152.000	55.600	133.000
39 CINNC OH	0.028	0.281	10435.000	48.400	100.000
40 COLUM OH	0.010	0.190	10848.000	60.700	114.000
41 DAYTN OH	0.015	0.309	10329.000	56.200	125.000
42 TOLED OH	0.001	0.143	11590.000	51.700	157.000
43 YTOWN OH	0.011	0.258	9928.000	52.100	150.000
44 TULSA OK	0.010	0.134	11642.000	58.200	82.000
45 PLAND OR	0.008	0.078	11377.000	62.900	42.000
46 PHILA PN	0.013	0.344	10431.000	50.600	89.000
47 PITTS PN	0.013	0.207	10536.000	53.400	124.000
48 REDDG PN	0.006	0.068	9695.000	43.300	89.000
49 PROVI RI	0.010	0.100	10208.000	45.900	128.000
50 CHATT TN	0.026	0.360	8336.000	47.600	70.000
51 MEMPH TN	0.049	0.392	10104.000	49.200	61.000

Table 5.8 (*Contd.*)

	DENS	NONW	IN69	EDUC	COLD
52 DALLS TX	0.028	0.258	12474.000	54.800	34.000
53 HOUST TX	0.032	0.266	11737.000	51.700	21.000
54 PASSA TX	0.018	0.005	11822.000	51.700	21.000
55 SANAN TX	0.062	0.086	9027.000	46.800	23.000
56 SALTC UT	0.015	0.032	10812.000	68.500	110.000
57 NFOLK VA	0.021	0.302	9236.000	48.300	31.000
58 RICHM VA	0.018	0.424	10620.000	47.100	68.000
59 SFATT WA	0.010	0.126	12557.000	67.800	32.000
60 CHARL WV	0.012	0.108	10856.000	52.800	95.000

	6SFT	XCAR	APRO
	16314.051	123491.313	39844.547
	975.743	3618.011	706.747
1 BIRMG AL	15079.500	129119.000	39517.699
2 MONTG AL	15030.398	128765.000	39264.801
3 PHOEN AZ	16116.699	120959.000	40696.199
4 TUCSN AZ	16054.102	120957.000	40395.500
5 LROCK AK	15186.500	129263.000	39630.301
6 LONGB CA	16079.102	120519.000	41050.398
7 OAKLD CA	16030.898	120345.000	41306.898
8 SANDI CA	16090.398	120865.000	40788.801
9 SFRAN CA	16030.898	120345.000	41306.898
10 HARTF CT	18240.500	121166.000	40740.000
11 NEWHA CT	18118.801	120707.000	40348.500
12 WATER CT	18255.801	120882.000	40413.301
13 WASHG DC	16219.500	126710.000	40232.000
14 ATLAN GA	15737.398	128113.000	40143.199
15 CHICA IL	16404.699	121525.000	39337.301
16 ECHIG IN	16295.000	121512.000	39144.000
17 INDIA IN	16261.102	121447.000	39100.199
18 SBEND IN	16198.398	121453.000	39005.500
19 DESMO IO	16244.699	121511.000	39096.000
20 DUBUQ IO	16153.102	121495.000	38978.102
21 TOPEK KA	16070.801	121291.000	38877.500
22 WICHI KA	16040.102	121060.000	38827.102
23 LEXNG KY	15555.602	128726.000	39981.301
24 LOUIS KY	15563.398	128982.000	40212.000
25 NEWOR LA	15119.199	128678.000	39532.602
26 BALTI MD	15724.500	128374.000	40248.398
27 DETRO MI	16419.898	121501.000	39346.500
28 GDRAP MI	16266.801	121560.000	39095.500
29 MINNE MN	16431.801	121751.000	39322.000
30 KCITY MO	16217.199	121345.000	39047.199
31 STLOU MO	16175.398	121333.000	39030.199
32 OMAHA NB	16177.398	121345.000	38997.801
33 CAMDN NJ	17976.199	119345.000	39194.500
34 JCITY NJ	18157.500	120490.000	39916.699
35 NEWRK NJ	18148.801	121000.000	40602.398
36 ALBUQ NM	16052.102	120684.000	40456.801
37 NYORK NY	18028.102	120486.000	40287.301

Table 5.8 (*Contd.*)

	6SFT	XCAR	APRO
38 AKRON OH	16307.500	121535.000	39152.102
39 CINNC OH	16160.301	121335.000	39006.602
40 COLUM OH	16194.898	121321.000	39035.602
41 DAYTN OH	16349.199	121493.000	39215.699
42 TOLED OH	16273.801	121546.000	39135.398
43 YTOWN OH	16232.602	121414.000	39032.500
44 TULSA OK	15467.898	129016.000	39958.602
45 PLAND OR	16006.199	121115.000	40881.301
46 PHILA PN	18187.398	120737.000	40271.699
47 PITTS PN	18287.898	120748.000	39978.602
48 REDDG PN	18399.699	121050.000	40029.699
49 PROVI RI	18237.699	120540.000	39969.000
50 CHATT TN	15181.398	129289.000	39708.500
51 MEMPH TN	15129.301	128846.000	39551.301
52 DALLS TX	15717.000	128359.000	40155.199
53 HOUST TX	15626.500	128489.000	40134.500
54 PASSA TX	15947.398	128755.000	40795.199
55 SANAN TX	15080.699	129045.000	39443.699
56 SALTC UT	16013.500	121539.000	40791.102
57 NFOLK VA	15177.000	128966.000	39734.602
58 RICHM VA	15640.699	128727.000	40184.699
59 SEATT WA	16040.199	120738.000	41333.699
60 CHARL WV	15233.301	129243.000	39718.398

	NO69	PA70	SO70
	0.076	102.300	26.917
	0.034	30.107	22.197
1 BIRMG AL	0.093	138.000	10.000
2 MONTG AL	0.016	91.000	7.000
3 PHOEN AZ	0.089	117.000	9.000
4 TUCSN AZ	0.028	104.000	7.000
5 LROCK AK	0.012	71.000	8.000
6 LONGB CA	0.182	102.000	35.000
7 OAKLD CA	0.053	69.000	10.000
8 SANDI CA	0.106	88.000	10.000
9 SFRAN CA	0.095	52.000	9.000
10 HARTF CT	0.077	67.000	57.000
11 NEWHA CT	0.072	100.000	40.000
12 WATER CT	0.037	95.000	17.000
13 WASHG DC	0.069	99.000	28.000
14 ALTAN GA	0.096	88.000	20.000
15 CHICA IL	0.160	58.000	73.000
16 ECHIG IN	0.086	189.000	87.000
17 INDIA IN	0.079	96.000	51.000
18 SBEND IN	0.031	99.000	10.000
19 DESMO IO	0.033	134.000	11.000
20 DUBUQ IO	0.072	194.000	16.000
21 TOPEK KA	0.023	97.000	8.000

Table 5.8 (*Contd.*)

	NO69	PA70	SO70
22 WICHI KA	0.064	95.000	6.000
23 LEXNG KY	0.062	71.000	12.000
24 LOUIS KY	0.096	117.000	23.000
25 NEWOR LA	0.061	79.000	7.000
26 BALTI MD	0.099	136.000	54.000
27 DETRO MI	0.116	128.000	38.000
28 GDRAP MI	0.090	77.000	13.000
29 MINNE MH	0.076	88.000	38.000
30 KCITY MO	0.045	84.000	6.000
31 STLOU MO	0.135	120.000	42.000
32 OMAHA NB	0.075	132.000	12.000
33 CAMDN NJ	0.128	114.000	69.000
34 JCITY NJ	0.065	108.000	75.000
35 NEWRK NJ	0.092	111.000	37.000
36 ALBUQ NM	0.148	102.000	6.000
37 NYORK NY	0.142	109.000	45.000
38 AKRON OH	0.038	68.000	70.000
39 CINNC OH	0.099	95.000	18.000
40 COLUM OH	0.087	97.000	22.000
41 DAYTN OH	0.057	102.000	25.000
42 TOLED OH	0.096	111.000	13.000
43 YTOWN OH	0.083	134.000	30.000
44 TULSA OK	0.033	110.000	8.000
45 PLAND OR	0.058	60.000	14.000
46 PHILA PN	0.024	144.000	78.000
47 PITTS PN	0.113	137.000	57.000
48 REDDG PN	0.081	121.000	30.000
49 PROVI RI	0.087	93.000	67.000
50 CHATT TN	0.042	127.000	18.000
51 MEMPH TN	0.078	86.000	17.000
52 DALLS TX	0.074	105.000	7.000
53 HOUST TX	0.105	90.000	19.000
54 PASSA TX	0.050	80.000	9.000
55 SANAN TX	0.065	58.000	8.000
56 SALTC UT	0.060	88.000	9.000
57 NFOLK VA	0.077	83.000	26.000
58 RICHM VA	0.088	89.000	24.000
59 SEATT WA	0.095	58.000	22.000
60 CHARL WV	0.092	183.000	27.000

fat consumption (6SFT) and a correlation of 0.23 with cigarette consumption. In other words, air pollution as measured by SO_2 might not be orthogonal with respect to diet and smoking. The implication is that diet and smoking probably must be included to obtain unbiased estimates of the effect of SO_2 on human health.

Empirical analysis

The first step in estimating the model of human health we have specified is to attempt to account for human adjustments to disease in the form of medical care (doctors per capita). Thus, we first estimate a reduced form equation which has as the dependent variable doctors per capita and as independent, exogenous explanatory variables: median age, percentage nonwhite, density, cold, per capita consumption of cigarettes, protein, carbohydrates, and animal fat (all exogenous variables from the dose-response function); as well as per capita income and education level (exogenous variables in the determination of the demand for doctors). This estimated equation is shown in Table 5.10 below.

Note that we have chosen linear specifications throughout the analysis. The linear form has several advantages. First, the entire modelling framework can be interpreted as providing a set of first-order approximations of the slopes (the effects) of the variables in the model. As a linear approximate system, the estimated effects, if unbiased, only hold true for the neighbourhood of the estimate – that is for values of the variables near the means of our sample. Since we do not know the precise form (presumably nonlinear) which our functions take, we are at least not implying more about our knowledge of effects than the data can support. However, if significant nonlinearities do exist over the range of the data in our sample (and some of the estimated effects seem to imply this), then we have introduced a specification error by choosing linear estimates.

The second step in our analysis, then, is to generate, from the estimated reduced form equation and from data on exogenous variables in the model, an estimated doctors per capita variable (DOCH) to replace actual data on doctors per capita (MDOC) in the estimation of specific dose-response functions. Table 5.10 summarizes our results, while Tables 5.12–5.21 give individual linear estimated dose-response functions where the first equation reported excludes the air quality variables and the second (for comparison) includes these variables. Note that the basic model actually excludes air quality. This reflects the approach taken; to first develop a model of human health based on variables which are hypothesized to have large effects – age, medical care, smoking, diet, etc. Once a basic model of satisactory explanatory power is specified, it then may be appropriate to test for variables such as air pollution which are hypothesized to have small effects.

We choose a 97.5% confidence level ($t \geqslant 2.0$) for the entire analysis. It should be noted that if actual doctors per capita are employed, the variable is highly nonsignificant both when used in total mortality or when used in any of the component diseases. However, as indicated in our summary of results shown in Table 5.10 the estimated two-stage doctors per capita variable is highly significant and has a uniform negative effect on mortality

Table 5.9 *Summary of Two-Stage Linear Estimates of Factors in Human Mortality Hypotheses not Rejected at the 97.5%, Confidence-Level (One-tailed t-test, $t \geqslant 2.0$))*

Variable (Sign of Hypothetical Effect)		*Total Mortality Rate*	*Vascular Disease*	*Heart Disease*	*Pneumonia and Influenza*	*Emphysema and Bronchitis*	*Cirrhosis*	*Kidney Disease*	*Congenital Birth Defects*	*Early Infant Diseases*	*Cancer*
Doctors/Capita*	(−)	−	−	−		−		−			−
Median Age	(+)	+	+	+	+		+	+			+
% Nonwhite	(+)	+		+			+	+		+	+
Cigarettes	(+)	+	+	+							+
Room Density	(+)	+			+		+	+			
Cold	(+)	+			+						+
Animal Fat	(+)			+							
Protein	(+)	+				+					+
Carbohydrates	(?)					−					
NO_2	(+)										
SO_2	(+)									+	
Particulates	(+)				+						
R^2		.82	.60	.77	.54	.39	.64	.54	.22	.55	.86

* Two-stage estimator employed.

Table 5.10 *Reduced Form Equation*

MDOC 55 — 10 11 13 14 21 24 54 25 27 41

VAR	*B*	*T*
X10-NONW	50.447	1.1020
X11-MAGE	1.3513	0.50439
X13-IN69	0.61649D-02	0.86708
X14-EDUC	1.9399	1.3418
X21-DENS	161.53	0.26107
X24-COLD	−0.12806	−0.53850
X54-CI68	0.45771	1.4919
X25-XPRO	0.22302D-01	1.4136
X27-XCAR	0.22804D-02	0.72804
X41-6SFT	0.24002D-01	1.9402
CONSTANT	−1691.3	−2.7124

R-SQUARE = 0.3877
SSR = 0.1062D+06 DF = 49

Table 5.11 *Total Mortality*

MO70 1 — 61 10 11 21 24 54 25 27 41

VAR	*B*	*T*
X61-DOCH	−0.53031D-01	−4.7501
X10-NONW	5.6092	5.0448
X11-MAGE	0.66172	12.360
X21-DENS	31.910	2.4494
X24-COLD	0.14370D-01	3.1093
X54-CI68	0.21896D-01	3.0758
X25-XPRO	0.19325D-02	3.7525
X27-XCAR	−0.82907D-04	−1.5347
X41-6SFT	0.36251D-03	1.5938
CONSTANT	−78.675	−3.7169

R-SQUARE = 0.8195
SSR = 49.74 DF = 50

MO70 1 — 61 10 11 21 24 54 25 27 41 31 57 60

VAR	*B*	*T*
X61-DOCH	−0.52797D-01	−4.3493
X10-NONW	5.6276	4.5620
X11-MAGE	0.65893	11.540
X21-DENS	31.772	2.3469
X24-COLD	0.14436D-01	2.9089
X54-CI68	0.21968D-01	2.8120
X25-XPRO	0.19196D-02	3.5522
X27-XCAR	−0.79431D-04	−1.3612
X41-6SFT	0.39783D-03	1.4508
X31-NO69	1.6457	0.35779
X57-SO70	−0.31302D-02	−0.34850
X60-PA70	0.10744D-02	0.20059
CONSTANT	−79.296	−3.5115

R-SQUARE = 0.8205
SSR = 49.48 DF = 47

Table 5.12 *Vascular Disease*

VA70 2 — 61 10 11 21 24 54 25 27 41

VAR	*B*	*T*
X61-DOCH	−0.70223D-02	−2.2186
X10-NONW	0.37954	1.2040
X11-MAGE	0.10936	7.2050
X21-DENS	1.7016	0.46071
X24-COLD	0.1769SD-02	1.3504
X54-CI68	0.30001D-02	1.4865
X25-XPRO	0.18542D-03	1.2699
X27-XCAR	−0.13460D-04	−0.87885
X41-6SFT	−0.84316D-04	−1.3075
CONSTANT	−5.5672	−0.92769

R-SQUARE = 0.5657
SSR = 3.998 DF = 50

VA70 2 — 61 10 11 21 24 54 25 27 41 31 57 60

VAR	*B*	*T*
X61-DOCH	−0.88088D-02	−2.6671
X10-NONW	0.63816	1.9014
X11-MAGE	0.11671	7.5127
X21-DENS	2.7540	0.74768
X24-COLD	0.20961D-02	1.5524
X54-CI68	0.42167D-02	1.9838
X25-XPRO	0.23976D-03	1.6306
X27-XCAR	−0.17117D-04	−1.0781
X41-6SFT	−0.18874D-04	−0.25297
X31-NO69	−0.86198	−0.68915
X57-SO70	−0.38911D-02	−1.5922
X60-PA70	−0.63071D-03	−0.43278
CONSTANT	−8.3456	−1.3583

R-SQUARE = 0.6022
SSR = 3.663 DF = 47

Table 5.13 *Heart Disease*

HA70 3 — 61 10 11 21 24 54 25 27 41

VAR	*B*	*T*
X61-DOCH	−0.22340D-01	−3.4204
X10-NONW	1.7509	2.6917
X11-MAGE	0.29627	9.4592
X21-DENS	9.3338	1.2247
X24-COLD	0.43566D-02	1.6113
X54-CI68	0.13129D-01	3.1525
X25-XPRO	0.66878D-03	2.2197
X27-XCAR	−0.17969D-04	−0.56857
X41-6SFT	0.42380D-03	3.1849
CONSTANT	−35.183	−2.8412

R-SQUARE = 0.7517
SSR = 17.03 DF = 50

HA70 3 — 61 01 11 21 24 54 25 27 41 31 57 60

VAR	*B*	*T*
X61-DOCH	÷0.19800D-01	−2.9132
X10-NONW	1.3603	1.9694
X11-MAGE	0.28122	8.7965
X21-DENS	7.4177	0.97861
X24-COLD	0.43300D-02	1.5583
X54-CI68	0.10868D-01	2.4847
X25-XPRO	0.57165D-03	1.8893
X27-XCAR	÷0.22071D-05	−0.67551D-01
X41-6SFT	0.39645D-03	2.5822
X31-NO69	4.8498	1.8842
X57-SO70	0.82843D-03	0.16473
X60-PA70	0.14052D-02	0.46855
CONSTANT	−32.823	−2.5960

R-SQUARE = 0.7737
SSR = 15.51 DF = 47

Table 5.14 *Pneumonia and Influenza*

PN70 4 — 61 10 11 21 24 54 25 27 41

VAR	*B*	*T*
X61-DOCH	−0.12925D-02	−1.2098
X10-NONW	0.18381	1.7274
X11-MAGE	0.19920D-01	3.8880
X21-DENS	2.9692	2.3816
X24-COLD	0.13030D-02	2.9460
X54-CI68	0.61524D-03	0.90310
X25-XPRO	0.70654D-04	1.4336
X27-XCAR	−0.11329D-05	−0.21914
X41-6SFT	0.38010D-05	0.17462
CONSTANT	−3.0478	−1.5046

R-SQUARE = 0.4108
SSR = 0.4556 DF = 50

PN70 4 — 61 10 11 21 24 54 25 27 41 31 57 60

VAR	*B*	*T*
X61-DOCH	−0.38115D-03	−0.37068
X10-NONW	0.13820	1.3226
X11-MAGE	0.16194D-01	3.3484
X21-DENS	2.6677	2.3264
X24-COLD	0.10428D-02	2.4807
X54-CI68	0.61816D-03	0.93415
X25-XPRO	0.46048D-04	1.0060
X27-XCAR	−0.10027D-05	−0.20286
X41-6SFT	−0.49261D-05	−0.21208
X31-NO69	0.55215	1.4180
X57-SO70	−0.47719D-03	−0.62722
X60-PA70	0.14272D-02	3.1456
CONSTANT	−2.1183	−1.1075

R-SQUARE = 0.5409
SSR = 0.3550 DF = 47

Table 5.15 *Emphysema and Bronchitis*

EM70 5 — 61 10 11 21 24 54 25 27 41

VAR	*B*	*T*
X61-DOCH	−0.13851D-02	−2.3989
X10-NONW	0.22533D-01	0.39184
X11-MAGE	0.49451D-02	1.7859
X21-DENS	0.92106D-01	0.13670
X24-COLD	0.18996D-03	0.79468
X54-CI68	0.53419D-04	0.14509
X25-XPRO	0.65261D-04	2.4502
X27-XCAR	−0.95199D-05	−3.4072
X41-6SFT	−0.17700D-04	−1.5046
CONSTANT	−0.90721	−0.82870

R-SQUARE = 0.3559
SSR = 0.1331 DF = 50

EM70 5 — 61 10 11 21 24 54 25 27 41 31 57 60

VAR	*B*	*T*
X61-DOCH	−0.13761D-02	−2.2419
X10-NONW	0.46333D-01	0.74278
X11-MAGE	0.51065D-02	1.7687
X21-DENS	0.17013	0.24853
X24-COLD	0.14392D-03	0.57352
X54-CI68	0.24382D-03	0.61719
X25-XPRO	0.66687D-04	2.4404
X27-XCAR	−0.10427D-04	−3.5335
X41-6SFT	−0.13868D-04	−1.0001
X31-NO69	−0.11515	−0.49533
X57-SO70	−0.47320D-03	−1.0419
X60-PA70	0.29115D-03	1.0750
CONSTANT	−0.96354	−0.84382

R-SQUARE = 0.387
SSR = 0.1265 DF = 47

Table 5.16 *Cirrhosis*

CI70 6 — 61 10 11 21 24 54 25 27 41

VAR	*B*	*T*
X61-DOCH	0.51923D-04	0.65875D-01
X10-NONW	0.22721	2.8943
X11-MAGE	0.173230D-01	4.5831
X21-DENS	2.1612	2.3497
X24-COLD	0.52436D-03	1.6070
X54-CI68	0.61784D-03	1.2293
X25-XPRO	0.73982D-04	2.0347
X27-XCAR	−0.77437D-05	−2.0303
X41-6SFT	−0.11197D-04	−0.69726
CONSTANT	−2.3252	−1.5559

R-SQUARE = 0.6258
SSR = 0.2479 DF = 50

CI70 6 — 61 10 11 21 24 54 25 27 41 31 57 60

VAR	*B*	*T*
X61-DOCH	0.31818D-03	0.37741
X10-NONW	0.18469	2.1558
X11-MAGE	0.16077D-01	4.0543
X21-DENS	1.9819	2.1080
X24-COLD	0.49340D-03	1.4315
X54-CI68	0.39600D-03	0.72987
X25-XPRO	0.65122D-04	1.7351
X27-XCAR	−0.67906D-05	−1.6755
X41-6SFT	−0.19734D-04	−1.0362
X31-NO69	0.24209	0.75825
X57-SO70	0.51883D-03	0.83173
X60-PA70	0.69311D-04	0.18632
CONSTANT	−1.9446	−1.2399

R-SQUARE = 0.6399
SSR = 0.2387 DF = 47

Table 5.17 *Kidney Disease*

NE70 7 — 61 10 11 21 24 54 25 27 41

VAR	*B*	*T*
X61-DOCH	−0.67302D-03	−2.9834
X10-NONW	0.90661D-01	4.0353
X11-MAGE	0.34110D-02	3.1531
X21-DENS	0.75879	2.8825
X24-COLD	0.73289D-04	0.78479
X54-CI68	0.10132D-03	0.70439
X25-XPRO	0.15723D-04	1.5110
X27-XCAR	0.47349D-07	0.43376D-01
X41-6SFT	0.63724D-05	1.3866
CONSTANT	−0.72766	−1.7013

R-SQUARE = 0.5419
SSR = 0.2031D-01 DF = 50

NE70 7 — 61 10 11 21 24 54 25 27 41 31 57 60

VAR	*B*	*T*
X61-DOCH	−0.55265D-03	−2.3310
X10-NONW	0.79829D-01	3.3134
X11-MAGE	0.30851D-02	2.7665
X21-DENS	0.71889	2.7189
X24-COLD	0.29075D-04	0.29997
X54-CI68	0.80286D-04	0.52619
X25-XPRO	0.12995D-04	1.2312
X27-XCAR	−0.20721D-06	−0.18181
X41-6SFT	0.12112D-05	0.22615
X31-NO69	−0.66609D-01	−0.74186
X57-SO70	0.26956D-03	1.5366
X60-PA70	0.97647D-04	0.93342
CONSTANT	−0.51502	−1.1677

R-SQUARE = 0.5743
SSR = 0.1887D-01 DF = 47

Table 5.18 *Congenital Birth Defects*

C/B% 8 — 61 10 11 21 24 54 25 27 41

VAR	*B*	*T*
X61-DOCH	−0.11009D-02	−0.95740
X10-NONW	−0.10484	−0.91545
X11-MAGE	0.90212D-02	1.6360
X21-DENS	0.51667	0.38505
X24-COLD	0.41358D-03	0.86881
X54-CI68	0.11415D-02	1.5569
X25-XPRO	0.32274D-04	0.60844
X27-XCAR	−0.15016D-06	−0.26987D-01
X41-6SFT	0.15405D-04	0.65758
CONSTANT	−1.3390	−0.61416

R-SQUARE = 0.1867
SSR = 0.5277 DF = 50

C/B% 8 — 61 10 11 21 24 54 25 27 41 31 57 60

VAR	*B*	*T*
X61-DOCH	−0.10806D-02	−0.88051
X10-NONW	−0.62417D-01	−0.50047
X11-MAGE	0.96362D-02	1.6693
X21-DENS	0.68174	0.49810
X24-COLD	0.29908D-03	0.59609
X54-CI68	0.15099D-02	1.9116
X25-XPRO	0.36136D-04	0.66141
X27-XCAR	−0.25284D-05	−0.42856
X41-6SFT	0.16833D-04	0.60717
X31-NO69	−0.47663	−1.0255
X57-SO70	−0.44966D-03	−0.49518
X60-PA70	0.46820D-03	0.86461
CONSTANT	−1.3072	−0.57256

R-SQUARE = 0.2205
SSR = 0.5058 DF = 47

Table 5.19 *Early Infant Diseases*

I/B% 9 — 61 10 11 21 24 54 25 27 41

VAR	*B*	*T*
X61-DOCH	0.39159D-03	0.13339
X10-NONW	0.89283	3.0537
X11-MAGE	−0.44748D-02	−0.31786
X21-DENS	5.8110	1.6964
X24-COLD	0.35758D-03	0.29424
X54-CI68	−0.13312D-02	−0.71117
X25-XPRO	−0.10427D-03	−0.76995
X27-XCAR	0.17641D-04	1.2419
X41-6SFT	0.15367D-03	2.5695
CONSTANT	0.68864	0.12373

R-SQUARE = 0.4741
SSR = 3.439 DF = 50

I/B% 9 — 61 10 11 21 24 54 25 27 41 31 57 60

VAR	*B*	*T*
X61-DOCH	0.21825D-02	0.73588
X10-NONW	0.77575	2.5739
X11-MAGE	−0.79126D-02	−0.56722
X21-DENS	5.4464	1.6467
X24-COLD	−0.47371D-03	−0.39069
X54-CI68	−0.12146D-02	−0.63634
X25-XPRO	−0.13747D-03	−1.0.412
X27-XCAR	0.98932D-05	0.9390
X41-6SFT	0.67486D-04	1.0073
X31-NO69	−2.0458	−1.8215
X57-SP70	0.43841D-02	1.9978
X60-PA70	0.17731D-02	1.3549
CONSTANT	4.1264	0.74792

R-SQUARE = 0.5484
SSR = 2.954 DF = 47

Table 5.20 *Cancer*

CA70 53 — 61 10 11 21 24 54 25 27 41

VAR	*B*	*T*
X61-DOCH	−0.71271D-02	−3.8356
X10-NONW	0.63382	3.4249
X11-MAGE	0.13235	14.854
X21-DENS	3.9772	1.8342
X24-COLD	0.17859D-02	2.3216
X54-CI68	0.50032D-02	4.2228
X25-XPRO	0.21038D-03	2.4545
X27-XCAR	−0.13166D-04	−1.4643
X41-6SFT	0.51683D-04	1.3652
CONSTANT	−9.5112	−2.6997

R-SQUARE = 0.8556
SSR = 1.378 DF = 50

CA70 53 — 61 10 11 21 24 54 25 27 41 31 57 60

VAR	*B*	*T*
X61-DOCH	−0.70763D-02	−3.4976
X10-NONW	0.64712	3.1475
X11-MAGE	0.13242	13.915
X21-DENS	4.0247	1.7837
X24-COLD	0.17298D-02	2.0913
X54-CI68	0.51394D-02	3.9471
X25-XPRO	0.21071D-03	2.3394
X27-XCAR	−0.14074D-04	−1.4471
X41-6SFT	0.51447D-04	1.1257
X31-NO69	−0.16472	−0.21498
X57-SO70	−0.16143D-03	−0.10784
X60-PA70	0.23494D-03	0.26317
CONSTANT	−9.4472	−2.5101

R-SQUARE = 0.8560
SSR = 1.374 DF = 47

rates in total mortality, vascular disease, heart disease, emphysema and bronchitis, kidney disease, and cancer. We conclude, then, from a properly structured hypothesis test, that we cannot reject the hypothesis that medical care has a highly important effect on human mortality.

Both the median age and percentage of nonwhite variables are widely significant across the estimated equations and show up with uniformly positive effects on mortality rates.

Cigarette consumption shows significant positive partial correlations with total mortality, vascular disease, heart disease and cancer, while room density and cold both show significant positive partial correlations with total mortality and pneumonia and influenza. Room density also shows significant positive correlations for cirrhosis and kidney disease.

The dietary variables show significance in total mortality, heart disease, and cancer – correlations between heart disease and saturated fats and between cancer and meat consumption (note the positive association for protein) have long been recognized – as well as in emphysema and bronchitis.

Again, however, it must be stressed, especially for the dietary variables, that collinearity abounds and the estimated effect may really not be related to the specified variable but to a highly collinear one. Similarly, an estimated effect may include the sum of the effects of several collinear variables. In other words, causality is not established by correlation. However, we cannot reject the hypotheses that doctors, cigarettes, and diet are all highly important in determining human mortality rates. Unfortunately, these variables have typically been excluded from previous aggregate epidemiological studies (Schwing *et. al.* (1974) do, however, include a smoking variable).

Turning to the air quality variables, only two significant partial correlations appear – between particulates and the pneumonia and influenza variable, and between SO_2 and the early infant disease variable. The latter of these effects is consistent with the work of Lave and Seskin (1977).

However, differences between our estimated air pollution effects as opposed to the Lave and Seskin (1977) work are profound. Lave and Seskin (1977) did not find a significant association between particulates and pneumonia. More importantly, Lave and Seskin (1977) found positive associations between air quality (specifically sulphate) and a cardiovascular disease mortality variable and between air quality and cancer mortality. Whether we use SO_2 or the highly collinear sulphate measure, we cannot accept the hypotheses that air pollution has any association with heart and vascular disease or with cancer mortality. Further, our estimated total effects of air pollution on human mortality are about one order of magnitude smaller than those shown by Lave and Seskin (1977).

We can summarize the results of our analysis as follows. When we *increase* each of the following significant variables by one per cent over their mean values in our sample, from the estimated total mortality equation the following percentage change in mean total mortality rate results: first for doctors per capita a 0.76 per cent *decline* in mortality rate; second for per capita cigarette consumption a 0.32 per cent *increase* in mortality rate; and third for per capita protein consumption a 6.7 per cent *increase* in mortality rate. These results suggest several observations. First, medical care, smoking, and diet appear to be enormously important factors in human health. Second, if one looks to a 100% decrease from mean levels for these variables, i.e. the impact on average total mortality of setting these variables to zero, one obtains a 76 % increase in mortality for a zero level of doctors per capita, a 32 % decrease in mortality for no smoking and a 670 % decrease in mortality for no protein in diet. Obviously, the last of these effects is impossible and suggests that we may only have linear approximations of highly non-linear effects. Further, some protein is required to sustain life. Thus, the estimates of mortality effects are likely to be valid only for relatively small changes in explanatory variables. Finally, the air pollution variables are insignificant in the total mortality equation – as one might suspect if air pollution has only a small effect on mortality rates. This is verified by the fact that the significant estimated effects of particulates on pneumonia and influenza, and of SO_2 on infant diseases are very small in terms of total mortality as compared to the effects of doctors, smoking, and diet.

Given these results, it is important to test the sensitivity of the model to changes in specification of included variables and structure. Two alternative formulations have been specified and tested. First, a version of the model which: first uses lagged diet (1955 dietary variable) as opposed to 1965 diet); second, employs a two-stage doctors per capita variable which includes air pollution in the reduced form equation; and third, adds lead and sulphate to the air pollution variables, produces essentially identical results both for the impact of medical care and air pollution on mortality. Sulphate air pollution is statistically insignificant across all diseases. The second alternative formulation is identical to the one presented in detail above but the air pollution variables are again included in the reduced form equation for doctors per capita. The results are consistent for the effect of medical care and for the positive associations between sulphur oxides and infant diseases and for particulates and pneumonia. More interesting, however, is a significant *negative* association which appears between doctors per capital and air pollution, in the reduced form equation. It appears that doctors may choose *not* to live in polluted cities (perhaps for aesthetic reasons). If this is the case, one can easily explain false positive associations between air pollution and mortality where medical care is excluded as an explanatory variable. If doctors avoid polluted cities, and if doctors do reduce mortality rates, then pollution could well be associated with higher mortality rates; but *not* because of any direct health effect of air pollution on mortality. Rather, failure to account for the locational decisions of doctors (supply and demand for medical-care) may well bias estimated epidemiological relationships. In fact, the negative association between doctors per capital and pollution is so strong, that when pollution is included in the reduced form equation for doctors, the estimated doctors variable used in the two-stage procedure becomes collinear with the pollution variables. This collinearity in some cases produced negative coefficients on the pollution variables in estimated dose-response relationships for some disease categories where pollution is used in the reduced form equation for doctors per capita. Thus, it is important that, in spite of this collinearity, stable *positive* associations are retained between pneumonia and influenza and particulates and between infant diseases and sulphur oxides. The inclusion or exclusion of air quality from the reduced form equation has little impact on the conclusions of this study. In part, this occurs because air pollution is collinear with diet. In fact, saturated fats and sulphur oxides are reasonable proxy variables for each other. It has been shown by McCarthy (1971) that the exogenous variables which are collinear with included exogenous variables may be excluded from estimated reduced forms with little loss in consistncy in a two-stage least squares procedure.

Another important question for analysis is the possibility that heteroskedasticity is present. At this point, we have only examined one disease category – cancer mortality – for this problem. An examination of the residuals plotted against several important explanatory variables (age, for example) showed no evidence of heteroskedasticity.

Finally, in interpreting the results, it should be observed that the associations we have found between mortality and air pollution are principally for diseases of the very young and very old – particularly susceptible groups within the population. Further, these effects are those which one would perhaps associate with short-term as opposed to long-term air pollution exposures. It may well be that aggregate epidemiology may be incapable of revealing the long-term consequences of air pollution exposures. Two problems are particularly significant here. First, lagged data or data on air pollution histories is not available for such studies. Second, it is nearly impossible to control for population mobility in such studies. Thus, even if one accepts the hypothesis that air pollution levels show enough persistence over time to reveal long-term effects, population mobility will still distort and confound attempts at estimating such effects. A partial remedy for these problems is, of course, to use data on individuals as opposed to aggregate data.

We now turn to an economic evaluation of the value of air pollution control in reducing mortality based on the value of safety approach described above.

A tentative estimate of the value of safety from air pollution control

Given all of the caveats discussed above concerning the validity of the estimated effects of air pollution on mortality, it is possible to construct benefit measures using the methodology outlined in a previous section above. The methodology is briefly summarized in Table 5.21.

First, to obtain national estimates, we must know the population at risk.

Table 5.21 *Methodology for Health Benefits Assessment*

Benefits = (Population at Risk) × (Value of Safety) × (Reduction in Health Risk)

Value of Safety Based on Consumer's Willingness to Pay

Low estimate:	$340,000	
Source:	Thaler & Rosen	(1975)
High Estimate:	$1,000,000	
Source:	Robert Smith	(1974)

Since our sixty-city sample is entirely urban and since air pollution is principally an urban problem we will use a population risk for 1970 of 150 million urban dwellers. As a range for the value of safety, we will employ Thäler and Rosen's (1975) estimate of $340,000 (in 1978 dollars) as a lower bound and Smith's (1974) estimate of $1,000,000 (in 1978 dollars) as an upper bound. Finally, to provide an estimate of reduced risk from air pollution control, we will assume an average 60% reduction in ambient urban concentrations both for SO_2 and particulates. Then, using the mean concentration of these pollutants in our sixty-city sample as a basis for calculation, we can derive the average reduction in risk of pneumonia mortality for a 60% reduction in particulates and the average reduction in risk of infant diseases for a 60% reduction in SO_2 from our estimated dose response functions for these diseases.

Multiplying the population at risk by the assumed value of safety, and then by the *average* reduction in risk, gives a crude approximation of the benefits for a 60% reduction in national urban ambient concentrations of particulates and SO_2, respectively. National urban totals and the value of the average individual risk reduction are shown in Table 5.22.

The value estimates as shown in Table 5.22 agrees surprisingly well with those developed by Lave and Seskin (1977) for national air pollution

Table 5.22 *Urban Benefits from Reduced Mortality: Value of Safety for 60% Air Pollution Control*

Disease	*Pollutant*	*Average Individual Safety Benefit (1978 Dollars/Year)*	*National Urban Benefits (1978 Billion Dollars/Year)*
Pneumonia	Particulates	29–92	4.4–13.7
Early Infant Disease	SO_2	5–14	0.7– 2.2
Total		34–106	5.1–15.9

damages. However, the dollar value is similar only because we use a range for the value of safety (derived from observed market behaviour of consumers) which is about an order of magnitude larger than the 'value of life' figure based on lost earnings which is employed by Lave and Seskin (1977). We, of course, reject the value of life notion, instead focusing on the measurable concept of value of safety. Since there is no evidence to suggest that society puts less value on safety for children, the aged or women than on employed heads of households, we feel that the best measures available now for the value of safety should be employed for all individuals. Eventually, more refined measures of the value that different individuals place on safety may become available. However, for the time being, these are the best valuations of the social worth of safety we can employ.

6

Economic Growth and Climate: The Carbon-Dioxide Problem

William D. Nordhaus

INTRODUCTION

The combustion of fossil fuels results in the emission of carbon dioxide (CO_2) into the atmosphere. It would appear that about 50% of this remains there. It is known that CO_2 in the atmosphere produces a 'greenhouse' effect, so that, other things remaining the same, an increase in CO_2 concentration leads to an increase in the mean global surface temperature.[1] The current concentration of CO_2 in the atmosphere is about 330 parts per million. It is thought that if the use of fossil fuels grows at about 3% to 4% per year the atmospheric concentration of CO_2 will rise to a level between 365 and 385 parts per million by the year 2000. In a well-known study Manabe (1971) estimated that, other things remaining constant, this will lead to an increase in the mean global temperature by 0.3°C to 0.6°C. In a subsequent study, Manabe and Weatherald (1975) argued that a doubling of atmospheric concentration of CO_2 would result in an increase in the mean global temperature by 3°C. Taken on its own 3°C, not to mention 0.6°C, may not appear as a significant increase. Unfortunately, it is thought that even a 0.6°C increase is sufficiently large to bring about changes in atmospheric circulation and the melting of sea ice; that is to say, it is feared that there is significant *climatic amplification* associated with increase in the mean surface temperature of the earth. The impact on agriculture could be deleterious in many parts of the globe, and the effect would be world-wide.[2] It is for such reasons that the CO_2 problem is taken very seriously by scholars of varied dispositions, and why we have felt Nordhaus's case-study to be particularly suitable for inclusion in this collection.

A general framework for analyzing the *intertemporal* economics of pollution control is developed in Mäler (1974) and in Chapter 8 of Dasgupta (1982). Each of these studies attempts to arrive at social cost-benefit rules that a society ought to follow as a guide in its choice of economic activity.[3] Such rules, not surprisingly, reflect both social objectives and technological and institutional constraints. To be sure also, they vary from place to place and from time to time and depend as well on the nature of the economic activity under study. In what follows we shall review briefly some of the issues that are involved in social cost-benefit analysis of pollution control.

Suppose that the emission of pollutants is a by-product of useful production – as in the case of CO_2 emission. We take it that the output (production of energy) is desirable and that the associated emission is undesirable. Now, broadly speaking, there are four ways of controlling the pollution: first, by having lower output; second, by investment in alternative technological specifications of production, so that less emission takes place per unit output – for example, investing in pollution abatement technologies (stack-gas scrubbers for removing sulphur dioxide produced during coal combustion and sewage treatment plants for household and industrial sewage), or relying on a substitute product which is relatively pollution free (solar energy as opposed to fossil-fuels as a source of energy); third, by cleaning up the environment after the pollutant has been emitted (the use of lime in lakes damaged by acid rains); and fourth, discharging the effluent in sites earmarked as pollution dumps. Each of these options, quite clearly, involves foregone benefits. To be sure also, not all options are in fact available for all pollution problems – for example, the last two ways are plainly not feasible for CO_2 emission. Any sensible study of pollution control must consider alternative options, using technical information that are pertinent for each of these four broad avenues.

We now come to the valuation problem. For our purposes here we may suppose that the social valuation of the flow of output poses no great problems. Very often, though, the social damages caused by the associated effluent discharge are extremely hard (if not possible) to evaluate. We are here thinking of damages to human health and increases in the risk of death.[4] It is not merely that we are uncertain about the effects of many pollutants on human welfare; there are often deep conceptual difficulties that one faces in trying to *value* such welfare losses. Nevertheless, cn many occasions – as illustrated in several of the case studies collected here – it can be done, and in this case one subtracts the damage from the benefit enjoyed from the output. One also subtracts the social costs involved in undertaking pollution control measures and, as outlined in our general Introduction, we emerge thereby with a criterion function which enables us to compare options.

In many instances, where environmental damage functions are overly difficult to estimate, short-cuts are often taken. This often takes the form of not referring to damage functions at all but instead of imposing *environmental standards*. We noted this in our General Introduction and suggested alternative justifications for such an approach. The imposition of environmental standards on a planning problem reflects social objectives: the standard in question being a level of pollution which, it is felt, it would be intolerable to exceed. (A detailed discussion of standards acting as objectives in a planning exercise is in Dasgupta (1982), Chapters 3 and 8.)

In Nordhaus's study of the CO_2 problem, there is no damage function in the planning exercise. Instead, an upper limit on the CO_2 concentration level is imposed – the upper limit being a given multiple of the existing concentration level – and the analysis is directed at maximizing the present discounted value of social benefits (Nordhaus calls it the minimization of the present discounted value of social costs), subject to the constraint that the CO_2 concentration level never exceeds this upper limit. As noted earlier, the third and fourth options are not available for the CO_2 problem. Therefore, Nordhaus has to limit himself to an exploration of the first two options, that is, reductions in the output of energy based on fossil fuels, and the production of energy from alternative sources.[5]

In his simulation study Nordhaus has chosen a planning horizon of 200 years, a discount rate of 10% per year, and his central computation has been carried out on the basis of an upper limit to the concentration level of CO_2 that is *twice* the existing level. As the author notes in the final section, there are two surprising results that emerge from the simulation run. First, although the time path of CO_2 emission is seriously constrained due to the imposition of the CO_2 constraint, total energy output (and hence energy consumption) is not; in fact, in later years (when non-fossil fuel production becomes most significant), energy output is higher than it would be if CO_2 emission is not subject to control. Second, the effect of a carbon constraint on *current* energy consumption is almost negligible; it is only in later periods of the simulation run that the optimal programme is noticeably different from the uncontrolled path.

Nordhaus's planning model is a linear programme. The optimal policy has a system of shadow (or accounting) prices associated with it. The shadow price of CO_2 emission is the tax rate which, if imposed, will in principle sustain the optimal programme. For his central simulation run, Nordhaus finds the shadow tax per ton to be low in initial years (1980–2000) (U.S. $0.14 per ton carbon at 1975 prices), becoming significant around about year 2020 and rising to about U.S. $87.00 at the end of the next century; (see Table 6.1 in Nordhaus). In 1975, prices per ton of carbon or carbon-based fuel was about U.S. $25 a ton for coal, $100 a ton for petroleum and $200 a ton for natural gas. The optimum carbon tax is therefore truly negligible in initial years, though rising rapidly.[6] Table 6.1 in Nordhaus's paper also presents the fact that the cost (in terms of increased energy prices from more expensive sources) due to the imposition of the CO_2 constraint is of the order of U.S. $87 billion. This is not a negligible figure, though perhaps not unduly large, given the potential gravity of the problem. And, as with all major global pollution problems, the question remains: how is agreement to be reached among nations with divergent interests?

Notes

1 The concentration of CO_2 is more or less uniform up to about 100 km above the earth's surface. While CO_2 is relatively transparent to solar radiation, it is a prime absorber of re-radiated energy from the earth's surface and helps to keep the surface temperature warm. This is the greenhouse effect.

2 A general warming of the earth's surface will not be deleterious for *all* regions; indeed some regions will probably benefit from warmer climate and greater rainfall. Revelle (1982) has an excellent non-technical discussion of the CO_2 problem.

3 There are, of course, a great many technical articles that have developed the intertemporal economics of pollution control (e.g. Keeler *et al.* (1972) and d'Arge and Kogiku (1973)). But treatises on environmental pollution tend on the whole to ignore intertemporal issues.

4 Mäler and Wyzga (1976) and Freeman (1979) discuss how environmental damages in many circumstances may be assessed.

5 It should be noted that Nordhaus, in his programming model, considers both solar and nuclear fission as alternatives to fossil fuels. It has been argued by some that a move from fossil fuels to nuclear fission would relieve us of the CO_2 problem, but plunge us into potential radiation hazards. It would be interesting to see the extent to which Nordhaus's results would differ if nuclear fission is not included as an option.

6 One expects that the tax rate in initial years would be higher if a lower rate was used for discounting future costs and benefits.

CASE STUDY

In contemplating the future course of economic growth in the West, scientists are divided between one group crying 'wolf' and another which denies that species' existence. One persistent concern has been that man's economic activities would reach a scale where the global climate would be significantly affected. Unlike many of the wolf-cries, this one, in my opinion, should be taken very seriously. This article will first given a brief overview of the climatic implications of economic activity with special reference to carbon dioxide, and then will present possible strategies for control. A more complete report with references to the literature on climatic change is contained in Nordhaus (1976).

It is thought that the economic activities which most affect climate are agriculture and energy. Of these, the latter is probably more significant, is certainly more easily analyzed, and will be discussed here. In the energy sector, emissions of carbon dioxide, particulate matter, and heat are of significance for the global climate.

Energy and climate

When we refer to climate, we usually are thinking of the average of characteristics of the atmosphere at different points of the earth, including the variabilities such as the diurnal and annual cycle. The important atmospheric characteristics for man's activities are temperature, precipitation, snow cover, winds and so forth. A more precise representation of the climate would be as a dynamic, stochastic system of equations. The probability distributions of the atmospheric characteristics is what we mean by *climate*, while a particular realization of that stochastic process is what we call the *weather*.

Recent evidence indicates that, even after several millenia, the dynamic processes which determine climate have not attained a stable equilibrium. One of the more carefully documented examples is the global mean temperature which over the last 100 years has shown a range of variation of five-year averages of about 0.6° C (see Figure 6.2 below). The disputes about the sources of such variations are reminiscent of business cycle theory – with theories mentioning everything from sunspots to quasi-periodic oscillations to the existence of many locally stable but globally unstable equilibria.

The overall observation of high amounts of 'red noise' – as is also the case for typical economic time series – has important implications for those who are concerned with climatic implications of man's behaviour. This implies that the climatic stability we generally assume should not be taken for granted; indeed, some have pointed out that the string of good harvests is the mid-1970s in the Midwestern U.S. is no more likely than the Dust Bowls of the 1930s. Moreover, given the slowly changing climatic patterns it is difficult to separate nature's red noise from the red signal associated with smoothly growing economic activity.

At what point is there likely to be a significant effect of man's activities on the climate? Many climatologists feel that the changes witnessed in the last century – the 0.6° range – have led to major, albeit not catastrophic events. It should be stressed that the changes in temperature are rather trivial. It is not the mean temperature change which is economically significant, but other variables such as degree – days, precipitation, and snow cover, and these tend to vary much *more* than global mean temperature. Examples of high amplification are changes in precipitation and changes in the latitude of monsoons with changes in temperature. (See Machta and Telegdos (1974) or Schneider (1976).) Given the amplification, it seems prudent to consider a change of 0.5° C as a significant change.

The inadvertent affects of man's activities on climate have been estimated using a variety of techniques. Although the estimates are uncertain, many authors place the date at which significant climatic change can occur as follows: for carbon dioxide such a change would come with about 20 % increase in atmospheric concentrations. According to recent projections, we shall probably reach this level in the 1985–1990 period (see Broecker (1974)). For industrial heat (sometimes called 'waste heat'), the estimates are less secure. Using the same methodology as for the carbon dioxide estimates, it is estimated that waste heat will lead to an increase of 0.5°C around 2080. For particulate matter, the matter is even more problematical because the *direction* of effect is uncertain. A rather mechanical exercise of projecting the growth of particulates at the rate of growth of energy consumption leads to the conclusion that particulates would have the significant 0.5° C effect by about 2030, but this procedure is extremely dubious. From these estimates, it appears that carbon dioxide will be the first industrial emission to affect climate on a global scale, with a 'significant' effect appearing sometime in the next twenty years; for this reason we will focus only on carbon dioxide in the present report.

The interaction between carbon dioxide and the climate is shown by the following: Combustion of fossil fuels leads to emissions of carbon dioxide into the atmosphere. Once in the atmosphere, the residence time appears to be very long, with approximately one-half of all industrial carbon dioxide still airborne. Because of the selective absorption of radiation, the increased atmospheric concentration is thought to lead to increased surface temperatures. The most careful study to date (Manabe and Wetherald (1975)) predicted that a doubling of atmospheric concentrations of carbon dioxide would lead to a global mean temperature increase of 3° C. The predicted temperature increase by latitude is shown in Figure 6.1, indicating that there is considerable amplification at high latitudes. In addition, in Figure 6.2 we have shown the predicted change in global mean temperature as a function of time, given the predicted emissions of carbon dioxide which we will discuss in the later part of this paper. The significant point to note is that there are predicted to be vary large increases in temperature in the coming decades, taking the climate outside of any temperature pattern observed in the last 100,000 years.

Control strategies

The outcome just described is the effect of an uncontrolled economy-climate system, that is one in which the economy and the energy system evolve simply on the basis of economic forces, without considering the feedback of economic activity through climate back to man. The problem

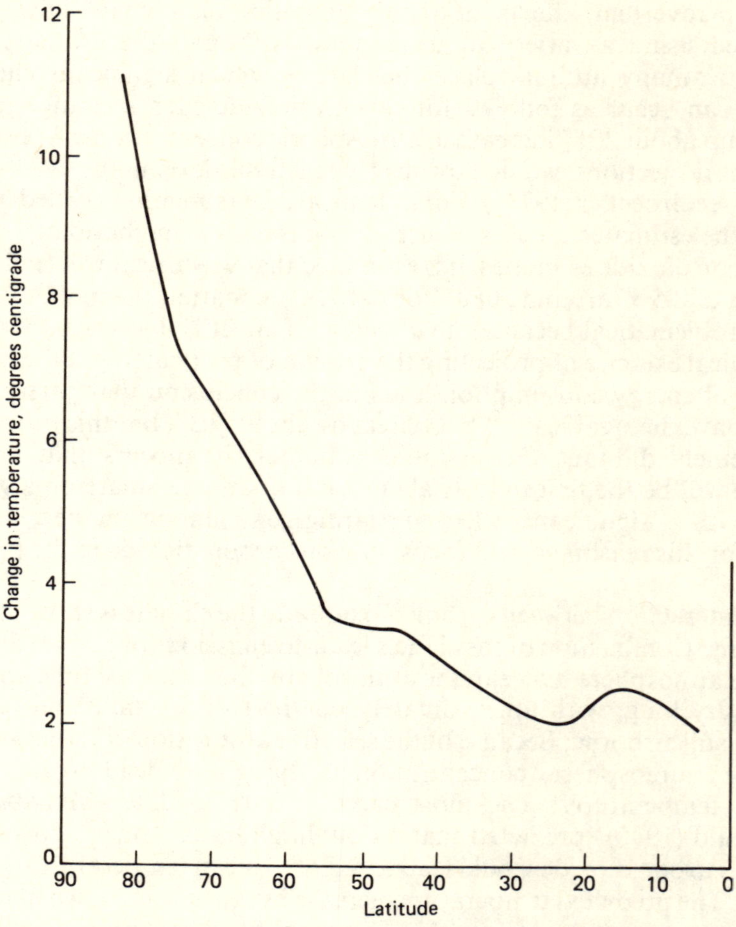

Figure 6.1 *Estimated Effect of Doubling of Atmospheric Carbon Dioxide on Surface Temperatures by Latitude*

Source: Manabe and Wetherald, 1975.

is the most extreme imaginable form of external diseconomy – one in which an individual burning a fossil fuel does not take into account the climatic consequences, and thereby affects not only the global climate, but also the climate for hundreds of years in the future.

We therefore investigate strategies for control of atmospheric carbon dioxide. A control strategy involves two aspects: On a scientific and aggregate level, the feasibility of control techniques must be explored. But there must also be a way to decentralize the controls so that nations, producers, and consumers have proper incentives to implement the control strategy on an individual level. We will consider briefly these two aspects.

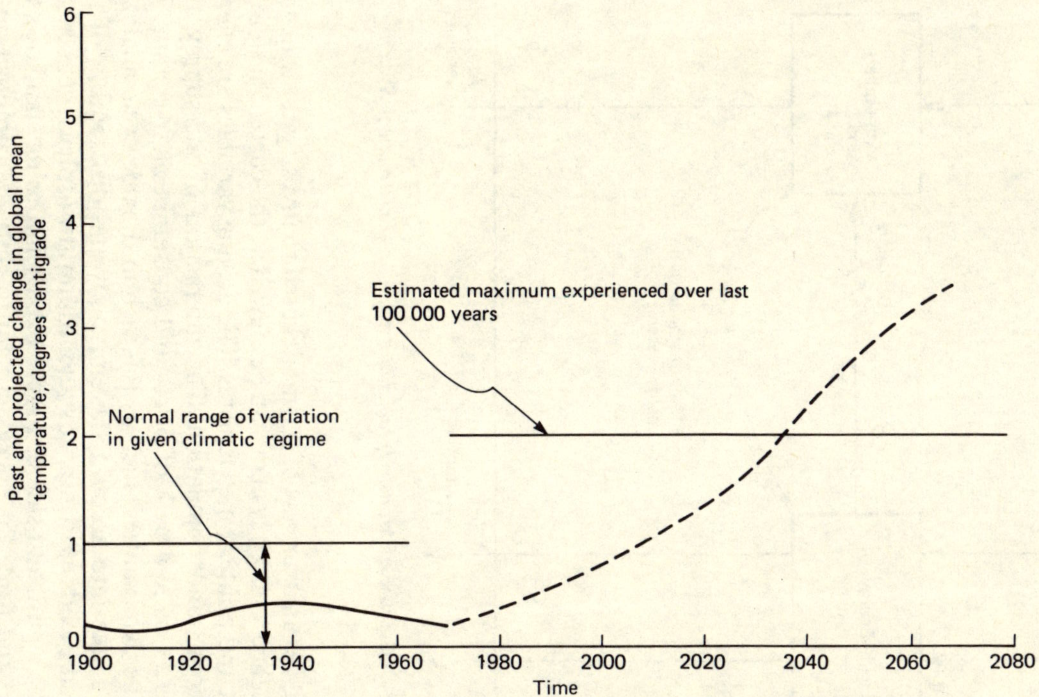

Figure 6.2 *Past and Projected Global Mean Temperature, Relative to 1880–84 mean*

Note: Figures up to 1970 are actual. Figures from 1970 on are projections using 1970 actual as a base and adding the estimated increase due to uncontrolled build-up of atmospheric carbon

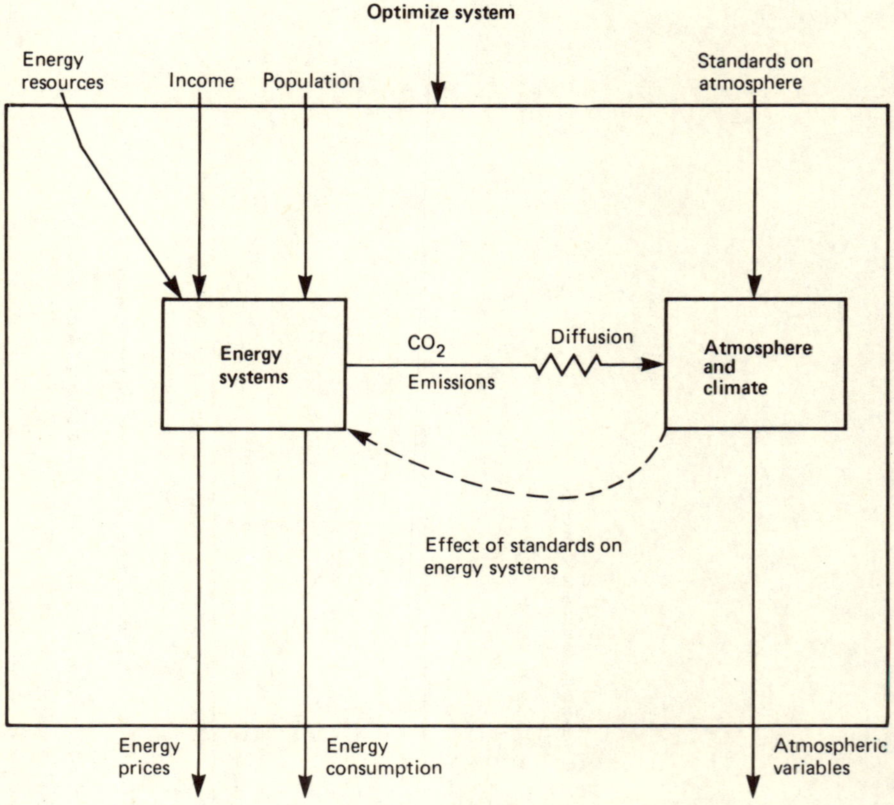

Figure 6.3 *Overview of Model Optimizing the Energy-Environment System*

Figure 6.3 gives an overview of the model used to investigate strategies. The block labelled 'energy system' can be viewed as the current system of mixed market and political mechanisms. The driving variables are energy resources, income, and population. The interaction of the supply and demand forces leads to a path of prices and consumption over time. To account for the externalities, such as the carbon dioxide cycle analyzed here, we must take into account the emissions and distribution of the effluent. This step leads us to impose standards on atmospheric concentrations, as on the right hand side of Figure 6.3. By imposing standards we close the loop and force the energy system to shift the composition of supply and demand. Outside the entire system there is yet another box, indicating that the entire system is being optimized.

There are three general approaches to the problem of keeping atmospheric concentrations to a reasonable level. The first strategy, which is the route chosen in the present paper, is to reduce emissions of carbon dioxide. This takes place by substituting non-carbon-based fuels for carbon-based fuels. A second strategy is to offset the effects of emissions of carbon dioxide. This can take the form of introducing the carbon into places where it has delayed climatic effect (such as compressing and pumping liquid CO_2 into the deep oceans), or of using climatic engineering to offset the effects (such as painting roofs and roads white). A third approach would be to use natural or industrial processes to clean out the carbon dioxide from the atmosphere *ex post* (such as by growing and pickling trees). To avoid the odour of science fiction, we have limited control strategies to the first strategy – reductions in demand and substitution in supply.

The final question in the optimization concerns the 'standards' imposed in Figure 6.3. Unfortunately, although considerable scientific concern has been expressed about future trends in carbon dioxide concentration, there are no attempts to suggest what might be reasonable standards. As a first approximation, however, it seems reasonable to argue that the climatic effects of carbon dioxide should be kept well within the normal range of long-term climatic variation. (Note that the increase is more than the 'significant level' discussed above.) According to most sources, the range of variation between distinct climatic regimes is in the order of 5°C, and at the present time the global climate is at the high end of this range. As shown in Figure 6.2, if global temperatures were more than about 2°C above the current value, this would take the climate outside of the range of observations which have been made over the hundred thousand years. Within a stable climatic regime, such as the current interglacial, a range of variation of 1°C is the normal variation.

Given the estimate of the effect of carbon dioxide, to keep the effect within the normal variation implies that a doubling of the atmospheric concentration of carbon dioxide is a reasonable upper limit to impose at the present stage of knowledge. We also test the sensitivity of our results to limits of fifty per cent and two hundred per cent increases. *It must be emphasized that the process of setting standards used in this report is deeply unsatisfactory, both from an empirical point of view and from a theoretical point of view.* We can only justify the standards set here as rough guesses and we are not certain that we have even judged the *direction* of the desired movement in carbon dioxide correctly, to say nothing of the absolute levels.

The second problem of controlling carbon dioxide is implementation on a decentralized level. Because of the externalities, there are no market or political mechanisms which ensure that the appropriate level of control will be chosen. The procedure in the present paper will estimate an efficient way of allocating energy resources so as to satisfy the carbon dioxide constraint. To implement this efficient path implies that we are implicitly putting a positive price on emissions of carbon into the atmosphere. In the real world, the policy can take the form either of taxing carbon emissions, or of physical controls (like rationing). In an efficient solution the two are interchangeable; in practice, the use of taxes is much simpler because the taxes tend to be much more uniform than the quantities. We therefore will concentrate on 'carbon taxes' as a way of implementing the global policy on a decentralized level.

The model used to calculate the effects of imposing standards is an extension of earlier work (see Nordhaus (1973) for a description of an early version of the energy model, and Nordhaus (1976) for the details of the carbon model). It can be written in highly oversimplified form as follows: The energy model attempts to simulate the market allocation process. Thus, let U_{it} be the present value of the marginal utility, in terms of income, of good i in year t; let c_{it} be the present value of the cost of good i in year t, both discounted at 10 per cent; and let x_{it} be the level of activity. Under suitable assumptions (see Samuelson (1953)) a market allocation can be described by the mathematical programming problem:

$$\underset{\{x_{it}\}}{\text{maximize}} \sum_{t=1}^{T} \sum_{i=1}^{n} [U_{it} - c_{it}]x_{it}, \tag{1}$$

subject to resource constraints,

$$\sum_{t=1}^{T} \sum_{i=1}^{n} A_{ij}x_{it} \leqslant \overline{R}_j, \qquad j = 1, \ldots, m, \tag{2}$$

where A_{ij} is the content of scarce resource j per unit activity of good i, and $\overline{R}_j$ is the amount of scarce resource R_j which is available. In the actual problem examined, the goods x_{it} are composed of different energy goods (6 different fuels used in 4 different sectors), for 2 different regions of the world (U.S. and the rest of the world), for 10 time periods of 20 years each.

Equations (1) and (2) describe the energy system. Suppose we now wish to examine the carbon cycle as well. To do this we add a second block of equations describing the emissions and diffusion. If $\gamma(ll, i)$ is the emissions per unit activity x_{it} into stratum ll, emissions in a given period, $E(ll, t)$, are

$$E(ll, t) = \sum_{i=1}^{n} \gamma(ll, i)x_{it}, \qquad ll = 1, \ldots, L. \tag{3}$$

Next denote $M(ll, t)$ as the total mass of carbon in a given stratum at the end of a period t and $D(i, j)$ as the transition probabilities of a unit mass moving from stratum i to stratum j. From the basic diffusion equations we have

$$M(ll, t) = \sum_{i=1}^{L} D(i, ll)M(i, t-1) + E(ll, t),$$
$$ll = 1, \ldots, L, \; t = 1, \ldots, T \tag{4}$$

Finally, we impose standard on the energy sector that the total mass in a given stratum should not exceed $St(ll)$:

$$M(ll, t) \leqslant St(ll), \text{ all } t. \tag{5}$$

To implement the controls, we add equation set (3), (4), and (5) to our original problem in (1) and (2) and solve the optimization problem.

Results

The first question to investigate is whether the carbon controls we have suggested are feasible. The question of feasibility rests on the existence of activities which equilibrate supply and demand with relatively low levels of carbon dioxide emissions. In reality, any non-fossil fuel energy source (fission, fusion, solar, or geothermal) will be an option for meeting the carbon dioxide constraint since non-fossil fuels have no significant carbon dioxide emissions. In the programme discussed above, we consider both solar and nuclear fission as an alternative to fossil fuels, but the results would be identical for any of the non-fossil fuels, with the same cost structure.

The second question refers to the quantities in the controlled and uncontrolled paths. Table 6.1 shows the calculated U.S. energy consumption and world carbon emissions along the uncontrolled and controlled paths. These show two surprising results: first, although the time path of

Table 6.1 *Energy Consumption, Carbon Emissions and Carbon Emission Taxes*

	1970 (Actual)	*1980*	*2000*	*2020*	*2040*	*2100*
Energy Consumption, U.S., 10^{15} btu/yr						
Uncontrolled CO_2	71	76.	92.	155.	250.	395.
100 per cent increase CO_2		76.	92.	142.	160.	405.
Global Carbon Emissions, 10^9 tons/yr						
Uncontrolled CO_2	4.0	6.9	10.7	18.4	40.1	45.4
100 per cent increase CO_2		6.9	10.7	16.6	16.0	4.9
Carbon emission tax ($/ton)						
Uncontrolled CO_2	0.00	0.00	0.00	0.00	0.00	0.00
100 per cent increase CO_2		0.14	1.02	8.04	67.90	87.15

Notes: Energy consumption use the U.S. Bureau of Mines conventions on conversions. Carbon emissions are tons of carbon dioxide, carbon weight, while carbon taxes are calculated dual variables in the efficient programme, and have the dimension of 1975 dollars per ton carbon weight of emission.

Source: Nordhaus (1976).

emissions is severely constrained, the total energy consumption is not. In fact, in later periods (when non-fossil fuel production becomes most significant), consumption is higher because of the lower thermal efficiency of non-fossil sources. Second, it is surprising that the effect of a carbon constraint on *current* energy consumption (and on the composition of consumption) is alomost negligible; it is only in the later periods that an efficiently designed programme leads to noticeable modifications of the energy system.

In an optimization framework, as in an economy, constraints have their costs in terms of the objectives of the optimization. The control programme takes the form of imposing upper bounds on the level of atmospheric concentrations, and associated with each of the constraints are shadow prices on emissions. The last row of Table 6.1 gives the shadow prices for carbon emissions for the controlled programme. The prices per ton start very low ($0.14 per ton carbon), become significant in the third period, and rise to a very high level of around $90 a ton (1975 prices) by the end of the next century. These should be compared with the prices per ton of carbon of carbon-based fuels, which are around $25 a ton for coal, $100 a ton for petroleum, and $200 a ton for natural gas. Put differently, the current implicit subsidy on carbon fuels is less than one per cent of the price, but without a control programme, that subsidy will be growing very rapidly.

We can also ask what the carbon dioxide constraints are costing *in toto*. Whereas the shadow prices give the cost on the margin, we can examine the attained value of the objective function in (1) to determine the overall cost. Table 6.2 gives the calculation of the discounted cost of meeting the three different constraints. Clearly the control of carbon dioxide is a very expensive operations – the medium control path 3 has discounted costs of $87 billion at 1975 prices. As a corollary, it is evident that the social return to new 'carbon control technologies' – the science fiction stories referred to earlier – would be very high if carbon dioxide were to be controlled.

Table 6.2 *Cost of Carbon Dioxide Control Programmes*

		Path		
	Uncontrolled	*200% Increase*	*100% Increase*	*50% Increase*
Discounted Total Cost, billions of 1975 dollars	$0	$30	$87	$540
Discounted Total Cost as Percentage of Discounted World GNP	0%	0.06%	0.12%	0.81%

Source: Nordhaus (1976).

It should also be noted that, since at the present the only proven large-scale and low-cost alternative to carbon-based fuels is nuclear fission, the outcome of the nuclear debate will significantly effect the prospects of carbon dioxide control. If nuclear fission were to be constrained along with carbon emissions, then, until major breakthroughs in alterative technologies become available, the growth rate of energy consumption would be effectively constrained to zero. Preliminary estimates indicate that the cost of prohibiting nuclear power along with a limitation on carbon dioxide concentrations is around five times the most restricted case in Table 6.2.

We have investigated an efficient programme for meeting certain carbon dioxide standards. These indicate that such programmes appear feasible and, moreover, require little change in the energy allocation for the first two 20-year periods, and only in the third period, starting around 2010, do significant modifications in the allocation take place. The modifications take the form of reducing fossil fuel use in the non-electric sector, and replacing it with non-fossil fuels. The efficient programmes analyzed here eventually have very high implicit taxes on carbon emissions and therefore on carbon-based fuels; the effect on energy prices (not presented here) or on total real income (presented in Table 6.2) are expensive but not unthinkable.

Subject to the limitations of the techniques used here, we can be relatively optimistic about the technical feasibility of a carbon dioxide control strategy. The central question for economists, climatologists, and other scientists remains: How costly are the projected changes in (or the uncertainties about) the climate likely to be, and therefore to what level of control should we aspire? And for students of politics, the question is: How can we reasonably hope to negotiate an international control strategy among the several nations with widely divergent interests?

References

Broecker, W. S. (August 1975), 'Climatic Change: Are We On the Brink of a Pronounced Global Warning?', *Science*, vol. 189, pp. 460–3.

Machta, L. and Telegados, G. (1974), 'Climate Forecasting', *Weather and Climate Modification*, New York.

Manabe, S. and Wetherald, R. T. (January 1975), 'The Effect of Doubling the CO_2 Concentration on the Climate of a General Circulation Model', *Journal of Atmospheric Sciences*, vol. 32, pp. 3–15.

Nordhaus, W. D. (1973–4), 'The Allocation of Energy Resources,' *B.P.E.A.*, pp. 529–70.

Samuelson, P.A., 'Market Mechanisms and Maximization', *Collected Papers*, Cambridge, Mass., pp. 425–504.

Schneider, S. (1976), *The Genesis Strategy*, New York.

7

A Socially Optimum Pricing Policy for a Public Water Agency

Gardner Brown Jr
C. B. McGuire

INTRODUCTION

The earliest work in social cost-benefit analysis was directed at water-resource projects. Nevertheless, in recent years the development of such analyses has been, for the most part, in the field of industrial and infrastructure projects in less developed countries. This is surprising, since the importance of water availability, e.g. for drinking and irrigation, in many parts of the globe is immense. The article by Brown and McGuire included here provides an admirable example of how social cost-benefit analysis can fruitfully be applied to the choice of the allocation of ground and surface water in competing regions.

Water, whether obtained from an aquifer or from surface flow, is a renewable resource. It has a particularly simple 'growth' function: with obvious qualifications, the annual recharge (or flow) rate is approximately constant over the annual cycle. Being renewable, it should not be surprising that there is some affinity between the problems of water management and those of fisheries. (See Dasgupta (1982), Chapter 6, for a more detailed account.)

Consider two adjacent districts, each of which has an aquifer to draw from and each of which also enjoys a steady flow of surface water. Let us suppose that groundwater cannot be transported from one district to the other but that surface water can, at negligible cost. Let us suppose also that there is a master agency in charge of allocating water to the two districts. A set of related questions we may ask is this: at what rate ought each district be tapping its aquifer; how should the surface flows be allocated between them; and what price should be charged by the master agency for water? This is the reduced form of the set of questions raised and answered by Brown and McGuire in their analysis of the problems facing the Kern County Water Agency in California in the early 1960s.

To help the reader follow the details of the Brown-McGuire article, it will prove useful to formalize the foregoing example. Suppose S_t^1 and S_t^2 are the stocks of ground-water in the two districts, respectively, at time t and suppose $\bar{X}^1$ and $\bar{X}^2$ are the recharge rates (assumed constant). Let X_t^1 and X_t^2 be the rates at which water is extracted in the two districts at time t and let $X_t^1 c(S_t^1)$ and $X_t^2 c(S_t^2)$ be the cost of drawing water. It is appropriate to assume that the unit cost of water extraction rises as the ground-water table falls and so $c(\cdot)$ is a *decreasing* function of the stock of groundwater. Let $\bar{Y}$ be the steady flow of surface water and suppose Y_t^1 and Y_t^2 are the rates of consumption of surface water by the two districts respectively. Thus, total rates of consumption of water by the two districts at time t are $(X_t^1 + Y_t^1)$ and $(X_t^2 + Y_t^2)$, respectively. Finally, let us assume that $B^1(X_t^1 + Y_t^1)$ and $B^2(X_t^2 + Y_t^2)$ are the gross benefit functions in the two districts from water consumption. (In the Brown-McGuire analysis the water is assumed to be used for irrigation purposes and so the benefit functions are obtained from the marginal value products of water in irrigation use.)

In their analysis Brown and McGuire eschew income distributional issues and therefore sum the net benefits functions of all districts. The flow of net social benefits is then $[B^1(X_t^1 + Y_t^1) + B^2(X_t^2 + Y_t^2) - X_t^1 c(S_t^1) - X_t^2 c(S_t^2)]$. Let r (assumed constant and positive) be the social discount rate. The problem facing the master agency is therefore this:

Choose X_t^1, Y_t^1, X_t^2, Y_t^2 (all non-negative), so as to maximize $\int_0^\infty [B^1(X_t^1 + Y_t) + B^2(X_t^2 + Y_t^2) - X_t^1 c(S_t^1) - X_t^2 c(S_t^2)] e^{-rt}\, dt$, subject to constraints

$$dS_t^1/dt = \bar{X}^1 - X_t^1 \quad (1)$$

$$dS_t^2/dt = \bar{X}^2 - X_t^2 \quad (2)$$

and

$$Y_t^1 + Y_t^2 \leqslant \bar{Y}, \quad (3)$$

where S_0^1 and S_0^2 are given as initial conditions.

In order to have a tractable problem we shall suppose, as Brown and McGuire do, that constant conditions prevail, so that the optimal pricing policy is a stationary one. The question may be asked, given that distributional considerations have been eschewed, what form of market failure requires the master-agency to impose taxes and not rely on the market mechanism for allocating water. The answer is that an individual farmer's groundwater withdrawal cost typically falls short of the social cost of pumping because water withdrawal by one farmer lowers the groundwater table and thereby increases the withdrawal cost of neighbouring farmers.

At a stationary state, $X_t^1 = \bar{X}^1$ and $X_t^2 = \bar{X}^2$ (see equations (1) and (2) above), and so the groundwater levels remain constant. Let λ^1 and λ^2 be the accounting (or shadow) price of *unextracted* groundwater in the two basins and let μ be the accounting price of surface water. Then it is easy to show that

$$c(S^1)+\lambda^1 = c(S^2)+\lambda^2 = \mu \tag{4}$$

and that this in turn equals the marginal social benefit of water consumption in each of the two districts. (See Brown and McGuire, equation (11).)

Thus, at an optimum stationary state, the master agency ought to charge μ for a unit of surface water and should impose λ^1 and λ^2 as water withdrawal taxes per unit extracted in the two districts, respectively. The point is that if the master agency were simply to impose a charge of μ for the use of surface water there would be a misallocation of resources, because the *private* (unit) costs of groundwater withdrawal in the two districts are $c(S^1)$ and $c(S^2)$, respectively. The withdrawal taxes, λ^1 and λ^2, therefore, need to be imposed on the farmers in the two districts so as to correct for the market failure mentioned earlier. It is in fact possible to show that

$$\lambda^1 = -\bar{X}^1(dc(S^1)/dS^1)/r \tag{5}$$

and

$$\lambda^2 = -\bar{X}^2(dc(S^2)/dS^2)/r. \tag{6}$$

(See Brown and McGuire, equation (14).) That is, the withdrawal tax on a given aquifer, to quote Brown and McGuire, ought to equal '. . . all increases in direct pumping costs, the variable costs, that follow from the increase in lift caused by pumping an additional acre-foot today' (p. 187).

Equations (5) and (6) are fundamental in groundwater management. Since they are similar we need to interpret the first of these only. Recall that we are at a steady state. The rate of groundwater extraction in the first district is $\bar{X}^1$. If a representative farmer in this district were to withdraw an additional unit of water the groundwater stock would *decline* marginally. Other things remaining the same this would mean that unit extraction cost in the district would *increase* marginally. This increase is $-dc(S^1)/dS^1$, (which is, of course, positive since $c(\cdot)$ is a decreasing function). Thus at each period the total increase in withdrawal cost in the district would be $-\bar{X}^1(dc(S^1)/dS^1)$. The present discounted value of this increased cost is therefore $-X^1(dc(S^1)/dS^1)/r$, which is the right-hand side of equation (5) and which is the tax that needs to be imposed on each farmer in the district for water withdrawal.

The Brown-McGuire article studies a model a good deal more complex than this example, and proceeds to estimate the taxes that are pertinent for the data they use for Kern County.

CASE STUDY

Introduction

Throughout the arid west, the real cost of developing new water supplies has tended to increase through time, because the rate of technological change has not kept pace with the increasing inaccessibility of untapped water resources. Under these circumstances we may reasonably expect to observe increased efforts to manage existing sources of water more efficiently.

A difficulty often encountered in the search for better resource decision rules is the identification and estimation of externalities. The economic model developed in this paper diagnoses a classic externality in an environment where both surface and groundwater are available to some water districts over time, whereas only surface water is available to others. The individual water districts are members of a master water agency whose responsibility it is to find answers to the following set of questions: What annual quantity of surface water should the master agency purchase from a supplier of water? What annual quantities of groundwater should be pumped in each member district? What prices, if any, should be charged by the master water agency for district purchases of surface water? What control should be exerted by the master agency over groundwater pumping? How should the annual quantity of surface water be allocated among the member districts? To the extent that they can be influenced, what should be the levels of the various groundwater tables? These conditions and questions fairly describe the Kern County Water Agency (K.C.W.A.) in the early 1960s. This agency is one of the principal contractors for water in the first stage of the California water plan. Although the K.C.W.A. will sell water for both urban and agricultural use, the application of the model is limited to the derivation of pricing policies for the irrigation districts.

In this model it is assumed that a stable environment (the year 1990) has been reached. The build-up of surface water deliveries has reached its peak, and this delivery rate continues unchanged in each succeeding year. Farm and land development, it is assumed, have reached a similar steady state. Agricultural technology and farm prices remain constant. Groundwater tables have by this time either risen or declined to the level at which they will be maintained hereafter, or have declined forever beyond economic reach. Surface water distribution systems are assumed to be completed. Each succeeding year is like the last one in all respects. Since nothing in the environment changes, the decisions made each year concerning surface water use, groundwater use, crop selection, and other important factors remain the same. However, even in a steady-state situation a farmer might quite reasonably decide, to rotate crops annually. The rotation plan, therefore, is a regular one.

Conceptualizing water planning problems in this context is not so far-fetched when it is realized that water projects are long-term experiments. In particular, the expiration date for the K.C.W.A. contract is 2035, so that the costs and benefits during the 1990–2035 period are important. Present decisions and plans for the intervening years will be influenced by future expectations, and some assumptions about future farm prices and technology must necessarily be made in the current planning period.

An indicator of welfare

If a correct pricing policy is to be found, there must be a measure of correctness, a success indicator defined explicitly enough to be stated in a formula that will yield numerical values. Various measures of welfare might be adopted. (a) Maximize gross revenue to K.C.W.A. If this welfare indicator is chosen, that water policy that brings in the most revenue to the master agency will be selected. Most revenue might mean gross average annual revenue or gross revenue over the future discounted at some particular interest rate. This indicator places a heavy weight on the importance of master agency's ability to meet its repayment obligations to the water supplier, without explicitly considering the cost of water. It appears to leave out the effect of the water policy on the farmer. Does he pay 'too much' for his water? Does he receive 'too small' an allocation? (b) Maximize profits to the master agency. This indicator is a simple modification of (a) and suffers from similar shortcomings. Total costs, both fixed and variable, are subtracted from total revenue. The first subtraction will have no effect on the ranking of different water policies. If a given number is subtracted from each element in a set of numbers, the original ranking is preserved. The second subtraction will affect the ranking, since those water policies that sometimes take less than the contracted allocation will result in smaller variable transportation charges. (c) Regarding the master agency and all the farmers within its political jurisdiction as a division and the employees, respectively, of a large hypothetical business firm, maximize total profits to the firm. There remains the question of good and bad ways to distribute the profit among the 'employees' (the farmers), but the issue of profit distribution can be separated from the total profit maximization and water pricing policy selection problem. Whatever view is held about fair distribution of profit, one can readily agree that total profit should be large. So long as profit distribution can be accomplished without affecting the implementation of the chosen water policy, then it is legitimate to break the whole problem into these two parts. The maximization of total profit to this hypothetical firm is the welfare indicator adopted in this model.

Allocative efficiency in the steady state

Three parts comprise the total profit to the hypothetical master water agency. First is the total gross benefits or savings accruing to farmers on being supplied with specific quantities of water. The second part (a negative one) is the total of purchase costs for surface water from the supplier plus the total of local distribution costs for this same water. The third part consists of total pumping and well costs for ground water.

Clearly, one should not maximize total profit for a single year, because it is often possible to increase one year's profit at the expense of another, nor can annual profit be added over the years. Commonly, the present value of the stream of profit over future years is calculated by discounting at a chosen rate of interest each future year's profit to the present. Alternatively, we could discount to the beginning of the steady-state regime to yield a 1990 value. This study follows the last procedure, using a constant rate of interest of 6%. In the steady state, when each year's profit is the same, say π, then the present value of the stream of future profits is simply $\pi/0.06$.

The model, the solution, and some implications for policy

Functions

Let us define

$h_i(x)$ = value of the marginal product of water in District i when x acre-feet of water are being applied. h is the long-run demand curve, with price expressed as a function of quantity demanded;

$F(x)$ = total annual cost to the agency of purchasing x acre-feet from the State;

$f_i(x)$ = total annual cost to District i of distributing x acre-feet of surface water;

$g_i(x, m)$ = total annual cost of pumping a total of x acre-feet at pumping lift in District i.

Parameters

Assume that the above functions have the following linear form:

$$h_i(x) = u_i - v_i x$$
$$F(x) = E + Dx$$
$$f_i(x) = e_i + d_i x$$
$$g_i(x, m) = a_i + b_i m + c_i m x$$

where u_i and v_i are the demand parameters price intercept and slope, respectively. E is the fixed annual bill from the State of the agency, and D represents those unit charges by the State that *do* depend on the amount of water purchased. e_i and d_i are the fixed and variable costs for distribution within districts. $(a_i + b_i m)$ is the fixed cost associated with the whole array of wells in District i when (the common) pumping lift is m. $c_i m$ represents the unit cost of pumping at lift m.

A_i and B_i are hydrological parameters in District i. A_i denotes the annual natural recharge of the aquifer underlying District i measured in feet of rise of the groundwater table; B_i denotes the decline of this groundwater table brought about by the pumping of 1 acre-foot of groundwater from this aquifier. 'Safe yield', that quantity of groundwater that can be pumped without changing the level of the ground table, is therefore A_i/B_i.

Total surface water availability in year t will be denoted $\bar{Y}_t$; r will denote the interest rate and we will write $R = 1/(1+r)$.

Variables

Define

Y_t = surface water (in acre-feet) purchased by the agency in year t;
y_{it} = surface water (in acre-feet) consumed by District i in year t;
z_{it} = groundwater (in acre-feet) consumed by District i in year t;
m_{it} = the pumping lift (in acre-feet) in District i at the end of year t. The initial lifts m_{i0} are assumed to be given.
T_i = tax charge per acre-foot of ground-water pumped in District i.
p = internal price charged by the agency for delivering at a turnout one acre-foot to a district.

The welfare function and optimization

In year t when y_{it} and z_{it} are the amounts of water consumed in total by farmers in District i, ($i = 1, \ldots, N$), the gross benefits to these farmers are

$$\int_0^{y_{it}+z_{it}} h_i(x)\,dx$$

Distribution costs in this district are $f_i(y_{it})$, and pumping and well-maintenance costs are $g_i(z_{it}, m_{i,t-1})$.

Summing over districts and adding in the cost to the agency of providing surface water, we have

$$W_t = \sum_{i=1}^{N} \left[\int_0^{y_{it}+z_{it}} h_i(x)\,dx - f_i(y_{it}) - g_i(z_{it}, m_{i,t-1}) \right] - F(Y_t) \qquad (1)$$

Consider now the period $t = 1, 2, 3, \ldots$ extending into the future. The present value (i.e., at the beginning of the period studied) of the stream of future years' welfare functions is then

$$W = \sum_{t=1}^{\infty} R^t W_t \qquad (2)$$

We wish to choose non-negative values for the variables Y_t, y_{it}, z_{it}, m_{it}

($i = 1, \ldots, N$ and $t = 1, \ldots$) so as to maximize W subject only to

$$\sum_{i=1}^{N} y_{it} = Y_t \text{ for all } t \tag{3}$$

$$Y_t \leqslant \bar{Y}_t \text{ for all } t \tag{4}$$

and

$$m_{it} = m_{i,t-1} - A_i + B_i z_{it} \text{ for all } i, t \tag{5}$$

Assume that D, the *variable* cost to the agency of surface water, is so small compared with demand and with costs of alternative supplies that it is never found optimal to use less than the full amount of surface water made available by the State. It is always the case that $Y_t = \bar{Y}_t$. For constraints 3 and 4 we can substitute the single constraint

$$\sum_{i=1}^{N} y_{it} = \bar{Y}_t \text{ for all } t \tag{6}$$

By successive substitution of $m_{i,t-1}$ in the expression for m_{it} we can also rewrite constraint 5 as

$$m_{it} = m_{i0} - tA_i + B_i \sum_{s=1}^{t} z_{is} \text{ for all } i, t \tag{7}$$

Differentiating the 'Lagrangian' L of our problem with respect to y_{it}

$$\frac{\partial L}{\partial y_{it}} = R^t[h_i(y_{it} + z_{it}) - f'_i(y_{it})] - \lambda_t \tag{8}$$

where λ_t is the multiplier, or 'shadow price,' associated with constraint 6. For y_{it} to be greater than zero, this derivative must be zero.

Differentiating with respect to z_{it}

$$\frac{\partial L}{\partial z_{it}} = R^t\left[h_i(y_{it} + z_{it}) - \frac{\partial}{\partial z} g_i(z_{it}, m_{i,t-1})\right] - B_i \sum_{s=t}^{\infty} \theta_{is} \tag{9}$$

where θ_{is} is the Lagrange multiplier for constraint 7. If $z_{it} > 0$, then $\partial L/\partial z_{it} = 0$.

Finally, the derivative of L with respect to m_{it} is

$$\frac{\partial L}{\partial m_{it}} = -R^{t+1} \frac{\partial}{\partial m} g_i(z_{i,t+1}, m_{it}) + \theta_{it} \tag{10}$$

which must be zero if m_{it} is at any but its minimal level.

Derivatives 8, 9, and 10 then allow us to recognize an optimal solution. If positive y_{it}, z_{it}, m_{it}, λ_t, and θ_{it} ($i = 1, \ldots, N$ and $t = 1, 2, \ldots$) can be found for which constraints 6 and 7 hold, and for which all the partial derivatives 8, 9, 10 are equal to zero, then these values maximize the welfare function W. This roughly correct statement ignores the possibility of certain 'corner' solutions, where one or more of the variables are equal to zero. In such a case, the respective derivative need not vanish; it suffices that it be $\leqslant 0$. The same revision holds if a variable is to be constrained from below by a value other than zero. For instance, suppose that m_{it} cannot have a value less than some number, say 100 feet. Either enter the constraint $m_{it} \geqslant 100$ explicitly into the problem or omit it, but check to see whether in the solution m_{it} is above or below 100. If it is above, the solution is correct; if it is below, m_{it} must be increased to 100 and it must be required that $\leqslant$ holds in constraint 10.

If the derivative 8 is to be zero

$$h_i(y_{it}+z_{it}) = f_i'(y_{it}) + R^{-t}\lambda_t \quad \text{for all} \quad i, t \tag{11}$$

The first term on the right is marginal distribution cost at current surface water use levels. The second term is a mathematical object used in testing for optimality. It is useful to interpret the multiplier λ_t as an 'internal' price (internal to the agency) that might be charged to districts by the agency for an acre-foot of surface water delivered in year t. A slight complication in this interpretation arises from the fact that λ_t is really the price charged *now* (i.e., at the beginning of the year 1 for water delivered in year t). λ_t is a *futures* price, whereas one ordinarily thinks in terms of *spot* prices. Replace the variable λ_t, the price of a year t surface water future, with p_t, the spot price in year t of surface water delivered in year t. Since we are assuming a world of certainty and a given discount factor R, it must be true that $R^t p_t = \lambda_t$. Substituting in 11

$$h_i(y_{it}+z_{it}) = f_i'(y_{it}) + p_t \tag{11'}$$

The rule then for a district decision-maker to follow would be: Buy from the agency that amount of surface water that equates the value of marginal product with the sum of marginal distribution cost and price to the agency. The rule for the agency is: Sell surface water to whatever district will pay the price, and set the price at that level that just clears the market.

For derivative 9 to equal zero

$$h_i(y_{it}+z_{it}) = \frac{\partial}{\partial z} g_i(z_{it}, m_{i,t-1}) + B_i R^{-t} \sum_{s=t}^{\infty} \theta_{is} \tag{12}$$

The first term on the right is the direct marginal cost of pumping at current levels of production and lift. To understand the second term, let us look at derivative 10. Equality there allows substitution for θ_{is} in (12), yielding

$$h_i(y_{it}+z_{it}) = \frac{\partial}{\partial z} g_i(z_{it}, m_{i,t-1}) + B_i \sum_{s=t}^{\infty} R^{s+1-t} \frac{\partial}{\partial m} g_i(z_{i,s+1}, m_{is}) \tag{12'}$$

The meaning of the second term is now clear: it is the sum of the discounted marginal effects of a change in z_{it} on future pumping costs via future pumping lifts. (In the case referred to earlier, when some m_{it} is constrained from below, $\leqslant$ can hold in (10) and hence $\geqslant$ in (12).)

For a district decision-maker the rule as regards groundwater would therefore be: Pump that amount of groundwater that equates value of marginal product with the sum of direct marginal pumping cost at current lift and discounted marginal effects of current pumping on future pumping costs.

Assuming that the demand curves and the cost functions have the simple linear form stated earlier, by substitution rules (11′) and (12′) become

$$u_i - v_i(y_{it} + z_{it}) = d_i + p_t \tag{11''}$$

$$u_i - v_i(y_{it} + z_{it}) = c_i m_{i,\,t-1} + B_i\left[\sum_{s=t}^{\infty} R^{s+1-t}(b_i + c_i z_{i,\,s+1})\right] \tag{12''}$$

The steady-state solution

The assumptions of constant demand and constant groundwater recharge mean that under an optimum water policy the system will, as time goes on, approach nearer and nearer to a steady-state operation. In this steady state, groundwater consumption, surface water consumption, and pumping lifts all remain the same from year to year. In this case, $y_{it} = y_i, z_{it} = z_t$, $m_{it} = m_i$, and $p_t = p$. Conditions 11″ and 12″ become

$$u_i - v_i(y_i + z_i) = d_i + p \tag{13}$$

and

$$u_i - v_i(y_i + z_i) = c_i m_i + (1/r)B_i\ (b_i + c_i z_i) \tag{14}$$

since

$$\sum_{t=1}^{\infty} R^t = \frac{R}{1-R} = \frac{1/(1+r)}{1-1/(1+r)} = \frac{1}{r}$$

Furthermore, if lift m_i is to remain constant, it must be the case that exactly the safe yield is pumped from the aquifer, that is, $z_i = A_i/B_i$.

Hence 14 can be rewritten

$$u_i - v_i(y_i + z_i) = c_i[m_i + (B_i b_i)/rc_i + A_i/r] \tag{14'}$$

If in the solution both $y_i > 0$ and $z > 0$, then equality must hold in both (13) and (14′). It follows that

$$p + d_i = c_i[m_i + (B_i b_i)/rc_i + A_i/r]$$

Solving for m_i, the only variable in this statement, we find

$$m_i = (p + d_i)/c_i - (B_i b_i)/rc_i - A_i/r \tag{15}$$

This is the level of the optimal lift in the steady state. The first term represents that value of lift at which *current* marginal pumping costs just equal marginal costs to the district of surface water. This would appear to be the optimum lift level to the district decision-maker, who was not aware of the effect on future pumping costs of today's pumping.

Taxes to equate social cost and private cost

The marginal costs discussed in the two preceding sections are *social* costs incurred by the master water service region. However, part of the marginal social cost of pumping does not enter into the individual farmer's calculation of marginal private cost. The part left out consists of two subparts, corresponding to the two rightmost terms in (14′).

The first is the present discounted value of all incremental fixed costs that follow from the increase in lift caused by pumping an additional acre-foot today. The second part is the present discounted value of all increases in direct pumping costs, the variable costs, that follow from the increase in lift caused by pumping an additional acre-foot today.

The individual farmer's choice of pumping intensity is determined only by changes in cost as a result of *his* pumping an additional acre-foot today at today's lift $c_i m_i$. If each farmer does not determine his annual groundwater withdrawals on the basis of the true marginal cost, ultimately pumping lifts and pumping costs will be too high and total social welfare, as defined, will not be maximized.

If a tax T_t just equal to the sum of these two ignored subparts is imposed on each acre-foot of groundwater pumped, marginal private cost will be precisely the same as marginal social cost, and the decisions resulting from each farmer's attempt to maximize his own profit will yield the desired social optimum. The rule, thus, for individual farmers is, in addition to rule 13

$$u_i + v_i(y_i + z_i) = c_i m_i + T_i \tag{16}$$

where

$$T_i = (1/r)[B_i b_i + A_i c_i] \tag{17}$$

or equivalently

$$T_i = c_i[(B_i b_i)/rc_i + A_i/r]$$

The last expression shows that the tax is just equal to c_t times the difference between optimal lift and that level to which the lift would go if farmers pumped groundwater until it competed (in *current* cost terms) with surface water.

Profit redistribution

The imposition of a pumping tax induces each farmer to act in the best interest of all. Note that the tax extracts from the farmer an amount just equal to the present value of the costs incurred by him if he were to act in his own best interest in the absence of the tax. It would appear, from any one farmer's point of view, hence from all, that there is little to commend the tax scheme. There is, however, a significant difference between the two situations. The future costs saved by the taxing scheme represent payment for additional resources necessary to pump water from a deeper groundwater table. All of these payments are losses to the system while the tax revenues remain in the system (the taxing agency). These revenues might be redistributed to the farmers, or they might be used to help to cover K.C.W.A.'s payments to the State if the market price for surface water is inadequate. In this latter case, the tax revenues are still not counted as social losses, because they would be making up for other kinds of taxes that would have to be imposed to cover the K.C.W.A. deficit.

If it is felt that the tax payments should be redistributed to the farmers, it is essential that the redistributive pattern adopted does not affect marginal groundwater pumping decisions.

Demand and cost estimates and the application of the model

Benefits to farmers

In the context of this steady-state model, the measurement of gross benefit to a farmer necessarily entails the estimation of a long-run demand function for water. Ideally, a price for water is posted and the farmer chooses those farm activities and selects that combination of factors, including the choice of a unique quantity of water, that maximizes his net revenue. The experiment is repeated, a different price is posted, and the farmer recalculates his most desirable factor-product combination, regarding land as his only fixed factor. The long-run water demand function is derived by repeating this experiment for all possible water prices.

A farmer's gross benefit will be taken to be the full area under the long-run demand curve. The measure of profit for a given water price is then the sum of the difference between the revenue from and the associated cost of the first annual acre-foot applied and subsequent acre-feet applied. A district annual water demand function is simply the aggregate of the individual water demand relations.

Two demand schedules have been estimated for each member district. In the first instance, linear water price-quantity relationships for potential member districts were fitted to the demand curves prepared by the California Department of Water Resources (*Calif. Dept. Water Resources*, 1963). The data underlying these relationships reflect the customary payment-capacity procedures followed by that agency.

The results of a recent farm budget study provide the basis for an alternative estimate of water demand for the nine probable agricultural water districts in the Kern County Water Agency (*Moore and Hedges*, 1963*a*, *b*).

In general, water demand schedules based on farm budget data are more elastic than the Department's demand estimates based on a crop budget analysis. This is not surprising, given the different estimating procedures of the two studies. The primary response to a change in water price is crop substitution according to the Department's procedure. The substitution of water for other inputs was not permitted. Moreover, a fixed level of water use was assumed for each crop. In contrast, the farm budget analysis permitted crop and factor substitution and the intensity of water use to vary in response to changes in the price of water.

Rarely, if ever, has there been an actual water demand study that fully satisfied the definition of a long-run demand curve. Thus, apart from unavoidable forecasting errors, further inaccuracies are introduced which may or may not be significant, depending on the comprehensiveness of the empirical demand analysis.

Estimates of water demand derived from the farm budget analysis (Case 1) are most consistent with the analytical requirements of the steady-state model, because a relatively greater set of critical farm enterprise decisions is regarded as variable.

Surface water cost

The annual cost to the K.C.W.A. for surface water from the State system has two components: a fixed and unavoidable unit cost for each acre-foot of the entitlement, whether used or not, and a variable transportation cost for each acre-foot of the annual entitlement actually delivered. Fixed costs play no role in the determination of the best use of water within the K.C.W.A. No decision by the K.C.W.A. could alter this part of the water bill.

For present purposes, variable surface water costs also play no significant allocative role, because a condition of demand in excess of the annual entitlement would exist for a price set at this level. The estimated annual fixed and variable cost of surface water, according to unpublished data, was estimated to be $16.7 million.

The cost of surface water to the farmer differs from the cost to K.C.W.A. because of local distribution costs. Annual district distribution costs will be of two parts, those that are fixed-interest on the fixed system, maintenance, and depreciation costs – and those that vary with the quantity of water transported. Since district distribution facilities have not been constructed, it is appropriate to regard all such costs as variable.

The cost of surface water to K.C.W.A. depends on the location of the diversion of the annual entitlement. During the planning period when the decision about diverting the entitlement is still open, certain costs are variable that later become fixed after this decision has been made. The intra-K.C.W.A. transportation cost of surface water is such a cost. For the allocative efficiency problem it is conceptually akin to the district distribution cost and is so treated in the present analysis. Let

$$d_i = d_i^* + d_i^{**}$$

where d_i^* is the unit cost of transporting water within the K.C.W.A., and d_i^{**} is the variable unit cost of the distribution system within district i.

Estimates of d_i^* and d_i^{**} in Table 7.1 are based on unpublished data from the *California Department of Water Resources* (1963).

Groundwater costs and parameters

Present knowledge regarding safe yields, water quality, overdraft, and other important dimensions of groundwater in the Kern County service area is incomplete. Nevertheless, estimates of annual safe yield are available for those districts overlying groundwater basins and are exhibited in Table 7.2.

The pumping lift of a particular district varies directly with the quantity of water withdrawn by pumps located in the district. A district's average pumping lift is also affected by water withdrawn from wells located outside a particular district if there is a hydrological interdependence between the two regions. Although such dependence may exist, insufficient information precluded its specification. To simplify the analysis further, it was assumed that the effects of pumping on groundwater tables are slow; this year's pumping has no effect until next year. A linear relationship between the change in lift and annual groundwater withdrawals was estimated from data prepared by *California Department of Water Resources* (1959, 1960*a*, 1960*b*) and *Boyle Engineering* (1963)

$$\Delta m = -A_i + B_i z_{it}$$

where Δm = change in lift. The estimated values of these parameters for each district are given in Table 7.2.

It will be recalled that the annual cost of pumping z acre-feet of water from one well in the K.C.W.A. region is given by

$$g(z, m) = a + bm + cmz$$

The parameters of this equation were estimated on the basis of linear relationships fitted to the empirical data published elsewhere (*Moore and Hedges*, 1962). To estimate the annual cost of pumping groundwater for a district, assume that one well pumps 1000 acre-feet annually. Thus the annual cost of pumping groundwater for a member district is

$$g_i(z_{it}, m) = a_i + b_i m + c_i m z_{it}$$

where $a_i = az_{it}/1000$; $b_i = bz_{it}/1000$; and $c_i = c$ (see Table 7.2).

The steady-state calculation

Given estimates for the parameters, a steady-state solution is readily found. From (13)

$$y_i = [(p + d_i - u_i)/-v_i] - z_i \qquad (18)$$

so that

$$\partial/\partial p(\sum y_i) = -\sum 1/v_i$$

Table 7.1 *Estimated Annual Water Demand and Distribution Cost Parameters for K.C.W.A. Member Districts*

	Estimated Number of Farms	Case 1: Farm Budget Survey Data		Case 2: Crop Survey Data		Local Distribution Cost: Capital Cost per acre-foot	Local Distribution Cost: Variable Cost per acre-foot	Local Distribution Cost: Transportation Cost per acre-foot
		u_i	v_i	u_i	v_i	d_i^{**}		d_i^*
Belridge W.S.D.	102	42.5	0.0001178	50.0	0.0002174	2	5	0.75
Lost Hills W.D.	73	42.5	0.0001663	42.5	0.0003864	1	3	0.00
Rosedale-Rio Bravo W.S.D.	38	42.5	0.0003194	50.0	0.0005555	3	4	1.70
Semitropic W.S.D.	93	42.5	0.0001305	45.0	0.0001500	4	2	1.20
West Kern W.D.	17	42.5	0.0007142	50.0	0.0001111	4	6	2.00
Antelope Plain W.D.	37	42.5	0.0003282	45.0	0.0004285	2	5	5.70
Wheeler Ridge – Maricopa W.S.D.								
No. 1	90	42.5	0.0001349	48.3	0.0001667	2	5	5.80
No. 2	45	42.5	0.0002698	4.05	0.0004285	3	4	11.25
Kern River Delta and Others	325	42.5	0.0003736	42.5[1]	0.0003736[1]	2	4	1.50

[1] No data provided in the original sources. It is therefore assumed to be equal to Case 1 estimate.

Table 7.2 *District Groundwater Parameters*

	Annual Safe Yield A_i/B_i, acre-feet	Pumping Lift M_{io}, ft	A_i, ft	B_i, ft/million acre-feet	a_i, \$	b_i, \$/ft	c_i, \$/acre-feet
Rosedale-Rio Bravo W.S.D.	3,300	218	0.62	189.0	1,320	42.9	0.025
Semitropic W.S.D.	63,000	260	3.99	63.3	25,200	819.0	0.025
West Kern W.D.	25,200	165	4.00	160.0	10,080	327.6	0.025
Wheeler Ridge – Maricopa W.S.D. 2	22,000	625	3.78	172.0	8,800	286.0	0.025
Kern River Delta and Others	347,000	205	18.50	53.0	138,800	4511.0	0.025

If surface water is priced at zero a total amount $\Sigma[u_i - d_i)/v_i - z_i]$ will be demanded. Hence the total quantity demanded at price p will be

$$\sum[(u_i - d_i)/v_i - z_i] - p\sum(1/v_i)$$

If this demand is to be equal to the supply $\bar{Y}$ it must be true that

$$p = \{\sum[(u_i - d_i)/(v_i - z_i)] - \bar{Y}\}/[\sum(1'/v_i) \qquad (19)$$

The market clearing price is calculated by (19) with the safe yield quantity A_i/B_i substituted for z_i. The individual y_i are then found by plugging p into (18). The remaining variables, the m_i, are then found from (15). Steady-state values for the y_i, p_i, m_i for the two alternative water demand estimates are presented in Table 7.3.

The use of the Department's steeper sloped district demand functions results in a relatively lower equilibrium p, consequently relatively smaller (numerically) m_i's. Different district demand functions result in differences that are small relative to the total surface water allocation, but of course absolute differences do exist. For example, Semitropic W.S.D. would take 16,000 acre-feet more per year if the Case 2 demand functions were the more accurate descriptions of actual future-water demand.

The value for the optimal lift in each district is given in Table 7.4. In the absence of a pump tax under Case 1 conditions, pumping lifts would vary between 708 and 1150 feet, depending on the particular district. When the pumping tax is imposed the socially optimum lift is lower, varying between 251 feet and 1054 feet.

The lift effect of the tax is directly related to the 'socialness' of the groundwater basin. The greater the annual safe yield of a basin is or the more numerous the pumping units are, the higher is the aggregated social cost of individual pumping. The difference in lift with and without the tax is about fifteen feet for Rosedale-Rio Bravo W.S.D., whose estimated safe yield equals 3300 acre-feet, whereas the difference is about 468 feet for the Kern River Delta region, whose estimated annual safe yield is 347,000 acre-feet.

The difference between the optimum lift for a district under Case 1 and Case 2 water demand conditions depends on the cost of surface water at the farm headgate. Thus, when the allocative efficiency price is \$3.85 per acre-foot greater for each district, Case 1 versus Case 2, the optimum lift in each district is 146 feet greater. From the foregoing remarks it follows that a district's total tax payment will be high or low, depending on the same yield of the groundwater basin it overlies. For Rosedale-Rio Bravo W.S.D. the total pumping tax would be \$1299; for the Kern River Delta region it is over \$4 million annually.

Given a maximum annual surface water entitlement, the solution values for y_i and p that bring about allocative efficiency do not guarantee that annual revenue will equal K.C.W.A.'s annual obligation. This condition

Table 7.3 *District Water Deliveries, Prices, and Lifts under Steady-State Conditions*

	Case 1 $p = \$10.50$			Case 2 $p = \$6.85$			Kern County Water Agency[1]		
	Annual Delivery	Annual Charge	Lift	Annual Delivery	Annual Charge	Lift	Annual Delivery	Annual Charge	Lift
	y_i, thousand acre-feet	$p + d_i^*$ \$/acre-feet	m_i, ft	y_i, thousand acre-feet	$p + d_i^*$, \$/acre-feet	m_i, ft	y_i, thousand acre-feet	$p + d_i^*$, \$/acre-feet	m_i, ft
Belridge W.S.D.	206	11.25	–	163	7.60	–	157	15.80	–
Lost Hills W.D.	168	10.50	–	82	6.85	–	95	15.20	–
Rosedale-Rio Bravo W.S.D.	70	12.20	752	59	8.55	606	60	12.00	744
Semitropic W.S.D.	127	11.70	607	143	8.05	461	171	11.10	583
West Kern County W.D.	3	12.50	799	3	8.85	652	30	17.30	990
Antelope Plain W.D.	59	16.20	–	59	12.55	–	60	15.00	–
Wheeler Ridge–Maricopa W.S.D.									
No. 1	142	16.30	–	172	12.65	–	151	17.30	–
No. 2	29	21.75	1054	24	18.10	908	84	24.00	1144
Kern River Delta and Others	309	12.00	251	406	8.35	105	150	12.00	251
Total	1111			1111			958		

Note: Individual entries may not sum to the total because of roundling error.
[1] *Leeds, Hill and Jewett, Inc.*, 1963.

Table 7.4 *District Lift Level and Tax Rate under Alternative Price Policies and Demand Specifications*

					Case 1		*Case 2*		*K.C.W.A.*	
	$(B_i b_i)rci$ *ft*	A_i/r, *ft*	T_i, *\$/acre-feet*	$T_i z_i$, *hundred dollars*	$(p+d_i)/c_i$, *ft*	m_i, *ft*	$(p+d_i)/c_i$, *ft*	m_i, *ft*	$(p+d_i)/c_i$, *ft*	m_i, *ft*
Rosedale-Rio Bravo W.S.D.	5	10	0.39	13	768	752	622	606	760	744
Semitropic W.S.D.	35	66	2.53	1,593	708	607	562	461	681	583
West Kern County W.D.	35	67	2.54	640	900	790	754	652	1092	990
Wheeler Ridge–Maricopa W.S.D.	33	63	2.40	527	1150	1054	1004	908	1240	1144
Kern River Delta and Others	160	308	11.72	40,670	720	251	574	105	720	251
Total				43,443						

would be met only if K.C.W.A. had originally contracted for an efficient quantity of surface water. Table 7.5 indicates that under either set of demand functions the optimum pricing policy results in an annual deficit. The pumping tax could (but not necessarily should) be used to meet the deficit. This policy could be justified if it was believed that beneficiaries should pay for the water and if it could be shown that the secondary beneficiaries received no gains from water importation that were not offset by equal costs. If the annual obligation still exceeded revenue the problem would become one of designing optimum lump sum charges, perhaps through an assessment tax on unimproved property. This issue is separate and is perhaps best solved by contracting for an optimum quantity of water in the first instance.

Table 7.5 *Annual Repayment Obligation and Sources of Revenue under Alternative Pricing Policies*

	Socially Optimum Pricing Policy		
	Case 1 Demand	*Case 2 Demand million dollars*	*K.C.W.A. Pricing and Tax Policy*
Total Annual Repayment Obligation	16.664	16.664	17.496
Total Annual Revenues from Water Charges	14.058	10.236	14.496
Deficit	2.606	6.428	3.000
Total Annual Pumping Tax Revenue	4.344	4.344	–
Total Annual Revenue from Assessments	–	–	3.000

In 1962, the Board of the K.C.W.A. searched for a pricing policy that would alleviate overdraft conditions in the groundwater basin and would ensure that its member districts contracted for an annual 1.1 million acre-feet, an amount for which the K.C.W.A. had contracted with the State of California (*Public Hearings*, 1964). To these ends it adopted a discriminatory pricing system, charging a lower price for surface water to districts without groundwater. Water charges were escalated through time. In addition, a property tax will return about $3 million annually. This pricing policy does not alone ensure the stabilization of groundwater supplies. Only if an irrigator were to act voluntarily against his own self-interest would the stabilization goal be achieved, because no strictures prevent prospective irrigators from pumping at overdraft intensities.

The optimum pricing policy would ensure that only the safe yield was actually withdrawn from any given groundwater basin; hence the stability of the groundwater supply is ensured. Moreover, if a pumping tax is not imposed, the K.C.W.A. region will lose an estimated $4.344 million annually, less the value added created by only those firms located within this region whose well drilling, maintenance, and operation activities would be expanded.

If the optimum pricing policy is to be of general use, several conditions must be met. First, there is an institutional requirement. A district that wishes to manage efficiently surface and groundwater supplies must possess a legal right to levy a pumping tax. A recent court decision in California upholds the right of agencies such as the K.C.W.A. to levy a pumping tax on some or all of its members (Orange County Water District v. Farnsworth). Not all public water districts have taxing powers broad enough to make a pumping tax a feasible policy option.

Second, in an actual problem setting, estimation must be feasible. Assumptions about the linearity of relationships are convenient, but the physical and economic setting may not be so benign. It is neither difficult nor expensive to perform a sensitivity analysis to test whether either this assumption or error of estimation has a significant effect on the solution values of the variables. If it is clear, for example, that nonlinear demand functions are in order, the steady state model is not vitiated, but the new algorithm would be more complicated and the solution would be reached most efficiently with the aid of a computer.

Acknowledgements

The research of the first author was supported in part by a grant from the Ford Foundation to the Graduate School of Business Administration, administered through the Center for Research in Management Science. Both authors wish to record their indebtedness for many profitable discussions to Neil Houston and Julius Margolis.

References

Boyle Engineering Company (1975), engineering and economic report on imported water supply project for Rosedale-Rio Bravo water storate district.

California Department of Water Resources (1959), report on proposed Rosedale-Rio Bravo water storage district.

California Department of Water Resources (1960), office report: supplement to information and data on proposed programme for planning and constructing state water facilities.

California Department of Water Resources (1963), feasibility of serving the Kern County Water Agency from the State Water Project.

Hedges, T. R. and Moore, C. V. (1962), *Economics of On-Farm Irrigation Water*

Availability and Costs and Related Farm Adjustments, Giannini Foundation Research Report no. 257, University of California.

Leeds, Hill and Jowett Inc. (1963), letter to Board of Directors, Kern County Water Agency.

Moore, C. V. and Hedges, T. R. (1962), *Some Characteristics of Farm Irrigation Water Supplies in the San Joaquin Valley*, Giannini Foundation Report no. 258, University of California.

Orange County Water District v. Farnsworth, 138 Ca. App. 2nd 518, 1956.

Public hearing on proposed zone(s) of benefit in the San Joaquin Valley portion of Kern County. Transcript of proceedings at the meeting of the Kern County Water Agency held in Bakersfield, California, 13 July, 9 September, 10 September, 12 October, 21 October, 22 October 1964.

8

Atmospheric Corrosion of Materials

V. Kucera, J. Ghullman and P. Swartlang

INTRODUCTION

Corrosion damage from exposure to air pollutants is probably one of the best studied fields in environmental cost-benefit analysis. Economists and engineers have developed several different approaches to measuring this damage. The one reported here has the virtues of being recent and very simple.

Corrosion damage is one component of the wider concept of productivity losses. In principle, such losses should be measured as the change in consumer surpluses and producer surpluses caused by exposure to pollution. However, in many cases it may be reasonable to assume that product prices are not affected by the pollution and a study of the effects on producer surpluses would be sufficient. In fact, most studies (including the present one) have made this assumption implicitly. If the assumption is not valid, which may be the case when all plants within an industry are affected, serious bias is introduced. For the damage considered in this case study, the assumption of constant prices seems to be valid.

The study we have chosen to include is a part of an O.E.C.D. study on sulphur oxide emissions in Northern and Western Europe.[1] The chapter on corrosion is based on an analysis at the Swedish Corrosion Institute. The O.E.C.D. study tries to make a complete cost-benefit analysis of sulphur emissions, and compares different scenarios with different emissions of sulphur dioxide. The control cost for reducing emissions in the different countries for the different scenarios are estimated by quite conventional but probably effective calculations on the cost of buying low sulphur fuels, the cost of desulphurization of fuels and stack gases etc. By using the studies carried out in O.E.C.D. on the long range dispersion of air pollutants, it has been possible to predict the deposition of sulphates in the various countries for the different scenarios. By using standard Gaussian plume models for the local dispersion of sulphur dioxide, it was possible to predict ambient ground level concentrations of SO_2 in various places within the region. Four different types of damage from sulphur were identified and quantified. These types were atmospheric corrosion of materials, agricultural crop damage, health effects and acidification of waters. To this the study adds certain intangibles, but no attempt even to quantify the physical size of the intangible damage was made.

Studies of corrosion damage are usually divided into two stages. In the first stage a dose-damage relationship is estimated which can be used to predict the amount of corrosion at different exposures to the airpollutant. The second stage contains an attempt to assess the monetary value of this corrosion damage. The O.E.C.D. study follows this scheme. It starts out by identifying the kinds of materials that are corroded from exposure to sulphur dioxide and for each of these materials a dose-damage relationship is estimated by simple regression analysis.

By applying the estimated dose-damage functions to the chosen scenarios the amounts of the different materials that are corroded can be predicted and by valuing these amounts by the present materials prices, O.E.C.D. obtains a monetary estimate of the corrosion damage. One can, however, raise very strong criticism against this procedure.

The way O.E.C.D. has chosen to measure the damage simply means that one calculates the cost of now replacing the corroded material. In reality, corrosion means that the lifetime of a material is shortened, so that the replacement must be made earlier than otherwise. Assume that the remaining lifetime of a material is ten years in the absence of pollution, but that pollution has necessitated its replacement after just two years (instead of ten) by a new substitute material which costs 100 units more, the present value of the replacement cost is:

$$\frac{a+100}{(1+r)^2}$$

where a is the cost of the old material and r is the interest rate. We assume that the new material is not affected by pollution, otherwise we should have considered future replacements. If the environment were not polluted, the present value of the replacement cost would have been:

$$\frac{a}{(1+r)^{10}}$$

The damage cost C is thus given by:

$$C=\frac{a+100}{(1+r)^2}-\frac{a}{(1+r)^{10}}$$

The approach taken by O.E.C.D. implicitly implies that in the absence of pollution, the materials would have an infinite life so that the second term in the expression for the damage cost can be neglected and that the interest rate is zero. Both these assumptions imply that the damage cost is biased upward in the O.E.C.D. calculations.

CASE STUDY

Introduction

The rate of corrosion of materials is determined by a number of factors both natural and man-made, of which humidity, temperature and atmospheric pollution are the most important. For metallic materials, the rate of corrosion in rural areas due to natural (i.e. climatic) factors are fairly similar for the whole temperate climatic zone of Europe, except in coastal areas where chlorides play an important role. Thus, it seems that any differences in corrosion rate can be assumed to be caused by air pollution.

The most important man-made pollutants when considering corrosion of metals are sulphur compounds, although the relative importance of the different sulphur compounds is not yet clear. Considerable work has been done in this field (for example, by Kucera *et al.*) and good data exist for the corrosive effect of dry deposition of sulphur dioxide (SO_2). For particulate sulphates (via dry deposition), no good damage function exists but, in the O.E.C.D. Programme on Long Range Transport of Air Pollutants, it was found that deposition takes place at a much slower rate than for SO_2 and the air concentrations are also lower. It is recognized that the effect of SO_4 in rain (via wet deposition) can probably be disregarded since rain has both a wetting and corrosive effect and a washing, therefore protective, effect.

For these reasons, this study only deals with the corrosive effects of SO_2. This does, of course, imply a certain simplification but it is believed that this approach reflects the major influence of different levels of sulphur pollutants on the damage cost of materials included in this study.

The effect of SO_2 on a number of materials is described and an attempt is made to assess the economic importance of this damage for particular materials. The economic importance of such damage is, of course, of major interest but it is realized that any reliable assessment is difficult. This analysis has been previously undertaken in two major studies.

A wide range of materials were considered at the outset of the study but, for some, only a qualitative description of the effects of SO_2 is given either because the quantitative data is not available, or because no major corrosion costs exist or because the material is of minor economic importance (in the present study). A quantitative assessment is made of the effects of corrosion on galvanized steel and paint coatings on steel and galvanized steel.

Materials excluded from cost assessment

1 *Carbon steel* is greatly affected by SO_2, thus it is generally surface-coated; if not, as for example in rails and wheels of railway carriages,

the size of the pieces is such that corrosion during their lifetime is of relative minor importance;

2 *Copper materials* are less affected by SO_2 and the damage is not sufficient to shorten the lifetime of any construction;

3 *Aluminium materials* have good resistance to SO_2;

4 *Nickel and nickel-plated steel* corrode at a high rate in SO_2 polluted atmosphere but their use is very restricted;

5 *Stainless steel* is resistant to SO_2 damage;

6 *Sandstone and limestone* are severely affected by SO_2 but no reliable dose-response relationship has been established, and it is difficult to assign an economic value to the damage, particularly since most of the damage is done to works of art whose cultural value is difficult to express in monetary terms, and this value is also reduced by the fact of being restored. It is, however, possible to use renovation and repair costs as a surrogate for cultural value. These aspects will be described in more detail later.

Materials included in cost assessment

1 *Zinc and galvanized steel* corrode at a rate related to the atmospheric SO_2 concentration (5–8).

2 *Paint coatings on steel and galvanized steel* are affected by SO_2 in terms of the length of life although in one study it was found that no significant relationship existed in rural and moderately polluted atmospheres.

Thus, it was decided to attempt a cost assessment of the corrosion damage of these materials caused by SO_2 pollution in O.E.C.D. Europe.

Damage functions

Zinc and galvanized steel

Figure 8.1 shows the results of four separate studies of the relationship between corrosion rate and SO_2 concentration from which that proposed by Hudson and Stanners was chosen because it was performed in the European temperate climate zone and was close to the mean of the four studies.

Paint coatings

A linear relationship between the length of life of paint coatings on zinc and steel and SO_2 concentration based on data given by Fink *et al.* was chosen for this study (Figure 8.2).

Length of life of materials

Calculation of the corrosion rate of zinc (i.e. on galvanized materials) as a function of atmospheric SO_2 is based on Hudson and Stanners' data

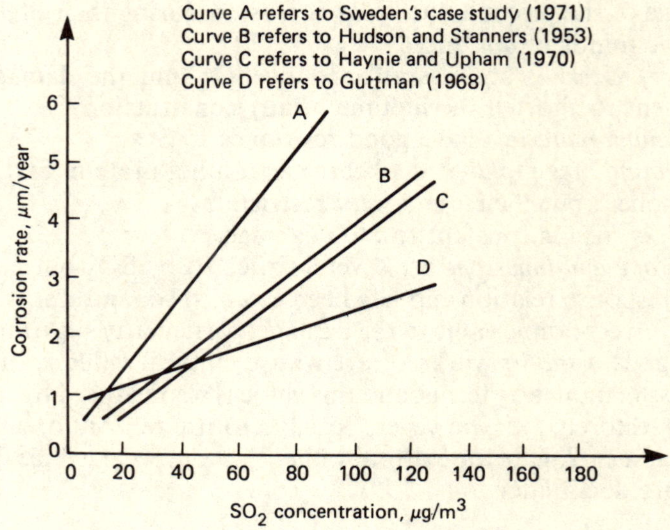

Figure 8.1 *Corrosion Rate of Zinc as a Function of the SO_2 Concentration in the Atmosphere*

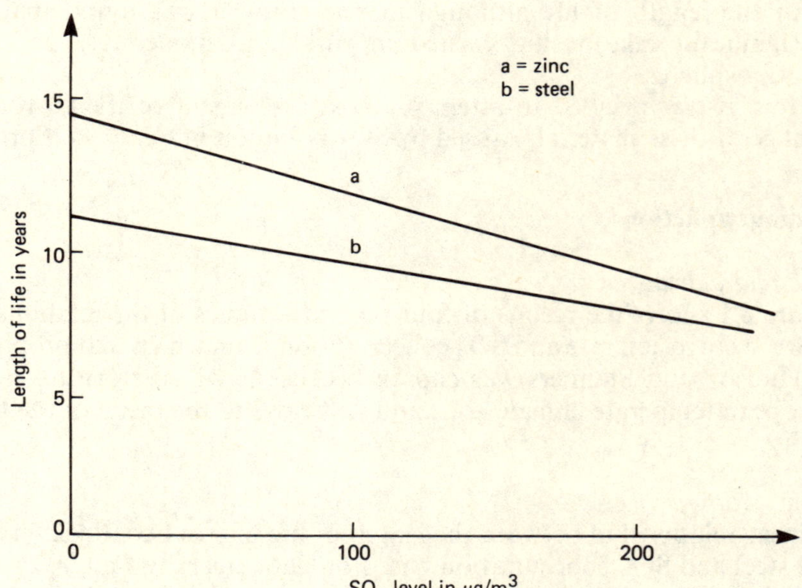

Figure 8.2 *Length of Life of Paint on Zinc and on Steel as a Function of the SO_2 Concentration in the Atmosphere*

Source: Based on results given by Fink *et al.*, 1971.

(Figure 8.1 Curve B). The length of life of paint on carbon steel and galvanized steel is calculated from Fink *et al.*'s data on time between repaintings. Details of the calculation are given in Appendix 8A but, in summary, the lengths of life (or corrosion rate) of paint or of zinc coatings are given by the following formulae:

No. of years for painted carbon steel =
$11.6 - 0.016 \times SO_2$ (in $\mu g/m^3$)
No. of years for painted galvanized steel =
$15.3 - 0.031 \times SO_2$ (in $\mu g/m^3$)
No. of years before painting of galvanized plate:

$$\frac{142}{2.46 + 0.204 \times SO_2 \text{ (in } \mu g/m^3)}$$

To illustrate these equations, the data for one of the largest cities give 1985 air quality varying from 95 $\mu g/m^3$ SO_2 under Case I to 62 $\mu g/m^3$ SO_2 Case II which corresponds to an increased lifetime of:

0.5 year for painted carbon steel;
1.0 year for painted galvanized steel;
2.9 years for unpainted galvanized steel.

Use of materials
For the purposes of this study, certain assumptions were made about the methods of application and maintenance procedures for these materials. These assumptions were chosen to reflect the practical use of these materials as closely as possible which implies the economically optimal use. The major assumptions for galvanized materials were that they were unpainted on initial exposure and that sheet and profile were to be painted and wire was to be replaced after some corrosion. For painted steel, it was assumed that time between repaintings was related to SO_2 concentrations, and that repainting took place at the economically optimal time. For all materials, it was assumed that they were used in proportion to the population (see Appendix 8B).

Cost estimates

Cost of corrosion and corrosion protection
The total cost of corrosion and corrosion protection (though not, of course, attributable to sulphur pollution alone) is a sum of the costs of painting carbon steel, corrosion of galvanized sheet, profile and wire and painting of galvanized sheet and profile. The following cost estimates based on 1979 Swedish prices for surface treatment (net of sales tax, but including social benefit charges) include the basic material cost for

galvanized wire only:

Galvanized sheet	0.6 $/m^2
Galvanized profile	5.0 $/m^2
Galvanized wire	4.0 $/m^2
Painted steel and galvanized materials	11.4 $/m^2

The length of life and costs have been calculated for each grid square in the network, and the total cost for each country is the sum of costs from all the grid squares covering the country. These calculations are detailed in Appendix 8C. Here it is sufficient to give the cost equation for a grid square for each material type:

Cost of painting carbon steel:

$$\frac{\text{Amount of painted steel (m}^2) \times \text{cost of painting (\$/m}^2)}{\text{length of life (years)}}$$

Cost of corrosion of galvanized wire per year:

$$\frac{\text{Amount of wire (m}^2) \times \text{cost of wire (\$/m}^2)}{\text{length of life (years)}}$$

Because galvanized sheet and profile are considered to exist in two modes namely 'zinc' and 'painted' (they start in the 'zinc mode' and after some corrosion has taken place they enter the 'painted mode') two separate equations are required, as follows:

Cost of corrosion of material in the zinc mode:

$$\frac{\text{Amount of material (m}^2) \times \text{cost of galvanizing (\$/m}^2)}{\text{length of life of galvanizing (years)}}$$

Cost of painting on galvanized steel:

$$\frac{\text{Amount of material in painted mode (m}^2) \times \text{cost of painting (\$/m}^2)}{\text{length of life of paint (years)}}$$

Amounts of material in use

To obtain national figures for the per capita consumption of paint per year and for the consumption of zinc for galvanized sheet profile and wire, the O.E.C.D. Annual Statistics for the chemical and non-ferrous metal industries were used. It is realized that these figures contribute some uncertainty to the calculation. This uncertainty is particularly relevant for zinc consumption since the statistics are available for the amount used for galvanizing in each country but they do not specify whether the galvanized material will be used in the country or exported. This is important in relation to the figures for smaller countries since some have a large industry and thus are exporters of galvanized material, while others import all such materials. For these reasons, the statistics for the United Kingdom, France and Germany were used to calculate an average per capita consumption for the smaller countries. In relation to paint, the per capita annual consumption is available for all countries but Switzerland, so the figure for Switzerland was taken to be equal to that of France which is close to the average (Appendix 8D).

Results

Costs of corrosion and corrosion protection have been calculated for each country using the three SO_2 emission scenarios. These are given in Tables 8.4 a–k.

The costs for all countries considered have been compiled in Tables 8.1 and 8.2 where it is shown that the difference in damage costs between Case I and II equals \$448 million (\$2.0 per capita), and between Case I and III equals \$964 million (\$4.3 per capita).

It should be mentioned that the costs calculated for the 1974 SO_2 levels are also based on 1985 materials usage and so are directly comparable to 1985 SO_2 levels. A comparison of the 1974 level with the level of Case III shows a reduction of \$1,389 million/year (\$6.1 per capita). Thus, the figures for reduction of costs per capita are comparable with those obtained in previous studies.

Limitation of the method

This method of cost calculation for corrosion and corrosion damage has one major advantage which is the availability of most of the input data. However, the accuracy of data on SO_2 concentrations in grid squares is questionable since those concentrations used are averages for urban areas within each grid square; within many grid squares there are areas with higher SO_2 concentrations and a much higher than average density of corroding materials. Because such situations are not covered in the calculations, there will be a degree of underestimation of costs for those grid squares containing areas with high SO_2 levels. The degree of underestimation could only be determined if a narrower grid square network were used.

One main source of error is in the amount of materials in use, and, since the cost of corrosion is directly related to this, it means that the cost estimate is subject to the same relative error as that in the amount of materials plus the systematic error in the method itself.

Table 8.1 *Estimated Costs of Corrosion and Corrosion Protection in some European O.E.C.D. Countries in 1985 (millions of U.S. dollars per year)*

SO – level / Country	Costs related to (galvanized material) (galvanizing and repainting)				Costs related to painting of Carbon Steel				Total Costs			
		1985				1985				1985		
	1974	*I*	*II*	*III*	*1974*	*I*	*II*	*III*	*1974*	*I*	*II*	*III*
Australia	38	44	40	35	443	445	443	442	481	489	483	477
Δ		–	4	9		–	2	3		–	6	12
Belgium and Luxemburg	94	86	72	50	712	707	701	692	805	793	773	742
Δ		–	14	36		–	6	15		–	20	51
Denmark	47	40	33	24	415	411	408	404	462	451	441	428
Δ		–	7	16		–	3	7		–	10	23
Finland	15	16	15	12	336	336	335	333	352	352	350	345
Δ		–	1	4		–	1	3		–	2	7
France	423	359	263	221	3 893	3 864	3 837	3 762	4 316	4 223	3 100	3 983
Δ		–	96	138		–	27	102		–	123	240

Netherlands	93	114	98	63	780	788	782	770	873	902	880	833
Δ		–	16	51		–	6	18		–	22	69
Norway	11	10	10	9	301	300	300	300	312	310	310	309
Δ		–	–	1		–	–	–		–	–	1
Sweden	30	27	23	21	747	747	745	743	779	774	768	764
Δ		–	4	6		–	2	4		–	6	10
Switzerland	25	24	21	20	469	469	467	466	494	493	488	486
Δ		–	3	4		–	2	3		–	5	7
United Kingdom	819	641	556	416	3 512	3 440	3 406	3 354	4 331	4 081	3 962	3 770
Δ		–	85	225		–	34	86		–	119	311
Western Germany	542	494	408	348	3 512	6 460	6 411	6 374	7 042	6 954	6 819	6 722
Δ		–	86	146		–	49	86		–	135	232
Total	2 136	1 855	1 539	1 219	18 110	17 967	17 835	17 639	20 247	19 822	19 374	18 858
Δ		–	316	636		–	132	328		–	448	864

Notes: The costs for the 1974 SO_2 levels are based on 1985 use of materials and are thus directly comparable to the 1985 SO_2 pollution alternatives. All figures refers to the year 1985 and are based on Swedish prices for 1979. The influence of SO_2 is obtained by comparing the pollution alternatives given. The differences in costs between Case I and Cases II and III in 1985 are specified and designated asΔ.

Table 8.2 *Cost Estimates* (1974 met year) 10^6 \$ per year

	Case I–II	*Case I–III*	*Case I–II in % of Total Cost for Corrosion and Corrosion Protection*
Austria	6	12	1.2
Belgium†Luxemburg	20	51	2.5
Denmark	10	23	2.2
Finland	2	7	0.6
France	123	240	2.9
Germany	135	232	1.9
Netherlands	22	69	2.4
Norway	0.4	1	0.1
Sweden	6	10	0.7
Switzerland	5	7	1.0
United Kingdom	119	311	2.9
Total	448	964	2.3
Total \$ per capita	2.0	4.3	

Other sources of error are the exclusion of materials older than 25 years, no consideration of withdrawal of materials from use, the exclusion of certain materials, and the assumption of constant production of corroding materials between 1975 and 1985.

Despite these limitations, it is concluded that the accuracy of these cost estimates is high compared to that in other damage areas, and the dose-response relationship is well supported by other studies.

Sandstone and limestone

As mentioned earlier, it is felt that these materials deserve special mention since there are a number of specific problems related to the corrosion damage of public monuments and other works of art.

Sandstone and limestone were, in the past, often used as building materials, especially in large constructions like churches and government buildings. They were also used for decorative purposes on entire buildings, portals, facades and for ornamentation. Such decoration is often of cultural interest and, as such, has a substantial cultural value.

Sulphur dioxide in the atmosphere affects limestone and sandstone containing calcium carbonate as a binder. When sulphur compounds are absorbed on these surfaces, a series of reactions begins and gypsum (calcium sulphate) is the end-product. Gypsum, which is more soluble than calcium carbonate, is then washed away by rain.

Another factor that can cause deterioration of sandstone and limestone is the increase in volume that takes place when a unit of calcium carbonate reacts to form one unit of gypsum since the latter has a volume 2.1 times that of the corresponding amount of calcium carbonate. Temperature variation and frost can also contribute to the deterioration of limestone and sandstone.

Some attempts have been made to establish a dose-response relationship between SO_2 concentration and corrosion of sandstone, but because sandstone and limestone of different origin can be affected differently by sulphur pollutants no reliable dose-response relationship has yet been established.

Attempts have also been made to estimate the costs of restoring affected objects and buildings; figures of several hundred thousand dollars have been suggested even for single small objects. Estimation of the total economic losses seems to be difficult because no regional inventories of the materials used have been taken. Moreover, any restoration implies a decrease in originality of the objects and therefore a decrease in cultural value, a loss that cannot be estimated in economic terms.

Experts consulted

In addition to Messrs V. Kucera, J. Ghullman and P. Swartlang (Swedish Corrosion Institute, Stockholm), whose work served as a basis for drafting this chapter, the following experts were also consulted by the O.E.C.D. Secretariat through the organization of workshops or otherwise:

Mr. Michael Benarie, I.R.C.H.A., Vert-le-Petit, France.

Mr. Richard Livingston, Environmental Protection Agency, Washington D.C., U.S.A.

Dr. Lucat, Director of Museum, Essan, Germany.

Appendix 8A
Length of life of materials

Galvanized materials

Using data for the corrosion rate of zinc published by Hudson and Stanners, and Guttman's method, to convert SO_2 concentrations recorded by the PbO_2 candle technique into $\mu g/m^3$, the observed corrosion rate K' has been fitted to a straight line in terms of SO_2 concentration by the method of least squares. The equation obtained is:

$$K' = 0.204 \times SO_2 + 2.46 \tag{1}$$

where K' is given in g/m^2 per year and the SO_2 concentration of the air is given in $\mu g/m^3$. The time t (years) needed for 10 m zinc ($71\, g/m^2$) to corrode can then be calculated from the following equation (Figure 8.A.1):

$$t = \frac{71}{0.204 \times SO_2 + 2.46} \tag{2}$$

It is difficult to calculate a confidence interval for equation (2) mainly because the scatter around the relations in (1) from which (2) is derived has two sources:

1 the scatter around the straight line (1);
2 the scatter around the assumed linear relationship between the SO_2 content of the air and the sulphur deposition on PbO_2 candles.

The scatter found around line (1) is very small; the correlation coefficient obtained is 0.99996 which is equivalent to a scatter of only a few per cent in estimated corrosion rate.

Guttman gives some information about the scatter around the relationship between SO_2 concentration in air and sulphur deposition on PbO_2 candles. This information, together with an estimation of scatter around the straight line (1), should allow it to be assumed that the value for length of life calculated from equation (1) is within about 20 per cent of the correct value.

Painted carbon steel and painted galvanized steel

Using Fink *et al.*'s data for time between repaintings the lengths of life of paint on carbon steel and on galvanized steel have been calculated by linear regression as functions of the atmospheric SO_2 concentrations (see Figures 8.2 and 8.3). The equations obtained are:

$$\text{Painted carbon steel} \quad -L = 11.6 - (0.016\, SO_2) \tag{3}$$

$$\text{Painted galvanized steel} \quad -L = 15.3 - (0.031\, SO_2) \tag{4}$$

where the SO_2 concentration is in $\mu g/m^3$ and L is the length of life in years. The error in the estimated lengths of life is probably less than two years. If the SO_2 concentration of the air is within the range 10–350 $\mu g/m^3$, (and probably also for lower concentrations), these equations should be appropriate in the temperate climatic zone.

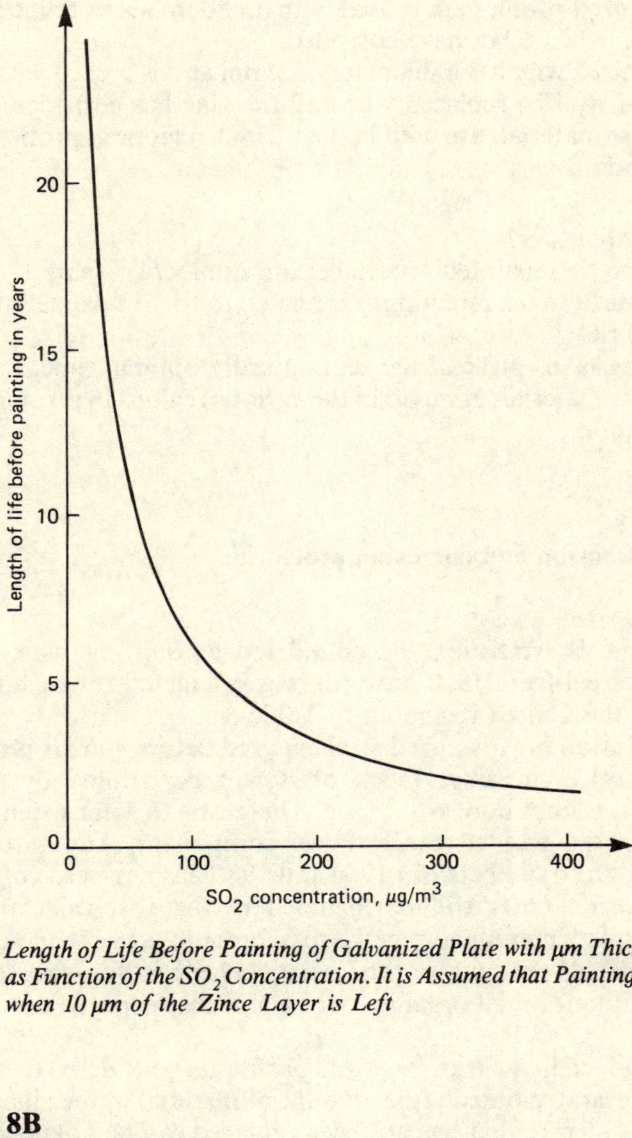

Figure 8.3 *Length of Life Before Painting of Galvanized Plate with μm Thick Zinc Layer as Function of the SO_2 Concentration. It is Assumed that Painting Takes Place when 10 μm of the Zince Layer is Left*

Appendix 8B
Use of materials

The following assumptions have been made about the use of materials:

Galvanized steel

1 Galvanized materials to be considered are initially exposed unpainted;
2 Galvanized sheet is coated with a 30 m layer of zinc and will be painted when 20 m have corroded away;

3 Galvanized profiles are coated with an 80 m layer of zinc and will be painted when 60 m have corroded;
4 Galvanized wire has a diameter of 3 mm and is coated with 30 m zinc layer – it will be replaced when all the zinc has corroded away;
5 All these materials are used in the various regions in proportion to the population.

Painted carbon steel
1 It has to be repainted after a certain number of years;
2 The time between repaintings is related to the atmospheric concentration of SO_2;
3 Painting takes place at the economically optimal time;
4 All these materials are used in the various regions in proportion to the population.

Appendix 8C
Cost of corrosion and corrosion protection

Galvanized steel
Using O.E.C.D. statistics, the cumulated amount of wire, sheet and profile, exposed from 1960 onwards was calculated for each country as shown for the United Kingdom in Table 8.3.

The exclusion of galvanized steel exposed before 1960 is probably not an important error since much of it will be painted by 1985, thus increasing the amount of paint used. Therefore, to some extent, it will be included in the painted carbon steel component. Any withdrawal of material put into use between 1960 and 1985 has not been considered so most corrosion costs will be included in the cost calculation. After discussions with manufacturers the total amounts were reduced by 50 per cent for sheet, 25 per cent for profile and 33 per cent for wire, so that only material without initial organic coating and that exposed outdoors were included.

As mentioned in the text, sheet and profile are considered to exist in two modes 'zinc' and 'painted' – the amount of material in the zinc mode and the amount of wire that has not been replaced can be obtained from the type of data illustrated in Table 8.3 when the length of life of the appropriate zinc coating has been calculated.

Galvanized wire
The following steps are used to calculate the cost of wire in a grid square:

1 the length of life of wire is calculated as $3 \times t$ (i.e. $3 \times$ time to corrode 10 m) from equation (2) in Appendix 8A by using SO_2 concentration;

Table 8.3 *Amount of Zinc Used for Galvanizing Plate, Wire and Profile Exposed in Unpainted Condition in the Atomosphere of the United Kingdom*

	Zinc Used, 1000 t					
	Plate		*Wire*		*Profile*	
Year	*Yearly Amount*	*Cumulated Amount*	*Yearly Amount*	*Cumulated Amount*	*Yearly Amount*	*Cumulated Amount*
1985	17.5	–	12.7	–	27.0	–
84	17.5	17.5	12.7	12.7	27.0	27.0
83	17.5	35.5	12.7	25.4	27.0	54.0
82	17.5	52.5	12.7	38.1	27.0	81.0
81	17.5	70.0	12.7	50.8	27.0	108.0
1980	17.5	87.5	12.7	63.5	27.0	135.0
79	17.5	105.0	12.7	76.2	27.0	162.0
78	17.5	122.5	12.7	88.9	27.0	189.0
77	17.5	140.6	12.7	101.6	27.0	216.0
76	13.0	157.5	10.5	114.3	27.0	243.0
75	8.4	170.5	10.4	124.8	27.2	270.0
74	16.4	178.9	11.8	135.2	26.6	297.2
73	18.1	195.3	13.1	147.0	26.1	323.8
72	16.5	213.4	12.7	159.7	27.8	349.9
71	15.6	229.9	12.2	171.9	29.3	377.7
1970	15.2	245.5	12.4	184.3	27.5	407.0
69	16.2	260.7	12.1	196.7	28.0	434.5
68	14.0	274.7	12.4	208.8	28.0	462.5
67	14.6	289.3	12.3	221.2	27.5	490.5
66	12.0	301.3	12.9	233.5	27.2	517.7
65	11.8	313.3	13.3	246.4	27.4	545.1
64	12.7	326.0	14.5	259.7	27.1	572.5
63	10.4	338.7	13.1	274.2	25.1	599.6
62	9.3	348.0	13.1	287.3	25.4	624.7
61	9.0	357.0	12.7	300.4	24.8	650.1

Note: The table, which is inserted as an example, is used for estimating the amounts of galvanized materials in the zinc mode and in the painted mode in individual grid squares using the length of life for respectively plate, wire and profile calculated by the use of equations in Appendix 8A.

2 the amount of wire is calculated from the length of life, the population and Table 8.3;
3 the cost of wire per year in the grid square is then calculated from:

$$\frac{\text{Amount of wire (m}^2) \times \text{cost of wire (\$/m}^2)}{\text{length of life (years)}}$$

Galvanized sheet and profile

Calculations for sheet and profile are made separately but using the same procedure and the following steps:

1 the length of life of the material in the zinc mode is calculated as $2 \times t$ for sheet and $6 \times t$ for profile from equation (2) in Appendix 8A;
2 if length of life is less than 25 years, part of the material is in the painted mode. The total amount of sheet and profile for the grid square in the 'zinc mode' and the 'painted mode' respectively is obtained from Table 8.3 and the population of the grid square.
3 the cost of corrosion of the material in the zinc mode is obained from:

$$\frac{\text{Amount of material (m}^2) \times \text{cost of galvanizing (\$/m}^2)}{\text{length of life of galvanizing (years)}}$$

4 the length of life of paint on galvanized steel is calculated from equation (4) in Appendix 8A;
5 the cost for painting on galvanized steel is then calculated from:

$$\frac{\text{Amount of material in painted mode (m}^2) \times \text{cost of painting (\$/m}^2)}{\text{length of life of paint (years)}}$$

Painted carbon steel
The cost of painting carbon steel has been estimated using the following calculations and assumptions:

1 the total consumption of paint for a country in the early 1970s is taken from O.E.C.D. statistics;
2 it is assumed that 15 per cent of the paint consumption is used for outdoor anti-rust painting;
3 it is assumed that paint layers are 100 m thick;
4 it is assumed that on average 67 per cent of the paint is solid dyestuff with a density of 2 kg/dm^3, hence the total surface of carbon steel painted in a country during one year can be estimated;
5 it is assumed that the amount of painted carbon steel surfaces per capita is the same over the whole country;
6 to estimate the total amount of painted surfaces in a country it is necessary to assume an average length of life of a coat of paint; in this study ten years has been chosen as a reasonable mean time for painting and repainting;
7 the total amount of painted carbon steel surfaces in a country is estimated as ten times the amount of steel surfaces painted during one year;
8 the length of life of paint on carbon steel in the grid square is calculated from equation (3) in Appendix 8A;
9 the cost of painting carbon steel in the grid square is then calculated from:

$$\frac{\text{Amount of painted steel (m}^2) \times \text{cost of painting (\$/m}^2)}{\text{length of life (years)}}$$

Appendix 8D
Amounts of material in use

The O.E.C.D. Annual Statistics relating to the chemical and non-ferrous metal industries form the basis for assumptions on the amounts of material in use in each country. Since this study is a forecast for the 1985 situation a zero-increase in production of galvanized sheet and paint has been assumed for 1977–1985 as the figures are lacking; production in 1973 (i.e. before the oil crisis) has been chosen as the basis for this assumption.

These statistics have been used to obtain a per capita annual consumption figure for paint and a figure for consumption of zinc in galvanizing sheet, profile and wire in each country. The former was fairly straightforward since paint consumption is given in kg/capita/year for all countries except Switzerland, where figures were lacking; the Swiss consumption was thus set at equal to that of France which was close to the average. The latter did, however, cause difficulties since statistics give the amount of zinc used for galvanizing in each country, but do not say where it is to be used. This creates a particular problem for small countries some of which have a large galvanizing industry and thus are exporters while others have no such industry and so must import all galvanized material. It was therefore decided to use only the statistics for the United Kingdom, France and West Germany and to use an average per capita consumption by these countries as the figure for the smaller O.E.C.D. countries.

Appendix 8E
Results

Estimated costs for the 12 European countries are given in Tables 8.4 a–k. They give the costs of corrosion and corrosion protection for both types of material under the three control scenarios (i.e. 1985 Case I, II and III). The influence of SO_2 is thus obtained by comparing the costs of these alternatives.

Two examples of calculations for individual grid squares are given in Table 8.5 – the urban area of Paris and the rural area of Alsace. Such results enable comparison to be made between areas in terms of influence of SO_2 on length of life of galvanized coatings and paint and hence on corresponding costs. In the same way, the figures for 300 individual grid squares have been calculated.

Table 8.4 a–k *Estimated Costs of Atmospheric Corrosion and Corrosion Protection (millions U.S. dollars per year) in Individual European O.E.C.D.-Countries in 1985*

a) Austria

		SO_2 level		
		1985		
Material	*1974*	*I*	*II*	*III*
Galvanized sheet	4	4	3	3
Galvanized profile	11	13	12	11
Galvanized wire	18	20	19	17
Painted galvanized sheet	5	7	6	4
Painted galvanized profile	–	–	–	–
Painted carbon steel	443	445	443	442
Sum of costs	481	489	483	477

b) Belgium-Luxemburg

		SO_2 level		
		1985		
Material	*1974*	*I*	*II*	*III*
Galvanized sheet	5	5	5	5
Galvanized profile	25	23	20	15
Galvanized wire	40	37	32	24
Painted galvanized sheet	22	21	15	6
Painted galvanized profile	1	–	–	–
Painted carbon steel	712	707	701	692
Sum of costs	805	793	773	742

c) Denmark

		SO_2 level		
		1985		
Material	*1974*	*I*	*II*	*III*
Galvanized sheet	3	2	2	2
Galvanized profile	12	11	9	7
Galvanized wire	20	17	15	12
Painted galvanized sheet	12	10	7	3
Painted galvanized profile	–	–	–	–
Painted carbon steel	415	411	408	404
Sum of costs	462	451	441	428

Table 8.4 (*Contd.*)
d) Finland

Material		*SO₂ level*		
		1985		
	1974	*I*	*II*	*III*
Galvanized sheet	1.3	1.4	1.4	1.2
Galvanized profile	4.8	4.8	4.5	4.6
Galvanized wire	7.7	7.7	7.3	5.8
Painted galvanized sheet	1.9	1.8	1.3	–
Painted galvanized profile	–	–	–	–
Painted carbon steel	335.8	335.8	335.3	333.3
Sum of costs	351.5	351.5	349.8	344.9

e) France

Material		*SO_2 level*		
		1985		
	1974	*I*	*II*	*III*
Galvanized sheet	19	18	17	15
Galvanized profile	72	66	55	46
Galvanized wire	217	188	145	122
Painted galvanized sheet	84	71	46	38
Painted galvanized profile	31	16	0	0
Painted carbon steel	3893	3864	3837	3762
Sum of costs	4316	4223	4100	3983

f) Netherlands

Material		*SO_2 level*		
		1985		
	1974	*I*	*II*	*III*
Galvanized sheet	6	7	6	4
Galvanized profile	26	30	27	19
Galvanized wire	41	49	44	32
Painted galvanized sheet	20	28	21	8
Painted galvanized profile	–	–	–	–
Painted carbon steel	780	788	782	770
Sum of costs	873	902	880	833

Table 8.4 (*Contd.*)
g) Norway

	SO_2 level			
		1985		
Material	*1974*	*I*	*II*	*III*
Galvanized sheet	1.0	1.0	1.0	0.9
Galvanized profile	3.6	3.2	3.2	3.0
Galvanized wire	5.7	5.2	5.1	4.8
Painted galvanized sheet	0.9	0.4	0.3	–
Painted galvanized profile	–	–	–	–
Painted carbon steel	301.2	300.5	300.3	300.0
Sum of costs	312.4	310.3	309.9	308.7

h) Sweden

	SO_2 level			
		1985		
Material	*1974*	*I*	*II*	*III*
Galvanized sheet	3	3	2	3
Galvanized profile	9	9	8	7
Galvanized wire	15	14	13	11
Painted galvanized sheet	3	1	–	–
Painted galvanized profile	–	–	–	–
Painted carbon steel	749	747	745	743
Sum of costs	779	774	768	764

i) Switzerland

	SO_2 level			
		1985		
Material	*1974*	*I*	*II*	*III*
Galvanized sheet	2	2	2	3
Galvanized profile	8	8	7	6
Galvanized wire	13	12	11	10
Painted galvanized sheet	2	2	1	1
Painted galvanized profile	–	–	–	–
Painted carbon steel	469	469	467	466
Sum of costs	494	493	488	486

Table 8.4 (*Contd.*)
j) United Kingdom

	SO_2 *level*			
		1985		
Material	*1974*	*I*	*II*	*III*
Galvanized sheet	22	22	21	20
Galvanized profile	163	147	134	109
Galvanized wire	382	310	274	215
Painted galvanized sheet	153	122	106	70
Painted galvanized profile	99	40	21	2
Painted carbon steel	3512	3440	3406	3354
Sum of costs	4331	4081	3962	3770

k) Germany

	SO_2 *level*			
		1985		
Material	*1974*	*I*	*II*	*III*
Galvanized sheet	30	33	32	31
Galvanized profile	160	156	143	129
Galvanized wire	163	152	134	120
Painted galvanized sheet	136	125	92	68
Painted galvanized profile	53	28	7	–
Painted carbon steel	6500	6460	6411	6374
Sum of costs	7042	6954	6819	6722

Note: All figures refer to the year 1985 and are based on 1979 Swedish prices. The influence of sulphur compounds is obtained by the comparison between the pollution alternatives given.

Table 8.5 *Examples of Results of Calculations Made for Individuals Grid Squares*

	1974	*1985 Case I*	*1985 Case II*	*1985 Case III*
PARIS (7.00 × 10⁶ inhab.)				
SO_2, $\mu g/m^3$	122.92	95.03	61.95	47.94
Lifetime ZNPL, years	5.15	6.49	9.40	11.59
Lifetime ZNWI, years	7.27	9.79	14.09	17.39
Lifetime ZNPR, years	15.45	19.48	28.19	24.77
Costs ZNPL, $/cap.	0.48	0.46	0.46	0.44
Costs ZNPR, $/cap.	3.72	3.35	2.76	2.23
Costs ZNWI, $/cap.	13:35	10.59	7.32	5.93
Lifetime ZP, years	11.43	12.31	13.35	13.79
Costs ZPPL, $/cap.	7.25	6.33	4.82	4.08
Costs ZPPR, $/cap.	4.03	2.28	0	0
Lifetime STPT, years	9.65	10.10	10.62	10.85
Costs STPT, $/cap.	87.07	83.25	79.12	77.50
COST, 10^6 $	811.82	744.32	661.80	631.70
ALSACE (4.92 × 10⁶ inhab.)				
SO_2, $\mu g/m^3$	9.65	9.43	6.93	4.83
Lifetime ZNPL, years	32.05	32.38	36.64	41.20
Lifetime ZNWI, years	48.07	48.56	54.96	61.80
Lifetime ZNPL, years	96.14	97.13	109.92	123.60
Costs ZNPL, $/cap.	0.34	0.33	0.30	0.26
Costs ZNPR, $/cap.	0.81	0.80	0.71	0.63
Costs ZNWI, $/cap.	2.15	2.12	1.88	1.67
Lifetime ZP, years	15.00	15.00	15.08	15.15
Costs ZPPL, $/cap.	0	0	0	0
Costs ZPPR, $/cap.	0	0	0	0
Lifetime STPT, years	11.46	11.46	11.50	11.53
Costs STPT, $/cap.	73.38	73.35	73.10	72.89
COST, 10^6 $	377.10	376.81	373.68	371.08

Code: ZNPL = unpainted galvanized plate.
ZNPR = unpainted galvanized profile.
ZNWI = unpainted galvanized wire.
ZP = painted galvanized material.
ZPPL = painted galvanized plate.
ZPPR = painted galvanized profile.
STPT = painted steel.
COST = total costs for the grid square considered.

References

Ekwall, G. and Alfort, S. (1975), *Einfluss des Keinheitsgrades der Vorbereitung Gemäss bis* 05 39 00 *auf die Kaltbarkeit von Korrosionsschutzbeschichtigungen*, Bulletin 73D, Swedish Corrosion Institute, Stockholm.

Fink, F. W. *et al.* (1971), *Technical-Economic Evaluation of Air Pollution Corrosion Costs on Metals in the U.S.*, Battelle Memorial Institute, Columbus, Ohio.

Fintling, E. and Hasselbohm, B. (1964), 'Corrosion of Metal-Coated Specimens in Swedish Climate', *Current Corrosion Research in Scandinavia*, Kemian Keskuzliitt, Helsinki.

Guttman, H. (1968), 'Effects of Atmospheric Factors on the Corrosion of Rolled Zinc', *Metal Corrosion in the Atmosphere*, American Society for Testing and Materials, Baltimore.

Haynie, P. H. and Upham, J. P. (1970), 'Effects of Atmospheric Sulphur Dioxide on the Corrosion of Zinc', *Materials Protection and Performance.*

Hudson, J. C. and Stanmore, J. F. (1953), 'The Effect of Climate and Atmospheric Pollution on Corrosion', *Journal of Applied Chemistry.*

Keane, J. D. (1969), 'Minimum Paint-Film Thickness for Economical Protection of Hot-Rolled Steel Against Corrosion', *Journal of Paint Technology.*

Kucera, V. (1976), 'Effects of Sulphur Dioxide and Acid Precipitation on Metals and Anti-Rust Painted Steel', *Ambio.*

Kulis, M. (1977), 'Durch Industrieemissionen verursachte Korrosionsschäden an Stahlbauten im Industriegebiet Ostrava', *Werkstoffe und Korrosion.*

Luckat, S. (1975), *The Conservation of Stone*, Proceedings of the Institute Syposium, Bologna.

O.E.C.D. (1979), *Programme on the Long Range Transport of Air Pollutants* (2nd ed.), Paris.

Royal Ministry of Foreign Affairs/Royal Ministry of Agriculture (1971), *Air Pollution Across National Boundaries*, Nordstedt and Sbner, Stockholm.

Skoulikidis, Th. N. (1979), *Corrosion Prevention and Control.*

Suhr. J. and Toft. L. (1979), Personal communication based on market inventory made by Hempel's Marine Paints, A/S.

9

Regional Residuals Management Models and The Lower Delaware Valley Case Study

Allen V. Kneese and Blair T. Bower

INTRODUCTION

One way of looking at the functioning of an economic system is to look at the throughput of materials and energy from raw materials and natural resources through mining and production operations to ultimate consumption and generation of wastes. The simple but fundamental physical idea of the indestructability of energy and mass means that all the mass that is going into an economic activity, independent of whether it is industrial production, individual consumption, waste management, etc. will leave that activity in exactly the same quantity but in other chemical forms. The whole mass of raw materials which during a time period is taken from the natural environment and used in economic activities will thus remain, as semi-finished products, as final products, as capital goods or as residuals, i.e. products that at the present do not have a profitable use. Ultimately, all the mass of the raw materials will be hennaged into residuals and the disposal of these residuals means the final return of the mass to the natural environment.

This circular flow of mass and energy is described in Figure 9.1. In this illustration, five boxes corresponding to production, capital accumulation, consumption, environmental protection, and the environment are shown. Primary resources such as petroleum, iron ore, lumber, water, are extracted from the natural environment and used as factors of production in the production box. The ultimate goal of production is of course the production of consumption goods and services. However, some of the produced goods are capital goods which are used as a factor of production. In the production process, residuals are generated which partly are recycled and perhaps undergo waste treatment before they are discharged into the environment.

The capital goods will ultimately undergo decay and will be scrapped.

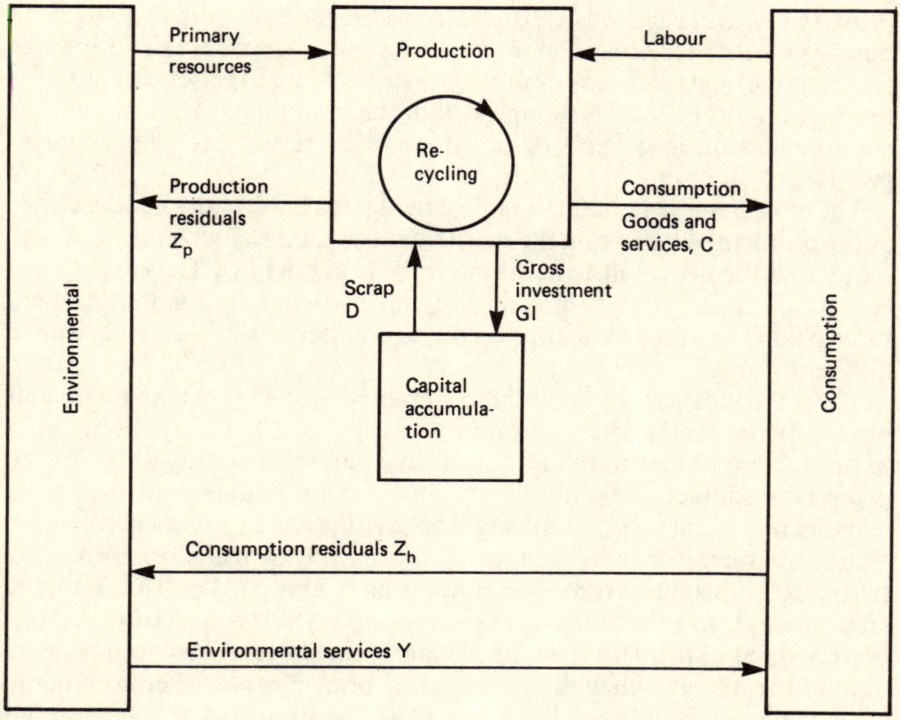

Figure 9.1

Parts of that flow of scrapped capital goods will be recycled but a part will be discharged into the environment.

Consumption in this model consists of consumption of services, either bought directly from the producers of such services or provided by consumption goods. The consumers thus buy a bundle of consumption goods and services *C*, consume the services that this bundle may yield and are left with wastes. These wastes or consumption residuals are either discharged directly into the environment, represented by the arrow z_h from the consumption box to the environment box, or transferred to the production box where the wastes are treated and raw materials recovered.

Wastes generated in the consumption and capital accumulation boxes enter the production box and are recycled or treated together with the residuals generated in the production process. The total flow of residuals from production to the environment is then given by z_p, and the total waste load is the sum of the consumption and production residuals.

The environment thus provides primary resources in the form of raw materials, ores etc. and waste disposal services for the residuals that these resources are transformed into by the economic system. Besides providing primary resources and waste disposal services, the environment provides a bundle of other services to mankind, life support services (air to breathe for example), recreational opportunities, aesthetic experiences, etc. The production of primary resources and the dumping of wastes in the environment do in general reduce these other services the environment provides.[1]

The environmental quality management problem can thus be described as the problem of balancing these different uses of the environment in such a way that the net result to mankind is the best possible. The role of cost-benefit analysis is to quantify in a common denominator the different service flows in order to facilitate a direct comparison of the value *s* of the different flows.

The classification of a specific commodity as a residual depends obviously on whether this commodity can beneficially be used as an input in production or consumption or not. In a market economy the prices on primary resources, labour and produced commodities will determine whether a particular commodity will be classified as a residual or an input. Waste treatment or 'residuals modification' means transformation of a particular substance from one form, which may be hazardous to the environment, to other forms which hopefully are less hazardous or can be recovered and used as inputs. There is therefore a trade-off between different residuals which is important to bear in mind when looking at environmental problems. By using a wet scrubber to reduce sulphur oxides in stack gases an air pollution problem will be transformed into a problem of disposing the sludge from the scrubber or by using effluent treatment plants which burn the sludge, a water pollution problem is transformed into an air pollution problem. The conventional division of environmental problems into air- water-and solid-waste pollution may in view of this trade-off lead rational environmental quality management astray. There is a strong need for approaches which could take a wider view of the environmental problems.[2]

The effects on environmental services from the discharge of residuals depend in general not only on the total amount of residuals emitted but also on their spatial distribution and the discharge of other residuals. The water quality in a watershed depends on where, for example, organic matter is discharged. If emitted upstream the effects on water quality will, other things being equal, be greater than if emitted close to the mouth of a river. But the effects from the discharge at one point will in general depend on the discharges at other points. Thus one should try to include all the sources and all the discharges that affect the environment in a region. This means that all plants and other economic units within a region should be simultaneously controlled, in contrast to environmental policy in many countries where pollution problems are approached plant by plant.

Very often environmental policy is aimed at the modification of

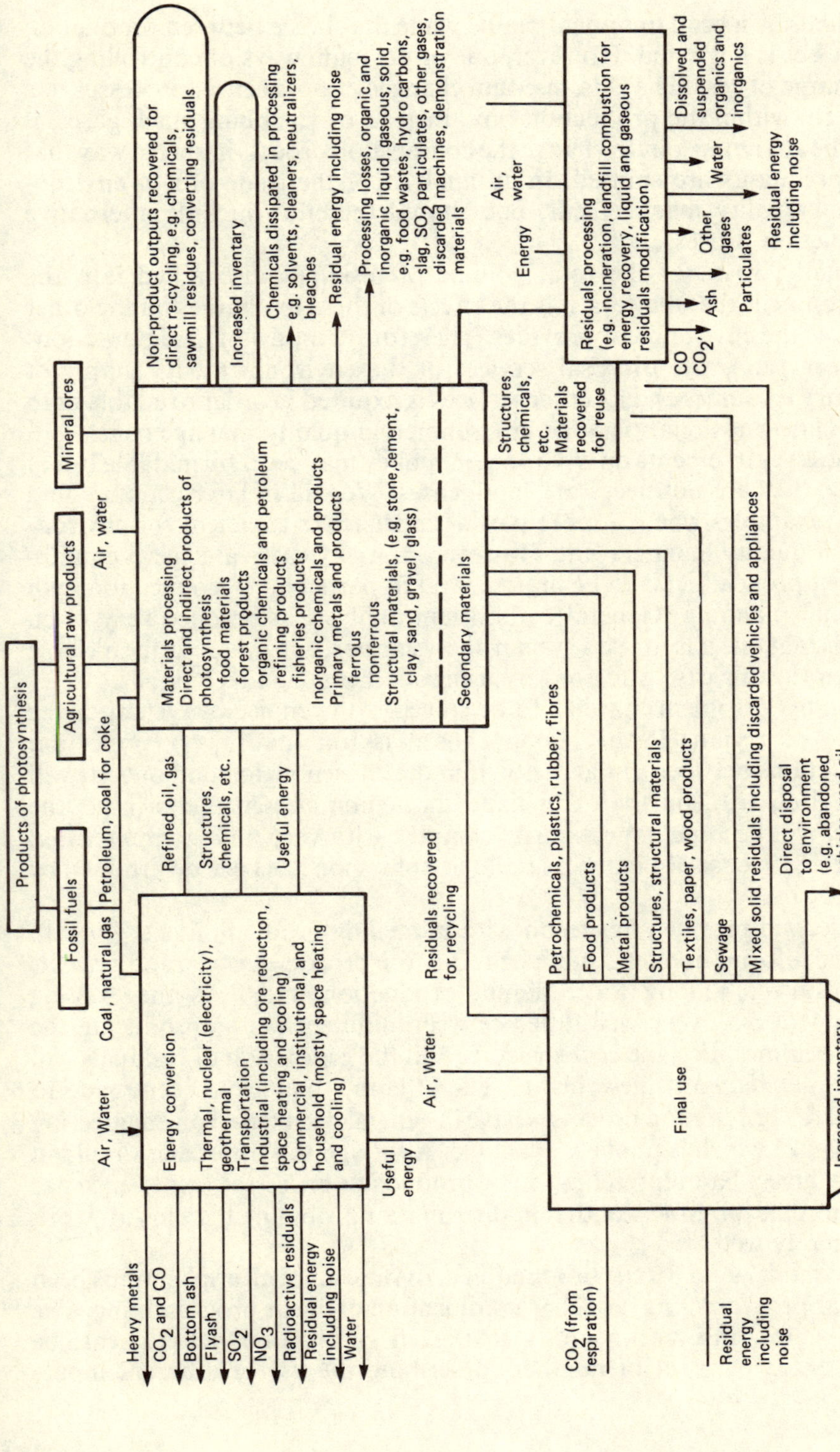

Note: Not all flows and activities are shown

Figure 9.2 *Materials and Energy Flows in a Society*

residuals in special treatment plants while the choice between production processes is neglected. However, one of the main ways of controlling the discharge of residuals is to institute changes in production processes, i.e. changes within the production box. Instead of scrubbing stack gases, it may be advantageous to change the combustion process in such a way that less pollutants are emitted. In an analysis of the trade-offs in environmental quality management, one should therefore include alternative production processes.

Finally, it is not the total volume of residuals discharged into the environment that matters; it is the effects of these discharges on the other services the environment provides. Therefore, a model of the interactions between the waste disposal services of the environment, its supply of primary resources and its other services is required in order to enable us to formulate a rational plan for environmental quality management.

These requirements on environment policy may seem formidable but of course they are not necessary in all cases. We will in later chapters find many examples where a more partial approach is sufficient for environmental quality management. However, in many cases a general equilibrium approach seems to be desired, and in particular in connection with regional planning. General equilibrium analysis in practice very often means that one has to use a system analysis approach, i.e. describe a whole system (in this case a region) by using mathematical techniques.

The first problem that has to be solved is the choice of system or the choice of region. If the region chosen is too small, very important interactions between discharges within the chosen region and outside will be neglected. If, on the other hand the region chosen is too large, the model will become unnecessarily complex with very high computer and information costs. In most cases the size of region has been determined by a watershed.

A second problem has to do with modelling production activities. In general information on available production processes, costs, and prices is decentralized among the different production units. As the existing equipment may very well differ between different plants producing the same commodities, the cost structure and the generation of residuals will also differ between these plants. The attempts that have been made to model the production processes have in general been based on engineering knowledge which is publicly available. Although this approach should in theory give a bad representation of production processes, experience has shown that in practice the approximations obtained seem to work sufficiently well.

The model used for the production activities has in all applications been a linear programming model or modification of linear programming. The idea behind this approach is that each production activity can be represented by a set of numbers describing the use of different inputs necessary to obtain one unit of output. If one is representing a production process in a pulp mill for example, the representation would give the amount of raw materials (wood), the electricity, the amount of fossil fuels, the amount of different kinds of chemicals, the amount of manpower, etc. necessary to produce one ton of pulp of a specified quality. In addition to this we can also have numbers giving the amounts of different residuals generated by the process (where each residual is defined not only by its chemical composition but also by the location of discharge). The representation of a production process thus contains all information necessary to carry out an economic analysis of the process, but it neglects completely the technical arrangements necessary to carry out the process. After all we are not interested in discussing the actual technical blueprint of the process, we are interested in the costs, the revenues and the effects on the environment.

The next assumption made is usually that it is possible to expand and contract such a production process continuously. Thus, in order to produce two tons of pulp, twice as much of the different inputs is needed and twice as many residuals is generated. However, in many cases the production possibilities are limited by existing capacity and in those cases it is unreasonable to assume that production can be changed continuously.

By introducing bounds defined by the existing capacities it is still possible to use linear programming to analyze such cases. If furthermore there are increasing returns to scale, i.e. if a doubling of production does not necessarily require twice as much of all inputs, linear programming cannot be used. Instead, an extension of linear programming has been applied, namely integer programming.

One of the first applications of a linear programming approach to environmental quality management was a celebrated study of the Delaware Estuary, U.S.A., in the beginning of the sixties.[3] The estuary was divided into 30 reaches and the Streeter Phelps oxygen equations were used to interconnect these different reaches. The transfer functions derived which forecasted the change in dissolved oxygen in one segment from changes in discharges of wastes in different segments (organic wastes measured as biochemical oxygen demand, B.O.D.) turned out to be linear. By estimating the cost of reducing the discharge of wastes in the different segments it was possible to formulate the water quality management problem as a linear programming problem where the objective was to minimize the total cost of reducing the waste discharges in the estuary while keeping certain predetermined levels of dissolved oxygen in the different reaches.

The output of the analysis was thus a least cost solution to obtain a given quality level in the estuary. Although this study only took into account waste treatment costs and water pollution, it gave some valuable insights into the efficiencies that could be gained by using a systems analysis approach.

By modelling the whole production processes as described above, it has been possible to integrate air and water pollution with solid waste. In the Delaware study referred to above very simple relations between discharges of organic wastes and dissolved oxygen levels were used. In order to take into account other water quality aspects as well as other water pollutants, more complex aquatic ecological models have been developed. In order to connect airborn emissions with ambient air quality use has been made of air pollution dispersion models which relate emissions to ground level ambient concentrations of pollutants. Research in this direction has been carried out in many countries and at many research institutes.[4]

The case study we have chosen to include in this volume is another study on the Delaware River carried out at the Resources for the Future by Walter O. Spofford, Jr., Clifford S. Russell and Robert A. Kelly. Their study is well documented in several papers but a very good description and evaluation of the whole case study is given in Spofford, Russell and Kelly, *Environmental Quality Management/An Application to the Lower Delaware Valley*, RfF, Washington D.C., 1976. Because of limited space we have selected summaries of this study written by two researchers who were involved in the project, Allen Kneese and Blair Bower. We have selected two chapters from their book *Environmental Quality & Residuals Management*.

It is important to recognize the size of the region under study. The population was a little more than 5.5 million and covers an area of about 12,000 square kilometres. The region is one of the most heavily industrialized areas in the United States with among other activities several petroleum refineries, five large steel mills, thirteen paper and pulp mills, many power plants and chemical plants of various types. It is obvious that the size of the region makes any modelling attempt very hazardous. Is it really possible to include all these activities in a model and still have a manageable model which gives interesting answers to the questions one may want to ask? Of course, it was impossible to include all activities which generate and discharge residuals into the air and the water, but the list of plants included is very impressive. All in all, the whole linear programming model of the generation of residuals and discharges contains more than 3,000 rows and almost 8,000 columns. In addition to this a linear transfer function for the dispersion of air pollutants and a non-linear aquatic eco-system model of the Delaware Estuary was used. Because of the non-linear natural system model a non-linear programming algorithm was developed for this model.

The two main problems experienced in this project seem to have been the availability of data and the cost of running the model. Very little data were publicly available when the project was initiated and substantial efforts were put into the search for the data. Moreover, it was impossible within the project to calibrate the models completely to the real world. However, it seems that new environmental legislation and efforts by the E.P.A. have improved the situation considerably in the United States. As technology may be uniform across national boundaries, this means that the growing availability of information in the U.S. may be of substantial value for similar enterprises in other parts of the world.

The other main problem has to do with the size of the model and the use of a non-linear eco-system model. The combination of these two factors implied substantial costs, partly monetary costs but also in terms of limited precision of running the complete regional model. Even with a linearized version of the model, each computer run would require a C.P.U. (central processing unit) time of about 35 minutes.

In spite of these obstacles, the project has shown that it is possible to construct large-scale operational models for regional environmental quality management. The main benefits from using such models have been discussed in the beginning of this introduction. It may be appropriate to conclude the introduction by pointing out some concrete outputs one can obtain from this kind of analysis. These are as follows:

1 total cost of meeting different environmental quality objectives;
2 marginal cost of meeting environmental quality objectives;
3 marginal cost of controlling different emissions;
4 the incidence of discharge controls on prices and to some extent distributional implications;
5 spatial distribution of pollution control costs;
6 guidelines on where and how to control residuals discharge.

Notes

1 In Dasgupta, this is discussed in more detail.
2 A more detailed picture of the materials' flows and tradeoffs is given in Figure 9.2.
3 For a description see, for example, Herfindahl and Kneese, *Economic Theory of Natural Resources*, Columbus, 1974.
4 For an overview of some models, see Bower (ed.), *Regional Residuals Environmental Quality Management Modeling*, Washington D.C., 1977.

CASE STUDY 1

It is useful to analyze integrated residuals management at the individual activity level because of the insights that such microlevel analysis can provide in and of itself, but also because it is essential to analyzing integrated residuals management on a regional level. Because actual decision-making having to do with managing residuals discharged from multiple sources takes place in particular geographic areas, a regional residuals-environmental quality management (R.E.Q.M.) strategy involves a mix of incentives that affect both the individual dischargers (to induce them to reduce discharges) and the management agency itself (when it acts in a collective way to modify residuals and when it acts directly to modify environmental quality) – all this directed toward improving ambient environmental quality.

The analysis of integrated residuals management at the microlevel provides information on the possible responses of individual dischargers. The task of *regional* R.E.Q.M. analysis is to combine the alternative residuals management options for the individual activities with collective management options and the transformations produced by natural systems to develop an optimal (however defined) regional strategy, a strategy which considers explicitly the distribution of both the benefits and the costs of improving ambient environmental quality.

When residuals are discharged, they are not only transported but they undergo various transformations in the natural systems which receive them. Accordingly, the impact that a given residuals discharge has on a particular receptor is a function not only of the amount and type of discharge but of where the discharger is located relative to the receptor and the specific characteristics of the receiving environmental media in that particular region. The latter include such factors as: air temperature, wind speed, the presence or absence of inversions; water temperature, water volume and flow, pre-existing biochemical composition; and land slope, infiltration capacity, soil type, and vegetative cover.

Thus, to analyze economic, technological, institutional, and ecologic aspects of residuals management in a region (a term which we purposely leave vague for the time being) requires a quantitative model[1] that incorporates salient aspects of the economy, technological options for reducing residuals discharges, the behaviour of the pertinent natural systems, and the location of receptors – and, for reasons explained previously, all this simultaneously for liquid, gaseous, solid, and energy residuals' streams. One of the principal activities of the Quality of the Environment programme at R.F.F. over the past several years has been to construct one such model and make an illustrative application of it to a particular region.

The objective of this chapter is to describe the particular type of conceptual R.E.Q.M. model developed by the R.F.F. team. This model is also known as the Russell-Spofford model. These terms will be used interchangeably in the following discussion. Constructing a quantitative model of this type necessarily involves extensive use of mathematics.

Since we are avoiding presentations of mathematical materials in the text, the reader interested in technical details of the regional application of the Russell-Spofford model will find a relatively complete, concise discussion of its mathematical structure in Appendixes 9A and 9B.

The model in general

A logical point of departure for understanding the kind of model needed for regional R.E.Q.M. is to consider first the programming model of residuals' management in an industrial operation presented in the previous chapter. Programming models have long been used in some industries to make scheduling, product design, and other management decisions. A straightforward but important extension of this type of industry model is made by constraining not only the availability to the industrial plant of ordinary resources but also of environmental resources; that is, limitations are placed on the amount of residual materials and energy that may be discharged to the air, water bodies, and on the land.[2] By this it is meant that the private internal costs imposed by policies, such as effluent standards or taxes, which are meant to diminish discharges and their associated external costs, can be determined for alternative levels of application of these policies. This is useful general information for regional R.E.Q.M. when costs are a consideration – that is to say, nearly always.

But such models of activities, useful as they are in themselves, say nothing about the quality of the environment. To make this connection, models of the effect of residuals discharges on the pertinent natural systems are needed. Making this step is often desirable, because there exist, or can be developed, reasonably acceptable models for the atmosphere and water bodies (including groundwater aquifers), which translate a quantity of a residual discharged at some point x to an ambient concentration at some point y. Similar models are possible for residuals-carrying runoff from land surfaces.

In constructing natural systems models, environmental media (by which we mean the atmosphere and water bodies) are usually divided conceptually into a number of grids or blocks within which environmental conditions are taken to be uniform. Each block is represented by differential equations describing the rates of flow of materials, energy, or both, across the boundaries of the blocks as a function of conditions within the blocks and the rates of biochemical and physical transformations or decay of these materials within the blocks as functions of the same conditions.

By means of such models, it is possible to include ambient environmental quality constraints in addition to effluent constraints in the regional analysis (or environmental quality constraints can be considered alone). Moreover, the dispersion-type natural system models are not limited to a single source of discharge. They can translate discharges from multiple point, area, and line sources to concentrations at multiple receptor points.[3] Natural systems models are discussed in more detail in Appendix 9B.

As part of the R.F.F. research programme on R.E.Q.M., a new aquatic ecosystem model of an estuary was developed by Robert Kelly. This model differs from the traditional dispersion-type model in that, in addition to converting weights of materials and quantities of thermal energy at points of discharge into concentrations of those materials at specified locations, it also converts them into measures of effects on living populations, such as zooplankton, algae, and fish. The last two are of more direct interest to environmental quality policy making than simple concentrations of residuals in the environment. Although it involves a large amount of computation, the availability of natural systems models therefore makes it feasible to minimize, for example, the overall private cost of achieving a specified ambient standard, or set of standards, either in terms of concentrations of materials or biomass of living species, or both, in a region. This is accomplished by means of a large regional mathematical model which encompasses aspects of the behaviour of the actual environmental systems (water bodies and the air mantle). Thus there exists, at least in rudimentary form, an economic-ecological model which in principle should be useful for R.E.Q.M. in, say, a river basin, a metropolitan airshed, or a groundwater basin.

But these seemingly straightforward extensions of well-established management science models raise fundamental questions and pose basic difficulties in trying to provide systems analyses useful for regional R.E.Q.M. There would appear to be four main questions: First, how far should the explicit incorporation of the various sorts of interdependencies among residuals and among media be carried? Second, how should the outputs (external costs avoided) of the management systems be evaluated, or should this even be attempted? Third, what is the appropriate objective or objectives? Fourth, how can and how should the model interact with actual and potential political structures?[4] The first question is particularly difficult in connection with R.E.Q.M. problems because of the genuine complexities involved and the prominence of 'ecological thinking' in the field. Hence, before discussing the particular regional R.E.Q.M. model used, some more general comments on this problem are relevant.

Simulation versus formal mathematical optimization

The 'frog in the hole in the bottom of the sea' chain of reasoning of some ecologists has led to visions of the R.E.Q.M. problem which push it beyond the bounds of any kind of successful modelling. Some years ago in an article on operations research, Robert Dorfman put the general point very well.

> As a result of complexity the operations analyst, like every other worker, lives nearly always near the end of his tether. He simplifies his problems as much as he dares (sometimes more than he should dare), applies the most powerful analytic tools at his command and, with luck, just squeaks through. But what if all established methods fail, either because the problem cannot be forced into one of the standard types or because, after all acceptable simplifications, it is still so large or complicated that the equations describing it cannot be solved? When he finds himself in this fix, the operations analyst falls back on 'simulation' or 'gaming'.[5]

All models are simulations in that some exogenous conditions are chosen, the model is run with the assumption that it mimics some part or parts of the real world and the behaviour of the actors therein, and an 'answer' is spewed out. In simulation models, relationships are given in the form of linked equations that are not solved analytically but computed numerically. Formal mathematical optimization models, however, are constructed to require analytical solutions, and, therefore, if there are a number of simultaneous relationships involved, they usually have to be primarily of a linear variety in order to make their solution feasible. To obtain this linearity, it is necessary to work with more or less good approximations of the actual functional relationships involved. Computer simulation can handle complex relationships beyond those manageable in mathematical optimization models, such as linear programming models. But one result of such ability is that much of any systematic method for finding a better answer in relation to the objective is lost, and the problem of choosing among alternative outcomes of the simulation can easily become very difficult.

Consider a small simulation model in which there are twenty-eight variables (an actual regional R.E.Q.M. model may easily have many hundreds, as the following chapter demonstrates), each of which may be set at any one of three levels. There are then 3^{28} possible systems, assuming all variables are independent. This amounts to approximately 23,000 billion. If it takes one minute of computer time to simulate each design, it could require about 50 million years to complete the simulation. Of course, no simulator would attempt a complete enumeration of outcomes in a large problem, but this calculation does suggest the complexities to be faced. The same complexity faces the modeller using mathematical optimization, but mathematical optimization provides a systematic method for finding a 'better and better' answer in relation to the chosen objectives. (However, complications arise when there are multiple optima, as is often the case for complex, regional R.E.Q.M. systems.)

Simulation may be appropriate if informed judgment can readily yield a relatively few alternative systems to analyze, or if there are sufficient constraints so that only a few possible options are to be analyzed. Neither of these conditions is likely to occur when large R.E.Q.M. systems are involved. Alternatively, simulation can be supplied with objective functions and one or another form of sampling used to generate a 'response surface'. But the principles of sampling for this type of problem are not well understood, and providing an adequate sample may itself be a very difficult problem if the number of variables and alternative levels is great and the response surface is irregular.

Be that as it may; even with mathematical optimization there is never a guarantee that the 'best' answer will be found if there are multiple optima; and the system may be sufficiently complex so that optimization may not be very efficient and – in the limit – may amount to nothing more than 'brute force'. Thus the line between mathematical optimization and simulation may virtually disappear. But clearly there are trade-offs between the two in terms of the types of output information produced.

The question of simulation versus mathematical optimization can be summarized by indicating the considerations to be taken into account in the choice of analytical approach, keeping in mind that combinations of simulation and mathematical optimization are possible.

1 Mathematical optimization imposes a valuable discipline on the modeller and the modelling process.
2 If ambient environmental standards are the targets to be achieved by the R.E.Q.M. strategy and there are a large number of dischargers, a large number of receptors, and a large number of possible discharge reduction options, then mathematical optimization will usually be the reasonable way to proceed.
3 If there are only a few major dischargers and a few options for reducing residuals discharges, simulation may be easier and efficient enough.
4 If there are many similar sources of residuals discharges, but only one or two options for reducing discharges at each source, and the objective is defined in terms of required reductions or percentage of reduction at the sources (rather than in terms of ambient environmental quality), simulation again may be easier and efficient enough.
5 Large mathematical optimization models are expensive and difficult, unless linear in nature. However, the assumptions necessary to make a linear model may do great violence to the real world, for example, result in unacceptable inaccuracies.

6 Large, nonlinear mathematical optimization models almost always (an estimated 90 per cent of the time) have multiple optima.
7 Synergistic and antagonistic effects are more difficult to handle in mathematical optimization than in simulation models.
8 Economies of scale or analogous increasing-return situations cannot be handled satisfactorily by any mathematical optimization technique.

Finally, it should be remembered that analyzing any complex R.E.Q.M. system by any approach involves obtaining, arranging, and handling large amounts of empirical data. In many cases the major problem is that of obtaining empirical data on activities – production processes, residuals generation, and residuals discharge reduction options and their costs – and on the effects of discharges on ambient environmental quality.

On the basis of such considerations, the modelling team at R.F.F. concluded that, with all the limitations, some form of mathematical optimization model was more likely than a simulation one to be useful for decision-making in the particular R.E.Q.M. case study described in the next chapter. Mathematical optimization models can also, of course, incorporate simulation submodels to provide descriptive linkages in a set of nested models, and the one developed by the team does (the aquatic ecosystem model mentioned above is a simulation model). But mathematical optimization does not sacrifice specifying a criterion function and thus results in an orderly approach to the optimal solution, for whatever objective or objectives are included in the criterion function. Selected parameters of the mathematical optimization model can be varied and new solutions found, and this would almost always be desirable in real decision-making situations, but the hallmarks of mathematical optimization models – an explicit objective function with constraints and a specific solution procedure – are not thereby abandoned.

Clearly it is necessary to recognize that regional R.E.Q.M. models can never be comprehensive in the sense that they consider all linkages and all alternatives. Therefore, great care must be taken to specify what aspects of reality are or are not included. In this connection a well-functioning market system can be of great help – a fact often ignored in the more ecologically orientated models – in that many aspects of resource use can be excluded from explicit consideration in R.E.Q.M. models on the grounds that they are appropriately handled by the market exchange system. The interface between these processes and the model as such is through the system of value weights generated by the market, that is, prices.[6] The model itself can then focus explicitly on those aspects of resource use where market exchange is known to fail seriously as an allocative device, for example, with respect to allocation of the common property resources of air, water, and associated ecological systems.[7]

Stochastic and dynamic elements are likely to be particularly difficult to handle adequately in mathematical optimization models. Inability to do so represents an important deficiency. Sensitivity analysis can help some, but the wise modeller will never let himself be lured into thinking that either on conceptual or empirical grounds his models will provide a complete basis for decision-making in a field as complex as R.E.Q.M. The mathematical models must be viewed as potentially helpful tools that constitute one element, albeit a major one, in a decision-making process – tools which can reveal nonobvious impacts of 'common sense' policies and go some distance in quantifying them. They must be built and used because the inherent logic of the problem demands it, and we have nothing better.

The R.E.Q.M. modelling research at R.F.F. began with a conceptual model developed by Clifford Russell and Walter Spofford. The original framework and a didactic application to a small hypothetical region have been described in detail.[8] We present here the basic features of that framework. Because the rationale for many of its features has been developed in previous chapters, and also exists in the appendixes to this chapter, we can be concise here. How this conceptual model was actually applied to a real region is described in the next chapter.

The conceptual Russell-Spofford model

The Russell-Spofford R.E.Q.M. model has the following components:

1 *residuals generation and discharge models* (activity models) which describe the factors influencing the generation, modification, and final discharge to the environment of liquid, gaseous, solid, and energy residuals from individual production and consumption activities, and the relevant production and residuals modification costs for one or more sets of prices of factor inputs to the activities;

2 *models of collective residuals modification activities*, which detail the inputs, outputs, and costs of activities (such as municipal incinerators, municipal sewage treatment plants, used-paper processing plants) that modify residuals collected and transported from several residuals-generating activities;

3 *environmental modification models*, which describe the options available for directly improving the assimilative capacity of the environment, such as low-flow augmentation and instream aeration, and their costs;

4 *natural systems models*, which translate the time and spatial pattern of residuals discharges into the resulting time and spatial pattern of ambient environmental quality in terms of residuals concentrations and population size or densities of biological species;

5 *damage functions*, which relate the time and spatial patterns of ambient residuals concentrations to the resulting impacts on receptors – man, animals, plants, structures – in physical, biological, physiological, and economic terms;
6 *evaluation and objective functions*, which specify how the inputs and outputs are to be evaluated and the structure and components of the objective function.

The second and third components are self-explanatory. Further comments on the other four components follows.

Activity models
Like the regional R.E.Q.M. model as a whole, activity models deal simultaneously with liquid, gaseous, solid, and energy residuals, recognizing explicitly the physical and economic links among them. They 'recognize', for example, that removing waterborne organic residuals by standard sewage treatment processes creates a sludge which, in turn, represents a solid residuals' problem; the sludge must either be disposed of on the land or burned, the latter alternative generating airborne particulates, other gaseous residuals, and a remaining solid residual. These models relate inputs and outputs of production processes and consumption activities at specified locations within a region, including: the unit amounts and types of residuals generated in the production of each product and in residential and commercial activities; the costs of changing these residuals from one form to another (as gaseous to liquid in the scrubbing of stack gases); the costs of transporting the residuals from one place to another; and the costs of any final-discharge-related activity such as landfill operations. Choices are possible among production processes, raw material input mixes, by-product production, materials recovery, and in some cases product mix and product specifications – all of which can reduce the total quantity of residuals requiring handling and disposal. That is, the residuals generated are assumed to be not fixed, either in form or in quantity. These models also allow for choices among modification processes and hence among the possible forms of the residual to be disposed of in the natural environment and among the locations at which such discharges are accomplished.

Natural systems models
Natural systems models – physical, chemical, and ecological – describe the fate of various residuals after their discharge into the natural environment. They may be thought of as transformation functions operating on the vector of residuals discharges and yielding another vector of ambient concentrations at specific locations in the area and, in the instance of the aquatic ecosystem model, as having an effect on living species as well as on ambient concentrations in the water body. Between

discharge point and receptor locations, the residual may be diluted in the relatively large volume of air or water in the natural world, transformed from one form to another (as in the decay of oxygen-demanding organics), accumulated or stored (as in the accumulation of organics in benthal deposits), and, of course, transported to another place. Fortunately, for many situations, the equations characterizing the transformation of residuals between discharge and receptor locations reduce to simple linear forms for steady state deterministic conditions, so that the linkage can be made via a coefficient.[9] The models which explicitly incorporate effects on living things are more complex and, as already mentioned, are in the form of simulation programmes.

Damage functions

The Russell-Spofford conceptual model includes a set of receptor-damage functions relating the concentrations of residuals in the environment and the effects on living things to the resulting damages, whether these are sustained directly by humans or indirectly through effects on material objects or on such receptors as plants or animals in which human beings have a commercial, scientific, or aesthetic interest. For the conceptual model, these functions relating concentrations and effects on species to damages are assumed to be expressed in monetary terms. The derivatives of these functions represent marginal damages, which could be summed for affected receptors for any particular discharge and thus provide an estimate of the appropriate effluent charge for that level of discharge by the specific discharger (given no synergistic and antagonistic relationships among residuals).

Assuming the damage functions are expressed in monetary terms, we can then explain the linkage between the components of the model and the method of optimum seeking in the following manner. The regional R.E.Q.M. model can be constructed as a linear programming model, which is solved initially with no restrictions or prices on the discharge of residuals. Using the resulting initial set of discharges as inputs to the natural systems models and the resulting ambient concentrations and effects on living species as arguments of the damage functions, as indicated above, the increment in damages can be determined as the change in damages associated with a unit change in a specific discharge. These incremental damages may then be applied as interim effluent charges on the discharge activities in the linear model, and that model solved again for a new set of production, consumption, modification, and discharge activities. The procedure is repeated until a position close to the optimum is found, that is, convergence occurs.[10]

In the real world, not all damage functions can be expressed in monetary terms, but let us assume that such damage functions could be found for all residuals, so that in fact a full-scale optimization is possible in the sense that no arbitrary ambient or discharge standards have to be specified. This leads us to another of the basic questions mentioned earlier. *Should* decision-makers, that is, representatives of the public – if there are any such representatives, with appropriate responsibilities, a matter to which we will return subsequently – accept this 'optimum' result as *the* basis for policy? It is pertinent to discuss this question because the conceptual model we are describing is in the format of traditional economic cost-benefit analysis which, in principle, aims at maximizing the efficiency or net benefit of the whole system. A necessary condition for this is that incremental damages be equated with incremental costs of management, as the solution just described would do. The two closely related issues raised by this general objective are: measurement of the value of inputs and outputs and the exact specifications of the objective function – the second and third questions raised earlier – to which we now turn.

Evaluation and objective functions

Modern welfare economics (that branch of economic theory which examines the normative properties of market economic systems) concludes that: first, if preference orderings of consumers and production functions of producers (the functions defining physically efficient combinations of inputs and ouptuts) are independent and their shapes appropriately constrained; second, if consumers maximize utility subject to given income and price parameters; and third, if producers maximize profits subject to those price parameters – a set of prices exists such that no individual can be made better off without making some other individual worse off. For any given distribution of income, this is an efficient state. Given certain further assumptions concerning the structure of markets, this Pareto optimum can be achieved via a market pricing mechanism and voluntary decentralized exchange.

The fundamental conceptual basis of cost-benefit analysis is this theorem (although it is not illogical to defend such analysis on more intuitive grounds). It is also the normative basis for the Russell-Spofford model under discussion. What cost-benefit analysis does, essentially, is to attempt to simulate a market result in which, for one reason or another, voluntary exchange does not exist and the resources allocation decision is made through the agency of government. For the most part the inputs to such a management programme – a project or a system of activities – are private goods purchased by the activities implementing the programme, and it is common practice to use market costs as acceptable estimates of social costs. Even this requires a long string of assumptions, for example, that all markets are in competitive equilibrium and there is no unemployment of resources in the economic system. Methods for relaxing some of these assumptions have been developed, but for present purposes we assume that costs are acceptably measured so that the discussion can be turned to the far more serious problem of benefit measurement.

In conventional cost-benefit practice, benefits are measured by making estimates of what consumers would be willing to pay in a market for alternative levels of the publicly provided good or service. As we mentioned, this means simulating a market result where none exists. For example, a mathematical function could be developed which relates incremental improvements in air quality to the 'willingness to pay' for them. Unfortunately, and especially when applied to R.E.Q.M. problems, this approach presents extremely difficult practical problems of measurement and requires some very heroic assumptions about distributional impacts.

In the case of private goods bought and sold in competitive markets, the matter of income distribution can be separated rather nicely from the problem of resources allocation. But the outputs of R.E.Q.M. actions are, as we have remarked several times, always public goods. This means that they are provided to large groups of people simultaneously (although different groups within a region, such as a metropolitan area, may receive significantly different amounts). For example, a reduction in sulphur dioxide (SO_2) may affect major parts of an entire city, and the amount I get if I am a resident of that part of the city is about the same as you get if you are a resident of the same part, and my breathing of the cleaner air does not deprive you of doing it simultaneously. This is different from a private good, in which case, if I eat it, you cannot. The technical name for this phenomenon is 'jointness in supply'.

Thus the income distribution problem associated with these public goods is particularly difficult because the use of the good cannot be differentiated among users on the basis of their voluntary choices in markets. When the supply of a public good (for example, air quality in a city) changes, both efficiency (resources allocation) and distribution (of goods and services) are inevitably affected, as we have seen. Consequently there is, in general, no way to be sure that equating incremental cost with the sum of incremental willingness to pay will yield a welfare maximum (this, we repeat, is the necessary condition for maximum net benefit). The pre-existing distribution of income cannot be maintained except through an elaborate system of side payments tailored to each individual. Such a system of payments is a practical impossibility. This is unlike an economy consisting solely of private goods where equality of marginal cost and price (marginal willingness to pay) can be unambiguously shown to be a necessary condition for a welfare maximum, in the sense of the central theorem. In such a private-goods-only economy, allocative and distributional questions can be neatly separated.

The distributional effect associated with the provision of public goods has been a hard problem for applied public economics, and several procedures have been used to circumvent it. One way is to assume that the marginal utility of income (the satisfaction a person gets from his last dollar of income) is the same for all individuals. This effectively wipes out distributional considerations, because total utility (or welfare) is unaffected by how the output is distributed among recipients. But most economists regard this assumption as grossly unrealistic.

The assumption most often made implicitly or explicitly by applied economists is that it is a mistake to consider individual public goods situations in isolation. Rather, the whole complex of public goods should be considered. Some will affect one group adversely and another group favourably and, on another occasion, vice versa. Thus, there will be many cancellations of distributional effects, and it then follows that the society that makes its decisions based on the efficiency criterion (maximum net benefit disregarding distribution) will be one in which most people will finally be better off than one in which criteria are used which foreclose efficient solutions. It is further assumed that public goods are a rather small part of the economy and that private goods are allocated (through tax and subsidy policy) in an ethically sanctioned way. No economist that we know of is completely happy with this set of assumptions, but it does provide a somewhat defensible basis for testing the efficiency of public decisions.[11]

The scope and difficulty of the empirical measurement required, plus our inability to handle distributional questions in an entirely defensible way, make it impossible to achieve Pareto-optimal allocations of public goods by simulating markets. Therefore, political entrepreneurs who are concerned with general taxation (the allocation between the public and private sectors) and the allocation of government budgets must, in a democratic society, assume general responsibility for deciding about the provision of public goods. Assessing willingness to pay in selected cases may, however, play a very useful role in helping to focus the political process, particularly when it can be shown that large overall efficiency gains are potentially possible. Such evidence gives incentives to political entrepreneurs and ammunition to the public. Moreover, and most unfortunately, the economic technician and the planner or management scientist are often forced to make allocative decisions on the basis of partial evaluations because no proper political institution representing the people involved exists to make such decisions.[12] An example of such an allocative decision is the question of who receives how much of what kinds of environmental quality and who pays how much. In recent times, one result of this has been strong public resistance, through nongovernmental means, when an effort is made to implement an allocation decision. This takes the form of milder or more aggressive forms of 'sabotage', often through the medium of the courts.

In the final analysis, the evaluation and allocation of public goods necessarily is a political problem in any society. This is true however useful the necessarily partial cost-benefit analyses made by technicians may be in aiding and even guiding the political process (or collective choice process as we like to call it). Final dependence cannot be put on disinterested evaluations of efficiency, even if there were a practical, politically sanctioned way of doing it, which there is not. To repeat, this is because such evaluation is necessarily partial and because it does not resolve adequately the distributional problems inherent in public goods situations.

The general point that evaluation of public goods is in the final analysis a political problem is clearly valid. But one cannot reasonably argue, we think, that our present political structures are adequate for solving environmental systems problems. This is surely one reason that the *value* problems associated with R.E.Q.M. have so often been converted into bogus technical problems. But to see what governmental arrangements might be more suitable, we must develop at least the rudiments of a theory of collective choice. One element of the R.F.F. Quality of the Environment programme in recent years has been the development of such a theory and its application to integrated R.E.Q.M. in a region.

Appendix 9A

Management model formulations and optimization scheme.[13] In this appendix we describe the mathematical structure of the overall Russell-Spofford model used in the application described in the following chapter. In Appendix 9B we discuss in some detail natural systems models, and in particular, the one incorporated in the application.

Model formulation

The objective function of the model is in the form of a cost minimization function. This does not mean that the management decision would be related to a single computed optimum. The model is formulated in this way for computational convenience. The coefficients in the objective function include: all the opportunity costs of traditional production inputs; all liquid, gaseous, and energy residuals modification costs; all collection, transport, and landfill costs associated with the handling and disposal of solid residuals; and all costs of directly modifying ambient environmental quality.

There are, basically, four types of constraints in the management model: first, traditional resource availability (inequality); second, continuity, or mass balance, relationships (equality); third, constraints (inequality) on the increased costs of certain consumer services (for example, electricity, sewerage, solid residuals disposal); and fourth, ambient environmental quality (inequality) constraints. The last, which involve the use of environmental models, are employed to constrain the levels of ambient environmental quality. They present the most difficulty and are therefore discussed in the greatest detail.

The regional R.E.Q.M. optimization problem is stated formally as

$$\min \{F = C(X, R)\} \tag{1}$$

subject to

$$g_i(X) = 0 \qquad i = 1, \ldots, m < n - q \tag{2}$$

$$g_i(X) \geqslant 0 \qquad i = m + 1, \ldots, p \tag{3}$$

$$h_i(X) = R_i \qquad i = 1, \ldots, q \tag{4}$$

$$R_i \leqslant S_i \qquad i = 1, \ldots, q \tag{5}$$

$$R_i \geqslant 0 \qquad i = 1, \ldots, q \tag{6}$$

$$X_i \geqslant 0 \qquad i = 1, \ldots, n \tag{7}$$

where $C(X, R)$ is, in general, a nonlinear objective function; $g_i(X) = 0$, $i = 1, \ldots, m$, is a set of linear equality constraints; $g_i(X) \geqslant 0$, $i = m + 1, \ldots, p$, is a set of linear inequality constraints; $h_i(X) = R_i, i = 1, \ldots,$ q, represents a set of environmental functions which relate residuals discharges to ambient concentrations of residuals (discussed in detail in Appendix 5B); X_i, $i = 1, \ldots n$, is a vector of decision, or management, variables, including production levels, residuals modification processes, and residuals discharges; R_i, $i = 1, \ldots, q$, is a vector of ambient levels of residuals concentrations and population sizes of species; and S_t, $i = 1, \ldots,$ q, is a vector of ambient environmental quality standards (for example, concentrations of sulphur dioxide and particulates in the atmosphere, and of algae, fish, and dissolved oxygen in the water).

Some of the necessary environmental functions, $h_i(X) = R_i$, are available in linear form, for example, the air dispersion relationships and Streeter-Phelps-type dissolved oxygen models. Others are available only in nonlinear analytical form, while still others are available in various other forms. For nonlinear aquatic ecosystem models, no analytical expressions – either linear or nonlinear – of the form $h(X) = R$ are available. The variables R_i, $i = 1, \ldots, q$, are expressible only as a set of implicit nonlinear functions and, hence, simulation and other iterative techniques must be used to compute their values. (These various environmental model types are discussed in Appendix 9B.) In general, the environmental constraint set, equation (4), represents a variety of functional forms, many of which are difficult, or even impossible, to deal with using traditional mathematical programming techniques.

Because the optimization scheme (described below) requires that all the constraints be linear, the environmental relationships are removed from the constraint set and dealt with in the objective function. This modification of the problem requires the use of the penalty function concept discussed below.

The new optimization problem may be stated formally as

$$\min\{F = C(X) + P(X)\} \tag{8}$$

subject to

$$g_i(X) = 0 \qquad i = 1, \ldots, m \tag{2}$$

$$g_i(X) \geqslant 0 \qquad i = m+1, \ldots, p \tag{3}$$

$$X_i \geqslant 0 \qquad i = 1, \ldots, n \tag{7}$$

where

$$P(X) = \sum_{i=1}^{q} p_i[S_i,\ R_i = h_i(X)] \tag{9}$$

and where $p_i(S_i, R_i)$, $i = 1, \ldots, q$, are the penalty functions associated with exceeding the environmental standards, S_i, $i = 1, \ldots, q$.

Although the optimization scheme used requires only that those constraints (environmental relationships) that are not of the linear form $R = A \cdot X$ be removed, we note from the formulation of the new problem, equations (8), (2), (3), and (9), that even the linear environmental models have apparently been removed as constraints. This is optional and depends upon the model formulation and its size. If model size (the number of rows and columns) is of no consequence and if the entire management model is contained within a single linear programme, it is more efficient to keep the linear environmental relationships as part of the constraint set. If size is a problem, or if it is otherwise desirable to divide the management model up into a number of smaller linear programmes to be solved sequentially, disposition of the linear environmental models is not as straightforward.

In order to separate a large linear programming problem into a series of smaller ones, either the smaller ones must be completely separable in the sense that none of the original constraints relates variables which are now located in different linear programmes, or one of the available decomposition techniques must be employed. No matter how the larger linear programme is subdivided, the environmental relationships, which involve all the liquid and gaseous residuals discharges throughout the region, invariably link the smaller programmes. Removing these relationships from the constraint set and placing them in the objective function is similar to the decomposition method known in the literature as 'price coordination' (Lagrange method) or 'dual feasible decomposition'.

The scheme used to eliminate environmental relationships from the constraint set and still meet the environmental quality standards, S_i, $i = 1, \ldots, q$, is known as a penalty or exterior point method (as opposed to a barrier or interior point method). The term derives from the fact that throughout the optimization procedure the vector of standards S, equation (5), is allowed to be violated, but only at some 'penalty' to the value of the objective function. The objective of the approach is to make this penalty severe enough in such a way that at the optimum the standards will be satisfied, within some tolerance, and the penalties reduced to essentially zero.

Because in the optimization scheme used the gradient is evaluated, it is necessary that the objective function equation (8) be continuous and have continuous first derivatives. A quadratic penalty function of the following form satisfies these requirements

$$p_i(X) = \max[(h_i(X) - S_i), 0]^2 \qquad i = 1, \ldots, q. \tag{10}$$

For computer applications, equation (1) may be written more conveniently as,

$$p_i(X) = \left[\frac{(h(X)-S) \rightarrow |(h(X)-S)|}{2}\right]^2 \qquad i = 1, \ldots, q, \tag{11}$$

a form which gives $p(X)_i = 0$ when $h_i(X) < S_i$.

The major difficulty with the penalty function expressed above as equation (10) is that, in general, it is not steep enough in the vicinity of the boundary and, consequently, the 'unconstrained' optimum is apt to lie substantially outside the feasible region. However, a slight modification to the P function remedies this situation. If $r > 0$, and $p_i(X) \neq 0$, the new penalty function

$$\frac{1}{r_i} p_i(X) \tag{12}$$

approaches infinity as $r_i \rightarrow 0$. Specifying a sequence of decreasing values for r has the effect of moving the unconstrained optimum closer to the boundary of the feasible region. From a computational point of view, it is sufficient that r only be made small enough to ensure that the unconstrained optimum is within a preselected distance of the boundary.

This procedure may be explained heuristically as follows. Given $r^{(1)} > 0$, where $r^{(1)}$ is usually chosen to be 1, $X^{(1)}$ is solved for using one of the available maximization techniques. Then, using $r^{(2)}$, $X^{(2)}$ is solved for, again using one of the available maximization techniques, and so on. When $X^{(k)}$ satisfies (within a specified tolerance) the original constraint set, the procedure is terminated, as this is also the optimal point for the original problem.

The optimization procedure

Thus far, a formal mathematical statement of the regional R.E.Q.M. problem has been presented, a penalty function method for eliminating all but the linear constraints discussed, and the problem restated in terms of a nonlinear minimum cost objective function and a linear constraint set, but nothing has been said about the nonlinear optimization procedure used. We now turn to this.

The procedure used is analogous to the gradient method of nonlinear programming. The technique consists of linearizing the response surface in the vicinity of a feasible point $X^{(k)}$. To do this, a tangent plane is constructed at this point by employing the first two terms of a Taylor's series expansion (up to first partial derivatives). This linear approximation to the nonlinear response surface will, in general, be most accurate in the vicinity of the point $X^{(k)}$ and less accurate as one moves farther away from this point. Because of this, a set of 'artificial' bounds is imposed on the system to restrict the selection of the next position along the response surface to that portion of the surface most closely approximated by the newly created linear surface. The selection of the appropriate set of artificial bounds is analogous to choosing a step size in other gradient methods of nonlinear programming.

Because the newly created subproblem is in a linear form, it is possible to make use of standard linear programming techniques for finding a new optimal point, $X^{(k+1)}$. This point locates the minimum value of the linearized objective function within the artificially confined area of the response surface. Because, in general, the linearized surface will not match the original nonlinear surface, the original nonlinear objective function must be evaluated at this point to determine whether or not this new point $X^{(k+1)}$ is, in fact, a better position than the previously determined one $X^{(k)}$ That is, the following condition must be satisfied

$$F[X^{(k+1)}] > F[X^{(k)}]$$

If this condition is satisfied, a new tangent plane is constructed at the point $X^{(k+1)}$, and a new set of artificial bounds is placed around this point. As before, linear programming is employed to find a new position $X^{(k+2)}$, which minimizes the linearized objective function, and so on until a local optimum is reached.

As has been pointed out, this optimization procedure requires that the objective function be linearized at point $X^{(k)}$. This is done according to the formulation explained in the following section.

Now that the essence of the optimization scheme used has been presented, including a discussion of the linear programming subproblem that must be both constructed and solved at each step along the ascent procedure, we can restate the management problem in these terms

$$\min\{F[X^{(k+1)}] = [\nabla C[X^{(k)}] + \nabla P[X^{(k)}] \cdot X^{(k+1)} + \gamma\} \quad (13)$$

subject to

$$g_i(X) = 0 \qquad i = 1, \ldots, m \quad (2)$$

$$g_i(X) \geqslant 0 \qquad i = m+1, \ldots, p \quad (3)$$

$$x_i \geqslant 0 \qquad i = 1, \ldots, n \quad (7)$$

$$x_j \leqslant \beta_j \qquad j = 1, \ldots, s \quad (14)$$

$$x_j \geqslant \alpha_j \qquad j = 1, \ldots, s \quad (15)$$

where γ is a constant and where β_j and α_j are, respectively, upper and lower bounds on the s discharge variables at the $(k+1)$th iteration. As mentioned previously, setting these bounds is similar to selecting a step size with other gradient methods of nonlinear programming. The efficiency of the optimization scheme depends directly on the selection of these bounds.

The linearized objective function equation (13) may be expressed in a slightly different form as

$$F = \left(\frac{\partial C(X)}{\partial X}\right)\cdot X + \left(\frac{\partial P(X)}{\partial X}\right)\cdot X + \gamma \tag{16}$$

In the R.E.Q.M. problem, $(\partial C(X)/\partial X)$ is a vector of linear cost coefficients associated with traditional production inputs – and residuals handling, modification, and disposal activities – and $[\partial P(X)/\partial X]$ is a vector of marginal penalties associated with the discharge of each residual.

Given that $R = h(X)$, equation (4), we see from equation (10) that

$$\frac{\partial P(X)}{\partial x_j} = \sum_{i=1}^{q} \frac{2}{r_i}(\max[(R_i - S_i), 0])\frac{\partial R_i}{\partial x_j} \qquad j = 1, \ldots, n \tag{17}$$

The term $2/r_i(\max[(R_i - S_i), 0])$ represents the slope dp_i/dR_i of the ith penalty function evaluated at the point R_i. The term $\partial R_i/\partial x_j$ represents the marginal response of the ith descriptor of the natural world (or ecosystem) to changes in the discharge of the jth residual. Equation (17) may be expressed more generally as,

$$\frac{\partial P(X)}{\partial x_j} = \sum_{i=1}^{q} \frac{dp_i}{dR_i}\cdot\frac{\partial R_i}{\partial x_j} \qquad j = 1, \ldots, n \tag{18}$$

or in matrix notation as

$$\frac{\partial P(X)}{\partial X} = \left(\frac{\partial R}{\partial X}\right)^T \cdot \frac{dp}{dR} \tag{19}$$

For linear environmental systems, $\partial R_i/\partial x_j$ is an element of the matrix of transfer coefficients A when the environmental functions are expressed linearly as

$$R = h(X) = A \cdot X \tag{20}$$

Hence, for the case of linear environmental systems, the marginal penalties may be expressed in matrix notation as

$$\left(\frac{\partial P}{\partial X}\right) = A^T \cdot \left(\frac{dp}{dR}\right) \tag{21}$$

where $(\partial P/\partial X)$ is a vector of marginal penalties, A is a matrix of environmental transfer coefficients, and (dp/dR) is a vector of slopes of the penalty functions evaluated at R.

For the case of nonlinear environmental models, the situation is similar except that evaluation of the environmental response matrix $(\partial R/\partial X)$ is somewhat more involved, and, in addition, because the response is nonlinear, it must be recomputed for each state of the natural world. Evaluation of the $(\partial R/\partial X)$ response matrix for the nonlinear aquatic ecosystem model not only involves taking derivatives of a system of implicit nonlinear algebraic equations, but it also involves using the chain rule for differentiating a series of interrelated functional forms.

One major problem with a large nonlinear programming problem of the type discussed here is that it may frequently by nonconvex. If this is so, then the procedure for solving it may fail to find the optimum optimorum and instead come to a halt at a lesser peak in the objective function.

Appendix 9B
Natural systems models[14]

In both the text and Appendix 9A, we have referred to models of natural environmental systems and the central role they play in analysis for R.E.Q.M. In this appendix we present a brief discussion of the various types of such models and the procedures by which they are incorporated in the larger model discussed in Appendix 9A.

Natural systems models – air and water dispersion, sediment and nutrient runoff from land, chemical reaction, and biological systems – may be used to describe the impact on the environment of energy and material residuals discharged from the production and consumption activities included in a regional R.E.Q.M. model. Generally, natural systems models are used to specify steady state ambient concentrations of residuals and population sizes of species, at various points in space throughout the region of interest, given a set of values for such environmental variables as stream flow and velocity, groundwater flow and aquifer characteristics, slope and soil erodability, wind speed and direction, atmospheric stability, and atmospheric mixing depth.

Some environmental models are easier to deal with than others within a mathematical optimization framework. In general, this depends on the mathematical structure of the model. In terms of the complexity involved, it is useful to distinguish among four broad categories of models: first, linear, explicit fractions; second, linear, implicit functions; third, non-linear, explicit functions; and fourth, nonlinear, implicit functions.

Two natural systems submodels were actually used in conjunction with the regional R.E.Q.M. model discussed in Appendix 9A. The first, a linear atmospheric dispersion model, was used to predict ambient concentration levels of sulphur dioxide and suspended particulates throughout the region. The second, a nonlinear aquatic ecosystem model, was used to predict ambient concentrations of various materials, and population sizes of certain species, throughout the water body involved, the Delaware Estuary. This model was developed at R.F.F. by Robert Kelly specifically for the regional R.E.Q.M. study. These two models represent the extremes of complexity for inclusion within a R.E.Q.M. model framework. A discussion of each will raise some of the important issues and will reveal some of the problems involved and how they were handled.

Atmospheric dispersion model

Of the various atmospheric quality models that are now available, physical dispersion models are the most advanced.[15] Chemical reaction models, such as those dealing with photochemical smog, are in the early stages of application. The most successful modelling efforts to date have been associated with predicting both steady and nosteady state distributions of sulphur dioxide, and particulates of 20 microns or more in diameter. Because of the availability of an existing air dispersion model, and the importance of these materials in the atmospheric environment of the region, ambient levels of sulphur dioxide and suspended particulates were selected to represent the air quality of the region.

The atmospheric model used in the R.E.Q.M. model is the dispersion model from the federal government's Air Quality Implementation Planning Programme (I.P.P.). This model is a point source Gaussian plume formulation. This formulation, which is based on mass continuity considerations, may be used to estimate ambient concentrations under deterministic, steady state conditions. For any given source-receptor pair, specified meteorological conditions, and discharge rate of unity, this nonlinear equation reduces to a linear coefficient relating ambient concentrations with residuals discharge rates. This is characteristic of physical dispersion type models.[16]

The necessary inputs to the atmospheric dispersion model are: $x-y$ coordinates of all sources and receptors in the region; residuals discharge rates for each source-point and area; physical stack height, stack diameter, stack exit temperature, and stack exit velocity for each point source; a seasonal joint probability distribution for wind speed, wind direction and atmospheric stability; mean seasonal temperature and pressure; and a mean atmospheric mixing depth for the period of interest. The output of this dispersion model represents arithmetic mean seasonal concentrations of sulphur dioxide and suspended particulates based on the probabilities of occurrence of a large number of discrete meteorological situations.

For a given set of meteorological conditions and physical parameters, the vector of mean seasonal concentrations of sulphur dioxide and particulates R may be expressed linearly, in matrix notation, as

$$R = AX + B \qquad (1)$$

where X is a vector of sulphur dioxide and particulate discharge rates; A is a matrix of transfer coefficients which specify, for each source-receptor pair in the region, the contribution to ambient concentrations associated with a residual discharge rate of unity; and B is a vector of background concentration levels. The matrix of transfer coefficients A is the output of the dispersion model.

The important thing to note from equation (1) is that the state of the natural world R is expressed directly in terms of linear, explicit algebraic functions. This particular mathematical form is relatively easy to deal with in an optimization framework. In fact, as is readily seen, equation (1) may be incorporated directly within the constraint set of a standard linear programme when one of the management objectives is to constrain ambient concentrations of residuals.

As indicated in equation (16) and the associated text in Appendix 9A, one of the requirements of the optimization scheme used is the availability of an environmental response matrix, $(\partial R_i/\partial x_j)$, $i = 1, \ldots, n$, $j = 1, \ldots, m$, where n is the number of designated receptor locations in the region and m is the total number of residuals discharges. This matrix may be obtained by differentiating equation (1) with respect to all the residuals discharges in the region, that is

$$\left(\frac{\partial R}{\partial X}\right) = A \qquad (2)$$

or simply the matrix of transfer coefficients.

Before leaving this section, we should point out that not all atmospheric quality models are as easy to deal with as the physical dispersion models, which are expressed in linear, explicit analytical form. Chemical reaction models such as for photochemical smog, would be significantly more difficult to handle within a mathematical optimization framework. The kinds of problems we would face with them are revealed in the discussion of a nonlinear aquatic ecosystem model which follows.

Aquatic ecosystem model

A variety of indicators are commonly used for describing the quality of a body of water. Among them are: bacterial counts, algal densities, taste, odour, pH, turbidity, suspended and dissolved solids, dissolved oxygen, temperature, and population sizes of certain plant and animal species. Because of the importance of dissolved oxygen to virtually all species of higher animals, the ease of measurement, and the relative ease with which it can be modelled for a river or estuary, its concentration has been, and still is, one of the most frequently used criteria for setting general water quality standards.

Streeter-Phelps-type dissolved oxygen models have been used for many years to predict water quality as a result of discharges of organic material (most notably, sanitary sewage). As we pointed out earlier, the steady state solution of such models results in a matrix of transfer coefficients which is exactly parallel in its use in the R.E.Q.M. model to that resulting from the steady state solution of the atmospheric dispersion model.

However, these models have three major deficiencies which the R.F.F. modelling team felt warranted the development of a more sophisticated aquatic ecosystem model. First, there is interest in the dissolved oxygen level only in so far as it is an accurate indicator of such things as algal densities and the population sizes of certain species of fish. To the extent that these densities and populations can vary independently of dissolved oxygen concentrations, we need information about them independently if policies on water quality are to be established intelligently. Second, materials other than organic (for example, nutrients and toxics) are known to have significant effects on aquatic ecosystems. Consequently, these inputs should be explicitly included along with the organics to evaluate more fully the impacts on the aquatic environment of residuals discharges. Finally, systems ecologists feel that aquatic ecosystem models based on at least some biological (or ecological) theory that includes the mechanisms of feeding, growth, predation, excretion, death, and so forth, are more reliable for prediction purposes than the more empirically based linear models of the Streeter-Phelps variety, even for predicting dissolved oxygen levels.

The aquatic ecosystem model developed at R.F.F. is based on a trophic level approach. The components of the ecosystem are grouped in classes (compartments) according to their functions, and each class is represented in the model by an endogenous, or state, variable. Eleven components (compartments) are designated in the model. The endogenous variables representing these eleven components are: nitrogen, phosphorus, turbidity (suspended solids), organic material, algae, bacteria, fish, zooplankton, dissolved oxygen, toxics, and heat (temperature). In addition, the following exogenous variables are considered: turnover rate (or advective estuary flow) and inputs (of the eleven chemical and biological materials above). Carbon is assumed not to be limiting and, hence, is not considered as either an endogenous or exogenous variable. Inputs to and outputs from a single reach of the model are illustrated in Figure 9.3; internal material flows within a single reach are depicted in Figure 9.4.

The inputs to the estuary model from the residuals discharges in the region are: organic material measured by its BOD_5, total nitrogen, phosphorus, phenols (toxics), and heat. The outputs are: densities of fish biomass, algal densities, and dissolved oxygen concentrations. The levels of these outputs are constrained, that is, environmental standards are imposed. In addition, concentrations of nitrogen, phosphorus, suspended solids, and organic material; temperature; and mass of bacteria and

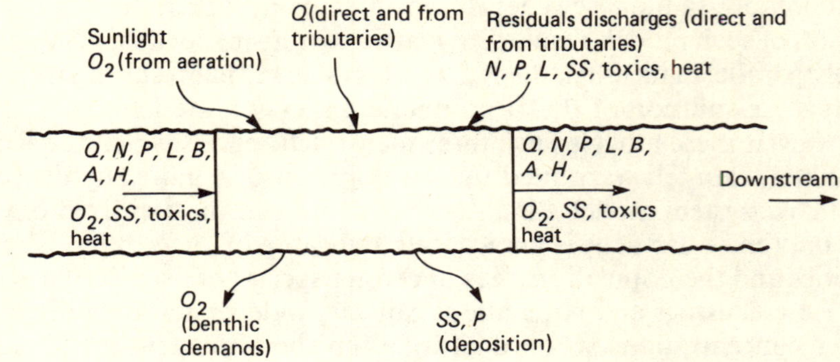

Notation: N = nitrogen $\quad$ H = zooplankton $\quad$ O = dissolved oxygen
P = phosphorus $\quad$ F = fish $\quad$ SS = suspended solids
A = algae $\quad$ L = organic matter (as BOD) $\quad$ Q = advective flow
B = bacteria

Figure 9.3 *Inputs and Outputs of a Single Reach: Delaware Estuary Eco-system Model*

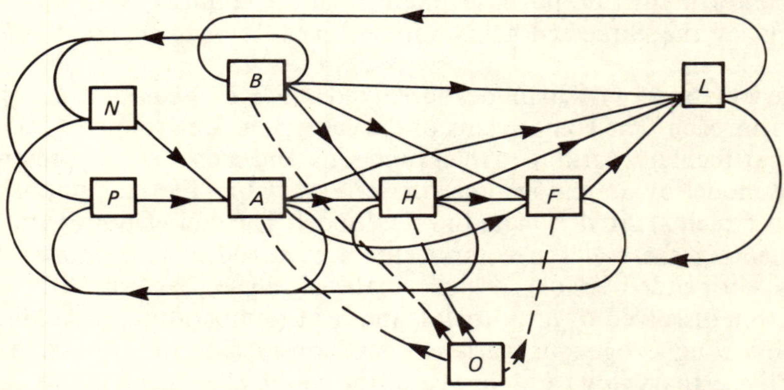

Notation: N = nitrogen $\quad$ H = zooplankton $\quad$ O= dissolved oxygen
P = phosphorus $\quad$ F = fish $\quad$ SS = suspended solids
A = algae $\quad$ L = organic matters (as BOD) $\quad$ Q = advective flow
B = bacteria

Note: The three remaining endogenous variables - heat (temperature), toxics, and suspended solids - are assumed to affect the rates of material transfers among the ecosystem components or 'compartments.'

Figure 9.4 *Internal Materials Flows within a Single Reach Delaware Estuary Eco-system Model*

Source: Spofford, Russell and Kelly, 'Operational Problems in Large-Scale Residuals Management Models', in Edwin Mills (ed.), *Economic Analysis of Environmental Problems*, National Bureau of Economic Research and Resources for the Future, 1975, p. 185.

zooplankton are also available as by-product outputs of this model.

The time rate of change of material in each compartment is expressed in terms of the sum of the transfers among other compartments and between adjacent sections of the estuary (since the material is distributed spatially as well as temporally). In order to ensure mass continuity of the materials considered, all materials entering and leaving a compartment are explicitly accounted for. By convention, oxygen is not included in the mass balances for species and materials, except, of course, for the oxygen balance itself. For the three nutrients – carbon (C), phosphorus (P), and nitrogen (N) – a mass balance is made on the individual chemical elements. For species, a mass balance is made on the total weight of carbon, phosphorus, and nitrogen. Fixed proportions of $C:P:N$ are assumed in the living components. The mathematical description of material transfers among compartments is based on the theoretical and empirical formulations given by Odum.[17]

Each compartment requires a separate differential equation to describe mass continuity, and, in general, these equations must be solved simultaneously. In this particular case, the differential equations are ordinary ones of the first order, nonlinear variety. In addition to these eleven equations, a set of similar differential equations is required for each reach of the estuary.

The general form of the differential equation set for the kth reach may be expressed as,

$$\left(\frac{dR}{dt}\right)^{(k)} = f[R(t)^{(k-1)}, R(t)^{(k)}, R(t)^{(k+1)}, X(t)^{(k)}] \tag{3}$$

where $(dR/dt)^{(k)}$ is a vector of time rates of change of the endogenous variables in the kth reach, $R^{(k)}$; and $X^{(k)}$ is a vector of residuals discharges into the kth reach.

Equation (3) is a set of ordinary nonlinear differential equations – one equation for each compartment and one set of compartmental equations for each estuary reach – that must be solved simultaneously. If one is interested in the transient (or nonsteady) states of the system, simulation techniques, that is, numerical integration (simulating over space and then time) furnishes a readily available means of solution. However, only the steady state solution was applied in the regional R.E.Q.M. model. There are two possibilities for determining steady state solutions, neither of which guarantees finding a stable point equilibrium: first, simultaneous simulation of a nonlinear differential equation set; and second, simultaneous solution of a set of nonlinear algebraic equations. If inputs to and outflows from each reach due to longitudinal diffusion are put aside, the system can be dealt with over time first, and then over space, starting with the uppermost reach and progressing systematically down the estuary.[18]

In this case, equation (3) for the kth reach would reduce to

$$\left(\frac{dR}{dt}\right)^{(k)} = f[R(t)^{(k-1)}, R(t)^{(k)}, X(t)^{(k)}] \tag{4}$$

Now only the eleven compartmental equations within each reach must be solved simultaneously. The state of the system within a particular reach depends only upon the inputs from upstream $R(t)^{(k-1)}$ and the residuals discharges to the kth reach $X(t)^{(k)}$ both of which may now be treated as exogenous inputs. In addition, if the resulting steady state solution $R^{*(k)}$ is independent of the time paths of rates of inputs, $R(t)^{(k-1)}$ and $X(t)^{(k)}$, equation (4) reduces to

$$\left(\frac{dR}{dt}\right)^{(k)} = f[R^{*(k-1)}, X^{*(k)}, R(t)^{(k)}] \tag{5}$$

Usually, ecological models are solved by simulation. Simulation of the differential equation set (a set of equations similar to equations (3) through (5)) poses no particular problem, but the steady state solution, if one exists at all, may take considerable time.

Even when a steady state solution can be found, an additional problem is that there may be more than one stable point equilibrium. To investigate this problem, an experiment was run with the ecosystem model. A random number generator was used to provide a set of random starting points. Twenty-five random starts resulted in the same steady state solution.

At steady state, $(dR/dt) = 0$, and thus the differential equation set above, equation (5), reduces to a set of nonlinear algebraic equations of the following form

$$0 = f[R^{*(k-1)}, X^{*(k)}, R^{*(k)}] \tag{6}$$

The endogenous variables $R^{*(k)}$ are implicitly expressed in this formulation.

To include this nonlinear aquatic ecosystem model within the regional R.E.Q.M. model, in addition to determining a set of steady state values, it is necessary to evaluate the response throughout the ecosystem to changes in the rates of the residuals discharges. That is, it is necessary to know, for example, the effect on algae in reach seventeen of an additional load discharged into reach eight, and so forth. In contrast to the linear steady state models, this requirement results in a considerable number of additional computations, but this is the key to being able to use these complex ecosystem models within the optimization framework.

The response matrix we wish to compute may, as has already been pointed out above, be expressed in matrix notation as $(\partial R/\partial X)$, where R is a vector describing the state of the system throughout the entire length of the estuary, and X is a vector of residuals discharges throughout the region. Using equation (6) for each reach of the estuary, and the relationship,

$$Z^{(k)} = q^{(k)} R^{(k-1)} + X^{(k)} \tag{7}$$

where $Z^{(k)}$ is a vector of inputs to the kth reach; $R^{(k-1)}$ is a vector of concentrations of materials in reach $(k-1)$; $q^{(k)}$ is the estuary advective flow rate into the kth reach; and $X^{(k)}$ is a vector of residuals discharges to the kth reach, a section of the system response matrix may be computed according to

$$\frac{\partial R^{(i)}}{\partial X^{(j)}} = \frac{\partial R^{(i)}}{\partial Z^{(i)}} \cdot \frac{\partial Z^{(i)}}{\partial R^{(i-1)}} \cdot \frac{\partial R^{(i-1)}}{\partial Z^{(i-1)}} \cdots \frac{\partial R^{(j+1)}}{\partial Z^{(j+1)}} \cdot \frac{\partial Z^{(j+1)}}{\partial R^{(j)}} \cdot \frac{\partial R^{(j)}}{\partial Z^{(j)}} \cdot \frac{\partial Z^{(j)}}{\partial X^{(j)}}. \tag{8}$$

From equation (7) we note that

$$\frac{\partial Z^{(k)}}{\partial R^{(k-1)}} = q^{(k)} I \tag{9}$$

and

$$\frac{\partial Z^{(k)}}{\partial X^{(k)}} = I, \tag{10}$$

where I is the identity matrix. Thus, the $[\partial Z^{(k)}/\partial R^{(k-1)}]$ terms are known a priori and are exogenous parameters in the ecosystem model.

The other terms $[\partial R^{(k)}/\partial Z^{(k)}]$ are evaluated from equation (6) according to the rules for differentiating implicit functions. That is

$$\left(\frac{\partial f}{\partial R}\right) \cdot \left(\frac{\partial R}{\partial Z}\right) = -\left(\frac{\partial f}{\partial Z}\right)$$

or

$$\left(\frac{\partial R}{\partial Z}\right) \cdot \left(\frac{\partial f}{\partial R}\right)^{-1} \left(\frac{\partial f}{\partial Z}\right) \tag{11}$$

This operation involves the inversion of the Jacobian matrix $(\partial f/\partial R)$. In addition, because the system of equations is nonlinear, the Jacobian matrix $(\partial f/\partial R)$ must be recomputed for each state of the natural world.

It should be clear, then, from the above discussion, that the major problems associated with including environmental models within the management framework is one of computer time. Nonlinear representations of the natural world increase the complexity and the number of calculations necessary for each iteration, but they also increase the realism, predictive capability, and information output of the R.E.Q.M. model.

Notes

1 It should be emphasized that there is a wide range in the degree of sophistication of quantitative models, from fixed coefficient, 'back of the envelope' type to complicated mathematical programming type models. The degree of model sophistication should be a function of the questions to be answered, the constraints in the given situation, and the analytical resources – personnel, time, data, computer facilities – available.

2 Similar extensions can, of course, be made to models of activities other than industrial: commercial, residential, agricultural, silvicultural and mining.

3 This paragraph is not meant to imply that either it is always necessary to develop such models or that it is always feasible to do so.

4 There is, of course, the important subsidiary question of how detailed the various submodels (activities and natural systems) should be.

5 See Robert Dorfman, 'Operations Research', *American Economic Review*, vol. 50, no. 4 (1960), p. 575.

6 This is not to say that these links – prices – can always be taken to be exogenous constants. They may be exogenous variables whose value depends upon the state of the R.E.Q.M. system. In this case a management model might be linked with an input-output model to capture secondary stresses in the system.

7 There are multiple objectives in most, if not all, decision contexts. It is highly unlikely that all of these can be incorporated in a single objective function. Consequently, the results of mathematical optimization models represent only part of the information that goes into the decision-making process.

8 See Clifford S. Russell and Walter O. Spofford, Jr., 'A Quantitative Framework for Residuals Management Decisions', in Allen V. Kneese and Blair T. Bower (eds.), *Environmental Quality Analysis: Theory and Method in the Social Sciences*, Johns Hopkins University Press, Baltimore, 1972.

9 It should be noted, however, that physical, chemical and biological interactions among residuals in the environment cannot be handled in this simple manner.

10 The regional R.E.Q.M. problem could also be stated in a completely general manner not suitable to numerical solution but perhaps easier to understand. The objective is to maximize, for a region, a complicated economic criterion function reflecting the costs of regional production, the benefits from regional consumption, the costs of residuals modification, and the external damages resulting from residuals discharges, with allowance for the 'assimilative' capabilities of the regional environment. In this form, the regional residuals management problem is a general nonlinear programming problem with both objective function and some constraints being nonlinear. For more detailed explanations of the general structure of the Russell-Spofford model, see Russell and Spofford, *A Qualitative Framework*.

11 Note that the same problem exists in nonmarket economics, where publicly provided goods (not necessarily 'public goods' in the strictest sense) comprise a larger portion of the economy and where prices are often structured to achieve specified social goals rather than economic efficiency.

12 It is also true, however, that, even where reasonably representative

governmental agencies exist, the politicians often fail to provide adequate guidance to the professional staffs.

13 This appendix is based on material prepared by Walter O. Spofford, Jr. and Clifford S. Russell.

14 This appendix is based on material prepared by Walter O. Spofford, Jr. and Robert A. Kelly.

15 For a description of these models, see, for example, H. Moses, *Mathematical Urban Air Pollution Models*, Report No. ANL/ES-RPY-001, Argonne, Illinois, 1969.

16 A model that reduces to a set of linear equations for steady state conditions is also available for analyzing the impact of organic residuals discharges on the dissolved oxygen regimes of streams. It is known as the Streeter–Phelps model. This type has frequently been used in water quality planning, but is not used in this study, having been replaced by the nonlinear aquatic ecosystem model.

17 See Howard T. Odum, 'An Energy Circuit Language for Ecological and Social Systems: Its Physical Basis', in Bernard C. Patten (ed.), *Systems Analysis and Simulation in Ecology*, vol. 2, Academic Press, New York, 1972.

18 Neglecting longitudinal diffusion, even in an estuary, is not as unreasonable as it first appears. Finite difference techniques for solving these differential equations introduce a numerical diffusion effect into the model. Inputs are immediately mixed in the volume, not because of any physical effects, but solely because of the numerical procedure. See Donald J. O'Connor and Robert V. Thomann, 'Water Quality Models: Chemical, Physical and Biological Constituents', in U.S. Environmental Protection Agency, *Estuarine Modeling*, stock no. 5501–0129, chapter 3, p. 138, 1971.

CASE STUDY 2

The residuals management and political modelling work done in the Quality of the Environment programme, although productive of a number of results in its conceptual phases, led naturally to an attempt to apply it in a realistic setting. A detailed description of this effort was published in an R.F.F. research paper *Environmental Quality Management: An Application to the Lower Delaware Valley*, by Walter O. Spofford, Jr., Clifford S. Russell, and Robert A. Kelly. This chapter has been adapted, and in many cases, quoted from that book.[1] The case study had several specific objectives. The order in which they are discussed does not imply relative importance.

One objective was to say something about the practical importance of including within a single analytical framework airborne, waterborne, and solid residuals. As we have shown, the regional residuals management problem cannot, in principle, be solved by considering air or water or solids in isolation because of the links among forms of residuals and discharge media that are implied by the conservation of mass and energy in production, use, and residuals modification processes. There was, however, no hard evidence on the quantitative extent of the linkages and the size of the costs implied by isolated solutions in real situations. The applied model was intended to be a good enough representation of an actual region to yield one piece of defensible evidence, at least on the extent of the linkages.[2] This model is referred to here as the Lower Delaware Valley model, or the regional R.E.Q.M. model.

A second objective was to generate information on the cost implications – both total regional costs and distribution of costs – of utilizing various types of collective facilities within a regional R.E.Q.M. context. Examples of such facilities are regional sewage treatment plants, instream aeration installations, and plants to produce paper from used paper products generated in multiple activities.

A third objective was to explore computational problems inherent in large-scale regional analyses; that is, how best to handle large amounts of data, how to aggregate with minimal loss of useful information, and how best to decompose large-scale models so that they become easier to compute.

A fourth objective was to produce an application with sufficient verisimilitude to see whether and how such models might work in an actual legislative and executive setting. Experimental work in this area was encouraging, but also indicated that the inclusion of the necessary information on the distribution of costs and benefits added significantly to the difficulties of constructing an applied regional R.E.Q.M. model and promised that in a real setting this information would add significantly to the model size. Making the extension include distributional information would permit an exploration of the degree to which the utility of the regional R.E.Q.M. model might be increased by the use of a political model that would allow potential legislative and executive users to explore distributional aspects efficiently. At the very least, this extension would permit the exploration of the costs of providing politically useful analysis on the distribution of costs and benefits of alternative physical measures for improving ambient environmental quality.

In the real world, the range of R.E.Q.M. strategies involved, the multiple sources and many types of residuals, and the varied distributions of effects and costs result in an almost infinite number of possible combinations. How can such complexity be represented and the results of analyses be communicated so as to make meaningful decisions possible? Developing data that would shed light on this question in a real situation was another closely related objective.

A final objective was to investigate the costs and benefits implied by incorporating a nonlinear model of the natural world, as discussed in the previous chapter and its appendixes, within a regional R.E.Q.M. model optimization framework. It was hoped to arrive at some basis for judging whether the increased computational costs and problems appear to be outweighed by some combination of greater accuracy and increased output of information relevant to policy making.

The region

The region chosen for the application of the conceptual and mathematical model explained in the previous chapter and its appendixes was the Lower Delaware Valley. This is a very complex area with many individual point and nonpoint sources of residuals discharges. It was chosen in preference to simpler regions where fewer data might be required for several reasons. First, its very complexity provides a severe test of whether the analytical approach can be applied. If it can be applied there, it should be possible to apply it almost anywhere. In addition, the approach could represent the kernel of a useful analytical too for policy making in one of the most important regions in the United States. Second, ties existed between R.F.F. and certain regional institutions, particularly the Delaware River Basin Commission. Third, this region has been extensively studied for other purposes, so that a body of pertinent information was available surpassing that for most other regions. Accordingly, even though the Lower Delaware Valley is very complex, its advantages in terms of data availability and familiarity were considered sufficient to offset the costs of complexity.

The region is defined by county boundaries as shown in Figure 9.5. It covers an area of about 4,700 square miles (approximately 12,200 square kilometres). The grid superimposed on the figure is used for locating dischargers and receptors of gaseous residuals in the model. It is related to the Universal Transverse Mercator Grid covering the United States. The region consists of Bucks, Montgomery, Chester, Delaware, and Philadelphia counties in Pennsylvania, Mercer, Burlington, Camden, Gloucester, and Salem counties in New Jersey; and New Castle County in Delaware. The major cities in the area are Philadelphia (conterminous with Philadelphia County); Trenton in Mercer County; Camden in Camden County; and Wilmington in New Castle County. There are 379 incorporated political jurisdictions – cities, towns, townships, boroughs, and divisions – in the eleven counties.

The 1970 population was little more than 5.5 million. Of this, 35 per cent was accounted for by Philadelphia alone, with Trenton, Camden, and Wilmington each accounting for 5 per cent. However, these figures do not fully indicate the extent of urbanization, for ten of the eleven counties – Salem being the exception – are over 70 per cent urbanized.[3]

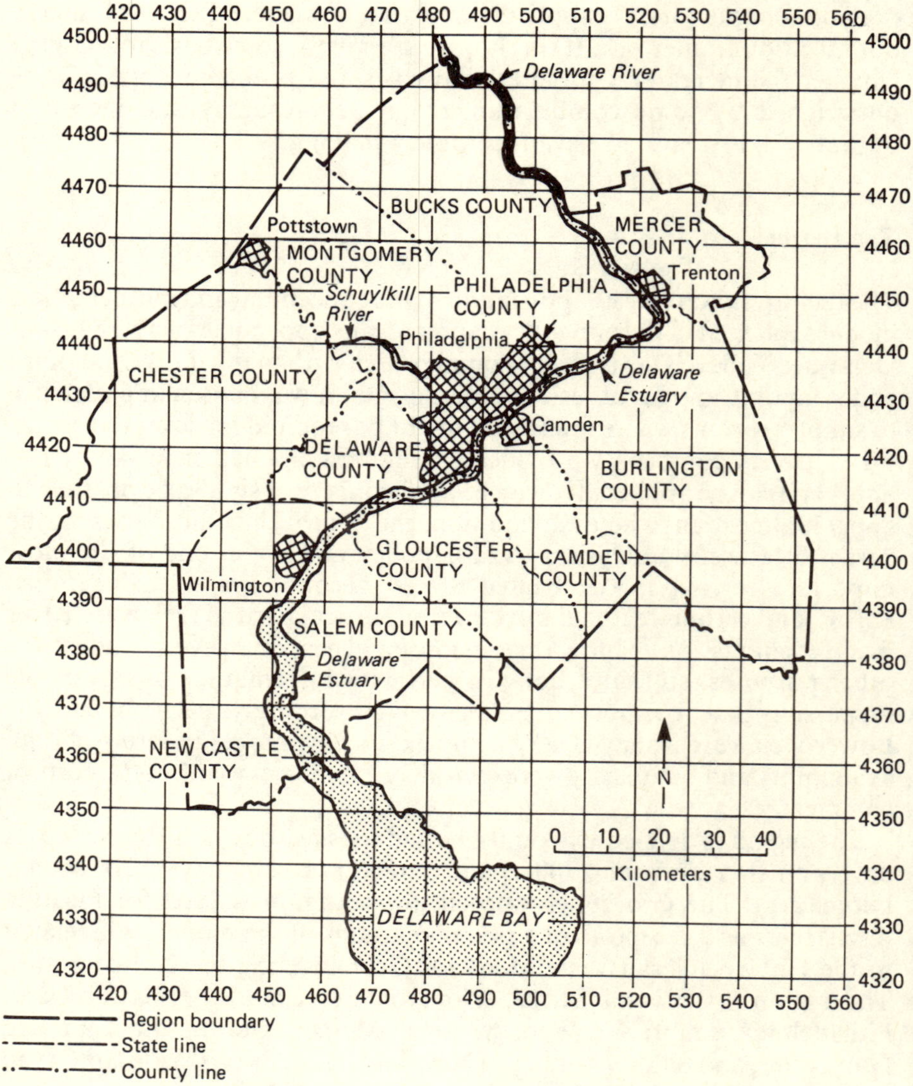

Figure 9.5 *Lower Delaware Valley Region*

Source: Spofford, Russel and Kelly, *Environmental Quality*, p. 4.

Population densities range to as high as over 15,000 per square mile in Philadelphia, and are 1,000 or greater for four other counties. In both Pennsylvania and Delaware, densities in the region are uniformly greater than the average for the respective states as a whole, but in New Jersey the suburban counties of Burlington and Gloucester, and rural Salem

County are all less densely populated than the average for the state.

Incomes are generally high in the region. Using median family income as an indicator, every county except Philadelphia has a higher median family income than the United States as a whole. Salem County has the lowest median income outside Philadelphia; Montgomery County has the region's highest median income. The difference between these two extremes is about $2,500 per family per year, or about 25 per cent of the lower figure. Thus, there are significant intraregional income differences, even at the highly aggregated level of counties. This suggests that the distributional implications of R.E.Q.M. strategies will be an important issue in the region. This presumption is accentuated by the fact that it is Philadelphia that sits in the centre of the largest industrial concentration, has the highest population density, and hence can be expected to have the greatest ambient environmental quality (A.E.Q.) problems, that also has the lowest per capita income base from which to pay for improving A.E.Q.

The region is one of the most heavily industrialized areas in the United States. It contains: seven large petroleum refineries; five large steel mills and many smaller ones; thirteen pulp and paper or paper mills with more than 100 tons per day output, and numerous smaller ones; fifteen large thermal electric energy-generating plants and two smaller ones; many large and small chemical and petrochemical plants of various types; and many other types of industrial operations, including foundries and automobiles and electronic assembly plants.

In 1968, there were seventeen municipal sewage treatment plants in the region with flows greater than one million gallons per day (mgd) discharging to the Delaware Estuary. (Seven of these plants had flows greater than 10 mgd.) In addition, 123 sewage treatment plants of various sizes discharged to the Schuylkill River and to the tributaries of the two major rivers.[4] In 1970 there were seventeen municipal incinerators and numerous landfills and dumps in operation in the region.

Surface waters

The major recipient of waterborne residuals in the Lower Delaware Valley region is the Delaware Estuary itself.[5] The estuary consists of the 85-mile stretch between the head of the tide at Trenton and the head of Delaware Bay at Liston Point, Delaware, Figure 9.6 shows the estuary and twenty of the twenty-two reaches into which it was divided for modelling purposes.

The flow of the river varies widely, from month to month and year to year. During the period from 1951 through 1972, for example, the monthly mean flow at Trenton varied from a low of about 1,550 cubic feet per second (cfs) in July of 1965 to a high of nearly 40,000 cfs in late spring of 1958. The mean annual flow for this period ranged from a low of about

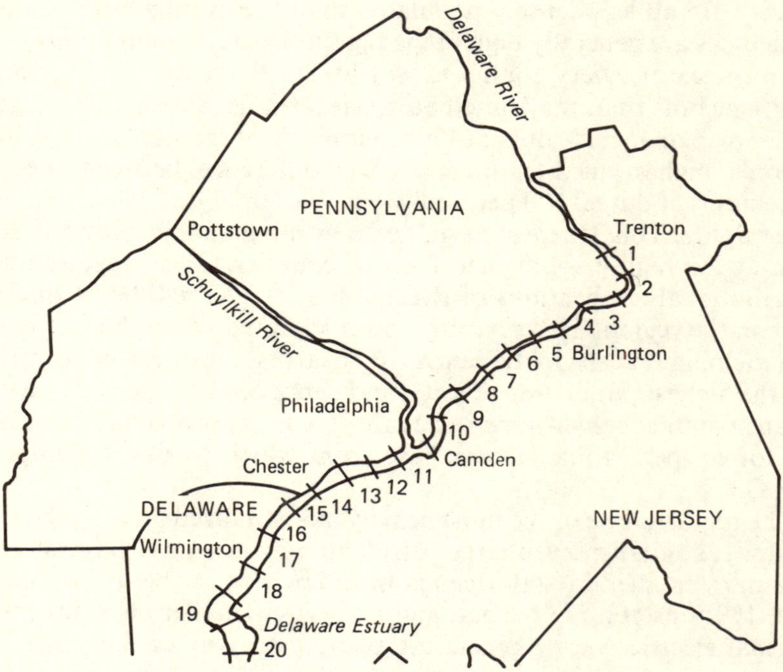

Figure 9.6 *Reach Locations for the Delaware Estuary Model*

Source: Kelly 'Conceptual Ecological Model of the Delaware Estuary', in B.C. Patten (ed.) *Systems Analysis and Simulation in Ecology*, New York Academic Press, 1976.

4,700 cfs for 1965 to a high of about 18,000 cfs for 1952. The mean discharge at Trenton over the sixty-year period from 1912 to 1972 was about 11,400 cfs.[6] The low flow period, and hence the period during which the river is most sensitive to residuals discharges, is July through October. The flow of the Delaware River at Trenton, used as the basis for the aquatic ecosystem model described later, corresponds to the mean flow for September 1970, that is, about 4,100 cfs. This flow is about 2.8 times as large as the seven-day, ten-year flow at Trenton of 1,500 cfs. Table 9.1 shows the estimated residuals discharges to the twenty-two reaches of the estuary for September 1970, and the heavy concentration of those discharges in a relatively few reaches. The maximum and minimum concentration in the estuary for that month are also shown.

The Schuylkill River is considerably smaller than the Delaware River. The mean discharge for the forty-seven-year period from 1926 to 1972 was about 1,800 cfs at Pottstown, Pennsylvania, approximately where the Schuylkill enters the Lower Delaware Valley region. (The mean discharge for the Schuylkill at Philadelphia over a thirty-four period was

Table 9.1 *Estimated Residuals Discharges to the Delaware Estuary, September 1970*

	Biochemical Oxygen Demand		*Nitrogen*		*Phosphorus*	
Sources	*Lbs/Day*	*Percentage of Total*	*Lbs/Day*	*Percentage of Total*	*Lbs/Day*	*Percentage of Total*
Industrial	385	41	117	53	7.93	15
Municipal	425	46	63.8	29	27.0	50
Tributaries	50	5	19.1	9	13.0	24
Storm water	76	8	20.5	9	5.76	11
Total (rounded)	936		220		53.7	

Distribution of September 1970 residuals discharges
83% of BOD_5 load is discharged into 27% of reaches
79% of N load is discharged into 27% of reaches
80% of P load is discharged into 27% of reaches

Measured ambient water quality resulting from September 1970 residuals discharges	(mg/l)
Minimum mean dissolved oxygen concentration:	1.2
Maximum mean BOD_5 concentration:	6.4
Maximum mean P (as P) concentration:	0.33
Maximum mean N (as TKN)[a] concentration:	2.5

Source: Blair T. Bower, ed., *Regional Residuals*–Environmental Quality Management Modelling, Research Paper R-7 (Washington, D.C., Resources for the Future, 1977) p. 61.
[a] NH_3 + organic N.

approximately 2,850 cfs.) The mean annual flow at Pottstown for the period 1951 through 1965 varied from a low of 840 cfs for 1965 to a high of 3,060 cfs for 1952. The monthly mean flow during this same period ranged from a low of 320 cfs in October 1963 to a high of 4,760 in February 1951. The seven-day, ten-year flow of the Schuylkill at Pottstown is about 240 cfs.

The major tributaries in the Schuylkill-Delaware river basins are still smaller, their mean annual flows ranging from a high of about 430 cfs for Brandywine Creek in Wilmington, Delaware, to a low of about 4 cfs for Blackbird Creek in Blackbird, Delaware. The flows in many of these tributaries are so low in some months of the summer that return flows from wastewater treatment plants currently comprise a major portion of the flows in the tributaries during low flow periods.

Atmosphere

The atmospheric 'resource' of the region does not lend itself to as simple a characterization as the flow relations for its watercourses. For the region as a whole, the seasonal prevailing wind pattern is roughly: winter and spring westerlies (and west-northwesterlies); summer southwesterlies; and autumn variability. In almost every month there are southwesterly winds along the stretch from roughly the Delaware state line to Camden, New Jersey. The net effect of these meteorological conditions, together with the spatial pattern of discharges of gaseous residuals, is a 'mountain' of poor quality air along the estuary from Wilmington to Trenton, with the highest concentrations over the Philadelphia-Camden area.

During the period from 1936 to 1965, atmospheric stagnations[7] over Philadelphia occurred most often during the month of September, with sixteen cases recorded out of a total of thirty-three; the next most frequent month was October with eight cases.[8] Episodes of poor air quality are often associated with atmospheric stagnations, although they are also dependent on residuals discharges during these adverse meteorological periods. During the two-year period 1957–1959, twenty-two 'air pollution episodes' were recorded in the Philadelphia area – four in the spring, two in the summer, eight in the fall, and eight in the winter.[9] From information on the frequency of atmospheric stagnations alone, proportionally more episodes would have been expected in the fall and fewer in the winter. However, discharges of sulphur dioxide and particulates in the Philadelphia area are typically higher in the winter than during any other period of the year.

During the 1967–1968 period, the maximum annual average concentration of sulphur dioxide (SO_2) and total suspended particulates (TSP) in the region were about 190 micrograms per cubic metre ($\mu g/m^3$) and about $150 \mu g/m^3$, respectively, measured at a station in Philadelphia. These compare with the U.S. primary ambient standards of $80 \mu g/m^3$ and $75 \mu g/m^3$, respectively. Table 9.2 shows the estimated discharges of SO_2 and particulates in the Lower Delaware Valley region for 1970.

The major discharges of SO_2 and particulates in the region are the petroleum refineries, steel mills, and power plants. Collectively, their SO_2 discharges in 1970 averaged about 1,760 tons per day, roughly 60 per cent of the total of about 3,000 tons per day. Their collective discharges of particulates averaged about 250 tons per day, roughly 40 per cent of the total of about 600 tons per day for the region. The power plants in the region clearly represent the largest set of dischargers of both SO_2 and particulates.

In 1970, area sources of SO_2 and particulate discharges accounted for about 25 per cent and 35 per cent respectively of the totals for the region. However, these sources typically discharge close to the ground and hence contribute proportionally more to ground level ambient concentrations than the relative magnitudes of their discharges would indicate. 'Area sources' of gaseous residuals are not tied to specific stack locations but were analyzed as though their discharges were uniformly generated over the different subareas identified.

For modelling air quality, the atmospheric conditions used represent the annual joint probability distribution of wind speed, wind direction,

Table 9.2 *Estimated Sulphur Dioxide and Particulate Discharges in the Lower Delaware Valley Region, 1970* (annual average in tons per day)

Discharger Category	*Sulphur Dioxide*	*Particulates*
Point sources (1,031 stacks)		
Petroleum refineries	410	66
Steel mills	19	58
Power plants	1,332	126
Other point sources	439	133
Total	2,220	383
Area sources (240 areas)		
Household heating[a]	214	25
Other area sources	550	191
Total	764	216
Total, all sources	2,964	599

[a] Estimated from the number of housing units and the household heating fuel types contained in the 1970 Bureau of the Census computer tapes.

Source: Based on EPA's 1970 inventory of gaseous discharges for the Metropolitan Philadelphia Interstate Air Quality Control Region, supplied by the Division of Applied Technology, Office of Air Programs, U.S. Environmental Protection Agency, Durham, North Carolina, and appearing in Spofford, Russell, and Kelly, *Environmental Quality*, p. 15.

and stability conditions for 1970, assumed to be uniform throughout the region.[10] For neither air nor water quality analyses, were conditions representing rare events used in the analyses. Ideally, explicit attention would also have been given to this aspect of regional R.E.Q.M.

The regional R.E.Q.M. model

The framework of the regional R.E.Q.M. model of the Delaware Valley Estuary is shown in Figure 9.7. There are three main parts of this model: a linear programming model of residuals generation and discharge (comprising both production and use activities), the natural systems models, and the environmental evaluation section. The regional R.E.Q.M. model is designed to provide at the least cost possible a way of: first, producing an exogenously determined 'bill of goods' at the individual industrial plants; second, meeting electrical energy and household and commercial space heating requirements for the region; and third, handling, modifying, and disposing of specified quantities of municipal liquid and solid residuals, subject to constraints on the distribution of ambient environmental quality – water, air, and landfills – over geographic units; and the distribution of consumer costs – electrical energy, heating fuel, sewage disposal, solid waste disposal, and regional instream aeration – over political jurisdictions.

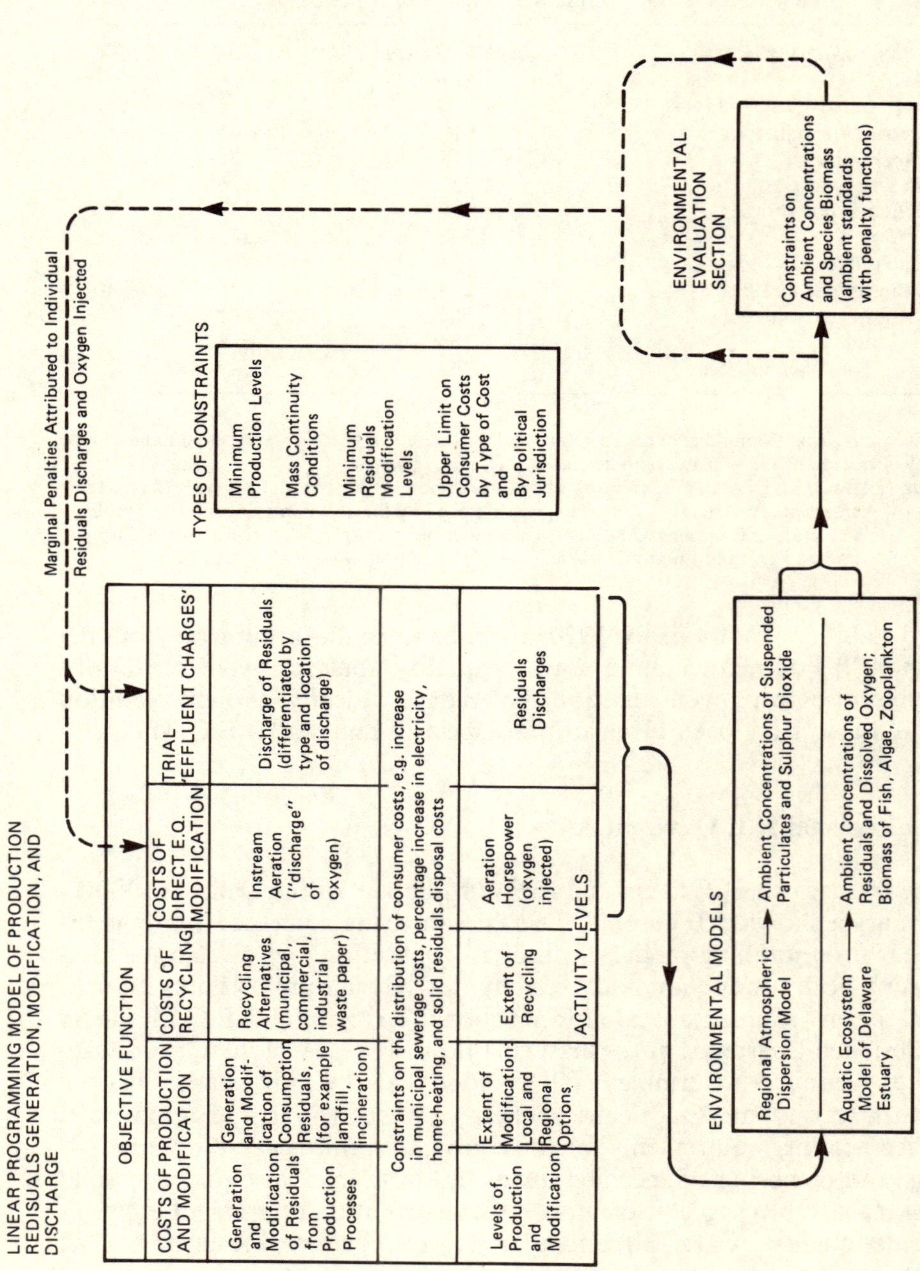

Figure 9.7 *A Regional R.E.Q.M. Model*

The three constraints can be exemplified by maximum concentrations of SO_2 and T.S.P. at a number of receptor locations in the region, minimum concentrations of dissolved oxygen and fish biomass in the estuary, maximum concentration of algae in the estuary, and restrictions on the types of landfill operations that can be used in the region. With respect to the latter category of constraints, the model permits constraining increases in: the cost of electricity by utility service area caused by all required discharge reduction activities, the cost of household heating caused by fuel switching, and municipal expenditures caused by increased liquid residuals modification and more expensive solid residuals management methods. However, credit is given for the sale of newsprint and linerboard produced from used newspapers and used corrugated containers, respectively, collected within the region, such production being an alternative to solid residuals disposal to landfills, incineration, or both.

Referring to Figure 9.7, in the upper left-hand block of the diagram is the basic driving force for the entire model, a linear programming model or residuals generation and discharge. It is in this part of the model that the minimum 'production' constraints are found. A key output of this part is a vector of residuals discharges identified by substance and location. This vector is fed into the environmental models, the model of the aquatic ecosystem, and the dispersion model for SO_2 and T.S.P. This section of the overall model, in turn, produces as output a vector of ambient environmental quality levels (for example, SO_2 in the thirty-seventh political jurisdiction). These concentrations are then treated as input to the 'evaluation' submodel found in the lower right of the figure. Here the concentrations implied by one solution of the residuals generation and discharge submodel are compared with the exogenously established ambient environmental standards imposed for the model run. An iterative procedure, based on the gradient method of nonlinear programming and on the use of penalty functions, was developed to meet the ambient standards within some specified tolerance, and to select a vector of residuals discharges that meets the constraints at least cost to the region.

The following are the main features of the Lower Delaware Valley model:

1 It is a mathematical model. It is intended to provide least cost ways of achieving various levels of A.E.Q. subject to constraints on production and use, A.E.Q., and consumer costs.
2 It reflects some of the nontreatment alternatives available for reducing the amounts of residuals initially generated, especially in production processes. In general, the amount (or form) of residual to be handled is not assumed to be fixed.
3 It deals with the three major forms of materials (liquids, gases, and

solids), heat, and the three receiving environmental media (watercourses, atmosphere, and land) simultaneously. The model reflects the conservation of mass and energy for the relevant residuals, accounting for material and energy flows as they are modified from one form to another in production, use, and residuals modification activities. Carbon dioxide and water vapour are ignored.

4 It is capable of incorporating various types of models of the natural world from the simplest linear transformations – for example, steady state Streeter-Phelps-type dissolved oxygen models – to complex simulation models of aquatic ecosystems.

5 It is a static, economic model so that time is not considered in the residuals generation and discharge portion of the model; capacity expansion and optimal timing are not explored; no new industries come into the region; and the population level and its distribution remain constant. The model output represents a 'snap shot' of the region for fixed conditions at a given point in time. A dynamic analysis of the effect on the region of economic and population growth cannot be made, but a comparative static analysis can be made.

6 The spatial distribution of activities in the region is fixed, although the effects of various distributions can be examined and compared.

7 Production and use activities in the region are deterministic and steady state.

8 The natural systems models are deterministic and steady state, although the ecosystem model is structured as a nonsteady state model, but the eventual steady state results are used in the calculations.

9 A single season (spring, summer, fall, winter, annual) is employed for the analysis, although the model can be operated for different seasons or time periods and the optimal solutions for each season compared.

10 Interactions among residuals in the atmosphere are assumed not to occur, and decay rates, where applicable, are independent of the quantities of the residual present and of the presence of other residuals.

To provide specific information on the geographic distribution of ambient environmental quality and of R.E.Q.M. costs to consumers throughout the region, the Lower Delaware Valley was divided into fifty-seven political jurisdictions with 1970 populations ranging from approximately 60,000 to 110,000. The objective was to make each jurisdiction as socially and economically homogenous as possible. To form these jurisdictions, some of the 379 cities, towns, boroughs, and townships that comprise the region were aggregated and others were subdivided; a few areas, such as major parks and military bases, were excluded. However, all fifty-seven political jurisdications are comprised of whole census tracts and are located entirely within the boundaries of individual counties and hence within states. Figure 9.8 shows the jurisdictions outside Philadelphia; Figure 9.9 those within Philadelphia.

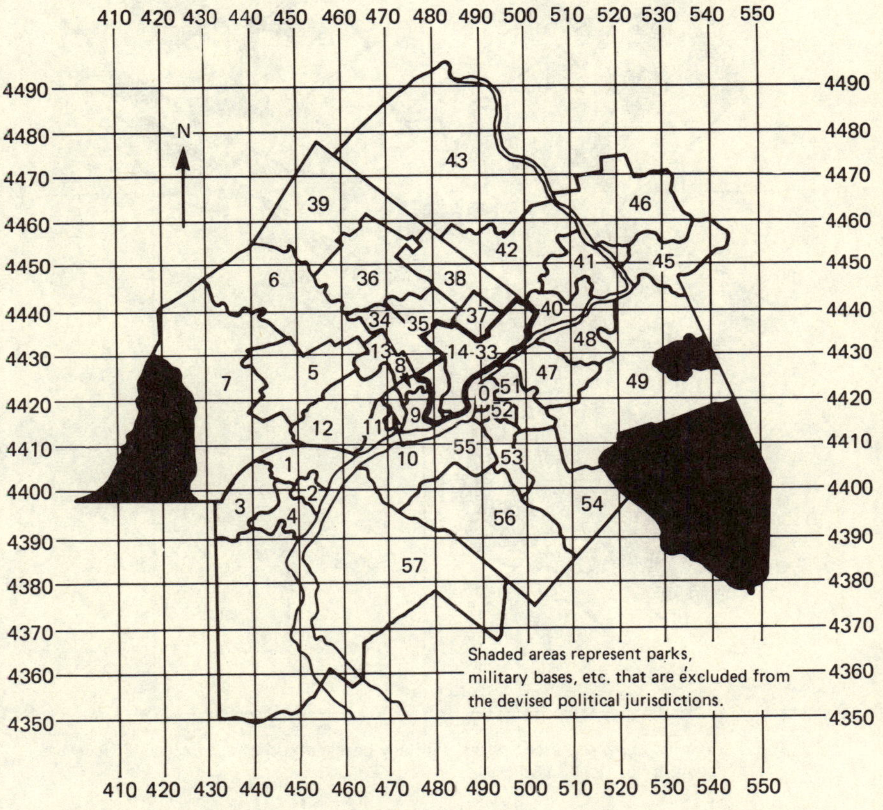

Figure 9.8 *Political Jurisdictions Devised for the Lower Delaware Valley Region*

For each political jurisdiction the following measures of ambient environmental quality and of increased consumer costs resulting from R.E.Q.M. are available: air quality (annual average ground level concentrations of SO_2 and T.S.P. at an arbitrarily selected location within each jurisdiction); landfill quality; and levels of increased consumer costs (uniform over each jurisdiction) for electrical energy, household and commercial heating, municipal sewage handling (including modification and disposal), and municipal solid residuals disposal. Ambient water quality in the estuary – in terms of concentration of dissolved oxygen,

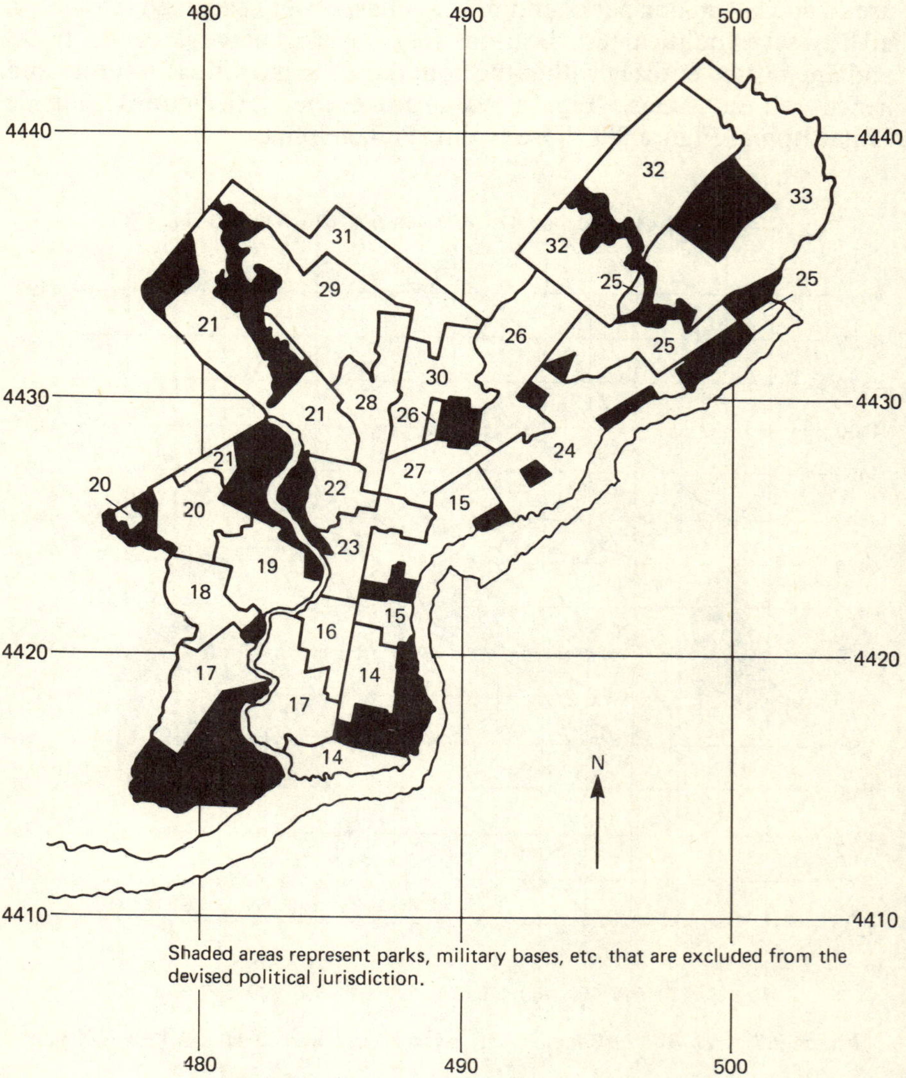

Figure 9.9 *Political Jurisdictions Devised for the Philadelphia Portion of the Lower Delaware Valley*

biomass of fish, and biomass of algae – is available for each of the twenty-two reaches shown in Figure 9.6 and is related to the fifty-seven political jurisdictions only indirectly. The allowable upper (or lower if appropriate) limits of these A.E.Q. indicators can be constrained.

The estuary is the only water body in the region that is described by a water quality model. Dischargers in the reach of the Schuylkill River included in the model are handled with specified discharge standards based approximately on state standards existing in 1968–70.[11] This arrangement does not permit liquid discharge trade-offs in this part of the region. Dischargers to other tributaries of the Delaware Estuary are dealt with in the same manner as dischargers to the Schuylkill. The stretch of the Delaware River above Trenton currently is of fairly good quality, and there appears to be little likelihood of major deterioration in the near future. Consequently, no water quality model of this part of the region was considered necessary.

Residuals generation and discharge models

The residuals generation, modification, and discharge submodel of the Lower Delaware Valley model is composed of six separate linear programming models arranged in individual modules. These modules are depicted in Table 9.3. The left-hand side of the table indicates the module number, for identification purposes only. (The M.P.S.X. designation derives from the particular computational routine used in the analysis.) Columns 1, 2, and 3 indicate the sizes of the individual linear programming modules – number of rows, number of columns, and number of residuals discharges, respectively. In total, in the model there are: almost 8,000 variables (columns); a little over 3,000 constraining relationships (rows); and almost 800 individual residuals discharges that enter the natural systems models. The residuals involved are biochemical oxygen demand (BOD_5), nitrogen, phosphorus, toxics (for which phenols comprise the proxy), suspended solids, and heat discharges to the estuary, and SO_2 and particulate discharges to the atmosphere. The fourth column describes the type and indicates the number (in parentheses) of

Table 9.3 *Lower Delaware Valley Model: Residuals Generation and Discharge Modules*

Module Identification	*Size of Linear Programme* Rows (1)	Columns (2)	Discharges (3)	*Description* (4)	*Per Cent Extra Costs for the 57 Political Jurisdictions (except as noted)* (5)
M.P.S.X.1	286	1,649	130	Petroleum refineries (7)	
				Steel mills (5)	
				Powerplants (17)	57 electricity
M.P.S.X.2	741	1,482	114	Household heat (57)	57 fuel
				Commercial heat (57)	57 fuel[a]
M.P.S.X.3	564	1,854	157	'Over 25 $\mu g/m^3$' dischargers (75)[b]	
M.P.S.X.4	468	570	180	Delaware Estuary sewage treatment plants (36)	46 sewage disposal (5 per household per year)[c]

Table 9.3 (*Contd.*)

Module Identification	*Size of Linear Programme* *Rows (1)*	*Columns (2)*	*Discharges (3)*	*Description (4)*	*Per Cent Extra Costs for the 57 Political Jurisdictions (except as noted) (5)*
M.P.S.X.5	951	1,914	88	Paper plants (10) Municipal incinerators (23) Municipal solid residuals handling and disposal activities	57 solid residuals disposal
M.P.S.X.6	229	395	117[d]	Delaware Estuary industrial dischargers (23)[e] Instream aeration (22)	57 instream aeration (absolute extra cost per day)[f]
Total	3,239	7,864	786		

Note: M.P.S.X. is a designation that derives from the particular computational routine used in the analysis. Figures in parentheses are the number of activities in the region for which residuals management options are included in the model.

Source: Spofford, Russell, and Kelly, *Environmental Quality* p. 29. The major sources of information and data used in the construction of the residuals generation and discharge models were: (1) ERA's 1970 inventory of SO_2 and particulate discharges in the Metropolitan Philadelphia Interstate Air Quality Control Region; (2) Delaware River Basin Commission for the municipal and industrial wastewater dischargers to the Delaware Estuary; (3) Regional Conference of Elected Officials' publications for municipal incinerators and for electricity districts and power plants; and (4) the 1970 U.S. Bureau of Census computer tapes for number of people and housing units by political jurisdictions, household heating fuel characteristics, and sewerage systems. The base period for data employed in this model is 1968 to 1970.

[a] The commercial heating requirements in this module are based on the differences between SO_2 discharges from area sources in the L.P.P. inventory of gaseous discharges and SO_2 discharges from the household heating model. Commercial heating requirements for political jurisdictions 19, 28, 29, 31, 32, 33, 37, and 44 are equal to zero.

[b] Includes each industrial plant whose gaseous residuals discharges result in maximum annual average ground level concentrations equal to or greater than 25 $\mu g/m^2$. To determine this group, all stacks in the Implementation Planning Program (I.P.P.) inventory were considered except those in M.P.S.X.1. The maximum annual average ground level concentrations of SO_2 and TSP were computed for each stack. For all stacks at the same x-y location (i.e. same plant), the maximum ground level concentrations were added together. Those plants resulting in maximum ground level concentrations, for either SO_2 or TSP, equal to or greater than 25 $\mu g/m^2$ were then placed in this category.

[c] The extra costs reported represent the *average* increase per household per year for each political jurisdiction. Jurisdictions 5, 6, 7, 36, 39, 43, 45, 46, 53, 54, and 56 do not discharge to the estuary at all.

[d] Does not include the 22 oxygen "discharges" from the instream acration option.

[e] Twelve of the Delaware Estuary industrial wastewater dischargers in M.P.S.X.6 are also represented by SO_1 and or T.S.P. dischargers in M.P.S.X.3, and the gaseous residuals discharges of another are included in M.P.S.X.6.

[f] The model currently reports the total regional absolute extra cost per day for instream acration. The cost is then allocated equally among the 57 political jurisdictions. Any other distribution is also possible.

activities in the region for which residuals management options are included in the model. The fifth column lists the information generated by the model on the distribution of extra costs for R.E.Q.M. Except for the costs of sewage disposal, there is one constraint for each type of extra cost and for each of the fifty-seven political jurisdictions into which the Lower Delaware Valley has been divided. For sewage disposal, there are only forty-six extra costs in the model, because eleven jurisdictions do not discharge any sewage directly to the estuary.

In the model, 297 point and nonpoint sources of gaseous and liquid residuals are provided with management options for reducing their discharges. The 183 point sources include 124 industrial plants and 59 municipal residuals-handling and disposal activities – 23 incinerators and 36 sewage treatment plants. The 124 industrial plants in turn include, among others, the 7 oil refineries in the region. 5 steel plants, 17 power plants, and 23 other industrial dischargers to the estuary. The 114 area (nonpoint) sources are 57 household activities and 57 commercial heating activities (one of each for each jurisdiction). The other point and nonpoint sources identified in the region that are not provided with residuals management options are incorporated as background dischargers.

The management options available to the various sources for reducing their discharges range from alternative production processes and raw material inputs to residuals modification at the 'end of the pipe'. Examples of these options are shown in Table 9.4. In addition to the management options for the individual activities listed in the previous paragraph, four collective residuals-handling and modification activities, and one direct modification of A.E.Q. activity are included: incineration, landfilling, regional sewage modification, and recycling of used newspapers and used corrugated containers represent the former; instream aeration, the latter.

The sources of residuals discharges included in the regional model do not encompass all residuals dischargers in the Lower Delaware Valley. Certain kinds of activities and the residuals generated by and discharged from them have not been included (for example, transportation, agricultural activities, and construction activities), except as background sources of residuals where appropriate. For certain kinds of A.E.Q. problems, these sources are important, and they could have been analyzed in an analogous manner. However, the activities that have been included in the model include the important dischargers of SO_2 and particulates to the atmosphere and the major dischargers of BOD_5, nitrogen, and phosphorus to the Delaware Estuary.

Natural systems models

The second major component of the regional R.E.Q.M. model consists of the natural systems models of the Delaware Estuary and of the air over

Table 9.4 *Residuals Management Options Available to Selected Types of Dischargers in the Lower Delaware Valley Model*

Type of Residual Discharger	*Management Option Available*	*Primary Residual Reduced*	*Secondary Residual Generated*[a]
Petroleum refineries	1. Secondary or tertiary wastewater treatment, and various reuse alternatives (cooling tower water makeup, desalter water, boiler feedwater)	BOD_5	Sludge
	2. Cooling tower	Heat	[b]
	3. Burn lower sulphur fuel	SO_2	None
	4. Refine lower sulphur crude	SO_2	None
	5. Cyclone collectors on catcracker catalyst regenerator (2 efficiencies: 70%, 85%)	Particulates	Fly ash
	6. Electrostatic precipitator, 95% efficiency	Particulates	Fly ash
	7. Sell, rather than burn, high sulphur refinery coke	SO_2 and particulate	None
	8. Sludge digestion and landfill	Sludge	[a]
Thermal power generating facilities	1. Cooling tower	Heat	[b]
	2. Burn lower sulphur coal	SO_2	None
	3. Limestone injection-wet scrubber, 90% efficiency	SO_2	Slurry
	4. Electrostatic precipitators (3 efficiencies; 90%, 95%, 98%)	Particulates	Fly ash
	5. Settling pond, 90% efficiency	Slurry	Solid 'ash'
Municipal sewage treatment plants	1. Secondary or tertiary wastewater treatment	BOD_5	Sludge
	2. Sludge digestion, drying, and landfill	Sludge	
	3. Sludge dewatering and incineration	Sludge	Particulates, Fly ash
	4. Dry cyclone collector (2 efficiencies: 80%, 95%)	Particulates	Fly ash
Municipal incinerators	1. Electrostatic precipitators (2 efficiencies; 80%, 95%)	Particulates	Fly ash

Notes
[a] A secondary residual is generated in the process of modifying a primary residual.
[b] Heat is rejected to the atmosphere along with water vapour.
[c] The secondary residual is digested sludge at a different location.

Source: Bower, *Regional Residuals*, p. 73.

the region. The former is a nonlinear ecosystem model of the Delaware Estuary, divided into twenty-two reaches as shown in Figure 9.6. (A general description of the model was given in the previous chapter, with a more detailed description in Appendix 9B.) Inputs of liquid residuals to the estuary model are: organics as biochemical oxygen demand (BOD_5), nitrogen, phosphorus, toxics (for which phenols are the proxy), suspended solids, and heat (in Btu). Outputs are expressed in terms of ambient concentrations of algae, bacteria, zooplankton, resident fish, dissolved oxygen, BOD_5, nitrogen, phosphorus, toxics, suspended solids, and temperature. Three of these outputs – algae, fish, and oxygen – can be constrained. These constraint levels are set exogenously to the regional R.E.Q.M. model and represent both a major driving force in the solution runs and one of the principal issues the R.E.Q.M. model is designed to study. Thus, the costs of meeting alternative sets of A.E.Q. levels can be viewed as the most important single output capability of the regional model. A diagram showing the structure of the Delaware Estuary ecosystem model in terms of materials flows is shown in Figure 9.4, and a summary of the model indicating relevant inputs and outputs is presented in Table 9.5.

With respect to air quality, the regional Delaware R.E.Q.M. model includes two 57×240 (57 receptor locations, one for each political jurisdiction, and 240 dischargers) air dispersion matrices – one each for SO_2 and T.S.P. These matrices relate annual average ambient ground level concentrations to discharges of SO_2 and particulates. The matrices are based on output of the air dispersion model contained in E.P.A.'s Implementation Planning Programme (I.P.P.). The air dispersion model was calibrated using equations developed in an unpublished E.P.A. study of the Philadelphia Metropolitan Air Quality Control Region. A summary of the air dispersion model, indicating relevant inputs and outputs, is shown in Table 9.6 (See p. 278.)

To keep the two air dispersion matrices as small and manageable as possible, all stacks at the same plant location in E.P.A. inventory of gaseous residuals discharges were aggregated to a single stack. This required computing the characteristics of a single stack that produced the same result as the group of stacks, that is, the same maximum ground level concentration as the group, using discharge rates from E.P.A.'s inventory. The discharge rate employed in the analysis for the single stack was the aggregate discharge of all the individual stacks.

Stack characteristics of the single stack (physical stack height, plume rise, and effective stack height) were determined for discharges of both SO_2 and particulates. In general, the two 'artificial' stacks computed on the basis of the above criterion differed substantially because the characteristics of the equivalent single stack depend on the relative discharge rates among the individual stacks. In developing the two air dispersion matrices, two different sets of single stacks were used, one for the SO_2 analysis and another for the particular analysis.

Table 9.5 *Delaware Estuary Ecosystem Model*

Endogenous variables (compartments – mg/l)	
Algae	
Zooplankton (herbivores, detritivores, and bacterivores)	
Bacteria	
Fish	
Dissolved oxygen (DO)	
Organic matter (as BOD_5	
Nitrogen	
Phosphorus	
Toxics	
Suspended solids	
Temperature (°C)	
Inputs of Residuals (lbs/day)	*Target Outputs*[a] (mg/l)
Organic material (as BOD_5)	Algae
Nitrogen	Fish
Phosphorus	Dissolved oxygen
Toxics	
Suspended solids	
Heat (Btu)	
Model	
Type: materials balance-trophic level	
Characteristics: deterministic, nonsteady state	
Calibration: based on average September 1970 flow at Trenton, N.J., of 4,150 cfs.	
Reaches	
Number: 22	

[a] The regional R.E.Q.M. model is operated for relevant minimum, or maximum, allowable ambient concentrations ('standards').

Source: Based on Kelly, 'Conceptual Ecological Model'; and Robert A. Kelly and Walter O. Spofford, Jr., 'Application of an Ecosystem Model to Water Quality Management: The Delaware Estuary', in C. A. S. Hall and J. W. Day, Jr., eds., *Ecosystem Modelling in Theory and Practice: An Introduction with Case Histories* (New York, Wiley, 1977).

Setting up the model runs

The operational objective in running the regional R.E.Q.M. model was to explore the effects on aggregate regional R.E.Q.M. costs and the distribution of those costs of the following decision variables: alternative requirements in the quality of landfills; alternative ambient water and air quality standards; an instream aeration option for directly improving estuary water quality; a regional sewage treatment plant option; and a regional recycling option for solid residuals management. For both air and water quality, there are two alternative sets of standards, a relatively easy (E) set to meet and a tight (T) set. For landfill operations, three alternative quality levels are specified: low, medium, and high. The sets of

Table 9.6 *Air Dispersion Model*

Endogenous variables (ground level, annual average ambient concentrations – $\mu g/m^3$)
Sulphur dioxide
Suspended particulates

Inputs of residuals (tons/day)
Sulphur dioxide
Particulate matter

Target outputs[a] ($\mu g/m^3$)
Sulphur dioxide
Total suspended particulates

Model
Type: Gaussian plume dispersion model from E.P.A's Air Quality Implementation Planning Programme (I.P.P.)
Characteristics: deterministic, steady state
Input requirements:
1. *Sources*
   For each stack:
   a. *x-y* coordinates
   b. Physical stack height
   c. Stack diameter
   d. Discharge rate for each gaseous residual stream with associated exist temperature and exit velocity
2. *Receptors*
   x-y coordinates of each receptor location
3. *Meteorological conditions*
   a. Annual joint probability distribution for wind speed (6 classes), wind direction (16 directions), and atmospheric stability (5 classes), using 1970 data for Philadelphia; the result is 480 discrete meteorological situations
   b. Mean temperature: 68°F (20°C)[b]
   c. Mean annual pressure: 1,017 millibars (30.3 inches of mercury).
   d. Mean maximum afternoon atmospheric mixing depth: 1,000 metres'

[a] The regional R.E.Q.M. model is operated for maximum allowable ambient concentrations ('standards').
[b] The mean temperature used in the model, 68°F, is roughly that for September. The mean annual temperature is 64°F.
[c] The mean maximum afternoon mixing depth used in the model, 1,000 metres, is the average for the months of May, August, and September. In June and July, the mean mixing depth is greater than 1,000 metres; from October to April, it is less than 1,000 metres. The effect of decreasing the mixing depth around the 1,000 metre level is to increase the concentrations predicted by the model.
Source: T.R.W. (Thompson Ramo Woolridge), Inc., *Air Quality Implementation Planning Programme*, vols. I and II (Washington, D.C., U.S. Environmental Protection Agency, November 1970) (also available from National Technical Information Service, Springfield, VA 22161,PB-198 299 and PH-198 300.

standards for the three media that are used in various combinations in the analyses, are shown in Table 9.7.

Analysis with the model involves specifying for each production run a combination of ambient environmental quality standards to be met and permitted regional residuals-handling and modification options. Most runs were arbitrarily stopped at between 29 and 35 iterations, although technically the optimum, even a local optimum, was not necessarily achieved.[12] However, experience indicated that at this number of iterations the ambient environmental constraints are met, if it is technically possible to meet them. This location is high up on the response

Table 9.7 *Air, Water, and Land Environmental Quality Standards for Production Runs of the Lower Delaware Valley Model*

Qualities	*Easy Standards (E)*	*Tight Standards (T)*
Water quality (milligrams per litre)		
Algae	3.00	2.00
Fish	0.01	0.03
Dissolved oxygen	3.00	5.00
Air quality (micrograms per cubic metre)		
Sulphur dioxide	120	80[a]
Suspended particulates	120	75[a]
Landfill quality		
L (low)	Open dump, but no burning allowed.	
M (medium)	Good quality sanitary landfill.	
H (high)	Good quality sanitary landfill with shredding, impervious layer to protect groundwater; treatment of leachate; measures to enhance aesthetics, such as fences, trees, etc.	

[a] For certain jurisdictions, it is technically impossible, as the model is constructed, to meet the stricter standard. Consequently, the following modifications were made to the stricter standards:

Political jurisdiction	*T.S.P.* ($\mu g/m^1$)	*Political jurisdiction*	SO_3 ($\mu g/m^1$)
14	76	16	83
15	82		
22	76		
23	79		
24	79		
27	81		
50	76		

Source: Spofford, Russell, and Kelly, *Environmental Quality*, p. 52.

surface and continuing beyond this point improves the objective function value only slightly. This is not meant to imply, however, that residuals discharge *patterns* would not change, perhaps even substantially if the run were to be continued beyond 30 iterations. Experiments in running the model beyond 30 iterations indicated that, although the *total* residuals discharges do not change much beyond the 30 to 35 iterations (because the ambient standards are being met), trade-offs in reductions among individual dischargers are still taking place.[13] Thus, a very relevant question is: how comparable are the results – costs and discharges – of the various production runs using output obtained from approximately the thirtieth iteration of each run?

Some seminal results of running the model

The combinations of decision variables used in selected runs of the model are indicated in Table 9.8, along with the number of iterations for each run and the resulting objective function values. The objective function values represent the additional costs ($ million per day) over base costs,

Table 9.8 *Characterization of Selected Production Runs of the Lower Delaware Valley Model and Resulting Values of the Objective Function*

	Standards[a]					Objective Function
Run Number	Air	Water	Landfill	Regional Options[b]	Iterations of Regional Model	Value[a] 10[a] $/day
1	T	T	H	+	34	1.20
2	T	E	H	+	35	1.18
3	E	T	H	+	29	0.42
4	E	E	H	+	30	0.36
5	T	T	M	+	35	1.16
6	T	E	M	+	34	1.14
7	E	T	M	+	30	0.37
8	E	E	M	+	30	0.31
9	T	O	H	+	35	1.12
10	O	E	H	+	30	0.11
11	O	T	H	+	16	0.14
12	E	O	H	+	30	0.26
13	E	T	H	O	30	0.52
14	E	E	H	O	30	0.35
15	E	T	H	O[d]	29	0.46
16	E	T	H	+[d]	30	0.39
17[e]	∞	O	H	O	1	1.19
18[e]	O	∞	H	O	1	0.34
19[e]	∞	∞	H	O	1	1.41
23	O	∞	H	+	1	0.36
25	O	O	H	O	1	0.034
26	O	O	M	O	1	0.016
Base Case	O	O	L	O	1	0

[a] Standards are *Air and water quality:* T = tight, E = easy, O = no standards, ∞ = extremely high marginal penalties on residuals discharges: *Landfill quality:* H = high, M = medium, L = low. (See Table 9.7.)

[b] The regional options include: two regional paper recycling plants (for newsprint and paperboard), two regional sewage treatment plants, and instream aeration. The options of using used newspapers at input to the newspring plant and used corrugated containers as input into the linerboard plant as alternatives for reducing solid residuals management costs are available in all runs. The regional sewage treatment plant option is available only in runs 15 and 16. + means instream aeration is employed in the run; O means instream aeration is not employed in the run.

[c] Increased costs are net of base costs.

[d] Regional sewage treatment plant option is also employed.

[e] Runs 20, 21, 22 are similar to runs 17, 18, and 19, respectively, except that medium quality landfills rather than high quality landfills are specified.

Source: Spofford, Russell, and Kelly, *Environmental Quality*, p. 81.

associated with improving the ambient environmental quality of the region – atmosphere, estuary, and landfills. The base case is the situation that existed in the Lower Delaware Valley during the period of roughly 1968 to 1970. The base cost was determined by using the Lower Delaware Valley R.E.Q.M. model with landfills of low quality throughout the region, and with only the physical restrictions on liquid and gaseous residuals discharges which existed in the 1968 – 1970 period. Thus the objective function value for the base case is zero.

The results of analyses illustrate: first, total regional costs to meet various combinations of ambient air, ambient water, and landfill quality standards; second, the effects of including regional facilities as components of regional R.E.Q.M.; third, linkages among forms of residuals and among the three environmental media; and fourth, distributions of changes in ambient environmental quality and of R.E.Q.M. costs. The first three are illustrated in Figures 9.10, 9.11, 9.12, 9.13, and Table 9.9, and associated text.

Costs and environmental quality standards

Figure 9.10 shows the total increased costs to the region of meeting: alternative air quality standards; alternative water quality standards; and alternative air and water quality standards simultaneously.

Water quality standards ($ million per day) \ Air quality standards ($ million per day)	O	E	T	∞
O	0.034[a] (#25)	0.26 (#12)	1.12 (#9)	1.19[a] (#17)
E	0.11 (#10)	0.36 (#4)	1.18 (#2)	
T	0.14 (#11)	0.42 (#3)	1.20 (#1)	
∞	0.34[a] (#18)			1.41[a] (#19)

Figure 9.10 *Total Increased Costs to the Lower Delaware Valley Region of Meeting Different Sets of Air and Water Quality Standards, with High Quality Landfills*

Note: Numbers in parentheses are production run numbers. For meaning of O, E, T, and ∞, see Table 9.7 and footnotes to Table 9.8.

Source: Spofford, Russell and Kelly, *Enviornmental Quality*, p. 60.

[a] Single iteration runs, the outputs of which are not dependent on the non-linear optimization algorithm. Aerators are not employed in these runs.

As expected, total costs to the region increase as the air and water quality standards become more stringent. Note that total costs to the region of meeting T-level water quality standards in the absence of any constraints on the discharge of gaseous residuals is substantially less than the costs of meeting T-level air quality standards in the absence of any constraints on the discharge of liquid residuals. This is due in part to the fact that most of the gaseous residuals dischargers in the region have been taken into account in the model, but only those liquid residuals dischargers which discharge their waterborne residuals to the Delaware Estuary have been considered. Nevertheless, it appears that 'cleaning up' the air will be a more pervasive and costly problem for the region than 'cleaning up' the water.[14]

Figure 9.11 illustrates the effects of different landfill qualities in conjunction with different sets of ambient air and water quality standards. The total incremental costs to the region of going from medium quality landfills to high quality landfills amount to between $40 thousand and $50 thousand per day, depending on the levels of air and water quality standards. However, as indicated by the module 5 costs, only $25 thousand to $30 thousand per day are attributable to the paper plant-solid residuals management module. Thus, landfill quality requirements impose substantial incremental costs on other, apparently unrelated, activities in the region. A second point to note from Figure 9.11 is that the water quality standards seem to have very little impact on the costs of paper production from paper residuals and on the costs of solid residuals management (module 5). However, the air quality standards appear to have a substantial impact on these costs.

Costs and regional facilities

The effects on total R.E.Q.M. costs of including regional options of instream aeration and regional sewage treatment plants are illustrated by the results of four runs – 3, 13, 15, 16. These runs all have T-level water quality standards, E-level air quality standards, and high quality landfills. When neither the instream aeration nor regional sewage treatment plant options is included, total regional costs are $520 thousand per day (run 13); with regional sewage treatment but no instream aeration, total regional costs amount to $460 thousand per day (run 15); with instream aeration but no regional treatment, costs are $420 thousand per day (run 3); and with both regional treatment and instream aeration, total regional costs are $390 thousand per day (run 16). Thus, the inclusion of regional facilities for residuals management can significantly decrease total regional costs to achieve specified levels of ambient environmental quality.

The input acitivity level of a regional newspaper plant illustrates how R.E.Q.M. conditions affect the economic feasibility of recycling used paper products in the region. Figure 9.12 shows the inputs to a 'new'

Total regional costs:
($million per day)

Water quality standards	High quality landfills — Air quality standards E	High quality landfills — Air quality standards T	Medium quality landfills — Air quality standards E	Medium quality landfills — Air quality standards T	Difference in costs — Air quality standards E	Difference in costs — Air quality standards T
E	0.36 (#4)	1.18 (#2)	0.31 (#8)	1.14 (#6)	0.05	0.04
T	0.42 (#3)	1.20 (#1)	0.37 (#7)	1.16 (#5)	0.05	0.04

Paper plant-solid residuals management (module 5) costs
($million per day)

Water quality standards	High quality landfills — Air quality standards E	High quality landfills — Air quality standards T	Medium quality landfills — Air quality standards E	Medium quality landfills — Air quality standards T	Difference in costs — Air quality standards E	Difference in costs — Air quality standards T
E	0.060 (#4)	0.079 #(2)	0.038 (#8)	0.054 (# 6)	0.022	0.025
T	0.071 (#3)	0.079 (#1)	0.040 (#7)	0.055 (#5)	0.031	0.024

Figure 9.11 *Total Increased Costs to the Lower Delaware Valley Region, with High and Medium Quality Landfills*

Note: For meaning of O, E, T, and ∞, see Table 9.7 and footnotes to Table 9.8. Numbers in brackets are production run numbers.
Source: Spofford, Russell and Kelly, *Environmental Quality*, p. 66.

newsprint plant under varying A.E.Q. standards. From this, two conclusions can be drawn. First, operation of the new newsprint plant is very sensitive to landfill costs, as would be expected. For low landfill quality coupled with no A.E.Q. standards (base case), the input to the plan is zero. However, for high landfill costs but still no A.E.Q. standards, the input is 550 tons per day (run 25). Under these conditions, substantial amounts of used newspapers are collected from single-family residences throughout the region, mostly in Philadelphia, in addition to the amounts currently being collected for recycling. Second, the new newsprint plant is sensitive to higher levels of both ambient water and air quality standards, that is, activity level reduces to zero for all combinations above E-E, except for E-water combined with T-air, because the costs of residuals management at

Water quality standards (tons per day) \ Air quality standards (tons per day)	O	E	T	∞
O	550 (#25)	500 (#12)	0.0 (#9)	0 (#17)
E	160 (#10)	155 (#4)	165 (#2)	
T	0.0 (#11)	0.0 (#13)	0.0 (#1)	
∞	0 (#18)			0 (#19)

Figure 9.12 *Quantities of Used Newspaper Input into New Newsprint Plant under Varying Environmental Quality Standards, with High Quality Landfills*

Note: Numbers in brackets are production run numbers. For meaning of O, E, T, and ∞, see Table 9.7 and footnotes of Table 9.8.

Source: Spofford, Russell and Kelly, *Environmental Quality*, p. 113.

the newsprint plant using used newspapers increase rapidly at higher A.E.Q. standards.

Linkages

One of the original objectives of applying the R.E.Q.M. modelling framework to the Lower Delaware Valley region was to investigate the linkages among gaseous, liquid, solid, and energy residuals, and among the various environmental media, in an existing situation. The evidence of linkages among the forms of residuals and among the three environmental media may be obtained from a comparison of: objective function values; magnitudes of materials *flows* in the region, such as fuels, residuals discharges, residuals transport (mixed solid residuals and sludge barging), and used paper products; capacities of *structures* such as municipal incinerators, regional sewage treatment plants, and add-on residuals modification devices (for example, electrostatic precipitators); or both.

Suggested evidence of linkages is presented in Figure 9.13. In part A of that figure, objective function values for the region are shown for varying combinations of ambient air and water quality standards, with high quality landfills. With existing ambient air quality standards (that is, the O level), it costs the region about $76 thousand per day to go from existing conditions to E-level water quality standards. When E-level air quality standards are imposed, the costs of improving water quality to the E-level

Part A

Total regional costs ($ million per day)

Water quality standards	Air quality standards: O	Air quality standards: E
O	0.034 (#25)	0.26 (#12)
E	0.11 (#10)	0.36 (#4)
T	0.14 (#11)	0.42 (#3)

Incremental regional costs ($ million per day)

Water quality standards	Air quality standards: O	Air quality standards: E
O to E	0.076	0.10
E to T	0.03	0.06

Part B

Total MPSX 1 costs ($ million per day)

Water quality standards	Air quality standards: O	Air quality standards: E
O	0.0 (#25)	0.11 (#12)
E	0.020 (#10)	0.15 (#4)
T	0.024 (#11)	0.17 (#3)

Incremental MPSX 1 costs ($ million per day)

Water quality standards	Air quality standards: O	Air quality standards: E
O to E	0.020	0.04
E to T	0.004	0.02

Figure 9.13 *Evidence of Linkages among Forms of Residuals: Lower Delaware Valley Model with High Quality Landfills*

Note: Numbers in brackets are production run numbers. For meaning of O, E, T, and ∞, see Table 9.7 and footnotes of Table 9.8.
Source: Spofford, Russell and Kelly, *Environmental Quality*, pp. 110–11

are about $100 thousand per day, a difference of about $24 thousand. Had there been no linkages at all between air and water, the increased costs would have been the same for both cases. In going from E-level water quality to T-level, the difference is larger: about $30 thousand per day when air quality is not considered, compared with about $60 thousand per day when the E-level air quality standard is imposed, a difference of about $30 thousand.

In part B, evidence is based on the costs from the first module (M.P.S.X. 1) containing the petroleum refineries, the steel mills, and the electric power plants. When no air quality standards are imposed, the cost to move from O-level to E-level water quality standards is about $20 thousand per day. When E-level air quality standards are imposed simultaneously, the incremental costs to achieve E-level water quality standards are about $40 thousand per day. In moving from E-level to T-level water quality standards when air quality standards are not imposed, the incremental cost is about $4 thousand per day. When E-level air quality standards are imposed simultaneously with T-level water quality standards, the incremental cost is about $20 thousand per day. Again, the linkages between air quality and water quality in the region are clearly indicated.

The final evidence of linkages presented here is the interrelationship between different levels of landfill quality and ambient air and water quality standards. Data are presented for two cases in Table 9.9, one for E-level air and water quality standards, and one for T-level air and water quality standards. As both panels of the table show, if there were no linkages between landfill quality and air and water quality, the difference

Table 9.9 *Relationship Between Solid Residuals Management Air and Water Quality Management: Lower Delaware Valley Model* ($ million, per day)

Panel A With easy (E) air and water quality standards		
Quality of landfill	*Total costs to region*	*Solid residuals management costs (M.P.S.X. 5)*
High quality landfill (#4)	0.36	0.060
Medium quality landfill (#8)	0.31	0.038
Difference	0.05	0.022

Panel B With tight (T) air and water quality standards		
Quality of landfill	*Total costs to region*	*Solid residuals management costs (M.P.S.X. 5)*
High quality landfill (#5)	1.20	0.079
Medium quality landfill (#5)	1.16	0.055
Difference	0.04	0.024

Note: Numbers in parentheses are production run numbers.
Source: Spofford, Russell, and Kelly, *Environmental Quality*, p. 57.

Table 9.10 *Distribution of Sulphur Dioxide Concentration by Political Jurisdiction for Selected Production Runs, with High Quality Landfills* (micrograms per cubic metre)

	Sulphur Dioxide			*Sulphur Dioxide*	
Political Jurisdiction	*Run 1 T-Level Ambient Air & Water Qual. Stds.*	*Run 3 E-Level Ambient Air & T-Level Ambient Water Qual. Stds.*	*Political Jurisdiction*	*Run 1 T-Level Ambient Air & Water Qual. Stds.*	*Run 3 E-Level Ambient Air & T-Level Ambient Water Qual. Stds.*
1	17	54	30	23	66
2	15	49	31	16	46
3	6	14	32	13	44
4	12	39	33	12	40
5	8	22	34	11	35
6	5	19	35	11	32
7	5	12	36	6	20
8	22	53	37	12	37
9	32[a]	68	38	9	27
10	25	58	39	4	12
11	28	64	40	11	46
12	15	42	41	9	34
13	11	32	42	7	24
14	56[a]	96[a]	43	4	11
15	42[a]	98[a]	44	13	40
16	83[a,b]	120[a,b]	45	10	34
17	64[a]	100[a]	46	8	20
18	35[a]	70	47	12	49
19	50[a]	91[a]	48	11	40
20	24	57	49	8	25
21	18	48	50	40[a]	87[a]
22	29	74[a]	51	20	64
23	38[a]	89[a]	52	27	71
24	29	103[a]	53	16	43
25	19	66	54	6	18
26	25	70	55	22	51
27	34[a]	94[a]	56	9	26
28	25	65	57	8	26
29	17	49			

Note: For locations of political jurisdictions, see Figures 9.8 and 9.9.
[a] Indicates the ten highest concentrations of SO_2.
[b] Indicates the minimum concentration of SO_2.
Source: Bower, *Regional Residuals*, p. 94.

Table 9.11 *Distribution of Dissolved Oxygen Concentration by Estuary Reach for Selected Production Runs, with High Quality Landfills* (millingrams per litre)

Delaware Estuary Reach	*Dissolved Oxygen*					
	Run 1[a]	*Run 2*[b]	*Run 3*[c]	*Run 13*[c]	*Run 15*[e]	*Run 16*[e]
1	8.6	8.6	8.6	8.6	8.6	8.6
2	7.7	7.7	8.0	7.9	7.9	7.9
3	6.9	6.6	7.2	7.0	6.9	7.2
4	6.3	6.0	6.8	6.2	6.1	6.5
5	5.9[d]	5.7	6.4	5.8[d]	5.4[d]	6.0
6	6.0	5.9	6.5	6.0	5.4[d]	6.0
7	5.9[d]	5.9	6.3	5.8[d]	5.3[d]	6.0
8	5.9	5.8	6.3	6.2	5.7	5.8[d]
9	6.4	6.1	6.7	6.8	6.3	6.2
10	6.8	5.3	7.0	7.8	7.5	7.1
11	5.3[d]	3.6[d]	5.1[d]	5.7[d]	5.2[d]	5.1[d]
12	6.1	3.7[d]	5.7[d]	6.3	6.0	6.1
13	5.7[d]	3.6[d]	5.4[d]	5.7[d]	5.3[d]	5.0[d]
14	5.7[d]	4.0[d]	5.5[d]	5.7[d]	5.3[d]	5.1[d]
15	6.1	4.5[d]	6.0[d]	6.0	5.5[d]	5.8[d]
16	6.4	5.2	6.3	6.0[d]	56	6.4
17	5.0[d,e]	3.0[d,e]	5.0[d,e]	4.9[d,e]	5.0[d,e]	5.0[d,e]
18	5.1[d]	3.4[d]	5.2[d]	5.4[d]	55	5.1[d]
19	5.7[d]	4.8[d]	5.8[d]	6.0	6.1	5.8[d]
20	6.1	5.8	6.1	6.1	6.2	6.1
21	6.2	6.2	6.3	6.3	63	6.3
22	6.6	6.6	6.6	6.7	6.7	6.6

Note: For location of reaches, see Figure 9.6.
[a] T-level ambient water and air quality standards.
[b] E-level ambient water and T-level ambient air quality standards.
[c] T-level ambient water quality and E-level ambient air quality standards.
[d] Indicates the eight lowest concentrations of dissolved oxygen.
[e] Indicates the minimum concentration of dissolved oxygen.
Source: Bower, *Regional Residuals*, p. 95.

between total regional costs (column 1) and the difference between solid residuals management costs (column 2) would have been the same. That they are substantially different indicates that linkages exist. Thus, substantial costs are imposed on other sectors when higher quality landfills are required, the linkages to these additional costs being through the air and water quality of the region.

Distributional effects
With respect to the distribution of ambient environmental quality, Table 9.10 shows the distribution of SO_2 concentrations among the fifty-seven

Table 9.12 *Distribution of Increased Consumer Costs by Political Jurisdiction for Selected Production Runs*

Political Jurisdiction	*Household Heating*		*Household Electricity*[b]		*Municipal Solid Residuals Management*[b]		*Municipal Sewage*	
	Run 1[a]	*Run 3*	*Run 1*	*Run 3*	*Run 3*	*Run 7*	*Run 1*	*Run 2*
	(percentage)						*($/household/year)*[c]	
	1	25.1	1.8	15.8[d]	2.4	19.2	7.7	0.5[a]
2	30.5	0.7	15.8[d]	2.4	19.4	7.8	43.5	8.0
3	29.0	0[e]	15.8[d]	2.4	19.3	7.7	5.9	1.1
4	23.0	0[e]	15.8[d]	2.4	19.4	7.8	1.0	0.2
5	33.9	0.6	13.6	4.5[d]	19.1	7.6	–	–
6	35.5	0[e]	13.6	4.5	19.1	7.7	–	–
7	16.8	0[e]	13.6	4.5	19.4	7.8	–	–
8	26.1	9.6	13.6	4.5	10.8	7.7	3.3	2.5
9	23.3	7.2	13.6	4.5	17.9	7.7	2.1	1.0
10	24.5	3.2	13.6	4.5	19.3	7.7	3.5	1.9
11	28.3	0.9	13.6	4.5	10.9	7.7	16.2	8.0
12	27.8	3.4	13.6	4.5	18.8	7.7	3.9	2.1
13	26.2	1.9	13.6	4.5	21.0	7.7	2.5	1.7
14	19.7	6.1	13.6	4.5	8.7	7.7	21.4	16.1
15	41.0	25.8	13.6	4.5	7.6[a]	7.6	16.2	12.2
16	31.4	18.5	13.6	4.5	17.3	7.7	15.4	10.6
17	16.4	7.4	13.6	4.5	8.1	7.7	19.3	13.1
18	21.7	8.2	13.6	4.5	17.5	7.7	18.8	12.8
19	50.4	28.5	13.6	4.5	20.1	7.6	14.4	9.8
20	22.2	6.3	13.6	4.5	20.4	7.7	16.8	11.4
21	25.6	6.3	13.6	4.5	8.6	7.6	16.6	11.6
22	31.7	15.2	13.6	4.5	20.4[d]	7.7	19.3	14.0
23	55.4[d]	30.0[d]	13.6	4.5	11.2	7.5	14.8	10.6
24	14.1	0.2	13.6	4.5	17.6	6.6[e]	8.0	7.1
25	10.4	0.5	13.6	4.5	17.8	6.6[e]	16.0	14.2
26	12.6	0.9	13.6	4.5	23.1	8.2[d]	15.0	13.4
27	25.5	4.8	13.6	4.5	20.5	7.7	22.1	16.7
28	29.8	5.1	13.6	4.5	20.4	7.7	15.6	13.3
29	33.9	1.6	13.6	4.5	10.7	7.6	17.9	14.1
30	16.5	2.7	13.6	4.5	20.6	7.7	15.6	13.9
31	17.2	2.7	13.6	4.5	20.3	7.7	15.7	13.6
32	9.9[e]	0.6	13.6	4.5	20.2	7.6	15.8	14.0
33	31.4	1.1	13.6	4.5	20.4	7.7	19.7	17.6
34	35.1	1.9	13.6	4.5	18.7	7.5	7.3	4.9
35	26.9	2.8	13.6	4.5	19.1	7.7	2.3	1.5
36	31.2	0.0	13.6	4.5	19.2	7.7	–	–
37	26.7	0.7	13.6	4.5	19.0	7.6	6.1	5.4
38	26.9	0.6	13.6	4.5	19.0	7.6	1.4	1.2
39	36.7	0.0[e]	n.a.	n.a.	19.2	7.7	–	–
40	36.7	0.2	13.6	4.5	19.1	7.6	8.3	1.3
41	31.3	0.0[e]	13.6	4.5	19.2	7.7	15.9	0.0[e]

Table 9.12 (*Contd.*)

Political Juris-diction	*Household Heating*		*Household Electricity*[b]		*Municipal Solid Residuals Management*[b]		*Municipal Sewage*	
	Run 1[a]	*Run 3*	*Run 1*	*Run 3*	*Run 3*	*Run 7*	*Run 1*	*Run 2*
	(percentage)						*($/household/year)*[c]	
42	29.6	0.3	13.6	4.5	19.3	7.7	1.8	1.6
43	33.1	0.0[e]	6.8	2.2	19.3	7.7	–	–
44	34.9	0.0[e]	2.9	0.4	19.4	7.7	48.2[d]	1.2
45	24.2	0.0[e]	2.9	0.4	19.2	7.7	–	–
46	25.0	0.0[e]	2.9	0.4	19.2	7.7	–	–
47	25.1	0.8	2.9	0.4	19.3	7.7	12.7	3.0
48	17.4	0.0[e]	2.9	0.4	19.5	7.8	11.5	0.0[e]
49	19.7	0.0[e]	1.4[e]	0.2[e]	19.4	7.8	2.9	0.0[e]
50	31.7	9.2	2.9	0.4	19.5	7.8	47.8	36.9[d]
51	20.6	4.1	2.9	0.4	19.3	7.7	20.7	13.6
52	29.5	6.0	2.9	0.4	19.4	7.8	4.4	3.2
53	22.3	2.8	2.9	0.4	19.4	7.8	–	–
54	25.6	0.7	10.6	1.3	19.3	7.7	–	–
55	25.9	5.0	2.9	0.4	19.5	7.8	6.6	4.5
56	19.2	0.2	10.6	1.3	19.5	7.8	–	–
57	28.2	0.0	10.6	1.3	19.6	7.9	0.5	0.1

Notes: For locations of political jurisdictions, see Figures 9.8 and 9.9. Dashes = not applicable. Standards for the runs are:

Run	*Air*	*Water*	*Landfills*
1	T	T	H
3	E	T	H
7	E	T	M
2	T	E	H

[a] Cost increases for household heating reflect the technological upper limits except in jurisdictions 1, 2, 7, 12, 35, 49, and 56. There is empirical evidence to suggest that at the 'optimum' for this run, all cost increases would be at their upper limits. Cost increases at the upper limits represent a situation where there is total conversion within the region to natural gas.

[b] The situation in which many jurisdictions have the same percentage cost increase reflects the fact that multiple jurisdictions are served by the same utility or solid residuals management agency.

[c] The costs of sewage disposal have been allocated in the model on the basis of both flow and BOD_5 load. BOD_5 concentrations in sewage have been assumed using different loading factors for urban, suburban, and rural areas. The average increased cost to jurisdictions for sewage disposal is computed on the basis of total sewage disposal costs divided by total housing units for each jurisdiction. Thus, all other factors the same, jurisdictions that are less than 100 per cent sewered will register smaller average increases than those that are 100 per cent sewered. This accounts for the apparent discrepancy in increased costs for jurisdictions served by the same sewage treatment plant.

[d] Maximum increases.

[e] Maximum increases.

Source: Bower, *Regional Residuals*, p. 97.

political jurisdictions for runs 1 and 3, the T-level air quality standards and the E-level air quality standards, respectively. The maximum concentration for both runs is found in political jurisdiction 16 (South Philadelphia). Of the ten highest concentrations for run 1, eight are located within Philadelphia (jurisdictions 14, 15, 16, 17, 18, 19, 23, and 27), one in Delaware County (jurisdiction 9), and one in Camden, New Jersey (jurisdiction 50). Although not shown in this table, the T.S.P. distribution for run 1 is similar to that for SO_2 in that of the ten highest concentrations, nine are located within Philadelphia (jurisdictions 14, 15, 16, 19, 22, 23, 24, 26, 27) and one in Camden (jurisdiction 50). Unlike SO_2, however, the maximum concentration of T.S.P. for runs 1 and 3 is found in jurisdiction 15 (in Center City Philadelphia). These results demonstrate that, for virtually all reasonable R.E.Q.M. strategies, the poorest air quality throughout the region, with respect to SO_2 and T.S.P. concentrations, will be found in the Philadelphia-Camden area.

The distributions of dissolved oxygen (D.O.) concentrations throughout the twenty-two-reach estuary for runs 1, 2, 3, 13, 15, and 16 are shown in Table 9.11. When E-level water quality standards are imposed (run 2), the eight reaches with the poorest water quality (which actually is fairly high quality), are all located between reaches eleven and nineteen, from the confluence with the Schuylkill River to below Wilmington. Using D.O. as an indicator of water quality, estuary water quality upstream from the confluence with the Schuylkill River is better than downstream. The reach with the poorest water quality is 17, near Wilmington, Delaware.

For the T-level water quality standard (D.O.$\geqslant$5.9 mg/1), the distributions of the reaches with poorer quality change (runs 1, 3, 13, 15, and 16). Now the eight reaches with poorer water quality are distributed between reaches 5 and 19, from above Philadelphia to below Wilmington, but the distributions differ depending on whether or not regional sewage treatment plants or instream aeration or both are employed. As before, the reach with the poorest water quality is 17, near Wilmington. As with the E-level standards, the poorest quality water is not found in the vicinity of Philadelphia.

With respect to the distribution of costs, Table 9.12 shows for each of the fifty-seven political jurisdictions:

1 the percentage increase in household heating costs with
  —T-level air and T-level water quality standards and high quality landfills (run 1), and
  —E-level air and T-level water quality standards and high quality landfills (run 3);
2 the percentage increase in household electricity costs under the same two conditions as above;

3 the percentage increase in municipal solid residuals management costs for
 —high quality landfills with E-level air and T-level water quality standards (run 3), and
 —medium quality landfills with E-level air and T-level water quality standards (run 7);

4 the increase in costs of sewage disposal per sewered household under
 —T-level water and T-level air quality standards with high quality landfills (run 1), and
 —E-level water and T-level air quality standards (run 2).

With respect to household heating costs, for the T-level air quality standards (run 1), the largest increase in costs, about 55 per cent, occurs in jurisdiction 23, in central Philadelphia. The next largest increase, about 50 per cent, occurs in an adjacent jurisdiction, number 19, also in Philadelphia. For the E-level air quality standards (run 3), the largest and next largest increases, about 30 per cent and 28 per cent, respectively, also occur in jurisdictions 23 and 19, respectively.

As for increases in household electricity costs, a different distribution exists. For the T-level air quality standards (run 1), the largest increase in costs, about 16 per cent, occurs in New Castle, Delaware (jurisdictions 1–4). The next largest increase, about 14 per cent, occurs in Chester, Delaware, Philadelphia, Montgomery, and Bucks counties in Pennsylvania (jurisdictions 5–42). In contrast, in Camden, New Jersey (jurisdictions 50–54), where the air quality is almost as poor as in Philadelphia, the increase in household electricity costs amounts to only about 3 per cent. For the E-level air quality standards (run 3), the situation reverses, and the Pennsylvania counties, including Philadelphia (jurisdiction 5–42), are associated with the largest increase in costs, about 4.5 per cent.

Different distributions among political jurisdictions of increases in household heating and household electricity costs reflect the fact that household heating is achieved largely by energy conversion on the site, whereas household electricity is produced in a few large plants in the region. The distributions are also affected by the location of each generator in relation to the receptors in the region, for example, the number of receptors that are downwind of the discharge. The electrical generating stations in New Castle County, Delaware, are upwind of much of the rest of the region; hence, their discharges have widespread effects.

There is relatively little variation among the jurisdictions in the increased costs of municipal solid residuals management. This is because, for all runs, all jurisdictions were required to maintain the same quality landfills, that is, high, medium, or low quality. Where a significant variation does occur, it is associated with the high landfill quality runs, such as run 3. Within this group of runs, the differences in increased costs among jurisdictions for the E-level air quality standards are substantially greater than those associated with the T-level standards. This is because, for the E-level air quality standards, seven municipal incinerators (out of a total of twenty-three), all available in Philadelphia, are used for solid residuals management. The result of this is that the solid residuals management costs of the six jurisdictions within Philadelphia that use these incinerators are approximately 50 per cent of those jurisdictions that do not have this option. However, when T-level air quality standards are imposed, some of the incinerators are not used, resulting in more uniform cost increases throughout the region.

With respect to municipal sewage disposal costs, among the ten jurisdictions exhibiting the largest average increased costs in terms of dollars per household per year, are Wilmington (jurisdiction 2), Trenton (jurisdiction 44), and Camden (jurisdiction 50). In fact, one of these three jurisdictions is always in the number one position – with the large increase in costs of municipal sewage disposal. The remaining seven of the ten highest cost jurisdictions are located within the city of Philadelphia.

Caveats and conclusions

Inevitably, in a research undertaking as large and complicated as that of developing and applying a regional R.E.Q.M. model to an existing complex region, limitations will be imposed on the analysis and difficulties will be encountered. This final section of the chapter consists of four parts: first, limitations presented as 'some caveats'; second, conclusions relating specifically to R.E.Q.M. for the Lower Delaware Valley region; third, some difficulties encountered; and fourth, conclusions relating to methodological issues in analysis for R.E.Q.M. But before proceeding it should be noted that from the beginning the application was intended to be illustrative and not operational, although the model is based on actual data from the region and on the best data available at the time the model as developed.

Some caveats

1 The model is largely based on publicly available data on unknown quality and has only been partially calibrated. No field measurements of any type were made by the modelling team, and the implications of the results presented here have not been assessed in the field.

2 The model reflects conditions that existed in the region about 1970. For example, fuel availability and costs in the model do not reflect recent increases resulting from worldwide changes in petroleum prices.

3 To keep the model as small as possible, all stacks at the same x-y location in E.P.A.'s inventory of discharges of gaseous residuals were aggregated. This aggregation procedure could have a substantial effect on the accuracy of predicted ground level concentrations, especially near large, multistack sources.

4 Some of the important industries in the region – particularly the petroleum refineries and the steel mills – are represented in the model by 'collapsed' versions of larger, generalized models of industrial operations. These collapsed versions were calibrated to the production levels of specific plants, but other, perhaps more important details peculiar to specific plants have not been included.[15]

5 The receptor locations chosen to represent ambient air quality over the fifty-seven political jurisdictions were not selected with respect to existing locations of residential areas or with respect to what might be critical locations within each of the jurisdictions. They were simply chosen to be roughly in the central portion of each jurisdiction.

6 Certain categories of residuals generators and dischargers, such as transportation, have not been incorporated in the model. Nonpoint sources of residuals discharges, such as agricultural and construction activities, have been included only as they affect background concentrations.

7 The costs reflected in the model are based on meeting standards expressed in terms of long-term average ambient concentrations (annual averages for air quality and low flow summer averages for estuary water quality), rather than on meeting shorter term peak concentration constraints. The impact on R.E.Q.M. strategies, R.E.Q.M. costs, and distribution of R.E.Q.M. costs of the latter consideration have not been assessed.

8 The predictions of ambient air quality for the region are based on the Implementation Planning Programme's (I.P.P.) dispersion model, on 1970 meteorological data for Philadelphia, and on the associated calibration relationships, all supplied by the U.S. Environmental Protection Agency. The results clearly depend heavily on these data and estimated relationships. However, time and the resources available precluded the possibility of investigating the sensitivity of the results either to alternative dispersion models or to alternative meteorological data.

9 The results reflect two optional physical measures for improving ambient air quality in the region that may not be realistic. First, complete conversion to natural gas in household and commercial heating activities is allowed in the regional model; it is also allowed in the electric power plants and some of the industrial plants. Second, barging of municipal sewage sludge to sea is allowed for the larger cities along the estuary.

10 Imports of gaseous residuals into the Lower Delaware Valley region are included only in terms of background concentrations. No limitations were imposed on the export of such residuals from the region. Given the increasing knowledge about the long-range transport of gaseous residuals, establishing constraints on the flows of gaseous residuals across the boundary of the region in the direction of the prevailing winds might have resulted in additional R.E.Q.M. costs to the region.

11 The R.E.Q.M. costs estimated in the model reflect actual resource costs to society for achieving the associated A.E.Q. standards; they do not reflect the actual cash flows that would be incurred by the individual dischargers. The latter are a function of the multiple and complicated subsidies and tax structures at federal, state, and local levels (such as federal grants to municipalities for sewage treatment plant construction and federal tax provisions allowing individual, industrial, and other operations to take rapid depreciation for investments in approved pollution control equipment). Thus, developing information on distribution of actual out-of-pocket costs to different dischargers would be even more difficult than the cost distribution information generated in this study.

Some conclusions: R.E.Q.M. for the Lower Delaware Valley region

1 All cases explored show: first, a substantial variation in air quality, in terms of SO_2 and T.S.P. concentrations, over the Lower Delaware Valley region; and second, a substantial variation in water quality, in terms of dissolved oxygen, algae, and fish biomass concentrations, throughout the Delaware Estuary. In general, the lowest concentrations of SO_2 and T.S.P. are in Bucks, Chester, and Montgomery counties in Pennsylvania; the highest in Philadelphia County in Pennsylvania and Camden County in New Jersey. With respect to dissolved oxygen, the highest dissolved oxygen levels are always found in reach 1 near Trenton, New Jersey; the lowest in reach 17, near Wilmington, Delaware.

2 Air quality over the Lower Delaware Valley region appears to be more of a problem than Delaware Estuary water quality for at least two reasons. First, in some areas of Philadelphia, it appears that it may be technologically difficult to achieve, and then to maintain, the federal primary annual average standards for SO_2 and T.S.P. Second, regional costs to achieve the federal primary ambient air quality standards would be six to eight times the regional costs of achieving ambient water quality standards in the estuary, that is, between $300 and $400 million per year versus about $50 million per year, respectively.

3 Ambient water quality standards in the estuary can be met in all cases examined by using various combinations of on-site residuals dis-

charge reduction, regional sewage treatment, and instream aeration. The regional alternatives appear to allow the region as a whole to meet the same ambient water quality standards at less cost than by relying on residuals discharge reduction measures at individual sites. However, all dishargers do not benefit to the same degree from the decreased cost. Indeed, some dischargers who are not serviced by the regional facilities actually pay more under management alternatives with regional facilities than when management alternatives are restricted to measures at individual sites and local municipal sewage treatment.

4 Under the conditions reflected in the model, roughly those of 1970, the rail haul alternative for disposing of solid residuals appears to be too expensive. However, as landfill sites become scarce (and hence more expensive), this alterntive will certainly become more attractive, as will increased recycling of used paper products.

5 Again, under 1970 conditions, it appears that new municipal incinerators are not economically feasible alternatives for solid residuals management, especially with the stringent standards that would be imposed on discharges of liquid and gaseous residuals from them.

6 Based on the analyses presented, there exists a variety of combinations of physical measures for meeting the regional A.E.Q. standards, and these combinations do not differ very much in total costs to the region. However, the distributions of levels of residuals discharge reduction, of residuals discharges, and of costs among dischargers, all vary substantially from combination to combination.

Some difficulties

Space limitations do not allow a detailed discussion of all the difficulties encountered in the development of a model for regional R.E.Q.M. analysis and its application to the Lower Delaware Valley region.[16] However, listing some difficulties along with some conclusions about methodology should provide useful insights.

1 Clearly, an analysis of a region as complicated as the Lower Delaware Valley requires large amounts of specific data, such as data on types and quantities of residuals discharges from individual point and nonpoint sources and costs of reducing such discharges to various degrees. Only a limited amount of such data was readily available, particularly with respect to costs for *individual* dischargers (in contrast to generalized cost functions for some typical processes used to modify liquid residuals, such as primary sedimentation and trickling filters). Similarly, relatively few actual observations of the biological aspects of ambient water quality associated with observed sets of residuals discharges were available. This meant that, for example,

even if a model of the aquatic ecosystem were constructed from first principles and published laboratory relationships, its calibration and verification would be difficult, and perhaps even impossible, given the lack of resources for primary data collection in the field.

2 Even if all the necessary data on both residuals discharges and ambient environmental quality had been available, the size of even the simplest model of the complex number, type, and distribution of activities in the region would be such as to involve significant computational costs. Computer costs are directly related to model size, which is in turn a function of: first, the number of activities in the region explicitly modelled; second, the incorporation of nontreatment residuals discharge reduction alternatives; third, the explicit consideration of the linkages both among liquid, gaseous, and solid and energy residuals, and among the three environmental media (atmosphere, watercourses, and land); and fourth, the provision of information on the distributions of ambient environmental quality and of R.E.Q.M. costs. Thus, in order to do analysis at all, ways had to be developed of aggregating data while minimizing the loss of important information.

3 The decision to incorporate a nonlinear aquatic ecosystem model of the estuary required the use of an heuristic, iterative nonlinear programming algorithm. This in turn resulted in potential problems of multiple optima and problems of determining the steady state values of the biological state variables in the aquatic model. To use an heuristic, iterative nonlinear programming algorithm effiiently requires the development of an efficient step size selector.

4 The size of the model and the use of an iterative nonlinear programming algorithm raised the problem of providing comparable outputs from one run to another. As noted previously, in order to save on computer expenditures, all runs in which the nonlinear algorithm was used were arbitrarily stopped near the thirtieth iteration, short of even a local optimum. Unfortunately, it appears that the rate at which the algorithm converges to an optimum is dependent on the levels of A.E.Q. standards specified, among other factors. For example, the algorithm appears to converge more slowly for the runs with stringent ambient air quality standards than for those with the less restrictive air quality standards. Thus, what is not known is exactly which iteration of one computer run would be 'comparable' to which iteration of another computer run, and under what conditions. However, large differences between costs and discharges near the thirtieth iteration of the different production runs *can* be compared and used for evaluation of alternatives; it is the small differences about which strong statements cannot be made.

5 Generating information on the distribution of costs involved in

achieving specified levels of ambient environmental quality was straightforward. However, real difficulty arose when an attempt was made to constrain simultaneously the levels of ambient environmental quality to be achieved *and* the levels of consumer cost increases.

6 The substantial volume of output information generated by such a model for such a complicated region – particularly when the distributional aspects are included –represents a very formidable problem in devising ways to present that volume of information so that it is understandable to the users, whoever they may be. This is perhaps the most difficult and challenging problem of all.

Methodological issues

Intermedia linkages and trade-offs Evidence of the importance of linkages and trade-offs among the ambient qualities of the three environmental media is provided by the results of the analyses. The examples presented demonstrate the kinds and extent of the interdependencies among residuals forms and among environmental media, but the question remains: is it really worth the effort to include these linkages explicitly in the analyses? One part of the question is how difficult and costly it is to include these linkages in the analysis of alternative regional R.E.Q.M. strategies. The other part of this question is how costly might it be to the region if these linkages were not considered explicitly.

With respect to the first part, the Lower Delaware Valley study indicates that the marginal costs of including the air-water-solids linkages are modest – to the extent that the costs can be separated at all. There were no problems in obtaining the linkage data themselves, such as fly ash generation rates in sludge incineration, or suspended solids loads created in wet stack-gas scrubbers. The one drawback of the linked models is their size, which has implications for the costs of analysis. But all things considered, the cost-benefit ratio for linked models appears very favourable to further development and application, especially where A.E.Q. standards are involved. The second part of the question is more difficult to answer, and no direct attempt was made in the study to obtain an answer.[17]

Nonlinear aquatic ecosystem models The potential value of using aquatic ecosystem models in analyses for R.E.Q.M. is substantial for those contexts in which the questions to be answered justify such models and the analytical resources to develop and apply them are available. Compared with classical linear dissolved oxygen models, the aquatic ecosystem models are potentially capable of providing additional information on the resulting state of the natural environment (such as algal densities and fish biomass). Also, they are alleged to provide more accurate predictions of dissolved oxygen over wider ranges of river flows and residuals discharges than the linear dissolved oxygen models. But there are substantial costs involved in incorporating them in a regional management model. For one thing, the inclusion of nonlinear ecosystem models within an optimization framework creates substantial computational problems and expense. In addition, at the current state of the art, these models do not provide accurate predictions at trophic levels above algae.

Whether or not it is worth the problems and expense of incorporating aquatic ecosystem models depends on the region being studied and the question being addressed. For the larger and more complex regions, a reasonable compromise at this time might be to use a linear, dissolved oxygen water quality model within the optimization framework. This would at least provide a relationship in the model between organic discharges and one indicator of ambient water quality. Then, using the optimal set of organic discharges from the regional model as input to an ecosystem simulation model, the implications for other water quality indicators, such as algal densities, could be investigated.

Another possibility would be to employ a linear phytoplankton model in the regional analysis. These models do exist, but they are not in as widespread use today as the nonlinear variety. In addition, certain restrictions must be placed on their use in the analysis because of the assumptions made in their development.

The feasibility of using nonlinear aquatic ecosystem models in regional R.E.Q.M. analyses would be enhanced by the development of efficient, large-scale, nonlinear programming algorithms that could deal with resource management problems of the type described here.

Distributional information The capability of providing information on the distribution of both R.E.Q.M. costs and ambient environmental quality is one of the most important features of the regional R.E.Q.M. model presented here. In most regions, the *distribution* of costs and of A.E.Q. will be a more important issue than regional economic efficiency. Unfortunately, the provision of this additional information is not without computational problems.

Relatively little difficulty was encountered in constraining levels of ambient environmental quality and generating information on the implied costs of the constraints by political jurisdiction in the region. However, real computational difficulty arose when the attempt was made to constrain the levels of ambient environmental quality and the levels of consumer cost increases simultaneously. There are two primary reasons for this difficulty. The first involves infeasible solutions, which are commonplace when both types of constraints are imposed. This will not be discussed here.

The second computational difficulty is associated with the fact that most nonlinear programming algorithms become less and less efficient as the optimum is approached. When the regional efficiency criterion is employed, it makes sense to stop these algorithms short of an optimum because only modest cost savings, in terms of percentage of total regional costs, are involved. However, significant shifts in the distribution of costs continue to occur with virtually every step in the approach to the optimum. Thus, stopping short of the optimum makes it difficult, if not impossible, to determine when comparable results of runs for different sets of conditions have been obtained. In addition, stopping short of the optimum makes it difficult to explore the trade-offs among the distributions of costs because these trade-offs occur at the flattest portion of the regional cost response surface, near the optimum. Therefore, for analysis of regional R.E.Q.M. where specific information on distribution of both costs and ambient environmental quality is desired, resort must be made to linear programming techniques with which optimum solutions can be obtained relatively efficiently. This means the elimination of nonlinear models of both the natural world and of residuals generation and discharge as components of regional R.E.Q.M. optimization models.[18]

Analysis with discharge standards The optimization model of the Lower Delaware Valley region had as its objective the achievement of specified A.E.Q. standards at least cost to the region. A logical question then is, how relevant is such analysis in the real world where not only A.E.Q. standards exist but where discharge standards or best management practices have been imposed on individual dischargers, stemming from federal and state regulatory activities? Structuring the analysis in a programming format enables it not only to be determined whether or not the A.E.Q. standards can be met, given the discharge standards and best management practices, but also enables the least-cost *additional* physical measures necessary to achieve the A.E.Q. standards, if they are not achieved by the specified discharge standards and best management practices, to be determined, and also enables the effects on R.E.Q.M. costs of changes in factor prices and technology to be efficiently investigated. In cases where the specified A.E.Q. standards will clearly be achieved by the specified discharge standards and best management practices, relatively little would be gained by adopting the programming methodology. Where they will not, the additional information generated by the methodology may well be worth the additional analytical effort.

Notes

1 See Walter O. Spofford, Jr., Clifford S. Russell and Robert A. Kelly, *Environmental Quality Management: An Application to the Lower Delaware Valley*, Research Paper R-1 (Washington D.C., Resources for the Future, 1976).

2 Available resources, including time, did not permit exploration of the second question.

3 The definition of 'urbanized' used by the U.S. Bureau of the Census is long and complex, but basically it amounts to counting as urbanized incorporated places of more than 2,500 inhabitants or of a density greater than 1,000 persons per square mile.

4 In the modelling application, 1970 was used as the base period, and the model structure reflects the situation in that year whenever possible. In some cases, such as sewage treatment plants, in which government surveys were the data source, the base year differs from 1970.

5 There are significant groundwater resources in the basin, particularly in the coastal plain section of Delaware. The Delaware River in the reach from Trenton to Philadelphia is the major source of recharge for the Magothy and Raritan aquifers, which provide significant sources of water for users in New Jersey. These and other aspects of groundwater in the region were not explicitly considered in the model.

6 Information provided by the Water Resources Division, U.S. Geological Survey, Reston, Virginia.

7 Atmospheric stagnations are defined here as periods of four or more days when the windspeed at anemometer level does not exceed 7.5 knots per hour.

8 See J. Korshover, *Climatology of Stagnating Anticyclones East of the Rocky Mountains, 1936–1965*, U.S. Department of Health, Education and Welfare, Public Health Service, Publication No. 999-AP-34 (1967).

9 See F. K. Davis, 'The Air Over Philadelphia', *Symposium: Air Over Cities*, U.S. Department of Health, Education and Welfare, Public Health Service, Technical Report A62–5 (November 1961), pp. 115–129.

10 This use of uniform wind rose and stability conditions for the region, in combination with the available source inventory data, produced distributions of ambient air quality similar to the measured annual averages.

11 Resources were not available to develop a water quality model of the Schuylkill River. Development of such a model was subsequently undertaken for the Environmental Protection Agency but was not completed in time to be utilized in the R.F.F. work.

12 At 1975 computer rates, it cost $1,220 for a 30-iteration run, or roughly $41 per iteration, operation on an IBM 370 model 165 and using 300K bytes of internal core storage. On average, one iteration takes 2.8 minutes of computer-processing unit time, 5.94 minutes of input-output time, has 13,400 read-write instructions, and prints 1,236 lines of output (minimum).

13 The one exception to the total discharges not changing much beyond the thirtieth iteration is the trade-off between instream aerators and BOD_5 discharges (and perhaps other discharges).

14 This is particularly true, because it was assumed at the time the model inputs were developed, that natural gas was available to all users at a relatively low price.

15 See the discussion of this point in footnotes 46 and 47 on pages 99 and 100 of Spofford, Russell and Kelly, *Environmental Quality*.

16 Various issues with respect to analysis for regional R.E.Q.M. are explored in Bower, *Regional Residuals*.

17 There is, however, some discussion of the issue in Spofford, Russell and Kelly, *Environmental Quality*.

18 This statement assumes that the nonlinearities are such that they cannot be converted into piecewise linear segments for inclusion in a linear programming model.

10

Option Value: Empirical Evidence from a Case Study of Recreation and Water Quality

Douglas A. Greenley
Richard G. Walsh
Robert A. Young

INTRODUCTION

If economists have been persistent in advocating that the correct criterion for choice under uncertainty is the maximization of *expected* (or *mean*) social net benefits, environmentalists have been vociferous in wanting to keep *future options* open. The literature on 'option values', of which the paper by Greenley, Walsh and Young is an example, studies the connection between these two decision criteria. (See Dasgupta (1982), Chapter 10.1, Arrow and Fisher (1974), Henry (1974) and Mäler (1977) develop the theory in a general manner.)

The environmentalist's concern with future options has a sound intuitive basis. The concern is founded on the recognition that the use of environmental resources may well have irreversible effects – so that decisions today will constrain the choices that are available later – *and* that it is desirable to insure against adverse states of nature. If everything that can be done can also be undone, one cannot but help keep one's options open. At the same time, if the future is known with certainty, there is no cost involved in foregoing one's future options. It is the twin presence of uncertainty and irreversibility that makes flexibility such an attractive feature of a planned course of action. The theoretical literature on environmental option values has analyzed the worth of flexibility in terms of expected social benefit, and thereby related the environmentalist's concern with the economist's prescription. The paper by Greenley, Walsh and Young attempts to measure this worth in curtailing mining activity in the South Platte River Basin, Colorado, U.S.A.

It should be emphasized that 'option value', as the term is used here, measures the value of keeping options open indirectly in terms of loss in expected welfare in the future. An alternative approach would be to define preferences directly on sets of options and thereby to build flexibility directly into the criterion of choice. (On this, see Koopmans (1964) and Kreps (1979).) A simple example of the idea of option values may help the reader understand the motivation behind the Greenley *et al.* analysis.[1]

Imagine two instants of time $t = 0.1$. There is a perfectly divisible asset (e.g. a forest) of size unity. The net social benefit from consuming a marginal unit of the asset at $t = 0$ is b_0. There are two possible states of nature θ_s ($s = 1, 2$). The state of nature is revealed at $t = 1$. If θ_1 prevails (the probability of this is assumed to be π) the net social benefit from consuming a unit of the asset is b_1. If θ_2 prevails (the probability of this is by definition $1-\pi$), net social benefit is b_2. The problem is to choose how much of the asset to consume now ($t = 0$) and how much to consume 'tomorrow' ($t = 1$) when the true state of nature will be revealed.

Since by hypothesis the decision-maker is risk-neutral (b_0, b_1 and b_2 are independent of the amounts consumed), it may seem reasonable to replace random variables by their *expected* (or *mean*) values. Let us see what this implies for the example at hand.

Let r (> 0) be the social rate of discount. From the vantage point of today ($t = 0$), $b_1\pi + b_2(1-\pi)$ is the expected marginal benefit from consumption 'tomorrow'. Let D_0 and $\tilde{D}$ denote the total quantity of the asset consumed at $t = 0$ and by $t = 1$ respectively. Since the act of consuming the asset is by hypothesis irreversible, we must have $0 \leqslant D_0 \leqslant \tilde{D} \leqslant 1$. Thus the planning problem is to choose D_0 and $\tilde{D}$ so as to maximize the present value of expected social benefits, which is:

$$b_0 D_0 + (\pi b_1 + (1-\pi) b_2)\tilde{D}/(1+r). \tag{1}$$

To have an interesting problem, suppose $b_1 < 0$, $b_2 > 0$ and $\pi b_1 + (1-\pi) b_2 > 0$. This last assumption means that it is expected that further consumption is desirable. Since we are choosing both D_0 and $\tilde{D}$ today, criterion (1) say, then we must plan to set $\tilde{D} = 1$. Therefore, optimal D_0 depends on the sign of b_0. If $b_0 > 0$ then choose $D_0 = 1$; if $b_0 < 0$ then choose $D_0 = 0$. But the main moral to emerge is that criterion (1) implies that the optimal amount of consumption today depends solely on the sign of b_0; that is expected net benefits of consumption today.

Let us now compute the true solution. The point to note first is that the amount to consume 'tomorrow' should be chosen only when tomorrow arrives, when in fact the true state of nature will be revealed. Let D_1 and D_2 be the amounts consumed tomorrow under states of nature θ_1 and θ_2 respectively. Because of irreversibility we must have $0 \leqslant D_0 \leqslant D_1, D_2 \leqslant 1$. The present value of *expected* social benefits is:

$$b_0 D_0 + \pi b_1 D_1/(1+r) + (1-\pi) b_2 D_2/(1+r). \tag{2}$$

The planner should choose D_0, D_1 and D_2 at $t = 0$. (Of course D_1 and D_2 are *planned* at $t = 0$.)

If one looks at (2) one notes that, because $b_1 < 0$, the planner will set $D_1 = D_0$ and because $b_2 > 0$, he should set $D_2 = 1$. Thus (2) reduces to

$$\{b_0 + \pi b_1/(1+r)\} D_0 + (1-\pi) b_2/(1+r). \qquad (3)$$

From (3) it is clear that the planner should set $D_0 = 1$ if $b_0 + \pi b_1/(1+r) > 0$ and $D_0 = 0$ if $b_0 + \pi b_1/(1+r) < 0$. But the criterion for having *positive* consumption today is stiffer under (2) and (3) than under (1), because the criterion now is $b_0 \geqslant -\pi b_1/(1+r)$, which is strictly positive.

What the example illustrates is that even a risk-neutral planner will require a rate of *current net social benefits* from asset consumption of at least $-\pi b_1/(1+r)$ (which is greater than zero) in order to foreclose society's options. Which is why $-\pi b_1/(1+r)$ is called the *option value.*

In their interesting paper, Greenley *et al.* have used the model of option value given above to estimate individuals' willingness to pay for the option to choose between two alternatives – either clean water, or polluted water from mining development – at some future time under conditions of sufficient knowledge as to the relative benefits of each (b_1 and b_2 in our notation). Details of the authors' sampling procedure for estimating b_1 and b_2 are given in their paper. Assuming a $6\frac{3}{8}$% rate of discount, and an infinite time horizon, the present value of annual benefits from water quality improvement in the South Platte River Basin was calculated to be nearly US \$1 billion. This estimate includes recreation use value of US \$414 million, existence value of US \$226 million, a bequest value of US \$153 million *and* an *option value* of US \$165 million.

Notes

1 The theoretical model in Greenley *et al.* (1981) is a generalization of the example in the text.

CASE STUDY[1]

Introduction

The environmental economics literature identifies several possibilities of willingness to pay for preservation of public non-market aspects of environmental quality which are distinct from the direct or immediate consumer surplus benefit from use of the natural environment. These preservation benefits include option, bequest, and existence demands as outlined by Krutilla (1967). *Option value* is defined as the willingness to pay for the opportunity to choose from among competing alternative uses of a natural environment in the future. *Existence value* is the willingness to pay for the knowledge that a natural environment is preserved. *Bequest value* is defined as the willingness to pay for the satisfaction derived from endowing future generations with a natural environment. Unfortunately, no empirical evidence bearing on the monetary significance of such benefits has been forthcoming to assist in the development of environmental policy. This paper provides what we believe to be the first measurement of option value, arising in this case from the assured choice of recreational use of preserved water quality in the presence of potential irreversible water quality degradation due to mining activity in the South Platte River Basin, Colorado.

Weisbrod (1964) originated the concept of option value. He wrote in rebuttal to Friedman's (1962) advocacy of a policy of cutting down the ancient redwoods in Sequoia National Park in the event that the present value of the stream of annual net benefits accruing to park visitors was found to fall below the current commercial value of redwood lumber. According to Weisbrod, option value was the amount of money economic men who anticipate visiting the park, but are uncertain and in fact may or may not make such a visit, would be willing to pay for an option which would guarantee their future access. If this value could be estimated, its magnitude would influence the public choice of whether or not the park should be preserved. An uncertain supply and demand situation coupled with prohibitively high costs of renewing production, once stopped, were identified as necessary conditions for the existence of option value.

Weisbrod's article generated a lengthy theoretical debate. Long (1969) argued that option value was equivalent to expected consumer surplus. Lindsay (1969) pointed out that Long had neglected Weisbrod's assumption of uncertainty of purchase. Using a game theoretic framework, Byerlee (1971) concluded that in the face of uncertain future demand, option value could be greater than, equal to, or less than consumer surplus. Cicchetti and Freeman (1971) responded by showing that when uncertainty in supply is also considered, a risk-averse individual would be willing to pay to preserve his future option of use. Schmalensee (1972) argued that an alternative risk is also borne if a natural environment is preserved – that of a very small future demand. Since the sign and magnitude of associated risk premiums are not generally known, he concluded that consumer surplus should serve as the appropriate proxy for option value.

Two later articles (Arrow and Fisher, 1974; Henry, 1974) showed that option value is distinct from consumer surplus and may attain significance even for a risk-neutral individual. Arrow and Fisher examined the question of whether or not the existence of option value for a risk-neutral individual necessarily led to a similar situation for society. They formulated a 'quasi-option' value model in terms of the aggregate benefits and costs that would be incurred by choosing various alternative environmental uses. It was concluded that, even in the aggregate, society should take cognizance of the presence of option value. The Henry model was based on individual willingness to pay for the assurance of selecting the preservation of an irreplaceable environmental asset facing an imminent irreversible commitment, until such time that sufficient information becomes available affecting the future option decision of selecting from among alternative uses.

We adopted the Henry model for our study. The specific objective of the study was to empirically test the application of the Henry framework in the measurement of benefits of water quality improvement. The benefits measured include:

1 Consumer surplus from enhanced enjoyment of water-based recreation activities;
2 Option value of assured choice of recreation use in the future by avoidance of irrevocable pollution by mineral and energy development;
3 Existence and bequest values for non-users.

Empirical estimates were derived using a simulated market bidding game.

Theoretical model

After Henry, consider a two time-period model defined in accordance with the following symbols:

N = The Nth individual
U = N's utility function
Y = N's income
CS = N's consumer surplus generated from use of the natural environment
D = Availability of the irreplaceable natural environment
$D = d$, the natural environment which is available
$D = d^*$, the natural environment has been appropriated for an alternative irreversible use and is unavailable
OV = Option value
i = States of the world, $i = 1, 2$
j = Time period, $j = 1, 2$
P_i = Probability that state i will occur (where $\sum p_i = 1$ for $i = 1, 2$)
C_j = Opportunity cost to retain the natural environment

The model is predicted on the following assumptions: first, that the future is uncertain; second, one use of the natural environment is more irreversible than the other; third, a decision is imminent as to which of the two competing uses of the natural environment will be chosen; and fourth, sequential decision-making takes place based on improved information acquired through time. Let

$$U = \sum_{j=1}^{2} \sum_{i=1}^{2} P_i^j U_i^j (Y_i^j, D^j) \tag{1}$$

be N's two period probability-weighted utility function. Assume an opportunity cost C^j must be paid to obtain $D^j = d$, that is, cost is imposed in the form of foregone alternatives if the natural environment is to remain available. C^1 and C^2 must be financed at instant 1 and instant 2, respectively, if $D^j = d$ is chosen. For simplicity of exposition C^j and Y^j are assumed known with certainty. The notation may then be simplified to $U_i^j(Y^j, d^*) = U_i^j(d^*)$ and in later equations, $U_i^j(Y^j - C^j, d) = U_i^j(d)$. Finally, assume that

$$\sum_{i=1}^{2} P_i^1 U_i^1 (d) < \sum_{i=1}^{2} P_i^1 U_i^1 (d^*) \tag{2}$$

This assumption specifies that if only the first period is considered, N will choose d^* so that the natural environment is not available. In this case the cost, C^1, of preserving the natural environment is greater than the associated benefits in period 1.

In the following case no new information is expected to become available between instant 1 and instant 2. A decision is made as if a 'timeless world' existed. Consumer surplus for N can be defined as the equating factor in

$$\sum_{i=1}^{2} P_i^1 U_i^1 (Y^1 - CS, d) + \sum_{i=1}^{2} P_i^2 U_i^2 (d) = \sum_{j=1}^{2} \sum_{i=1}^{2} P_i^j U_i^j (d^*) \tag{3}$$

N will be willing to pay an amount CS at instant 1 to have d. Even after payment of CS, the individual will still receive the same expected utility as if the natural environment were not available.

N will choose the preserved natural environment as opposed to the development alternative if $CS > C^1$. No CS term need appear in the second period term of the preservation alternative since no change in information occurs between the two periods. As long as C^1 is paid at instant 1 the natural environment will be available in all following periods because of the static situation. In this case CS is the present worth to N of the preserved natural environment for all time.

Now assume that new information enters between instant 1 and instant 2. Individual N will know with certainty at instant 2 which state of the world will obtain. Assuming a sequential decision-making process takes place the following question must be answered: How much will N be willing to pay at instant 1 both to enjoy the natural environment through period 1 and to have the option of choosing under conditions of certainty at instant 2 whether or not to retain the natural environment?

The preceding question can be answered by referring to the following equation

$$\sum_{i=1}^{2} P_i^1 U_i^1 (Y^1 - CS^1 - OV, d) + \sum_{i=1}^{2} P_i^2 \max[U_i^2(d), U_i^2(d^*)] = \sum_{j=1}^{2} \sum_{i=1}^{2} P_i^j U_i^j (d^*) \tag{4}$$

The terms CS^1 and OV balance equation (4). At instant 1 individual N will be willing to pay CS^1 to enjoy the natural environment during period 1. In addition, N is willing to pay an amount OV to choose, at instant 2, either the preserved environment or the irreversible alternative with full knowledge of which state of the world will obtain. In equation (4) CS^1 results from the enjoyment of the preserved natural environment through period 1 only. The magnitude of OV in period 1 is a function of P_i^2, $U_i^2(d)$, and $U_i^2(d^*)$ in period 2 as they exist at instant 1.

In considering the term ($\max[U_i^2(d), U_i^2(d^*)]$) four possible cases can occur:

(a) $U_1^2(d) > U_1^2(d^*)$ and $U_2^2(d) < U_2^2(d^*)$
(b) $U_1^2(d) < U_1^2(d^*)$ and $U_2^2(d) > U_2^2(d^*)$
(c) $U_1^2(d) < U_1^2(d^*)$ and $U_2^2(d) < U_2^2(d^*)$
(d) $U_1^2(d) > U_1^2(d^*)$ and $U_2^2(d) > U_2^2(d^*)$

For example, if situation (a) evolves then:

$$\sum_{i=1}^{2} [P_i^1 U_i^1 (Y^1 - CS^1 - OV, d)] + P_1^2 U_1^2(d) + P_2^2 U_2^2(d^*) = \sum_{j=1}^{2} \sum_{i=1}^{2} P_i^j U_i^j (d^*) \tag{5}$$

The inequality

$$P_1^2 U_1^2(d) + P_2^2 U_2^2(d^*) > \sum_{i=1}^{2} P_i^2 U_i^2(d^*) \tag{6}$$

exists because maximum values of $U_i^2(d)$ and $U_i^2(d^*)$ were chosen. Therefore, $OV >$ zero and d will be chosen at instant 1 if $CS^1 + OV > C^1$. The magnitude of OV is determined precisely by the difference between the right and left-hand expressions of inequality (6). In cases (b) and (c) OV will likewise be positive. Only in case (d) will option value equal zero. None of the four possible situations will produce a negative option value.

Option value is irrelevant to the decision-making process as long as $CS^j > C^j$. The option to use the environment in the future has been preserved free of cost. Option value is a free by-product as long as the user benefit of the preserved environment exceeds the opportunity costs of preservation. It is for this reason that inequality (2) is required. This expression states that if the first period is considered by itself, development is preferred over preservation. Under this condition it is necessary to include explicit consideration of the second period in order to determine the proper course of action at the beginning of period one. Henry extended the original analysis to an infinite number of sequential decision-making time periods. This empirical investigation, however, was limited to two time periods.

Empirical procedures

The contingent valuation approach was utilized in this study. The U.S. Water Resources Council (1979) has approved use of the method for valuation of recreation resources. Respondents answered 'yes' or 'no' to dollar increments in willingness to pay, contingent on hypothetical changes in water quality with the highest acceptable value presumed to correspond to the point of indifference between income and the environmental amenity. Many economists share Freeman's (1979) reservations about the approach, primarily because of the potential for strategic behaviour by respondents, which may bias the results in the direction of a preferred policy. Utilizing market-related data has been preferred by most analysts in the past, since such analyses are based on actual behaviour rather than responses to hypothetical situations.

It is notable that objections to the contingent valuation approach have been primarily theoretical, as empirical evidence of systematic bias is at best inconclusive. Davis, who pioneered the iterative bidding procedure in a study of the recreation benefits of the Maine woods, concluded that the reported values were not significantly different from those obtained by the market-related travel cost approach (Knetsch and Davis, 1966). Randall and associates developed refinements in the contingent valuation technique and presented a persuasive case for its effectiveness in the valuation of environmental quality. They studied the benefits from improved air quality and other environmental amenities in the Four Corners area of New Mexico (Randall *et al.*, 1974) and the Glen Canyon National Recreation Area (Brookshire *et al.*, 1976). They found no measurable strategic behaviour by environmentalists compared to other respondents. Replication of the studies resulted in similar values. Bohm (1972) conducted a controlled experiment comparing five alternative measures of willingness to pay for a public good, including actual immediate payment in cash of the stated willingness to pay. He found no significant difference in values reported by five groups, each presented with an alternative willingness to pay format. Bohm (1979) concluded that the theoretical objections to the contingent valuation approach could be resolved by application of an interval method. Two benefit functions would be derived, based on minimum and maximum incentives to misrepresent willingness to pay. The midpoint of the interval would represent the most acceptable value.

The willingness to pay measure of the value of improved water quality was selected over the alternative, willingness to sell or accept compensation for reduced quality. The appropriate question depends on the resource decision to be made. Congress in P.L. 92-500 determined that polluting rights are not for sale. Thus, the question of what level of compensation would be required to allow recreationists to remain no worse off than before pollution of recreation water resources is of only peripheral interest. A number of studies including Bishop and Heberlein (1979) have found that willingness to sell values including actual cash sales are considerably higher than willingness to pay, whether the latter is measured by contingent valuation or the travel cost approach. This would be the expected result, as willingness to pay would be constrained by limited household income and time budgets as well as other variables (Gordon and Knetsch, 1979).

A random sample of 202 resident households in Denver and Fort Collins, Colorado, were interviewed in their homes during the summer, 1976. A comparison of sample and population demographic characters of Denver and Fort Collins showed little sample bias. Racial minorities and young adults between 18 and 24 years of age were slightly under-represented. At the outset of the interview, respondents were shown colour photos of three stream sites (labelled A, B, and C) in the River Basin and were provided technical information about the degree of heavy metal pollution at the sites. The colour photos were selected to represent the range of water quality in the River Basin and to limit variations in composition so that water quality would be the sole basis for differentiation. Technical information about heavy metal concentration served as an index of water quality. The U.S. Geological Survey (Wentz, 1974; Moran and Wentz, 1974) found that Site C exceeded heavy metal concentration recommended for drinking water; Site B exceeded heavy metal concentration recommended for fish and wildlife survival; and no heavy metals were present at Site A. Ideally, colour photos should include a visual depiction of all water quality parameters which could influence perception of suitability for water-based recreation. Colour photographs can realistically depict evidence of visual pollution such as heavy metal mine drainage, algae, weeds, and sediment but not odour nor the presence of harmful chemicals and bacteria which can only be inferred from visual attributes. They have the advantage of allowing respondents to choose the specific characteristics of water quality which relate to their recreation experience.

The two methods of payment employed lend realism and credibility to the simulated market situations. The general sales tax and the residential water-sewer fee represent established routinized methods of paying for public services such as water quality improvement. Most respondents could readily conceive that pollution abatement may be financed by either approach. The sales tax measure was considered superior to the water-sewer fee in reducing the effects of the free-rider problem. Tourism is the third largest industry in the River Basin and sales taxes paid by tourists are an important source of revenue to state and local units of government. While payment of water-sewer fees are a monthly routine for property owners, renters do not pay directly. Of course, water-sewer fees are paid indirectly by renters and tourists alike in the purchase prices of goods and services. Nonetheless, residential property owners are likely to conceive of a proper range for water-sewer charges and recent experience with escalating fees may have resulted in understatement of their willingness to pay for water quality. To avoid these possible biases, Davis (1963) recommended the general cost of recreation activities as a hypothetical payment method. However, this was not deemed a suitable approach for measuring non-use preservation values.

We hypothesized that the starting point at which the bidding began would not produce any significant bias. If the starting dollar amount resulted in a negative response, it simply would be lowered until an acceptable level was reached. The starting point was 50 cents per month for the water-sewer fee with incremental changes of 50 cents per month. The sales tax iteration began at one-half cent per dollar of expenditure with incremental changes of one-quarter cent. Respondents were shown an Internal Revenue Service tax rate schedule with the estimated annual sales tax paid by household size and income categories. The starting points generated revenue of $6 per year in water-sewer fees and $25 per year in sales tax for a typical household of four with an average income of $13,500 per year.

Respondents were informed that the payment reported would be used for water quality improvements to enhance recreational enjoyment. The definition of recreational enjoyment was left to each individual. Any definition of water-based activities provided might have omitted an activity for which the respondent would be willing to pay. As a result, respondents conceived of water-based recreation broadly to include swimming, boating, fishing, sightseeing, picnicking, camping, hiking, driving, and other leisure time activities within view of lakes and streams.

It was specified that all waterways in the River Basin would be improved to level A by 1983 and preserved at that level indefinitely. The Federal Water Pollution Act Amendments of 1972 designated recreation as one of the principle benefits of the water quality programme and set a national goal of providing water suitable for contact recreation by 1983. This deadline was since been extended.

The hypothetical situation posited was designed to be as realistic as possible. Irreversible water quality conditions exist in several areas of the state, as a result of past mining practices and the prohibitive cost of rectifying the damage.[2] The imminent possibility of expanding mining development and the incumbent high probability of irreversible water quality impairment in the River Basin provided an appropriate setting for investigating the empirical significance of option value. Bishop (1977) noted that a similar potential exists in the adjacent Colorado River Basin.

An introductory scenario explained the potential mining development and the probable consequences to water quality. The two alternative uses of the waterways were set forth and substitution possibilities were minimized. The option value questions took the following form:

> In the near future, one of two alternatives is likely to occur in the South Platte River Basin. The *first alternative* is that a large expansion in mining development will soon take place, creating jobs and income for the region. As a consequence, however, many lakes and streams would become severely polluted. It is highly unlikely, as is shown in Situation C, that these waterways could ever be returned to their natural condition. They could not be used for recreation. Growing demand could cause all other waterways in the area to be crowded with other recreationists.
>
> The *second possible alternative* is to postpone any decision to expand mining activities which would irreversibly pollute these waterways. During this time, they would be preserved at level A for your recreational use. Furthermore, information would become available enabling you to make a decision with near certainty in the future, as to whether it is more beneficial to you to preserve the waterways at level A for your recreational use or to permit mining development. Of course, if the first alternative takes place, you could not make this future choice since the waterways would be irreversibly polluted.
>
> Given your chances of future recreational use, would you be willing to pay an additional ____ cents on the dollar in present sales taxes every year to postpone mining development? This postponement would permit information to become available enabling you to make a decision with near certainty in the future as to which option (recreational use or mining development) would be most beneficial to you.[3] Would it be reasonable to add ____ to your water bill every month for this postponement?

Similar although much abbreviated questions were asked separately with respect to benefits from enhanced enjoyment of current water-based recreation use and non-use preservation values including the existence and bequest of clear water resources in the River Basin (Walsh *et al.*, 1978).

Results

Table 10.1 summarizes the responses to the survey. The sales tax values will be emphasized for ease of exposition, followed by a comparison with water-sewer fee estimates. Willingness to pay additional sales taxes for the option to choose to engage in water-based recreation activities in the future was estimated as $23 annually per household. This is the mean population-weighted value for the 80 per cent of sample households who expect to continue to use waterways in the River Basin for recreation activities in the future. Of the 202 households surveyed, about 20 per cent were unwilling to pay because they did not expect to engage in water-based recreation activities in the future. About 60 per cent were willing to pay some positive amount of sales tax for option value. Thus, the mean option value of $23 includes 20 per cent who reported zero values. Those reporting zero values felt that water quality preservation was unnecessary, as their households were not believed to be harmed by water pollution. Others rejected the bidding game itself. Some considered it unfair to expect those adversely affected by water pollution to pay the costs of improvement. Others said taxes were already too high and expressed little confidence in the ability of responsible government entities to implement an effective programme of water quality preservation. Some were dissatisfied with the hypothesized mechanism of payment for water quality.

Water quality improvement shifts the demand curve for water-based recreation activities. The economic benefit generated is consumer surplus delineated as the area between demand curves with and without water pollution (Freeman, 1979). The 80 per cent of households interviewed who engage in water-based recreation activities in the River Basin reported they were willing to pay an average of $57 for water quality to enhance the enjoyment of these activities. This figure is quite similar to Oster's (1977) estimate of the annual recreation benefits from improved water quality in the Merrimack River Basin as $12 per resident or $48 for a family of four in 1973. Adjusted for inflation to 1976, that estimate is well within the 95 per cent confidence interval of our estimate for the South Platte River Basin.

The economic significance of option value and the other preservation values is that they shift the vertical intercept of the demand curve for water quality preservation. The inclusion of option value shifted the demand curve for water quality preservation in the River Basin by an average of $23 per year, equal to a 40 per cent increase in the current recreation use value of water quality. Summing the two values, the total recreation-derived benefit of improved water quality to the 80 per cent of the households who expect to continue to use waterways in the River Basin for recreation activities averaged $79 annually. To put this in perspective, it was equivalent to approximately $5 per household recreation activity day in 1976.

Additional preservation benefits to the general population residing in the River Basin (existence and bequest value) were defined to include the satisfaction derived from knowledge of the existence of a natural waterway ecosystem and its bequest to future generations. About 20 per cent of the households interviewed who do not use the River Basin for recreation activities reported they were willing to pay an average of $25 annually for knowledge of the existence of the natural aquatic ecosystem and $17 annually to bequest clean water to future generations, for a total non-user value of $42 annually. Estimates of these values also were obtained from recreation users, premised on the hypothetical assumption of certain knowledge they would not engage in water-based recreation activities in the River Basin. Not surprisingly, responses of present users were larger than for non-users. Average existence value of recreation users was $34 and bequest value $33, for a total non-use value of $67 annually, or 60 per cent more. Existence and bequest value estimates reported by recreation users are the values which would remain in the absence of recreation use. We believe these preservation values should not be added to recreation use and option values because of the high probability of upward bias. As a first approximation, the existence and bequest value estimates for non-user households were extrapolated to all residents of the River Basin, including recreation users.

Table 10.2 shows our estimates of total annual recreation and aesthetic benefits of water quality aggregated over the 576,435 households residing in the River Basin. Based on Willingness to pay an additional sales tax, total annual benefits were estimated as $61 million, including option value of $10.5 million, recreation use value of $26.4 million, existence value of $14.4 million, and bequest value of $9.8 million.

Assuming a 6 3/8 per cent discount rate and an infinite time horizon, the present value of annual benefits from water quality improvement in the River Basin was calculated as nearly $1 billion. This estimate includes option value of $165 million, recreation use value of $414 million, existence value of about $226 million and bequest value of $153 million.

These present value estimates are premised on the assumption of constant annual benefits. This may be a reasonable forecast of recreation and aesthetic benefits for the foreseeable future in an economy beset with energy shortages, high prices, and near stable incomes. However, outdoor recreation has grown at an average annual rate of 5 per cent per year during the previous decade. If the historic 5 per cent annual growth rate continued to the year 2000, the present value of water quality in the River Basin would increase by about 15 per cent to $1.1 billion.

Tables 10.1 and 10.2 show that willingness to pay for water quality was quite sensitive to the method of hypothetical payment. Residents sampled reported willingness to pay only about one-quarter as much in water-sewer fees as in sales tax for the option value of water quality. Respondents were more reluctant to participate in the water-sewer bill estimation procedure, and may have perceived inequities. Everyone,

Table 10.1 *Resident Household Willingness to Pay Additional Sales Tax and Water Service Assesments for Water Quality Preservation in the South Platte River Basin, Colorado* (mean values in 1976 dollars)

Water Quality Preservation Values	*Water Fee/ Month* (dollars)	*Tax Rate* (cents)	*Annual Dollars* *Water Fee*	*Sales Tax*[a]
		Denver Metropolitan Area		
Option Value	0.50	0.39	6.00	18.31
95% Confidence Interval			(4.58–7.51)	(13.27–23.36)
Per cent of Total Value	17.7%	15.5%	17.7%	16.5%
Number Reporting	83	88		
Bequest Value[b]	0.46	0.42	5.52	16.43
95% Confidence Interval			(3.93–7.22)	(6.67–26.19)
Per cent of Total Value	16.3%	16.7%	16.3%	14.8%
Number Reporting	14	15		
Existence Value[c]	0.54	0.70	6.48	26.03
95% Confidence Interval			(4.78–8.07)	(1.78–50.29)
Per cent of Total Value	19.1%	27.9%	19.1%	23.5%
Number Reporting	14	15		
Recreation Value[d]	1.32	1.00	15.84	50.18
95% Confidence Interval			(12.99–18.69)	(42.94–57.43)
Per cent of Total Value	46.8%	39.8%	46.8%	45.2%
Number Reporting	85	85		
Total Preservation and Recreation Value	2.82	2.51	33.84	110.95
		Fort Collins		
Option Value	1.00	0.85	12.00	22.60
95% Confidence Interval			(5.68–18.14)	(20.11–47.99)
Per cent of Total Value	24.0%	25.1%	24.0%	22.9%
Number Reporting	78	89		

Table 10.1 (*Contd*)

Water Quality Preservation Values	*Water Fee/ Month* (dollars)	*Tax Rate* (cents)	*Annual Dollars* *Water Fee*	*Sales Tax*[a]
Bequest Value[b]	0.42	0.40	5.04	18.42
95% Confidence Interval			(2.70–7.31)	(−9.70–46.53)
Per cent of Total Value	10.1%	11.8%	10.1%	12.4%
Number Reporting	9	9		
Existence Value[c]	0.58	0.50	6.96	22.17
95% Confidence Interval			(5.37–8.63)	(5.33–49.66)
Percent of Total Value	13.9%	14.8%	13.9%	14.9%
Number Reporting	9	9		
Recreation Value[d]	2.16	1.63	25.92	74.00
95% Confidence Interval			(11.79–40.06)	(51.07–96.94)
Per cent of Total Value	51.9%	48.2%	51.9%	49.8%
Number Reporting	89	89		
Total Preservation and Recreation Value	4.16	3.38	49.92	148.64
	South Plate River Basin[e]			
Option Value	0.64	0.52	7.68	22.60
Per cent of Total Value	20.1%	19.0%	20.1%	18.6%
Number Reporting	161	177		
Grouped T-Value[f]	1.01	1.51		
Bequest Value[b]	0.45	0.41	5.40	16.97
Per cent of Total Value	14.1%	15.0%	14.1%	14.0%
Number Reporting	23	24		
Grouped T-value[f]	0.88	1.55		
Existence Value[c]	0.55	0.64	6.60	24.98

Per cent of Total Value	17.2%	23.3%	17.2%	20.6%
Number Reporting	23	24		
Grouped T-Value	0.99	1.69		
Recreation Value[d]	1.55	1.17	18.60	56.68
Per cent of Total Value	48.6%	42.7%	48.6%	46.8%
Number Reporting	174	174		
Grouped T-Value	0.81	1.32		
Total Preservation and Recreation Value	3.19	2.74	38.25	121.23

[a] From U.S. Internal Revenue Service (1974).

[b] Willingness to pay estimate for a sub-sample of non-recreationists for the benefit derived from the assurance that future generations will have access to a preserved natural environment in the South Platte River Basin, Colorado.

[c] Willingness to pay estimate for a sub-sample of non-recreationists for the benefit derived from the knowledge that a preserved natural reserve exists as a habitat for various species of potentially unique flora and fauna.

[d] Defined as any water-associated recreation benefit derived from preservation of a high level of water quality by 1983.

[e] Weighted by population. The Denver Metropolitan Area population of 1,267,000 persons excluding Boulder County was 72.7 per cent of the 1,742,900 persons in the South Platte River Basin in 1976.

[f] Tests the significance of difference between grouped mean values. At the 5 per cent level, there is no statistically significant difference between the Denver and Fort Collins mean option value estimates.

Table 10.2 *Annual and Present Values from Water Quality Preservation in the South Platte River Basin, Colorado* (1976 dollars)

Water Quality Preservation Values	*Denver Metropolitan Area*		*Fort Collins*		*South Platte River Basin*	
	Annual Value	*Present Value*[a]	*Annual Value*	*Present Value*[a]	*Annual Value*	*Present Value*[a]
Option Value						
Water Fee	2,042,682	32,042,078	193,236	3,031,153	3,581,687	56,183,321
Sales Tax	6,161,700	96,654,102	548,307	8,600,896	10,526,153	165,116,132
Bequest Value						
Water Fee	2,366,693	37,124,596	94,615	1,484,157	3,118,513	48,917,856
Sales Tax	6,981,107	109,507,561	348,562	5,467,634	9,782,102	153,444,736
Existence Value						
Water Fee	2,732,107	54,920,408	132,461	4,125,956	3,792,942	59,497,134
Sales Tax	11,060,147	173,492,502	419,523	6,580,752	14,399,346	225,872,099
Recreation Value						
Water Fee	5,330,492	83,615,571	417,390	6,547,290	8,658,460	135,818,977
Sales Tax	16,886,624	264,888,216	1,191,622	18,692,110	26,399,220	414,105,414
Total Recreation and Preservation Value						
Water Fee	12,471,874	207,702,653	837,702	15,188,556	19,151,602	300,417,288
Sales Tax	41,089,578	644,542,381	2,508,014	39,341,392	61;106,821	958,538,381

[a] Discounted at 6.3/8 per cent. This was the discount rate recommended for water resource development projects in 1976 (U.S. Water Resources Council, 1979).

including tourists, pays sales taxes whereas only property owners and indirectly renters, pay water-sewer bills. Moreover, recent experience with escalating water-sewer fees may have resulted in understatement of willingness to pay for water quality.

Conclusion

The purpose of this study was to develop and apply a procedure for measuring option value and other preservation values of water quality, compared to benefits from water-based recreation activities. The results of the study provide an empirical test of Weisbrod's (1964) proposal that option value and other preservation values should be added to the aggregate consumer surplus of recreation activities to determine the total benefit of environmental amenities to society. In the absence of such an estimate, insufficient resources would be allocated by society to preservation of unique environments such as pristine mountain streams in the South Platte River Basin. The Henry (1974) model of option value was successfully tested in which respondents reported willingness to pay for the option to choose between two environmental alternatives, either clean water or polluted water from mining development, at some future time under conditions of sufficient knowledge as to the relative benefits of each.

Notes

1 Research conducted with funds provided under E.P.A. Grant R 803206-01-5 and by the Colorado State University Experiment Station. The authors acknowledge the helpful suggestions of Anthony Fisher, John Krutilla, John McKean, Anthony Prato, and Alan Randall.

2 Historically, gold, silver, lead, and zinc mines have been major sources of water pollution, including sediment, acidity, and havy metals. Irreversible drainage of pollutants flow from both abandoned and active mine shafts, mill sites, slag piles, and tailing ponds. Uranium, molybdenum, and other metals are extensively mined in the River Basin. Recently, gold and silver mining have also expanded in response to higher prices. The River Basin also contains two large coal fields. Increased diversion for irrigation, industrial, and domestic consumption concentrates effluent load.

3 This scenario does not identify the specific time interval necessary for the attainment of full knowledge of the economic impact of the optional environmental choices available if the second alternative is selected. The interval required for the collection and dissemination of the appropriate information was uncertain. The question explicitly specifies that the option benefit assessment would continue for an indefinite period until the required information was available. This approach is consistent with the theoretical

model which requires that the first period in state 2 be of sufficient length to allow for collection of the necessary information.

References

Arrow, K. J. and Fisher, A. C. (May 1974), 'Environmental Preservation, Uncertainty and Irreversibility', *Quarterly Journal of Economics*, LXXXVIII, pp. 312–19.

Bishop, A. Bruce (October 1974), 'Impact of Energy Development on Colorado River Water Quality', *Natural Resources Journal*, XVII, pp. 649–71.

Bishop, Richard C. and Heberlein, Thomas A. (December 1979), 'Measuring Values of Extra-market Goods: Are Indirect Measures Biased?', *American Journal of Agricultural Economics*, III, pp. 926–30.

Bohm, Peter (June 1972), 'Estimating the Demand for Public Goods: An Experiment', *European Economic Review*, III, pp. 111–30.

Bohm, Peter (1977), 'Estimating Access Values' in Wingo and Evans (eds.) *Public Economics and the Quality of Life*, Resources for the Future, Baltimore.

Bohm, Peter (1979), 'Estimating Willingness to Pay: Why and How?', *Scandinavian Journal of Economics*, LXXXI, pp. 142–53.

Brookshire, David, S., Ives, Berry C. and Schultze, William D. (1976), 'The Valuation of Aesthetic Preferences', *Journal of Environmental Economics and Management*, III, pp. 325–46.

Byerlee, D. R. (August 1971), 'Option Demand and Consumer Surplus: Comment', *Quarterly Journal of Economics*, LXXXV, pp. 523–7.

Cicchetti, C. J. and Freeman III, A. M. (August 1971), 'Option Demand and Consumer Surplus: Further Comment', *Quarterly Journal of Economics*, LXXXV, pp. 529–39.

Conrad, Jon M. (1980), 'Quasi-Option Value and the Expected Value of Information', *Quarterly Journal of Economics*, XCIV, pp. 813–20.

Davis, Robert K. (October 1963), 'Recreation Planning as an Economic Problem', *Natural Resources Journal*, III, pp. 239–49.

Freeman III, A. Myrick (1979), *The Benefits of Environmental Improvement: Theory and Practice*, Resources for the Future, Baltimore.

Friedman, Milton (1962), *Capitalism and Freedom*, University of Chicago Press, Chicago.

Gordon, Irene M. and Knetsch, Jack (February 1979), 'Consumer's Surplus Measures and the Evaluation of Resources', *Land Economics*, LV, pp. 1–10.

Greenley, Douglas A. (1979), *Recreation and Preservation Benefits from Water Quality Improvement*, Ph.D. thesis, Colorado State University, Fort Collins.

Henry, Claude (1974), 'Option Values in the Economics of Irreplaceable Assets', *The Review of Economic Studies: Symposium on the Economics of Exhaustible Resources*, pp. 89–104.

Knetsch, J. L. and Davis, R. K. (1966), 'Comparison of Methods for Recreation Evaluation' in Kneese and Smith (eds.) *Water Research*, Resources for the Future.

Krutilla, John V. (September 1967), 'Conservation Reconsidered', *American Economic Review*, LVII, pp. 777–86.

Linddsay, C. M. (May 1969), 'Option Demand and Consumer's Surplus', *Quarterly Journal of Economics*, LXXXIII, pp. 345; 52.
Long, M. F. (May 1967), 'Collective Consumption Services of Individual Goods: Comment', *Quarterly Journal of Economics*, LXXXI, pp. 351; 2.
Moran, R. E. andWentz, D. A. (1974), *Effects of Metal-Mine Drainage on Water Quality in Selected Areas of Colorado, 1972–3*, Colorado Water Resources Circular No. 25, Colorado Water Conservation Board, Denver.
Oster, Sharon (December 1977), 'Survey Results on the Benefits of Water Pollution Abatement in the Merrimack River Basin', *Water Resource Research*, XIII, pp. 882; 4.
Randall, Alan, Ives, Berry and Eastman, Clyde (1974), 'Bidding Games for Valuation of Aesthetic Environmental Improvement', *Journal of Environmental Studies*, I, pp. 132–49.
Schmalensee, R. (December 1972), 'Option Demand and Consumer's Surplus: Valuing Price Changes under Uncertainty', *American Economic Review*, LXII, pp. 814; 24.
U.S. Internal Revenue Service (December 1972), *1975 U.S. Individual Income Tax Returns*, 1975 Optional State Sales Tax Tables, Washington D.C.
U.S. Water Resources Council, *Procedures for Evaluation of National Economic Development (NED) Benefits and Costs in Water Resource Planning*, Federal Register, Washington D.C.
Walsh, R. G., Greenley, D. A., Young, R. A. *et al.* (January 1978), *Option Values, Preservation Value and Recreational Benefits of Improved Water Quality: A Case Study of the South Platte River Basin, Colorado*, U.S. Environmental Protection Agency, Socioeconomic Environmental Studies Series, E.P.A.-600/5-78-001, Research Triangle Park.
Weisbrod, B. A. (August 1964), 'Collective-Consumption Services of Individualized–Consumption Goods', *Quarterly Journal of Economics*, LXXVIII, pp. 471–7.
Wentz, D. A. (1974), *Effects of Mine Drainage on the Quality of Streams in Colorado, 1971–2*, Colorado Water Resources Circular No. 21, Colorado Water Conservation Board, Denver.

11

Input-Output Analysis and Air Pollution Control

Robert E. Kohn

INTRODUCTION

Suppose Y is the output of some economic activity (e.g. annual output of electricity in a region) and suppose that currently the pollution that is emitted due to this is P. Call $\alpha = P/Y$ the emission-output ratio. Suppose that it is now desired that total pollution emission be reduced to $\bar{P}$ ($< P$) without lowering output. We wish to estimate the cost of this move. Let C be the cost of abating the excess pollution ($P - \bar{P}$). In an important article Leontief (1970) noted that C *under*estimates pollution abatement costs for the reason that the additional *production* of pollution control equipment is itself a source of additional pollution, which in turn must be abated . . . and so on. Therefore, the cost incurred in ensuring that total pollution is $\bar{P}$ is greater than C, say C' – the sum of the direct cost (C) and the indirect cost ($C' - C$).

The question arises whether the indirect cost, $C' - C$, is significant as compared to the direct cost C. In his article Leontief provided a numerical example to indicate that it may be significant. He asked us to imagine a region in which 30 grams of air pollution is a maximum allowable flow ($\bar{P}$ = 30 grams). Currently, however, 60 grams are being emitted (P = 60 grams). A pollution abatement sector is therefore created to eliminate the excess pollution ($P - \bar{P}$). The direct cost of this is \$3.00 per gram. It follows that total direct cost C = \$90.00. However, the inputs required by this pollution abatement programme increases the production activities of other sectors which are also a source of pollution. Leontief computed the various multiplier effects in his input-output example and showed that in fact not 30 grams, but 33.93 grams of pollution must be eliminated. At \$3.00 a gram this means that total cost of abatement C' = \$101.80. Thus $(C' - C)/C = 11.80/90.00 \simeq 12\%$.

In his article Leontief restricted himself to a hypothetical example with a view to showing that the indirect effect can indeed be significant. The article that follows in this collection, by Robert Kohn, is an attempt at estimating the total cost of pollution abatement in an actual situation – the

St. Louis airshed. Kohn's investigation is rich in design. He recognizes that there are many processes for controlling pollution and that they are not combined in fixed proportion across all production activities. He notes at the beginning that the indirect costs associated with pollution abatement may urge one to expand the level of control and may alter the optimal mix of control methods. Thus, in estimating C' and C Kohn solves two optimal programming problems. His framework is as follows.

Suppose there are N techniques for controlling air pollution ($j = 1, \ldots, N$). To give an example, the jth technique – pertinent for a steel plant – may consist of electrostatic precipitators for the basic oxygen furnace primary cleaners for the blast furnaces and dry cyclone collectors for the sintering operations. Suppose next that there are M production units, that is, M sources of pollution. A typical example of one is a steel mill, or a power plant. Let S_i ($i = 1, \ldots, M$) be the output level of source i. Thus, S_i is the number of tonnes of steel produced at the plant in question, the number of tonnes of coal burnt at the power plant (i.e. the number of kilowatts generated), and so on. Let U be a $M \times N$ matrix connecting pollution control techniques to sources of pollution. Thus the typical element U_{ij} is 1 if the jth technique is defined for pollution source i, and is zero otherwise. Let X_j be the intensity with which technique j is used, expressed in units of output of the source at which j has been installed. Let K_j be the cost of operating technique j at unit intensity. Suppose finally that there are P pollutants and that E is a $P \times N$ matrix whose typical element E_{tj} is the quantity of pollutant t ($t = 1, \ldots, P$) per unit of activity associated with technique j.

Kohn is concerned with locating the least cost method of producing a given vector of outputs $\bar{S}_i$ ($i = 1, \ldots, M$) subject to the constraint that pollution discharges do not violate given *emission standards*.[1] Suppose $\bar{A}_t$ ($t = 1, \ldots, P$) is the emission standard on pollutant t. It follows that to calculate the direct cost C of optimum pollution abatement one must solve the following linear programme (see Kohn, p. 327):

$$\left.\begin{array}{l}
\text{Choose } X_j \ (j = 1, \ldots, N) \text{ so as to} \\
\qquad \text{minimize } \sum_{j=1}^{N} K_j X_j \\
\text{subject to the constraints:} \\
\qquad \sum_{j=1}^{N} U_{ij} X_j = \bar{S}_i, \qquad i = 1, \ldots, M \\
\qquad \sum_{j=1}^{N} E_{tj} X_j \leqslant \bar{A}_t, \qquad t = 1, \ldots, P \\
\text{and} \qquad X_j \geqslant 0, \qquad j = 1, \ldots, N.
\end{array}\right\} \quad (1)$$

Let X_j^* $(j = 1, \ldots, N)$ be the solution of (1). Then $C = \sum_{j=1}^{N} K_j X_j^*$.

However, the foregoing linear programme does not take into account the fact that the production of pollution abatement equipment is itself a source of pollution. Thus suppose that anti-pollution activity level X_j results in an *increase* in the output level of source i by the amount $\sum_{j=1}^{N} R_{ij} X_i$, where R_{ij} is a typical element of a $M \times N$ matrix, R.[2] The complete problem then is this:

$$\left.\begin{aligned} &\text{Choose } X_j \ (j = 1, \ldots, N) \text{ so as to} \\ &\text{minimize} \sum_{j=1}^{N} K_j X_j \\ &\text{subject to the constraints:} \\ &\sum_{j=1}^{N} (U_{ij} - R_{ij}) X_j = \bar{S}_i, \qquad i = 1, \ldots, M \\ &\sum_{j=1}^{N} E_{tj} X_j \leqslant \bar{A}_t, \qquad t = 1, \ldots, P \\ &\text{and} \quad X_j \geqslant 0. \end{aligned}\right\} \quad (2)$$

Let $\bar{X}_j$ $(j = 1, \ldots, N)$ be the solution of (2). Then $C' = \sum_{j=1}^{N} K_j \bar{X}_j$.

In applying this framework to the St. Louis airshed Kohn finds that $(C^\circ - C)/C \simeq 2.3\%$; that is, the indirect effect of pollution abatement is negligible.

Notes

1 Contrast this with the CO_2 study by Nordhaus where the standard set on CO_2 was on its concentration level.

2 In Kohn's notation (p. 328, equation (3)), $R = FGH$.

CASE STUDY

Introduction

Some significant research on economics of the environment is taking place in the field of input-output analysis. Leontief has published an important article relating pollution abatement to the economic structure.[1] Isard and his associates are expanding the input-output scope to include ecologic commodities and environmental processes.[2] Miernyk and others have presented papers on the impact of pollution and pollution control on regional economies.[3]

The present paper is, essentially, an empirical sequel of Leontief's. In that article, we are presented with the hypothetical model of a region, in which 30 grams of air pollution is a maximum allowable flow. Because 60 grams are being generated by economic activities, an antipollution sector is created to eliminate the excess emissions. The cost of abatement is \$3.00 per gram; thus it might appear that the total cost of pollution control would be \$90.00. This, however, is not the case. The inputs required by the antipollution sector generate increases in the production levels of other sectors which are themselves sources of pollution. When the various multiplier effects are taken into account, it is found that 33.93 grams of air pollution must be eliminated. The total cost of abatement is therefore \$101.80.[4]

Let us define some terms suggested by Leontief's example. The cost of reducing air pollution to some predetermined allowable level, ignoring the economic impact of abatement itself, is Z. The cost of achieving the allowable levels, taking into account the additional flow of pollution resulting from abatement activities, is Z'. For purposes of analysis we then define *the abatement multiplier* as the ratio, Z'/Z. In Leontief's hypothetical model, the abatement multiplier is \$101.80/\$90.00, or 1.131.

The Leontief model assumes a single pollution control process or a fixed combination of processes. In reality, there are many processes for controlling pollution and it is unlikely that they are combined in fixed proportions. The extent to which the abatement multiplier necessitates an expanded level of control and alters the optimal mix of control methods will be investigated in the context of a specific model.

The writer has developed a linear programming model in which maximum allowable flows of five separate pollutants in the St. Louis airshed are specified.[5] A set of air pollution control method activity levels is selected which achieves the allowable flows at the least cost, Z. The abatement multiplier, Z'/Z, for the St. Louis airshed will be calculated, using this same model in conjunction with an input-output study of the St. Louis region.[6]

The value of Z' is determined by augmenting the cost-effectiveness model with appropriate feedbacks. The feedback steps are as follows (the symbols in parentheses are matrix products which will be defined subsequently):

(Hx), the value of economic inputs associated with any set of control method activity levels, x;

(GHx), the changes in regional production levels necessary to sustain any set of control method activity levels;

($FGHx$), the changes in the levels of polluting activities associated with changes in production levels;

(E^*FGHx), the changes in emission flows (assuming the base year level of control) corresponding to changes in the levels of polluting activities.

The efficient set of control methods, x_0, is now that set which eliminates excess pollution, including the incremental pollution associated (directly and indirectly) with pollution control itself, at the least cost, Z'.

It is presumed that a cost-effectiveness model can be a useful guide for regulatory agencies in selecting an efficient strategy for achieving a predetermined set of air quality goals. In this paper, we investigate the significance of the abatement multiplier for such policy making. This research should provide insight as to how individual cost models and input-output studies can be made more useful for environmental planning. It may also enable us to evaluate the feasibility of incorporating a pollution control sector in the structure of an input-output model.

The linear programming model for determining Z

In matrix notation, the linear programming model for air pollution control is:

$$\begin{aligned} \text{minimize} \quad & Z = cx; \\ \text{subject to} \quad & Ux = s; \\ & Ex \leqslant a, \\ & x \geqslant 0, \end{aligned} \tag{1}$$

where x is an $(N \times 1)$ vector of air pollution control method activity levels and c is a $(1 \times N)$ vector of unit control costs. The vector s is an $(M \times 1)$ vector of pollution source levels, such as the number of tons of coal burned per year in a particular power plant, and the $(M \times N)$ matrix U is a distributive matrix which equates control method activity levels to pollution source levels. The element u_{ij} is 1 when the jth control method is defined for the ith pollution source and zero otherwise. Thus, there are as many 1's in any row of the U matrix as there are control methods defined for the pollution source which corresponds to that row. For the sum of control method activity levels to equal the corresponding pollution source level, it is necessary that both are measured in the same units, that the control method set include M control methods representing the activity levels of the M existing types of control (or noncontrol), and that each control method be uniquely defined for a single pollution source. The element, e_{ij}, of the $(P \times N)$ matrix E is the quantity of pollutant i emitted per activity unit of control method j, and the $(P \times 1)$ vector a is the allowable annual emissions for the P pollutants in the airshed. A simple example which illustrates the model is presented in the appendix to this paper.[7]

Model 1 was implemented as follows. The vector s contains projected levels of 94 polluting sources for the St. Louis airshed in 1975. These levels were projected from observed growth rates or from estimates by industrial representatives. The control method vector x, which includes over 215 alternative control methods in addition to the 94 existing control methods, and the emissions matrix E were developed from available engineering data, with control method costs, c, based on 1968 prices. The allowable annual emission flows, a, were derived from official maximum allowable concentrations for five pollutants in the St. Louis airshed.[8] The annual cost of achieving the air quality goals in 1975 wa found to be an estimated $35.3 million over and above the cost of abatement that would be expended given the existing, preregulatory level of control.[9]

The linear programming model for determining Z'

The increase in polluting activities associated with pollution abatement is Δs. The cost of eliminating excess pollution, including the incremental emissions associated with Δs, is the solution of:

$$\begin{aligned} \text{minimize} \quad & Z' = cx; \\ \text{subject to} \quad & Ux = s + \Delta s; \\ & Ex \leqslant a, \\ & x \geqslant 0. \end{aligned} \tag{2}$$

The increase in polluting activities, Δs, is assumed to be a linear function of abatement,[10]

$$\Delta s = FGHx, \tag{3}$$

where F is an $(M \times L)$ matrix, whose element f_{ik} is the change in polluting level i per dollar change in sales of sector k; G is an $(L \times L)$ matrix of intersectoral multipliers, where g_{kK} is the increase in sales of sector k per dollar increase in final demand sales of sector K; and H is an $(L \times N)$ matrix whose element h_{Kj} is the value of inputs from sector K per activity unit of control method j. Substituting for Δs in model 2 and moving $FGHx$ to the left-hand side gives:

$$\begin{aligned} \text{minimize} \quad & Z' = cx; \\ \text{subject to} \quad & (U - FGH)x = s; \\ & Ex \leqslant a, \\ & x \geqslant 0. \end{aligned} \tag{4}$$

There may be some incompatibility here in combining an open input-output model, where all production sectors can expand simultaneously, and a cost-effectiveness model in which full employment is implicitly assumed. No attempt will be made here to formulate additional assumptions which might ensure the internal consistency of the model. Most likely such assumptions would allow for an inflow of resources into the airshed. Note that while the costs, cx, are the value of national resources allocated to abatement, it is only the impact on local economic activities, s, that is examined. The effect of pollution control in the St. Louis airshed on pollution levels and pollution control costs in *other* airsheds is ignored.

The procedures used to calculate the H, G, and F matrices are now described.

The H matrix

The H matrix was implemented to conform with the sector classification in Liu's *Interindustrial Structure of the St. Louis Region, 1967* (see footnote 6). Although Liu distinguished 23 sectors, it was found impractical to allocate each unit control cost among 23 component inputs. Accordingly, six direct input sectors were selected, resulting in an H matrix with 6 nonzero and 17 zero rows. The six sectors are listed in rows 1 through 6 of Table 11.1. The remaining inputs, which were assumed to have no intersectoral impact, are noted in rows 7 through 10. This table includes selected control methods from the model and the inputs associated with these control methods. The entries in rows 1 through 6 typify elements h_{Kj} of the H matrix and denote the requirements from sector K (rows 1 through 6) per unit of activity of control method j (columns 1 through 8).

The inputs which would be purchased from the chemical, petroleum, and rubber sector include, for example, the increased cost of low sulphur fuel oil (see column 2), dolomite for wet scrubbing stack gases (see column 5), gasoline and diesel fuel for refuse hauling and landfilling equipment (see column 7), etc.

The value of inputs from the machinery sector represents purchases of scrubbers, dust collectors, afterburners, etc. (for convenience all machinery is assigned to the nonelectric machinery sector), while the purchase of automotive control devices and refuse hauling vehicles are attributed to the transportation equipment sector. Although these capital expenditures may be made within the space of five to seven years, the 1975 sector purchases are assumed to be equal to the annual depreciation of the equipment. Since the latter is, in general, based on a longer equipment life than seven years, the purchases from these two sectors may be understated for the year 1975.[11]

A negative purchase from the mining sector represents the value of coal replaced by natural gas (see column 3) while a positive value is the incremental cost of low sulphur coal (see column 4).

The transportation, communication, and utilities sector includes the purchase of natural gas for air pollution control, both as a substitute for coal and a fuel for afterburners. In the case of the dolomite wet scrubbing control method (see column 5), purchases from this sector represent the value of scrubbing water and of electricity to power pumps and fans.

Purchases from the household sector are for labour to maintain and operate control equipment. A negative purchase from the household sector (see column 3) indicates a saving of labour associated with a particular control method.[12]

Miscellaneous unallocated inputs include such items as the equipment and facilities for maintaining control equipment, the nonlabour costs for disposing of nonrecyclable by-products such as dolomite waste (see column 5), the cost of outside soil for landfilling (see column 7), the value of recovered steam in the operation of a carbon monoxide waste heat boiler, etc. While such costs should be allocated to primary sectors, there are other unallocated costs which should not. For example, the saving in household labour when domestic furnaces are converted from coal to natural gas would have no traceable impact on regional economic activity although it is assigned a dollar value.

Although the values of recovered chemicals (e.g. elemental sulphur, ammonium nitrate fertilizer) are included as negative purchases from the chemical, petroleum, and rubbr sector, this was not done in the case of sulphuric acid (see row 8) obtained as a result of controlling sulphur dioxide from power generation and lead smelting. It is assumed here that this output represents additional sales of sulphuric acid and has no impact on regional activity other than the inputs required for the operation of the recovery processes.

One of the sectors which should be included as a primary demand sector is local government. It is a limitation of this model that the costs of government regulation and enforcement have been omitted. These could effect the optimal control solution both by altering relative control method costs and through the pollution feedbacks from the expansion of the local government sector.

The opportunity cost of capital (see row 9) represents ten per cent of the total investment in control equipment from the machinery and transportation equipment sector.[13] For example, the upgraded electrostatic precipitator for a specific category of cement plant (see column 8) requires an incremental capital investment of $.50 per barrel of cement produced. It is assumed here that capital investments in control equipment are additional expenditures in the region and do not replace other planned investments. Hence, there is no feedback on polluting levels in the airshed.[14]

Another economic cost which is assumed to have no current impact on regional activity is the scarcity premium for natural gas (see row 10). This represents the excess of the social value of natural gas used for pollution control over its regulated market value.[15] The costs in the final row of

Table 11.1 *Value of Inputs per Activity Unit for Selected Control Methods* (dollars)

Control Method	*Crankcase and Exhaust Controls for 1970 through 1975 Model Automobiles (1)*	*Maximum Sulphur Content of 1% for Residual Fuel Oil Burned by Industry (2)*	*Conversion of Travelling Grate Stokers with Cyclone Dust Collectors from Coal to Natural Gas by Industrial Firms (3)*	*Maximum Sulphur Content of 2% on Coal Burned by Industry in Travelling Grate Stokers with Electrostatic Precipitators (4)*	*Wet Scrubbing of Stack Gases at Meramec Power Plant with Dolomite (5)*	*Cat-Ox System to Convert Sulphur Dioxide at Portage des Sioux Power Plant to Sulphuric Acid (6)*	*Hauling of Waste to a Sanitary Landfill Instead of Burning It On-Site (7)*	*Upgraded Electrostatic Precipitators for Cement Plant with Current Collection Efficiency of 96.4% (8)*
Control Method Activity Unit	*One thousand gallons of gasoline burned*	*One thousand gallons of residual fuel oil burned*	*One ton of coal burned*	*One ton of coal burned*	*One ton of coal burned*	*One ton of coal burned*	*One ton of waste disposed*	*One barrel of cement produced*
(1) Value of direct inputs from chemical, petroleum, and rubber sector	0	5.00	0	0	.22	0	.30	0
(2) Value of direct inputs from nonelectric machinery sector	0	0	0	0	.19	.58	0	.04
(3) Value of direct inputs from transportation equipment sector	9.23	0	0	0	0	0	1.50	0

(4) Value of direct inputs from mining sector	0	0	−5.27	2.50	0	0	0	0
(5) Value of direct inputs from transportation, communication, and utilities sector	0	0	11.27	0	.20	.36	0	n*
(6) Value of direct inputs from household sector	3.70	0	−1.57	0	.15	.24	7.20	.01
(7) Miscellaneous unallocated inputs	91	0	−.06	0	.05	.27	1.16	.01
(8) Sulphuric acid produced from sulphur dioxide	0	0	0	0	0	−1.34	0	0
(9) Opportunity cost of capital	4.62	0	0	0	.39	1.16	1.00	.05
(10) Scarcity premium for natural gas	0	0	3.80	0	0	0	0	0
Total Control Method Unit Cost	18.46	5.00	8.17	2.50	1.20	1.27	11.16	.11

* *n* less than one half cent.

Table 1 are unit control costs from the vector *c*. Each is the sum of input values in that column.

The G matrix
The *G* matrix is taken directy from Liu's input-output study and contains intersectoral multipliers for the St. Louis region. A portion of this matrix is repoduced in Table 11.2. Each entry shows, per dollar of direct sales of inputs for pollution control by the sector at the top, the total dollar value of production directly and indirectly required from the sector on the left. These multipliers are based on a model in which the household and local government sectors are endogenous.

It is assumed here that the technology, trading patterns, and relative prices for 1967 are applicable to 1975, although Miernyk notes that an input-output structure with fixed coefficients should be projected no more than two or three years.[16]

The F matrix
The *X* vector in Leontief's model represents sector activity variables and his emission factors, a_{gi}, relate directly to sector levels.[17] However, it is convenient in air pollution control models to identify polluting activities, *s*, across conventional sector classifications. Many of the 94 separate polluting activities defined in this model occur in each of the industrial sectors (e.g. the combustion of coal in various types of stokers, evaporation of industrial solvents, combustion of diesel fuel in trucks, disposal of refuse by open burning, etc.). To define each of these pollution sources according to sector as well as type would multiply the control method set enormously. In order then to relate polluting levels, as defined in the present model, to input-output multipliers based on a conventional economic sector classification, a conversion matrix is required. The *F* matrix fills this need.

The coefficients of the *F* matrix indicate changes in polluting levels associated with changes in sector sales. They are illustrated in Table 11.3 for selected pollution sources.[18] In the case of petrol burned in motor vehicles (see row 1), it was assumed that the ratio of petrol consumption in 1967 to the value of retail trade services in that same year, which was 643.52 thousand gallons per million dollars of sector activity, is a constant.[19] The production of cement, primary steel, grain handling, and sulphuric acid were assumed to be proportional to the sales of the respective standard industrial code classification sector, with the constant of proportionality based on 1967 levels.[20]

The combustion of coal in industrial furnaces was based on the sales of thirteen industry sectors. It ws estimated, for example, that the food, tobacco, and kindred products sector used 96.3 tons of coal per million dollars of sales in 1967.[21] It was projected that in 1975, given the same level of pollution control as existed in 1963, which was the base-year in the pollution model, approximately 6.5 % of the industrial coal burned in the St. Louis region would be burned in traveling grate stokers with cyclon controls. Accordingly, for every million dollars in sales by the food, tobacco, and kindred products sector, (96.3) × (.065), or 6.26 tons of coal would be burned in this furnace category (see row 2, column 1). Because the combustion of industrial coal in pulverized coal furnaces equipped with 90 % efficient electrostatic precipitators represents 39.0 % of the projected coal combustion in 1975, the corresponding coefficient for this polluting activity is larger (row 3, column 1).

It could have been assumed that coal combustion in individual power plants is proportional to sales of the transportation, communications, and utilities sector. However, this would mean that a million dollars in sales of natural gas for air pollution control would have the same impact on power plants as would the sale of a million dollars of electricity. To avoid a serious distortion in the model, it was assumed that the sale of natural gas had no direct effect on power plant activity. This required a separate accounting of natural gas and electricity inputs for air pollution control. The coefficient relating coal combustion at the Meramec Power Plant to a million dollars of electricity sales (row 4, column 17) was obtained as follows. It was assumed that a million dollars in sales to industrial users represents 93,620,000 kilowatt hours of electricity.[22] The Meramec Power Plant, which burns approximately .000427 tons of coal per kilowatt hour produced will supply an estimated 6.5 % of the area's power requirements in 1975. Accordingly, the appropriate element of the F matrix is (93,620,000) × (.000427) × (.065), or aproximately 2,600 tons of coal per million dollars of sales of electricity.

The sale of natural gas as well as electricity would affect power plant activity via the impact on other economic sectors. For example, it was estimated that 381,950 kilowatt hours of electricity are required by the paper and printing sector per million dollars of sales.[23] The f_{ik} coefficient of the Meramec Power Plant for this industrial sector is therefore (381,950) × (.000427) × (.065), or 10.6 tons of coal per million dollars in sales by the paper and printing sector (see row 4, column 4).

It was estimated that for each million dollars of sales by the primary metals sector, there would be 96.2 tons of nonrecycled solid waste generated.[24] Assuming, in the absence of regulatory activity, that 24.3 % of solid waste in the St. Louis region is disposed of by on-site open burning,[25] it was estimated that (96.2) × (.243), or 23.38 tons of waste would be burned on industry property per million dollars of metal sales (see row 6, column 8).

The effect of the F matrix is to relate directly the level of a polluting activity to the production level of either a single economic sector, or in the case of coal and refuse burning, to a linear combination of sector levels.

Table 11.2 *Selected Elements of the Matrix of Intersectoral Multipliers for the St. Louis Region*

	Chemicals, Petroleum, and Rubber Products (5)	*Machinery (except electrical) (10)*	*Transportation Equipment (12)*	*Mining (15)*	*Transportation, Communication, and Utilities (17)*	*Household (22)*
(1) Food, tobacco, and kindred products	.0243	.0513	.0216	.0544	.0525	.0892
(2) Textiles and apparel	.0047	.0101	.0043	.0108	.0102	.0173
(3) Lumber and furniture	.0011	.0026	.0010	.0024	.0024	.0037
(4) Paper and printing	.0135	.0158	.0079	.0183	.0207	.0233
(5) Chemicals, petroleum, and rubber products	1.0613	.0126	.0063	.0137	.0119	.0201
(6) Leather products	.0007	.0017	.0007	.0017	.0016	.0027
(7) Stone, clay, and glass	.0138	.0038	.0017	.0040	.0040	.0063
(8) Primary metals	.0019	.0346	.0166	.0071	.0046	.0022
(9) Fabricated metals	.0066	.0271	.0057	.0163	.0050	.0060
(10) Machinery (except electrical)	.0008	1.0255	.0062	.0067	.0018	.0010
(11) Electrical machinery	.0014	.0026	.0022	.0017	.0036	.0020
(12) Transportation equipment	.0048	.0122	1.0165	.0114	.0121	.0181
(13) Miscellaneous manufacturing	.0018	.0037	.0083	.0025	.0029	.0034
(14) Agriculture	.0013	.0028	.0012	.0030	.0029	.0049

(15) Mining	.0028	.0014	.0008	1.0262	.0029	.0014
(16) Construction	.0057	.0112	.0048	.0128	.0189	.0166
(17) Transportation, communication, and utilities	.0887	.1168	.0561	.2865	1.2178	.1676
(18) Wholesale trade services	.0118	.0306	.0094	.0213	.0219	.0234
(19) Retail trade service	.0571	.1419	.0561	.1332	.1309	.2082
(20) Finance, insurance, and real estate	.0680	.1429	.0613	.1807	.1619	.2245
(21) Business, personal, and other services	.0540	.1153	.0484	.1285	.1309	.1833
(22) Household	.3938	.8674	.3665	.9249	.8756	1.5313
(23) Local government	.0240	.0491	.0199	.0535	.0672	.0745

Source: B. C. Liu, *Interindustrial Structure of the St. Louis Region, 1967* (St. Louis: St. Louis Regional Development Corporation, 1968), Table V—1.

Table 11.3 *Detail of the Matrix for Relating Increased Polluting Levels to an Increase in Sector Sales of One Million Dollars*

	Food, Tobacco, and Kindred Products (1)	*Textiles and Apparel* (2)	*Lumber and Furniture* (3)	*Paper and Printing* (4)	*Chemicals, Petroleum, and Rubber Products* (5)	*Leather Products* (6)	*Stone, Clay, and Glass* (7)	*Primary Metals* (8)	*Fabricated Metals* (9)	*Machinery (except electrical)* (10)
(1) Thousands of gallons of gasoline burned in automobiles	0	0	0	0	0	0	0	0	0	0
(2) Tons of coal burned by industry in travelling grate stokers with cyclone controls	6.26	1.24	3.75	22.83	20.59	6.59	53.16	19.55	2.26	4.45
(3) Tons of coal burned, by industry in pulverized coal units with 90% efficient electrostatic precipitations	37.56	7.42	22.38	136.35	123.02	39.34	317.57	116.79	13.48	26.55
(4) Tons of coal burned in the Meramec Power Plant	7.93	2.55	4.95	10.60	20.01	6.06	55.06	38.58	9.18	4.44
(5) Tons of coal burned in the Portage des Sioux Power Plant	32.59	10.48	20.33	43.71	82.23	24.91	226.51	158.54	37.71	18.26
(6) Tons of waste disposed of by on-site open burning	13.24	15.42	60.11	10.44	39.56	43.57	181.31	23.38	19.38	26.93
(7) Barrels of cement produced in cement plant with 99.4% efficient electrostatic precipitators	0	0	0	0	0	0	43210.	0	0	0
(8) Tons of primary steel produced in basic oxygen furnaces	0	0	0	0	0	0	0	1470.6	0	0
(9) Tons of grain handled and processed in elevators	1869.2	0	0	0	0	0	0	0	0	0
(10) Tons of sulphuric acid produced by the contact process	0	0	0	0	701.55	0	0	0	0	0
(11) Tons of dry cleaning solvents used	0	0	0	0	0	0	0	0	0	0

Electrical Machinery (11)	*Transportation Equipment* (12)	*Miscellaneous Manufacturing* (13)	*Agriculture* (14)	*Mining* (15)	*Construction* (16)	*Transportation, Communication, and Utilities* (17)	*Wholesale Trade Services* (18)	*Retail Trade Services* (19)	*Finance, Insurance, and Real Estate* (20)	*Business, Personal, and Other Services* (21)	*Household* (22)	*Local Government* (23)
0	0	0	0	0	0	0	0	645.52	0	0	0	0
2.78	3.37	3.35	0		0	0	0	0	0	0	0	0
16.50	20.10	19.99	0	0	0	0	0	0	0	0	0	0
10.46	6.23	9.19	3.19	17.46	3.66	2600.[a]	8.03	9.22	13.42	16.06	12.12	7.18
42.98	25.60	37.77	16.08	71.74	15.03	10710.[a]	33.01	37.89	55.16	66.01	49.83	29.50
26.93	11.68	2.40	0	38.05	5.51	8.79	12.19	18.92	5.63	17.32	24.97	31.60
0	0	0	0	0	0	0	0	0	0	0	0	0
0	0	0	0	0	0	0	0	0	0	0	0	0
0	0	0	0	0	0	0	0	0	0	0	0	0
0	0	0	0	0	0	0	0	0	0	0	0	0
0	0	0	0	0	0	0	0	3.29	0	0	0	0

[a] Tons of coal burned per million dollars of electric power sold.

The FGH matrix product

The *ij*th element of the *FGH* matrix product represents the change in source level *i* per unit of control method *j* activity. This element has the form,

$$\sum_{k=1}^{L} \sum_{K=1}^{L} f_{ik} g_{kK} h_{Kj}.$$

For example, when one ton of waste, customarily burned on-site, is hauled away for landfill disposal (see Table 11.1, column 7), the increased combustion of gasoline in automobiles is an estimated (643.52) (.0571 × .30 + .0561 × 1.50 + .2082 × 7.20) (10^{-6}), or approximately .001 thousand gallons (see Table 11.2, row 19 and Table 11.3, row 1).[26]

It should be noted that there are other feedbacks of abatement activity on polluting levels which are not included here. If the private costs of control are added to the selling prices of pollution-related intermediate and final goods and services, there may be substitutions which reduce the levels of polluting activities.[27] Furthermore, the abatement of pollution may result in technical efficiencies which reduce the level of polluting activities.[28]

Results: the abatement multiplier

The abatement multiplier is a measure of the increase in the cost of pollution control caused by input-output feedbacks of the control technology on the vector of polluting activities. It is defined as the ratio of Z' to Z. If we let x_0 represent the optimal control method solution of the feedback model, (4), the minimized cost of pollution abatement, Z', is the product cx_0. This cost was found to be \$36.1 million, which compares to a cost of \$35.3 million for the original model (1) in which the feedbacks were ignored. The abatement multiplier is therefore equal to 1.023.

The factors which determine the size of the abatement multiplier will be investigated here. It will be useful to examine the following: x_0, the optimal set of control methods; Hx_0, the total value of direct inputs for abatement; GHx_0, the increase in economic sector production levels $FGHx_0$, the changes in polluting source levels; and E^*FGHx_0, the additional emissions which must be eliminated.[29]

Optimal control method activity levels, x_0

Selected activity levels of the x_0 vector are listed in Table 11.4. These are compared to corresponding activity levels from the solution of the original model. The fact that control method activity levels do not increase in the same proportion demonstrates that there is a shift in abatement technology. Because the efficient control method set is altered as the level

Table 11.4 *Optimal Activity Levels of Selected Control Methods in the Original Model and the Feedback Model and Total Cost of Abatement*

Control Method	*Control Activity Level in the Original Model*	*Control Activity Level in the Feedback Model*	*Ratio of Control Levels (feedback model to the original model)*
Exhaust control device for 1970 to 1975 model automobiles	545,638,000 gallons of gasoline combustion controlled	548,319,000 gallons of gasoline controlled	1.005
Crankcase evaporation control device for 1970 to 1975 model automobiles	25,885,000 gallons of gasoline combustion controlled	40,249,000 gallons of gasoline controlled	1.555
Upgraded electrostatic precipitators for industrial pulverized coal furnaces	444,000 tons of coal combustion controlled	444,615 tons of coal combustion controlled	1.001
Conversion of travelling grate stokers with cyclone controls from coal to natural gas	106,030 tons of coal combustion controlled	173,185 tons of coal combustion controlled	1.633
Desulphurization process for the Meramec Power Plant	730,000 tons of coal combustion controlled	740,330 tons of coal combustion controlled	1.014
Conversion of burning dumps to sanitary landfill	455,000 tons of refuse burning controlled	455,516 tons of refuse burning controlled	1.001
High energy wet scrubber for blast furnaces	1,417,500 tons of iron production controlled	1,417,846 tons of iron production controlled	1.000
Annual cost in 1975 for all air pollution control method activity levels combined	$35.3 million	$36.1 million	1.023

of control is increased, it is clear that the abatement multiplier as defined in this paper differs from conventional input-output multipliers, which are based on fixed technological relationships.

The major change in the control method solution is a 15 per cent overall increase in the quantity of natural gas required for pollution control. For travelling grate stokers equipped with cyclone collectors, there is a sharp increase in the substitution of natural gas for coal (see Table 11.4). Another control method, representing the conversion of a different category of stoker from coal to natural gas, entered the basis in the second solution.

Direct inputs for pollution control, Hx_0

Of the \$36.1 million in annual costs of pollution control, only \$24.1 million are assumed to have an input-output feedback. This is the sum of the nonzero elements of the matrix product Hx_0, which are listed in the upper part of Table 11.5. The larger the portion of Z° which reflects direct purchases in the region the greater will be the abatement multiplier. In a more elaborate model all of the 'miscellaneous unallocated inputs' would be assigned to appropriate input-output sectors and the abatement multiplier would be larger.

If the recovered by-product sulphuric acid were to diminish current production of sulphuric acid in the chemical sector, this would reduce the

Table 11.5 *Value of Direct Inputs for an Efficient Set of Air Pollution Control Methods in the St. Louis Airshed in* 1975 (millions of dollars)

Inputs	*Value of Inputs*	
Assigned to an Input-Output Sector (Hx_0)		
Chemicals, petroleum, and rubber products sector	.4	
Machinery sector	6.7	
Transportation equipment sector	8.7	
Mining sector	−13.0	
Transportation, communication, and utilities sector		
Electric power only	3.2	
Natural gas, etc.	13.3	
Household sector	4.8	
Subtotal		24.1
Not Assigned to an Input-Output Sector		
Miscellaneous unallocated inputs	1.6	
Credit for by-product sulphuric acid produced from sulphur dioxide	−11.9	
Opportunity cost of capital	19.4	
Scarcity premium for natural gas	29	
Subtotal		12.0
Total value of inputs		36.1

sum of elements of the product Hx_0, and the abatement multiplier accordingly. A sensitivity test with the model indicated that if the $11.9 million worth of recovered sulphuric acid were to replace an equal valued quantity of commercial sulphuric acid production in the airshed, the abatement multiplier would decline to 1.011.[30]

Increases in sector production, GHx_0

As a consequence of the direct demand for inputs, Hx_0, there are secondary or derived demands as well. The equilibrium set of increased activity levels, GHx_0, is presented in Table 11.6. Note that it requires $54.1 million in increased production levels to supply the $24.1 million of direct inputs for abatement. The $19.0 million increase in demand for household

Table 11.6 *Increased Indirect and Direct Economic Activities Associated with an Efficient Set of Air Pollution Control Methods in the St. Louis Airshed in 1975* (millions of dollars)

Economic Sector	*Increased Activity Levels* (GHx_0)
Food, tobacco, and kindred products	1.1
Textiles and apparel	.2
Lumber and furniture	.1
Paper and printing	.4
Chemicals, petroleum, and rubber products[a]	.6
Leather products	[a]
Stone, clay, and glass	.1
Primary metals	.4
Fabricated metals	.1
Nonelectric machinery	6.9
Electrical machinery	.1
Transportation equipment	9.1
Miscellaneous manufacturing	.1
Agriculture	.1
Mining	−13.3
Construction	.3
Transportation, communication, and utilities	18.5
Wholesale trade services	.5
Retail trade services	2.9
Finance, insurance, and real estate	3.0
Business, personal, and other services	2.6
Households	19.0
Local government	1.3
Total of all sectors	54.1

Note: The $11.9 million in sales of recovered sulphuric acid, a by-product of pollution control, are not included in this table.

[a] Less than $50,000.

services suggests that pollution abatement could create employment for 2,500 people.[31]

A sensitive test was performed to determine the relative significance of the *derived* demand for inputs on the size of the abatement multiplier. When the G matrix was omitted (or, in effect, replaced by a $[23 \times 23]$ identity matrix), the abatement multiplier declined from 1.023 to 1.014. While the feedbacks associated with indirect inputs account for less than half of the abatement multiplier, it can still be observed that the larger the input-output multipliers, the larger will be the abatement multiplier.

Increases in polluting activity levels, $FGHx_0$

The increases in pollution source levels, assumed proportional to increases in corresponding economic sector activity levels, are represented by a (94×1) matrix product, $FGHx_0$. Selected elements of this matrix product are contained in Table 11.7.[32] It will be observed here that the largest percentage increases are for the power plants which supply the electricity needed for pollution control.

The percentage increases in pollution source levels are substantially less than the 2.3 per cent of Z' over Z. Essentially, this is because a portion of emissions associated with the original pollution source levels is allowable, whereas all emissions associated with the increased levels must be eliminated. However, the comparatively small percentage increases in Table 11.7 help to explain why the abatement multiplier in the present study is as small as it is.

Additional emissions, E^*FGHx_0

The increase in air pollutants associated with the vector of increased pollution source levels, $FGHx_0$, is found by premultiplying the latter by a $(P \times M)$ matrix, E^*. The element, e_{ij}^*, of this matrix is the emission flow of pollutant i per activity unit of control method, j, where j is the existing or base year control state for pollution source j. The E^* matrix is contained in the E matrix and is used here for explanatory purposes only. These incremental emissions, elements of the (5×1) matrix product, E^*FGHx_0, are contained in Table 11.8. It is not surprising that the largest percentage increases in the pollution reduction requirements are for nitrogen oxides and sulphur oxides, which are the major pollutants from the larger power plants in the St. Louis airshed. As noted earlier, the most significant impact of pollution control will be the increase in power generation.

The percentage increases in required emission reductions, which range from .3 to 2.1 per cent, are less than the 2.3 per cent increase in abatement costs (or Z' to Z). This is in contrast to the Leontief example, where the cost of pollution abatement increases by the same per cent as the increase in the quantity of pollution which must be eliminated. Because pollution control is represented by Leontief as a constant cost industry, the

Table 11.7 *Estimated Production Levels for Selected Pollution Sources and Increases in these Levels Associated with an Efficient Set of Air Pollution Control Methods in the St. Louis Airshed in 1975*

Pollution Source	*Estimated Production or Consumption Level for 1975*	*Increase Because of Pollution Control* ($FGHx_0$)	*Percentage Increase*
(1) Combustion of gasoline in automobiles and light duty trucks	1,137,000,000 gallons of gasoline	1,841,000 gallons of gasoline	.2
(2) Diesel fuel used by railroads	40,800,000 gallons of fuel	385,000 gallons of fuel	.9
(3) Combustion of coal by industry in pulverized coal furnaces equipped with electrostatic precipitators	583,000 tons of coal	625 tons of coal	.1
(4) Combustion of coal in residential stokers	428,000 tons of coal	1,330 tons of coal	.3
(5) Combustion of coal at the Meramec Power Plant	730,000 tons of coal	10,330 tons of coal	1.4
(6) Combustion of coal at the Labadie Power Plant	5,500,000 tons of coal	77,840 tons of coal	1.4
(7) Refuse burned in municipal incinerators	357,000 tons of refuse	405 tons of refuse	.1
(8) Grain handled and processed in elevators	2,400,000 tons of grain	2,110 tons of grain	.1
(9) Crude oil processed in refineries	137,606,000 barrels of crude oil	50 barrels of crude oil	*
(10) Rock and gravel crushed, screened, conveyed, and handled	4,000,000 tons of rock	1,225 tons of rock	*

* Less than .05%.

Table 11.8 *Projected Emissions in the St. Louis Airshed in 1975 in the Absence of Additional Abatement, Allowable Emissions, and Incremental Emissions from Pollution Control* (emissions in millions of pounds)

Pollutant *(1)*	*Projected Emissions in* 1975 *in the Absence of Additional Abatement* *(2)*	*Allowable Annual Emission Flows*[a] *(3)*	*Required Reductions in Emission in* 1975 *(4)*	*Incremental Emissions Because of Abatement* (E^*FGHx_0) *(5)*	*Percentage Increase in Required Reductions* *(6)*
Carbon monoxide	4202.2	2335.2	1867.0	6.1	.3
Hydrocarbons	1518.8	994.5	524.3	2.3	.4
Nitrogen oxides	415.4	303.5	111.9	2.4	2.1
Sulphur dioxide	1389.6	400.4	989.2	11.3	1.1
Particulates	299.6	135.8	163.8	.9	.5

Note: Emissions from stacks higher than 600 feet are adjusted down to ground level equivalent emissions.

[a] The allowable flows are based on the following air quality goals (annual averages at the St. Louis Continuous Air Monitoring Programme Station): carbon monoxide, 5.0 ppm; total hydrocarbons, 3.1 ppm; nitrogen oxides, .069 ppm; sulphur dioxide, .02 ppm; suspended particulates, 75.0 $\mu g/m^3$.

marginal cost of eliminating one gram of pollutant does not change. In the present model, the cost of abatement increases more than the pollution reduction requirements because of increasing costs. This would not have been the case if each of the nonzero control method activity levels had increased by the same proportion (see Table 11.4). Because of the rising cost of pollution control, the abatement multiplier is larger than it would otherwise be.

Summary of factors which affect the size of the abatement multiplier

The abatement multiplier has been introduced as a device by which to measure the feedbacks of pollution abatement on the flow of emissions. It abatement and the optimal set of control method activity levels are more sensitive to factors other than the abatement multiplier. There are important cost and emission parameters in the model which are only estimates. These include data which characterize the technologies for desulphurizing power plant stack gases and controlling nitrogen oxides from automobiles. Relatively small changes in these would have a more substantial impact on the optimal solution than do the abatement feedbacks. In addition, minor changes in certain air quality goals or in the formulas which describe the relationship of emission flows to pollutant concentrations would have a more important impact on the control solution.

It is not clear whether the size of the abatement multiplier might not also be sensitive to such changes in parameters. One such sensitivity test was performed. The allowable emission flows (see Table 11.8, column 3) were reduced 10 per cent for each pollutant in the model. The new values of Z and Z' were respectively $55.5 million and $56.7 million. While this test confirmed the increasing costs of pollution abatement, the abatement multiplier changed very little, and in fact, declined slightly.[33]

Although the value of 1.023 for the abatement multiplier for the St. Louis model appears to be small, it should be noted that the incremental control costs of $.8 million are 1.5 per cent of the sum of incremental economic activities, which would be $54.1 million. In contrast, the total cost of abatement from this model is only .1 per cent of the projected total value of economic activity in the St. Louis region in 1975. Thus the ratio of control costs to economic activity is far greater at the margin than are the corresponding totals. It is apparent that the assumption of fixed maximum allowable pollution flows implies that increased economic activity will require significantly higher expenditures for environmental control.

Results: shadow prices

The pollutant shadow prices presented in Table 11.9 indicate the increase in the total cost of abatement associated with a decrease of one pound in the corresponding allowable annual emission flow. The pollutant shadow

Table 11.9 *Shadow Prices Generated by the Linear Programming Models*

Constraints	*Shadow Price in the Original Model*	*Shadow Price in the Feedback Model*
	Pollutants	
Carbon monoxide requirement	$.00428 per pound	$.00432 per pound
Hydrocarbon requirement	.02476 per pound	.02482 per pound
Nitrogen oxides requirement	.32639 per pound	.33333 per pound
Sulphur dioxide requirement	.02193 per pound	.02220 per pound
Particulate requirement	.07748 per pound	.07941 per pound
	Inputs from Input-Output Sectors	
Chemical, petroleum, and rubber products sector	0	.01811 per dollar
Nonelectric machinery sector	0	.01110 per dollar
Transportation equipment sector	0	.00494 per dollar
Mining sector	0	.01236 per dollar
Transportation, communication, and utilities sector		
Electricity only	0	.17132 per dollar
Natural gas, etc.	0	.01422 per dollar
Household sector	0	.01423 per dollar

can be concluded from the above analysis that the abatement multiplier is larger:

1 the greater the portion of pollution control costs which represent current direct purchases of inputs;
2 the less the replacement of existing production by recycled pollutants;
3 the larger the input-output multipliers;
4 the larger the ratios of polluting activities to sector levels (the less a region imports the larger these ratios will be);
5 the greater the emissions associated with polluting activities;
6 the more steeply rising are the costs of pollution abatement.

It should be stressed that this study of the abatement multiplier is based on a specific model of a specific airshed. Any conclusions must be viewed as tentative because they may be sensitive to parameters and data unique to the particular model. It is likely, however, that the cost of pollution prices from the feedback model incorporate the incremental pollution control costs associated with abatement. To the extent that control costs in the model correspond to control costs that would be borne by polluters, these shadow prices functioning as emission fees would theoretically achieve the optimal control solution x_0 via decentralized decision making.[34]

The merger of linear programming and input-output analysis produces the unique set of shadow prices at the bottom of Table 11.9. These indicate the pollution control costs in the St. Louis airshed associated with an increased production of $1.00 by the corresponding economic sector.[35] If for example, the chemical, petroleum, and rubber products sector would increase its sales by $1.00, pollution control costs in the airshed would rise by 1.8 cents. The sale of an additional dollar of electricity would increase control costs by 17 cents.[36] A dollar increase in annual sales by the transportation equipment sector, which imports a large per cent of its inputs, would raise total costs of abatement in the airshed by half a cent. These costs reflect the fact that final demand sales by any sector increase the production level of other sectors.

The shadow prices of the inputs have a second interpretation. If the pollutant shadow prices were used as emission fees, an increased production of $1.00 by an economic sector would involve incremental control costs and emission fees in the airshed equal to the shadow price.

Implications of this research for cost-effectiveness models for environmental planning

Abatement feedbacks

It is appropriate that the feedbacks of pollution abatement on the levels of polluting activities be included in cost-effectiveness models. Not only is the cost of abatement higher because of these feedbacks, but adjustments in the control solution may result. This was illustrated in this paper by the revisions in the optimal control method set (Table 11.4) when feedbacks were incorporated.

While the inclusion of input-output multipliers improves the model, there is some question as to whether the increased accuracy is sufficient compensation for the immense computational effort involved. It was observed in this paper that 60 per cent of the feedback impact could be captured by incorporating only the direct inputs and not the indirect inputs to abatement (i.e., by omitting the *G* matrix).[37] Moreover, a substantial portion of the primary feedback could be incorporated through electricity inputs alone, thereby further simplifying the model.

If it were anticipated that large quantities of recovered sulphuric cid were to replace existing commercial acid production, it would be advisable to incorporate this abatement feedback into a cost of control method. The present research suggests that certain inputs have a more significant feedback effect than dó others, and that the latter might, for simplicity, be ignored.

Measurement units for pollution source levels

Emission factors are generally based either on inputs (i.e., tons of coal burned, gallons of diesel fuel consumed, etc.) or on outputs (i.e. tons of steel manufactured, number of airplane landing and take-off cycles, barrels of cement produced, etc.).[38] As a result, it is typical to measure polluting levels in terms of both inputs and outputs. This asymmetry, apparent in Tables 11.1, 11.3, 11.4, and in the example used in the appendix, is in contrast to the uniformity found in input-output analysis.

Some thought should be given to expressing the levels of polluting activities in future cost-effectiveness models in terms of either inputs or outputs, but not both. If output units are used, the cost-effectiveness model could more readily be related to input-output tables as well as other data arranged according to a standard industrial classification. Although the possibility of basing pollution coefficients on output units would eliminate the need for the *F* matrix used in the present model, it would also increase the dimensions of the control method vector.[39]

Implications of this research for input-output models for environmental planning

Aggregation of economic sectors

One of the problems encountered in this research relates to the aggregation of industries in the input-output model. The aggregation of all utilities in a single sector required special handling to separate the very different impacts of natural gas and electricity purchases. The fact that the chemical and petroleum industries, both major sources of air pollution in the St. Louis airshed, were included in the same sector of Liu's input-output model was a distinct limitation. The input-output models being developed for environmental studies should avoid aggregating industries with significantly different pollution characteristics.

The pollution abatement sector

Leontief has expanded the input-output structure with an additional row for pollution output and an additional column for pollution abatement. The feasibility of treating air pollution control as a constant cost industry is challenged in the present paper. Whereas there are no capacity constraints on interindustry sales in an open input-output model, there are significant capacity constraints on pollution control processes *when abatement occurs at the source.*[40] Thus there are only so many underfeed stokers which can be converted from coal to natural gas, so many new automobiles which can be factory equipped with the latest pollution control equipment, etc. As these upper limits become binding, successive levels of abatement are attained at rising marginal costs. If, for example, the pollutant shadow prices for the original model (see Table 11.9) were *average* costs, the cost of pollution control in the original model would be the vector product of these costs and the corresponding required reductions in pollutant emissions (see column 4 of Table 11.8), or more than $90 million a year. This demonstrates the extent of increasing costs, for clearly, a substantial amount of pollution abatement would have to occur at much smaller costs than these shadow prices for the annual cost of abatement to be $35.3 million. If, because of increasing costs, it is not feasible to incorporate pollution control sectors in input-output models, it may be that future research relating economic activity and pollution control costs will depend on interfaced input-output and cost-effectiveness models such as the one presented in this paper.

Appendix: numerical illustration of the model

To clarify the model, consider the following example with two pollution sources, three pollutants, four economic sectors, and five control methods. This hypothetical airshed contains two sources of air pollution; a steel mill producing 1,000,000 tons of steel a year and a power plant whose annual consumption of coal is 2,000,000 tons. The vector of polluting production levels is:

$$s = \begin{bmatrix} 1{,}000{,}000 \\ 2{,}000{,}000 \end{bmatrix}.$$

Desirable air quality can be achieved in this airshed if total annual emissions do not exceed 8,000,000 pounds of particulates, 40,000,000 pounds of sulphur dioxide, and 35,000,000 pounds of nitrogen oxides. The vector of allowable emission flows is

$$a = \begin{bmatrix} 8{,}000{,}000 \\ 40{,}000{,}000 \\ 35{,}000{,}000 \end{bmatrix}.$$

The steel mill currently emits 7 pounds of particulates, 13 pounds of sulphur dioxide, and 2 pounds of nitrogen oxides per ton of steel produced. These emission occur in the operation basic oxygen furnaces, blast furnaces, sintering machines, coke ovens, and during the combustion of fuel oil, natural gas, and coke oven gas. The power plant currently emits 3 pounds of particulates, 118 pounds of sulphur dioxide, and 20 pounds of nitrogen oxides per ton of coal burned. Thus annual emissions in the airshed are well in excess of allowable flows for all three pollutants.

The present state of control (x_1) at the steel mill includes electrostatic precipitators for the basic oxygen furnaces, primary cleaners for the blast furnaces, and dry cyclone collectors for the sintering operations. The present pollution control method (x_4) at the power plant is an electrostatic precipitator.

The alternative control methods for the steel mill are (x_2) high energy wet scrubbers for the blast furnace, which would cost an additional \$.10 per ton of steel output, and (x_3) the high energy wet scrubbers for the blast furnace plus electrostatic precipitators for the sintering operations, which would add incremental costs of \$.25 per ton of steel output. The alternative control method (x_5) for the power plant is a desulphurization process costing an additional \$1.20 per ton of coal burned. The row vector of control method costs is, $c = [\$.00\ \$.10\ \$.25\ \$.00\ \$1.20]$. Each of the alternative control methods would be used in combination with the existing control method. However, because it is the *incremental* cost of pollution control which is being minimized, the existing control methods are, for convenience, assigned zero costs.

The alternative control methods for the steel mill reduce particulate emissions from 7 to 4 pounds per ton of steel for the first alternative (x_2) and from 7 to 3 pounds for the second alternative (x_3). The desulphurization process (x_5) would reduce emission from the power plant to 2 pounds of particulates, 12 pounds of sulphur dioxide, and 16 pounds of nitrogen oxides per ton of coal burned. The matrix of emission factors is therefore:

$$E = \begin{bmatrix} 7 & 4 & 3 & 3 & 2 \\ 13 & 13 & 13 & 118 & 12 \\ 2 & 2 & 2 & 20 & 16 \end{bmatrix}.$$

The distributive matrix which equates the sum of control method activities for each pollution sources to the production level of that source is:

$$U = \begin{bmatrix} 1 & 1 & 1 & 0 & 0 \\ 0 & 0 & 0 & 1 & 1 \end{bmatrix}.$$

The linear programming model in standard form is:

$$\begin{array}{llllllll} \text{minimize} & Z = \$.00x_1 + \$.10x_2 + \$.25x_3 + \$.00x_4 + \$1.20x_5 \\ \text{subject to} & x_1 + & x_2 + & x_3 & & & = & 1{,}000{,}000 \\ & & & & x_4 + & x_5 & = & 2{,}000{,}000 \\ & 7x_1 + & 4x_2 + & 3x_3 + & 3x_4 & 2x_5 & = & 8{,}000{,}000 \\ & 13x_1 + & 13x_2 + & 13x_3 + & 118x_4 + & 12x_5 & = & 40{,}000{,}000 \\ & 2x_1 + & 2x_2 + & 2x_3 + & 20x_4 + & 16x_3 & = & 35{,}000{,}000 \\ & x_1, & x_2, & x_3, & x_4, & x_5 & = & 0 \end{array}$$

The optimal solution is $x_1 = 0$ tons of steel, $x_2 = 971{,}698$ tons of steel, $x_3 = 28{,}302$ tons of steel, $x_4 = 28{,}302$ tons of coal, $x_5 = 1{,}971{,}698$ tons of coal and $Z = \$2{,}470{,}283$.[41]

The input-output feedbacks associated with pollution control are now included. In this simple example, there are only four economic sectors: a primary metals sector, a machinery sector, an electric power sector, and a household sector. Assume that the annual purchases of local inputs for pollution control are as follows. Each activity unit of control method x_2 requires \$.03 worth of inputs from the machinery sector, \$.01 from the electric power sector, and \$.02 from the household sector. Each activity unit of control method x_3 requires \$.10 worth of inputs from the machinery sector, \$.02 from the electric power sector, and \$.04 from the household sector. Each activity unit of control method x_5 requires \$.20 worth of inputs from the machinery sector, \$.20 from the electric power sector, and \$.15 from the household sector. The matrix of input requirements is accordingly:

$$H = \begin{bmatrix} 0 & 0 & 0 & 0 & 0 \\ 0 & .03 & .10 & 0 & .20 \\ 0 & .01 & .02 & 0 & .20 \\ 0 & .02 & .04 & 0 & .15 \end{bmatrix}.$$

Because no direct inputs are purchased from the primary metals sector, the first row of the H matrix contains only zeros. Because no *incremental* inputs are required for the two existing control methods, columns 1 and 4 contain only zeros. The input requirements for the existing control methods are already incorporated in sector production levels.

The matrix of intersectoral multipliers is determined from a regional interindustry flow model. For this example, it is assumed that:

$$G = \begin{bmatrix} 1.010 & .040 & .005 & .002 \\ .002 & 1.030 & .002 & .001 \\ .100 & .120 & 1.220 & .170 \\ .600 & .870 & .880 & 1.530 \end{bmatrix}.$$

Polluting activities are related to sector levels as follows. For every dollar of sales by the primary metals sector, .0015 tons of steel are produced and .0010 tons of coal are burned at the power plant to provide electricity to the primary metals sector. For every dollar's worth of sales by the machinery sector, by the electric power sector, and by the household sector, .0002, .07, and .0004 tons of coal, respectively, are burned at the power plant. The matrix of coefficients relating pollution source levels to sector sales is:

$$F = \begin{bmatrix} .0015 & 0 & 0 & 0 \\ .0010 & .0002 & .0700 & .0004 \end{bmatrix}.$$

The model with input-output feedbacks is the same as the previous model except that the U matrix is replaced by a $[U - FGH]$ matrix. In the present example, this matrix is:

$$[U - FGH] = \begin{bmatrix} 1 & .999998 & .999994 & 0 & -.000014 \\ 0 & -.001378 & -.003115 & 1 & .979173 \end{bmatrix}.$$

The optimal solution is $x_1 = 0$ tons of steel, $x_2 = 889{,}257$ tons of steel, $x_3 = 110{,}774$ tons of steel, $x_4 = 23{,}357$ tons of coal, $x_5 = 2{,}020{,}290$ tons of coal, and $Z' = \$2{,}540{,}967$. As a consequence of the feedback effect annual steel production rises 31 tons and coal combustion at the power plant increases 43,647 tons a year. The abatement multiplier in this example is \$2,540,967/\$2,470,283, or 1.03.

Comment

Frederick M. Peterson, University of Maryland

Using input-output analysis, Leontief showed that polluton abatement activities generate some pollutants themselves by requiring inputs.[1] For instance, the fans and pumps needed to clean the air use electricity, and the production of this electricity causes additional air pollution. Leontief's illustration raised two empirical questions. Is a significant amount of pollution caused by abatement activities? Do planners have to consider the Leontief effect?

For Kohn's air pollution study of St. Louis, the answer is no. If Kohn's results are supported by other findings, the Leontief effect will be reduced to a theoretically interesting, but empirically unimportant phenomenon. Planners will be able to ignore the effect or dispose of it with a few back-of-the-envelope computations.

Kohn's computations were exhaustive. He included the Leontief effect in a linear programming model of the St. Louis airshed. The model picked the control techniques that achieved a set of emission standard at least cost.[2]

The Leontief effect added only 2.3 per cent to the cost of achieving the standards, a small percentage compared to the other errors and uncertainties that an environmental planner faces. Half of this percentage was achieved without an input-output model, by considering only direct inputs to abatement activities. Kohn showed this by replacing his G matrix with an identity matrix. Kohn assumed that sulphuric acid recovered from power plants and lead smelters was additional production rather than a substitute for existing production. When he tried the alternate assumption that sales were constant and that virgin production was reduced, the Leontief effect was cut from 2.3 per cent to 1.1 per cent.

Kohn's estimates of the Leontief effect may be low, but the bias is probably small. The effects of abatement activities were fed back through only six of the twenty-three sectors in the model, as is reflected by the seventeen zero rows in the H matrix. This means that inputs from the seventeen sectors had no direct or indirect effect on pollution. To the extent that abatement activities used inputs from these sectors and caused additional pollution, the Leontief effect was understated. It is probably true, as Kohn argued, that these sectors are not important, but it would be nice to have enough details in the paper to check his argument. Generally, the paper lacks sufficient detail for the reader to find out what is happening.

Another area where more information is needed is Kohn's treatment of interregional imports. Kohn ignored the effect of pollution control in the St. Louis airshed on pollution levels and pollution control costs in other airsheds, an omission that probably decreased the observed Leontief effect. If St. Louis imports abatement machinery from Cleveland and increases Cleveland's pollution control bill, the additional cost to Cleveland must somehow get back to St. Louis in the form of higher machinery prices. Even if the costs are not passed back, the effect in other regions should be estimated. It seems that Kohn could do this with knowledge of the import sector in Liu's interindustry model.

If Kohn wanted to estimate the size of the Leontief effect, one would think that a reasonable estimate could have been obtained with back-of-the-envelope calculations. By making a crude guess at the direct inputs needed for abatement, estimating the pollution generated, and doubling the figure to account for indirect flows, he would probably have gotten an estimate between 1 per cent and 3 per cent, low enough to forget about elaborate modelling and computation. Back-of-the-envelope calculations are very useful for environmental problems. Claims are constantly being made about the importance of this or that environmental effect, and many of these claims can be disposed of by a few calculations with approximate engineering data that are readily available.[3]

The fact that the Leontief effect was small and might have been estimated with simpler computations does not totally erase the importance of Kohn's paper. He did not build the model just to estimate the size of the Leontief effect. He also wanted to advance the art of environmental modelling, which he did. He included pollution abatement activities in an input-output model, demonstrated how linear programming can be used to find the least cost way of achieving ambient standards, an calculated some interesting shadow prices that could be used to achieve the least-cost solution with a set of taxes.

Notes

1 See Wassily Leontief, 'Environment Repercussions and the Economic Structure: An Input-Output Approach', *The Review of Economics and Statistics*, August 1970, pp. 262–71.

2 See Walter Isard, C. Choguill, J. Kissin *et al.*, *Ecologic and Economic Analysis for Regional Planning*, The Free Press, New York, 1971.

3 See William H. Miernyk, 'Environmental Management and Regional Economic Development', *Annual Meetings of the Southern Economic Association and the Southern Regional Science Association*, Miami Beach, Florida, November 6, 1971. J. R. Norsworthy and Azriel A. Teller, 'Estimation of the Regional Interindustry Effects of Pollution Control', *Winter Meetings of the Econometric Society*, New Orleans, Louisiana. 26–29 December 1971. David L. Raphael and Ernest E. Enscore, Jr., 'The Direct and Indirect Impact of Regional Air Pollution', *Annual Meeting of the Air Pollution Control Association*, Cleveland, Ohio, June 1967.

4 See Wassily Leontief, 'Environmental Repercussions', p. 268.

5 Robert E. Kohn, 'A Linear Programming Model for Air Pollution Control in the St. Louis Airshed', Ph.D. dissertation, Washington University, 1969.

6 Ben-chieh Liu, *Interindustrial Structure of the St. Louis Region*, 1967, St. Louis Regional Industrial Development Corporation, 1968.

7 The model is described in more detail in Robert E. Kohn, 'Optimal Air Quality Standards', *Econometrica*, Volume 39, November 1971, pp. 983–95.

8 The relationship of the annual average concentration of a pollutant to the total annual emissions of that pollutant in the airshed is based on a *proportional model* which is defined on page 15,490 of 'Requirements for Preparation, Adoption and Submittal of Implementation Plans', *Federal Register*, Volume 36, Number 158, August 1971. An alternative approach,

in which annual emissions are related to ambient air concentrations by means of Gaussian diffusion formulae is used in Robert E. Kohn, 'Industrial Location and Air Pollution Abatement', *Journal of Regional Science*, Volume 14, Number 1, April 1974, pp. 55–63.

9 It is the economic impact of incremental costs of abatement that are examined in this paper. For simplicity, the costs of existing control methods are taken as zero and the costs of alternative control methods for any pollution source are incremental costs over and above that of the existing control method. The *total* annual cost of abatement would be in excess of $45 million.

10 Ayres and Kneese have called attention to the increase in water and soil polluting activities which may be a consequence of air pollution abatement. See R. U. Ayres and A. V. Kneese, 'Production, Consumption, and Externalities', *American Economic Review*, Volume 59, June 1969, pp. 282–97. This aspect of air pollution control was examined empirically in Robert E. Kohn, 'Joint Outputs of Land and Water Wastes in a Linear Programming Model for Air Pollution Control', *1970 Social Statistics Section, Proceeding of the American Statistical Association*, Washington D.C., 1971, pp. 207; 14. In the present paper it is the increase in *air* polluting activities as a consequence of the control of air pollution itself which is being examined.

11 The assumption that equipment expenditures in any year are equal to depreciation would be more appropriate for a steady state economy.

12 One control method which eliminates local labour is the transfer of a portion of power generating capacity to a mine mouth location outside of the region. So that the results of this paper may be as general as possible, this particular interregional transfer of labour is ignored here.

13 The sensitivity of the model to the opportunity cost of capital is examined in Robert E. Kohn, 'Air Quality, the Cost of Capital, and the Multi-Product Production Function', *Southern Economic Journal*, Volume 38, October 1971, pp. 156–60.

14 In their regional impact model, Norsworthy and Teller, 'Regional Inter-industry Effects of Pollution Control', p. 18, use the opportunity cost of capital as a proxy for purchases from the machinery and construction sectors. They treat depreciation as a cash flow to households and imports. In the present study, only the impact of actual production activities are considered.

15 The scarcity premium for natural gas is discussed in Robert E. Kohn 'Application of Linear Programming to a Controversy on Air Pollution Control', *Management Science*, Volume 17, June 1971, pp. 609–21.

16 See William H. Mierynk, *The Elements of Input-Output Analysis*, Random House, New York, 1965, p. 33.

17 Leontief, 'Environmental Repercussions', p. 271.

18 For convenience, the coefficients in Table 11.3 are related to *millions* of dollars of sector activity.

19 Petrol consumption in the St. Louis region in 1967 was an estimated 857,143 gallons (Kohn, 'A Linear Programming Model', p. 553) and retail

trade services in that year totalled 1,350,862,000 (Liu, *Inter-industrial Structure*, Table IV–1). The reader is cautioned that the F matrix, like the G matrix, is based on the assumption that the technological relationships and relative prices that prevailed in 1967 are applicable for 1975.

20 Four categories of cement plants are included in the model. It is assumed that the older plants (see, for example, column 8 in table 1) are at capacity, so that any increases in cement production will take place in newer plants equipped with 99.4% efficient electrostatic precipitators. To this limited extent, the present study incorporates a normal advance in abatement technology.

21 Extrapolated from data in *1963 Census of Manufacture, Volume 1, Summary and Statistics*, Washington D.C., Department of Commerce, 1966, pp. 45, 7–92, and in *1967 Census of Manufacture*, Missouri, Washington D.C., Department of Commerce, 1970, pp. 26–14, 26–15, 26–16.

22 The average price of electricity sold to industrial users by Union Electric Co. in 1967 was \$.010682 per kilowatt hour. See *1967 Annual Report*, St. Louis, Union Electric Co., 1967, p. 26.

23 A breakdown of power shipments to St. Louis industrial sectors was provided by Union Electric Co. and Illinois Power Co. The breakdown of power shipments to nonindustrial sectors was estimated from data in Liu, *Interindustrial Structure*, Table IV-1.

24 Waste production data are based on a study by the Institute of Industrial Research, University of Louisville, *Louisville, Ky-Ind. Metropolitan Region Solid Waste Disposal Study, Volume 1, Jefferson County, Kentucky* (Cincinnati, Ohio, Department of Health, Education and Welfare, 1970), pp. 6, 7, 25, 95, 96.

25 Relative polluting activity levels in the St. Louis airshed in 1975 are taken from Kohn, 'A Linear Programming Model'.

26 The previously noted exception for the transportation, communication and utilities sector can be formally stated. For elements $\sum_k \sum_x \mathrm{f}_{in}\ \mathrm{I}_{kk}\mathrm{h}_{ki}$, in which both subscripts k and K denote the transportation, communication and utilities sector, the coefficient h_{kj} is the value of the eletricity input only. When subscript k refers to any of the other economic sector, h_{kj} represents the combined value of natural gas, water, and electric power inputs.

27 This type of feedback is programmed into the model in Robert E. Kohn, 'Price Elasticities of Demand and Air Pollution Control', *Review of Economics and Statistics*, Volume 54, November 1972, pp. 392–400.

28 Raphael and Enscore, 'Impact of Regional Air Pollution', have modified an input-output model for Clinton Country, Pennsylvania so that the technical coefficients describing the production structure are altered by air pollution levels. In addition, certain sector levels, e.g. the production of cleaning services, are a function of pollutant concentrations. Because the technological and human effects of air pollution are not as well known as the costs of abatement, cost-effectiveness models for air pollution control are more satisfactorily implemented with empirical data than are cost-benefit models. However, when the costs of abatement are thoroughly investigated,

it becomes apparent that the damage effects of air pollution cannot be ignored, even in a cost effectiveness model.

29 The matrix E^* will be defined subsequently.

30 Recovered sulphuric acid is valued at one-half to one-third the value of commercially produced sulphuric acid depending on whether it is a by-product of power generation (and relatively pure) or of lead smelting. Assuming a fixed dollar demand for sulphuric acid, it would take two to three tons of recovered acid to replace one ton of commercial acid production. This feedback effect was implemented by treating by-product sulphuric acid as a negative input independently of the chemical, petroleum, and rubber products sector. The savings in indirect inputs associated with a dollar reduction in the projected level of commercial acid production are then included as negative direct inputs. These include a reduced demand by sulphuric acid producers for labour, machinery, water, power, and elemental sulphur.

31 This is based on the annual income per manufacturing employee in the St. Louis SMSA in 1967 (*1967 Census of Manufactures, Missouri*). This does not include any decreases in employment due to higher operating costs and prices. For a study of adverse impacts of abatement on employment, see Robert J. Kohn, 'Labor Displacement and Air Pollution Control', *Operations Research*, Volume 21, September–October 1973, pp. 1063–1070.

32 Some of the values in Table 11.7 can be checked by the reader. The increased combustion of petrol in cars and light duty trucks (row 1) is the product of the $_{fik}$ coefficient 643,520 gallons, in Table 11.3 (row 1, column 19) and the equilibrium increase in the value of retail trade services in Table 11.6, \$2.9 million. (The discrepancy in results is due to rounding.) The increase in the combustion of coal in pulverized coal furnaces equipped with electrostatic precipitators (see Table 11.7, row 3) is verified by multiplying the $_{fik}$ coefficients in row 3 of table 11.3 by the corresponding sector increases in Table 11.6 and summing. To verify the increased coal combustion at the Meramec Power Plant, the corresponding $_{fik}$ coefficients in row 4 column 17 must be multiplied by the product of 3.17 million (the value of direct, electrical input for pollution control in the feedback model) and the transportation, communication and utilities sector self-multiplier, 1.2178 (see Table 11.2). This special case is explained in footnote 26.

33 The decline in the multiplier should not be too surprising. None of the first five factor which explain the size of the abatement multiplier are necessarily related to the level of abatement. Although the marginal costs of pollution control are likely to increase as abatement levels are increased, they could, in a linear programming context, be fairly constant for any specific small range equal to E*FGHx.

34 The reader who is interested in calculating the government revenue from these emission taxes can multiply the rates in Table 11.9 time the corresponding allowable flows in Table 11.8. He may be surprised to find that the total annual revenue is more than four times the annual cost of abatement.

35 The shadow prices for inputs were obtained as follows. The constraint,

$[U - FGH]x = s$, was incorporated in the model in two equations, $Ux - FGy = s$ and $Hx - y = 0$, where the elements of y are values of direct inputs for abatement supplied by the separate economic sectors. The shadow prices of the elements of the null vector represent the incremental cost of abatement associated with a dollar increase in sales for the corresponding economic sector.

36 Alternatively, the additional cost of abatement associated with the sale of one kilowatt hour of electricity to industrial, commercial, or residential customers would be .18 cents.

37 It should be noted that the shadow prices for the inputs (see Table 11.9) may in some cases be largely attributable to multiplier effects. If, for example, derived demands are excluded from the model (this is the case where the G matrix is omitted), a dollar in sales by the nonelectric machinery sector would increase total cost of abatement by only .1 cents, far less than the 1.1 cents noted in Table 11.9.

38 See *Compilation of Air Pollutant Emission Factors* (Revised), (Research Triangle Park, Environmental Protection Agency, 1972).

39 This has been done in Wassily Leontief and Daniel Ford, 'Air Pollution and the Economic Structure: Empirical Results of Input-Output Computations', *Fifth International Conference on Input–Output Analysis*, Geneva, Switzerland, January 1971.

40 This may be more applicable to air pollution than water pollution control.

41 The solution of this example problem is awkward. It would be difficult to install control devices for an arbitrary fraction of a plant's production. Although an integer programming solution would be more realistic, it was found that in the standard linear programming model, divisibility occurs in no more rows than there are binding pollutant requirements (in this example, the nitrogen oxides requirement is not binding). The larger the number of pollution sources, M, in comparison to the number of pollutants, P, the smaller will be the relative importance of the problem of divisibility. In the actual model, the operation of basic oxygen furnaces, blast furnaces, sintering machines, coke ovens, the combustion of coke oven gas, the combustion of fuel oil, and the combustion of natural gas by industry are all treated as individual pollution sources, each with separate production levels and with control method coefficients based on the units in which the corresponding production is measured (i.e. tons of pig iron, tons of sinter, millions of cubic feet of coke oven gas, gallons of fuel oil, etc.). These various activities were combined so as to limit the size of the x vector in the example.

42 See Wassily Leontief, 'Environmental Repercussions and the Economic Structure: An Input-Output Approach', *Review of Economics and Statistics*, vol. LIII (August 1970), pp. 262–71.

43 The model is hard to master. There is much unorthodox terminology, such as an 'air pollution control method activity level' which is an amount of some input consumer or output produced that causes pollution. To understand the model, it is suggested that the reader study the numerical illustration in the Robert E. Kohn, 'Optimal Air Quality Standards', *Econometrica*, vol. 39, November 1971, pp. 983;87.

44 For an example, it has been claimed that insulating homes does not save energy because energy is required to make the insulation, but simple calculations show otherwise. With typical temperature differentials between the inside and the outside of the home, the insulation can be shown to save more energy in a single year than was required to make it.